Student's
Vegetarian
Cookbook

Student's Vegetarian Cookbook

*Quick, Easy, Cheap,
and Tasty Vegetarian Recipes*

Carole Raymond

REVISED

THREE RIVERS PRESS • NEW YORK

Published by Three Rivers Press, New York, New York.
Member of the Crown Publishing Group, a division of Random House, Inc.
www.randomhouse.com

THREE RIVERS PRESS and the Tugboat design are registered trademarks of Random House, Inc.

A previous edition of this work was published by Prima Publishing in 1997.

Printed in the United States of America

The information for pages xxiii and xxiv was compiled by EarthSave International. Used by permission.

Library of Congress Cataloging-in-Publication Data
Raymond, Carole
    Student's vegetarian cookbook : quick, easy, cheap, and tasty vegetarian recipes / Carole Raymond.
        p.   cm.
    Includes index.
    1. Vegetarian cookery. 2. Quick and easy cookery. 3. Low budget cookery. I. Title.
TX837.R3793 2003
641.5'636—dc21   2003006863

ISBN 0-7615-1170-9
10 9 8

Second Edition

*To my mother, Rose, and stepfather,
Henry, and to Yoda and Lucky*

Contents

11. Various Vegetables and Stir-Fries 189

12. Desserts and Quick Breads 215

Preface

Welcome to vegetarian cooking. There has never been a better time to appreciate the sights, smells, flavors, and textures of a meatless diet.

More and more people are recognizing how vegetarian cooking will benefit their health and please their palates. As markets fill with broader arrays of wholesome foods, even the student or first-time cook can easily turn a basketful of vegetables, grains, and other simple ingredients into delicious, quick, and inexpensive meals. Consider some of the bonuses of vegetarian eating:

- Eating vegetarian means that you can make a great meal with all the necessary nutrients and no meat in just one entree. Pasta, pizza, tacos, quesadillas, fajitas, stir-fries, simple one-pot soups, salads, creamy polenta with sautéed vegetables, a bowl of chili, or a baked potato topped with steaming vegetables; all these foods can easily fill the center of any plate.

- For the health-conscious, vegetarianism will help you look and feel great. Vegetarian meals are lower in fat than meals that revolve around meat, and this may explain why vegetarians are on the average trimmer than their meat-eating counterparts. Eating lots of vegetables is appealing because it helps combat the "Freshman 15," the mythical number of pounds a first-year college student is expected to gain eating high-calorie fast food.

- If you like to eat, but don't like cleaning up, vegetarian cooking has another bonus. Without the animal fat that sticks to pans and plates when you cook meat, cleanup is a snap.

- Cultures all over the world center their cuisine on plant foods. As you dip into vegetarian cooking, your plate will fill with the accumulated flavors of many culinary traditions.

If you are just starting out, you may need a helping hand over a few small hurdles. *The Animal Rights Handbook* estimates that the average American will eat 1 calf, 3 lambs, 11 cows, 23 hogs, 45 turkeys, and 1,097 chickens in a lifetime. You probably grew up thinking of meat as the virtual pillar of the American way of life. The government promoted it, your third-grade teacher placed steaks and drumsticks squarely in the middle of the food chart, and television told us meat would make us "real people."

The dominant meat-eating culture is often ignorant about and consequently maligns vegetarians. Here are some of the myths commonly associated with vegetarianism and the facts that dispel them.

- *Vegetarians are weak and frail.* Some of the planet's largest and strongest animals live by eating vegetables—after all, elephants, bulls, gorillas, and stallions are all vegetarians. There are many renowned vegetarian athletes, including Dave Scott, one of the greatest triathletes in the world.

- *Vegetarians do not get enough protein.* You can get all the protein you need just by eating a variety of foods every day. The average American diet far exceeds healthy protein requirements.

- *Vegetarians are a tired lot.* If you are looking for more energy, you will get it from eating complex carbohydrates like whole grain pasta and whole grain bread, not from meat.

- *Humans are naturally carnivores.* Human beings are primates whose teeth, intestinal structure, and dietary needs are ideal for eating plant foods, not flesh. (Many believe that eating meat began during the Ice Age when plant food became scarce.)

- *Health professionals find vegetarian eating a questionable choice.* The Physicians' Committee for Responsible Medicine recently called for four new food groups (whole grains, vegetables, fruits, and legumes) and lists dairy products and meat as optional.

Calcium and Vegetarianism

Calcium is an important nutrient for building strong bones that will last a lifetime. Vegetarians get their calcium from the same place cows do, from green things that grow in the ground and from calcium-fortified food. Milk and cheese are also excellent sources of calcium, but the definitive word about how much you need isn't in yet, so in the meantime, it makes sense to be moderate in the amount you choose. Here is a list of calcium sources to help guide your choices.

Excellent Sources of Calcium

Bok choy
Calcium-fortified orange juice
Calcium-fortified tofu (processed with calcium sulfate)
Calcium-fortified soy milk
Calcium-fortified rice milk
Calcium-fortified breakfast cereal and snack bars
Collard greens
Firm cheese: cheddar, Parmesan, Jack, part-skim
    mozzarella, Swiss
Kale
Nonfat dairy milk
Nonfat yogurt

Good Sources of Calcium

Black beans
Broccoli
Corn tortillas

Dried figs
Navy beans
Sesame seeds
Tahini (sesame butter)

Minor Sources of Calcium

Butternut squash
Carrots
Lentils
Oranges
Sweet potato

Building a healthy skeleton requires more than only calcium. Bones, like muscles, respond to use. When you exercise, they become stronger. Vitamin D is also part of the story. It is essential to help you absorb calcium, and you can get it from your diet and the sun, which triggers cells in the skin to manufacture the vitamin. So when you're outside jogging or walking, you're building strong bones, too.

Fast-Forward

Learning your way out of a meat-eating culture, especially as a beginning cook, can appear daunting. Luckily, attitudes are changing. Many people now recognize that a meat-based diet paves the road to many forms of illness, for both humans and the environment. A well-balanced vegetarian diet can provide all the nutrients we need. Many people quickly discover that vegetarian meals surpass their taste expectations.

No matter how much you love to eat, there are times when you don't feel like squarely facing the stove. Here's a list of 10 quick meals that set aside the sauté pan and instead rely on a can opener, commercial grocery options, and frozen vegetables.

Top 10 List of No-Time-to-Cook Meals

1. Celebrate Soup—Turn a simple cup or can of soup into a filling meal. Add some extras: cooked pasta, rice, beans, or frozen vegetables.

2. Hearty Green Salad—Start with a bag of commercially prepared, prewashed salad greens. On a bed of greens, add slices of tomato and carrots. Sprinkle with canned kidney beans, sunflower seeds, or grated cheese. Drizzle with dressing.

3. Pasta and Sauce—Boil up a pot of noodles. Open a jar of pasta sauce; heat it in a saucepan with a handful of frozen mixed vegetables. Pour the sauce mixture over the noodles and sprinkle with Parmesan cheese.

4. Chili on Toast—Heat $3/4$ cup commercial vegetarian chili with a handful of frozen corn. Toast a slice of whole grain bread. Spoon hot chili over the toast, and top with optional extras: grated cheese or yogurt, salsa, green onions, chopped cilantro.

5. Tacos—Fill a warm corn tortilla with creamy refried beans, lettuce, tomato, salsa, and a sprinkle of grated Cheddar cheese. Fold and eat.

6. Popular Pizza—Make a gourmet pizza in minutes. Spread a ready-made frozen pizza shell or seasoned Boboli with prepared pizza sauce. Drain the liquid from a jar of marinated artichoke hearts. Top the sauce with the artichokes, thin onion slices, olives, bell pepper rings, and tomato slices. Scatter cheese on top, and bake according to pizza crust directions.

7. Hot Baked Potatoes—Pick your favorite or try all four:
   - Taco Potato: Top a potato with warm canned black beans, salsa, and grated cheese.
   - Sauced Potato: Open the potato wide and mash the inside with a fork. Pour on $1/2$ cup warm commercial veggie soup (such as split pea, lentil, or minestrone).

- Veggie Potato: Top the potato with a mixture of steamed frozen vegetables, a squeeze of lemon juice, salt, and pepper.
- Sweet Potato: Mix 1/2 cup of plain yogurt with a teaspoon of tahini, and spoon it over a baked or steamed sweet potato; sprinkle with chopped green onions, and add a side of seasoned rice.

8. Virtual Burgers and Hot Dogs—Veggie burgers and tofu dogs (available in most commercial supermarkets) are a quick fix. Neither has the taste nor texture of their meat counterparts, so if that's what you expect, get ready for something different. Layer a bun or piece of bread with fresh lettuce, tomatoes, and sliced onion. Add the burger or tofu dog and top with your favorite condiments.

9. Tangy Yogurt—Add a handful of granola and sliced fruit to an 8-ounce container of yogurt. Stir and eat.

10. Whipped Drinks—In a blender, whip up a meal with soy milk and fresh fruit. Ripe bananas and berries make a good beginning.

When you are ready for more food adventures, the *Student's Vegetarian Cookbook* will give you the tools you need to bring a world of fresh and varied tastes onto your table. Grab a cutting board and follow these recipes to good health and great eating!

Acknowledgments

Thank you to Richard, Camela, and Jonathan; and to my friends, Toni Barrientos, Phyllis Beals, Anna Beck, Nancy Byles, Roberta Gross, Lee Johnson, and Patti Walther. Special thanks to Roberta Miller.

Special thanks also to my editors, Denise Sternad and Marjorie Lery, and everyone else at Prima and Three Rivers Press who helped make this book a reality.

Introduction
"It Bugs Me"

Celebrated author Andrei Codrescu, whose keen observations of American culture can be heard regularly on National Public Radio, has this to say in his book *Zombification: Stories from National Public Radio* (St. Martin's Press) about how eating meat affects the planet, animals, and your health and why building yet another Burger King bugs him.

> *Number one, they kill cows; number two, the cows they kill graze on the sites of murdered forests; number three, the cows they kill that killed the forests are full of hormones; number four, the hormone-filled cows they kill that killed the forests are full of bad-for-your-heart fat; number five, the bad-for-your-heart-hormone-filled-forest-killing-dead-cows are wrapped in bad-for-the-earth-plastic.*

What is a Whopper or Big Mac worth, and are you willing to pay the price? Here are facts from EarthSave International about eating meat that may disturb you:

- Livestock consume 70 percent of U.S. grain production. Twenty million people die each year as a result of malnutrition and starvation. Americans could feed 100,000,000 people by reducing their intake of meat by just 10 percent.

- One acre of prime land can produce many pounds of edible product. Here are a few examples:
    30,000 pounds of apples
    40,000 pounds of potatoes
    50,000 pounds of tomatoes
    250 pounds of beef

- Livestock—cattle, poultry, goats, sheep—totaling 15 billion worldwide now outnumber people three to one. Livestock graze on half of the world's land mass. The explosion of livestock populations has resulted in a parallel explosion of animal wastes that pollute surface and ground water. U.S. livestock produce 230,000 pounds of excrement per second. The amount of waste created by a 10,000-head feed lot is equal to the waste of a city of 110,000 people.

- World livestock production is now a significant factor in the emission of two of the four global warming gasses: carbon dioxide and methane. Every steak we eat has the same effect as a 25-mile drive in a typical American car.

- Each year, an estimated 125,000 square miles of rainforest are permanently destroyed, bringing about the extinction of approximately 1,000 plant and animal species.

- Producing 1 pound of feedlot steak results in the loss of 35 pounds of topsoil. It takes 200 to 1,000 years to form 1 inch of topsoil.

- It takes 2,500 gallons of water to produce 1 edible pound of beef. It takes 49 gallons of water to produce 1 edible pound of apples.

- Eighty percent of the meat produced in the United States contains drugs that are passed on to you when you eat it.

- Animal products contain large quantities of saturated fat and cholesterol and have no dietary fiber. The U.S. Surgeon General has stated that 68 percent of all diseases are diet related. A diet rich in fruits, vegetables, and grains (and free from animal products) can prevent, improve, and sometimes cure breast cancer, osteoporosis, prostate cancer, impotence, and obesity.

- Seventy-five percent of federal poultry inspectors say they would not eat chicken.

Organic Food

One of the greatest changes in grocery stores in recent years has been the popularity of organic food. It is expensive, but as the demand continues to increase, organic products will become more affordable. In the fall of 2002, the United States Department of Agriculture's (USDA's) rules for the production and labeling of organic food became effective. The regulations prohibit the use of genetic engineering, irradiation, and sewage sludge in certified organic production and handling of food. In general, the use of all synthetic substances, along with petroleum-based fertilizers, is prohibited, and organic food cannot be mixed with nonorganic varieties in stores.

The Genetically Modified Organisms (GMO) Controversy

The current revolution of biotechnology in food production is at the center of one of the planet's most important debates. Technology now enables food producers to go beyond the natural boundaries of nature by transferring genes from one species to another species. For example, moth or fish genes can be engineered into plants to make them more pesticide resistant. Many people feel we need to evaluate this new technology before we proceed further. The United States still does not require labeling of genetically engineered foods; however in Europe, the European Union has strict regulations that refuse to accept GMO crops from the United States. Change is on the way in this country. Recently, Oregon introduced a ballot measure requiring labeling, but so far voters have rejected the proposal.

What Can You Do?

Each individual has the opportunity to make a difference in creating a sustainable world for ourselves and future generations.

There is no way to escape the ecological cost of the choices we make, but there are ways to cut the price.

One of the significant choices you can make is to eat a vegetarian diet. This cookbook will teach you how to select and prepare fresh produce and other staples for vegetarian eating. The recipes collected here will help you to cook simple everyday meals to add to your list of lifelong favorites.

CHAPTER 1

Shop Smart—
Cook Smarter

Having food in the kitchen is 90 percent of the cooking battle, so begin your vegetarian adventure with a trip to the supermarket. Check out natural food stores and ethnic groceries. Look for supermarkets and neighborhood co-ops that sell items from bins where you scoop out what you need. Without the excess packaging on the product, you save a lot of money and there is less to recycle. Farmer's markets are a great place to find cheap, often organically grown, fresh fruits and vegetables.

When you buy fresh fruits and vegetables, buy them in small quantities. That way you won't find yourself staring at rotting produce in the refrigerator, and if you shop more than once a week, you'll find it easier to buy food that suits your mood.

As you roll your cart down the supermarket aisles, you'll see that the layout is anything but accidental. Some displays are set up to create a mini–traffic jam, so everyone pauses long enough to add more items to their carts. Look out for "endcap" displays designed to encourage impulse shopping. Market researchers have found that when background music slows from 108 beats per minute to 60 beats per minute, supermarket sales increase by 40 percent. Do most of your shopping at the perimeter of the store where you'll find the freshest, most healthful foods. Enjoy the tunes, eat the free food samples, and shop with your own plan in mind.

Compare the price of the store labels with the same brand-name item. Store labels are usually cheaper and comparable or better in quality. Big food manufacturers pay supermarkets enormous slotting fees to gain shelf space, and brand-name advertising budgets can reach over $100 million for a single product. As the consumer, you absorb the cost. Larger-sized packages are usually, but not always, cheaper. Two 14-ounce cans of tomatoes may be cheaper than one 28-ounce can. Handwritten signs along the aisles often make shoppers think a product is on sale when it may not be. Get to know the price of the foods you buy so you will know a bargain when you see it.

Check the expiration dates on perishable foods like dairy products, cereals, and bread. The freshest product is usually in the back of the display, and a handwritten sign by a perishable item may be a way to get you to buy a product that is about to expire.

In the cereal aisle, the ready-to-eat, whole grain cereals are usually on the bottom shelf, while the overprocessed, sugar-laden cereals are lined up at eye level. Read the labels and look for whole grain cereals like Shredded Wheat and Grape-Nuts. Buying cereal grains like old-fashioned rolled oats and cooking them yourself will save you money, and they make hearty meals.

When you arrive at the checkout stand with a basketful of fresh vegetarian food, it may surprise you to find that your grocery bill is less than you expected. Dollar for dollar, you get a lot more grains, beans, fruits, and vegetables than you do meat.

A Guide for Picking and Keeping
Some of the Best Stuff at the Market

The market can be an overwhelming place to a new vegetarian. How do you know you are getting the freshest produce? What does a parsnip look like? And where is the tofu? Here is a guide that will help you overcome any anxiety you may have about selecting and storing fresh, ripe fruits, vegetables, soy foods, and whole grains.

Fresh Produce

Buy fruits and vegetables individually rather than in prepackaged sacks or containers—that way you avoid wilted and bruised produce. Even if they are a bargain, chances are you will end up discarding some. When you get home, remove fruit from plastic bags, because plastic holds moisture and causes fruit to mold. Unlike fruit, most vegetables last longest tightly wrapped in plastic. Produce keeps best refrigerated. Store vegetables in their own crisper. If they are sitting with fruit, the ethylene gas from the fruit can cause premature brown spotting on vegetables. Do not wash fruits, particularly berries, before storing, because it hastens their deterioration. Wash fruit immediately before serving.

Apples   If you find apples on sale, but the color is less than perfect, the quality of the fruit is probably still good inside. Avoid any that are soft or have bruised spots. Refrigerated apples will keep for 2 weeks or more.

Artichokes   Choose an artichoke that feels heavy for its size and has compact, fresh-looking leaves. Dark outer leaves sometimes indicate cold-weather damage. Don't let that stop you from buying it. Eating an artichoke is a unique experience (See "Deconstructed Artichoke" on page 190).

Arugula　　This calcium-rich green grows almost any time of the year. The mature leaves add piquancy to salads and soups. Arugula will keep for a few days in the refrigerator.

Asparagus　　Look for tightly closed, compact tips, and firm brittle stalks. They are best eaten as soon as possible. Before cooking, snap off the tough lower stem ends and discard them. Rinse stalks under gently running water to remove any sand.

Avocados　　You know an avocado is ripe when it yields very slightly to the pressure of your thumb. If you bring home one that's not quite ready for eating, you can hasten the ripening process by putting the avocado in a paper bag with a banana, at room temperature. Once ripe, avocados spoil quickly. A ready-to-eat avocado will keep in prime condition in the refrigerator for 4 to 7 days. To prepare an avocado, slice it in half lengthwise. Remove the seed. Cut lengthwise and crosswise slices in the flesh, making a grid. Scoop the avocado cubes out of the shells with a spoon.

Bananas　　When buying bananas, buy some that are ripe, some not quite ripe, and a few green ones. That way they will be ready when you are. After a banana is ripe (but never before), put it in the refrigerator. (Once chilled, they won't sweeten.) Don't worry if the skin darkens after refrigeration. The fruit will still be good inside. A banana is in prime eating condition when it is dotted with brown "sugar" flecks.

Beans　　Green beans can be yellow or green depending on their variety. Their color should be bright, and they should snap easily and have a velvety feel. They will keep for about 5 days, refrigerated. Steam or stir-fry them until they are crisp-tender, and serve seasoned with salt and pepper and a splash of lemon juice.

Beets Beet roots should be smooth and firm. They will keep for about 2 weeks in the refrigerator. Peel and then shred or grate raw beets and toss them into salads. If preparing cooked beets, trim the leaf stem to about 1 inch, and boil or steam them with their skins on until tender. Lightly squeeze the beets when they are cool, and they will easily slip out of their jackets.

Broccoli For the best flavor, choose broccoli with dark green florets and tiny buds. Yellowing florets and large thick stems are signs that broccoli is past its prime. Broccoli is delicious lightly steamed, sautéed, used in stir-fries, and even eaten raw.

Brussels Sprouts Look for small, firm, compact heads with bright green color. Avoid large puffy ones or heads with dark spots or insect damage. Overcooking results in mushy, bitter-tasting vegetables. These minicabbages are tastiest when lightly steamed for 5 to 7 minutes. Cut off the stem end before steaming. Serve with a squeeze of lemon juice, and season with salt and pepper.

Cabbage Green and red cabbage have survived since prehistoric times. They are versatile, cheap, and will surprise you with how much flavor they add to vegetarian meals. Select a small, bright-colored, firm head that feels heavy for its size. Cabbage will keep for more than 2 weeks, refrigerated.

Cabbage, Chinese This is a generic name for a variety of greens used in Asian cooking. Two of the most popular are bok choy and celery cabbage. Look for bok choy with dark green leaves and thick white stems. Celery cabbage should be uniformly light green. The entire vegetable is usable. Chinese and celery cabbage are good in stir-fries and soups, or eat them steamed or sautéed as a side dish.

Cantaloupe In selecting a cantaloupe, be sure its exterior is covered with a creamy-colored netting. A large smooth spot is a bad sign, and the stem end should be smooth without rough fibers showing. Most important, it should have a sweet aroma. Wrap cut melons in plastic, and do not remove the seeds until you are ready to eat the melon, since the seeds keep the melon moist.

Carrots Look for carrots that are firm, not flabby. If the carrot is large and has a thick neck, the lighter-colored core will be large and thick too. For eating purposes, the core should be small because the good taste comes from the deep orange outside that stores the sugar. Carrots do not need peeling.

Cauliflower Buy compact white heads free of speckles and smudges. Eat cauliflower raw or cooked. It keeps for about a week, refrigerated.

Chiles Look for chiles with smooth, tight skins. Refrigerated in a plastic bag, fresh chiles will keep for about 5 days. The heat of a chile is in the ribs and seeds that are inside, and the heat can vary widely among the different kinds. Cut the chile open like a book; if you want to turn down the heat, remove ribs and seeds. Avoid touching your eyes or face while handling chiles.

Corn Fresh sweet corn is a summer crop that holds up well when frozen, so enjoy it year-round. Buy frozen corn in bags, because then it is easy to scoop out just what you need.

Cucumbers When selecting cucumbers, make sure you know what *not* to buy. Overmature cucumbers have a puffy, dull appearance. The skin of most supermarket cucumbers is coated with wax, so peel them before eating. Eat cucumbers raw.

Eggplants Choose eggplants that are firm and have shiny, dark skin. The cap should look fresh and green. Never eat eggplant raw—it contains a toxin called solanine. Cooking eliminates the danger. Once cooked, you can eat the skin too. Eggplants submit to almost any cooking technique.

Garlic Look for good-sized garlic with plump cloves free of soft spots. It is easier and faster to peel one or two big cloves than six tiny ones. Unpeeled garlic will stay fresh for weeks. Store garlic in a cool, dry place, but not in the refrigerator. Refrigerate jars of prepared garlic packed in oil. To prepare fresh garlic, first remove a clove from the bulb. Peel the clove by putting it on a cutting board and gently smashing it with the side of a large knife. The skin will slip off, and the flattened garlic will be easy to use. If you need small pieces, chop or mince by rocking your knife blade across the garlic. Hold down the front of the knife with the palm of your hand and cut, repeatedly pushing the garlic pieces back into a heap as you go.

Ginger Do not let these knobby-looking roots scare you. Ginger is a fragrant addition to many vegetarian meals. Covered with plastic wrap, it will keep refrigerated for 2 weeks. You can also freeze ginger and grate it frozen. If the roots are large, you do not have to buy the whole thing; just break off an inch or two. Thin-skinned gingerroot needs no peeling. The strongest flavor is just beneath the skin.

Grapefruit Choose grapefruits that are firm, spring to the touch, and feel heavy for their size. A heavy grapefruit indicates that it is full of juice. Grapefruit keeps for up to 8 weeks, refrigerated.

Grapes Good grapes have a velvety, powdery appearance. Too much handling will give grapes a smooth and shiny look. If the stems look dry and brown, they are past their peak flavor.

Greens (collards, kale, chard, mustard)   Collards and kale are both members of the cabbage family. They look tough and leathery, but once cooked, they become almost silky and soft. Chard is a member of the beet family. To prepare greens, first discard any yellow or damaged leaves. Strip the leaves from large or tough stems and discard the stems. To cut the leaves, stack, bundle, or crumple them together with one hand while you slice with the other hand. Use greens in soups and stir-fries, or steamed as a yummy side dish drizzled with olive oil and a squeeze of lemon. Mustard greens are good in stir-fries and salads, and their peppery taste adds spark to a sandwich. Look for bundles with small, young leaves.

Kiwi   This fruit softens at room temperature and is ready to eat when it yields slightly to the touch. Eat kiwis peeled or unpeeled. After washing the kiwi, you'll barely notice the peel on thin slices. Scoop kiwis from the half shell, or eat them like apples, skin and all. (The skin is slightly tart.) Store ripened kiwis in the refrigerator. They will last up to 3 weeks. One fuzzy, lime-shaped, green fruit offers 125 percent of the vitamin C you need each day.

Leeks   Leeks are a member of the onion family but less pungent in taste. They resemble giant scallions and are good for soups and marinated vegetable plates. Use only the white and light green part near the bulb. Rinse well under running water to remove the sand and gravel that collect in their overlapping leaves. They are sold in bunches of three or four, or you can buy just one.

Lemons and Limes   The best lemons and limes have a fine-textured skin and are heavy for their size. Avoid fruit that is soft or spongy feeling. Look at the stem; that's where signs of aging begin. Get more juice from the fuit by gently rolling it on the counter and applying pressure with your hand before you cut it. This helps break the interior cells of the fruit. If you don't have a lemon squeezer, insert a fork into the center of a cut lemon or lime and twist to juice.

Lettuce   Lettuce is about the only produce that has managed to avoid becoming a processed food. You will not find it canned, frozen, or dehydrated. Forget iceberg lettuce, those tight round heads that look like green bowling balls. (It costs less and keeps longer than other kinds of lettuce, but it's the least nutritious and according to some, the least flavorful.) Pick dark green romaine, Boston, Bibb, or loose-leaf lettuces (redleaf and greenleaf).

Mushrooms   There are many varieties of mushrooms, but creminis or Italian mushrooms are the ones you are sure to see in most markets. Choose mushrooms with closed caps when they open and look like umbrellas, it is a sign they have been hanging around the store too long. Store mushrooms in a paper bag in the refrigerator, never in plastic; they will keep for several days. Just before using fresh mushrooms, wipe them with a paper towel. Don't wash them because they'll become waterlogged and have less flavor when cooked.

Onions   The most common onions used for cooking are white or yellow. Sweet onions, like Bermudas, are good raw in salads and sandwiches. Choose onions that have their protective skin, are symmetrical, and are heavy for their size Avoid those with soft or discolored spots and "sprouters"; they are old. Store onions in a cool, dry place, and always keep a few on hand. If you only need half an onion, chop the whole thing, and store what's left in the refrigerator. It will keep for several days, and you'll have a head start on tomorrow's meal. If chopping an onion causes your eyes to water, chilling the onion in the refrigerator for a few minutes will help ease the problem. Onions contain a substance called sulfur oxide. When it comes in contact with the moisture in your eyes, it forms a compound similar to sulfuric acid. That's why your eyes burn.

Oranges   Do not depend on color to determine whether an orange is ripe and ready to eat. Instead, look for oranges that are firm and feel heavy for their size; this indicates lots of juice. Store them in the refrigerator for up to 6 weeks.

Parsnips   Most people grow up without tasting parsnips. Try one if you are feeling adventurous. Parsnips look like an off-white carrot and have a unique nutlike flavor and a mild fragrance. Look for smooth, firm, well-shaped roots that are small to medium in size; large ones are likely to have woody cores, which must be removed. Peel them before using. They add sweetness to stews and soups and are tasty steamed, sautéed, or baked. They will keep for several weeks in the refrigerator.

Pears   Growers pick pears before they are ripe, and they wind up in the produce department rock hard and bitter tasting. To achieve the sweet, buttery flavor that makes pears so delicious, ripen them in a warm place for 2 to 3 days or longer. Putting them in a perforated paper bag hastens the ripening process. They are ready to eat when the flesh around the stem yields to gentle pressure.

Peas, Garden, and Chinese Snow Peas   Most peas sold in markets are frozen. They are one of the few vegetables that hold their taste when processed. Chinese snow peas are tiny inside, and the pod is tender, so they are eaten whole. One of the best ways to enjoy fresh peas is to eat them raw. Use fresh peas as soon as possible.

Peppers, Bell   Red, green, or yellow—they are all good. The green ones are usually the cheapest, and you can often use them interchangeably. However, for roasted red peppers, there is no substitution.

Potatoes   Russet potatoes have a brown skin and are good for baking. White and red potatoes are good for all-around use: boiling, frying, mashing, and roasting. Watch out for potatoes with a greenish cast; they will taste bitter. Buy a few at a time if you are cooking for one person, and store them in a cool, dry place. It does not take long for a big bag of potatoes to start sprouting and grow moldy. Pare off potato eyes, green spots, and blemishes before using. You don't need to peel potatoes.

Radishes   Buy firm, bright-looking radishes with green crisp leaves and smooth, firm roots.

Spinach   If you buy spinach by the bunch, float the leaves in a big pot or bowl of water. The sand that clings to the leaves will sink to the bottom.

Sprouts, Mung Bean   The freshest sprouts are pearl-white and have not started to turn yellow. Store them for only 1 or 2 days in a sealed plastic bag in the refrigerator. Use them in stir-fries.

Squash, Summer   Zucchini is the best known, and it's available year-round. Choose squash that are small for their size, crisp, and free of wrinkled skin. They will keep refrigerated for a week.

Squash, Winter   Look for hard skin that shows no signs of softening or cracking. You will find winter squashes available in the supermarket year-round. Uncut squash will keep for months in a cool, dry place. Green and orange-colored winter squash can be a meal by themselves, used in soups, or stuffed with grains. Acorn and butternut are a good beginner's choice. Don't peel a squash before baking it. Simply cut in half and cook it cut-side down. Raw squash added to soups and stews will require peeling.

Tomatoes   Choose tomatoes that are firm to the touch. Store ripe tomatoes in the refrigerator. Don't bother to peel them. If you use only a portion of a tomato, store the remainder cut-side down on a ceramic or glass dish to keep it from becoming slimy.

Turnips and Rutabagas   These are close relatives, and they are interchangeable. Choose roots with firm, smooth skin, and avoid very large ones, which may be woody and pithy. It is best to peel them before using because the skin can be chewy. Like carrots, they make good snacks eaten raw. They are delicious tossed into soups or stews, steamed, sautéed, and baked. They will keep refrigerated for 1 to 2 weeks.

Yams and Sweet Potatoes   What American supermarkets call a yam is in fact a variety of sweet potato. (A true yam has a hairy, woody, brown exterior, and it is not widely available in the United States.) Do not substitute a true yam for a sweet potato. The light-color sweet potato you find in most supermarkets has a pale yellow flesh and is dry and crumbly when cooked. The darker variety sweet potato, often mislabeled as a yam, has a dark orange flesh and is sweet and moist when cooked. Look for firm, plump, blemish-free potatoes. They'll keep for a few weeks stored in a cool, dry place. Do not refrigerate them unless they are already cooked. Sweet potatoes can be peeled and eaten raw for a snack or grated and eaten raw in salads. They lend themselves to baking, boiling, and roasting. Don't peel whole sweet potatoes or yams before baking, but do peel them for stews and soups.

Soy Foods

Just as whole kernels of wheat become flour for bread, pasta, and cookies, soybeans come in a variety of forms. Look for the following soy foods as you shop.

Miso Miso is a thick puree made from the fermentation of soy beans, salt, and various grains ranging in flavor from light to hearty.

White or rice miso is mild and relatively sweet, red or barley miso is savory, and dark soy miso is thick and strongly flavored. Miso adds rich flavor to soups, spreads, stews, and sauces. You will find it in natural food stores and Asian markets.

Soy Cheese Made from soy milk, soy cheese is similar but not identical to dairy cheese. Some soy cheese has casein added to make it melt when heated, and casein is a milk product. If you are a vegan looking to avoid all animal products, read the label on the cheese before tossing it into your shopping basket. You will find soft varieties of soy cheese gently whipped into a consistency much like cream cheese, and firm cheese similar to mozzarella and Cheddar.

Soy Milk This dairy-free beverage is made by blending soaked whole soybeans with water and straining out the pulp. Use it in the same way you use cow's milk. Various brands taste surprisingly different from one another. If you don't like the first one you try, sample several others before you make a final decision about whether soy milk is for you. In cooked food—such as soup—there is little taste difference between soy milk and cow's milk. Lightly sweetened, plain, or vanilla soy milk is delicious poured on cereal, and it makes yummy chocolate pudding or "milk" shakes. Most soy milk is hermetically sealed to last months before opening; once opened, soy milk keeps for about 7 to 10 days in the refrigerator. Look for brands made from organic soybeans and fortified with calcium.

Soy Sauce   The best soy sauce has no sugar, food coloring, or chemical additives. Both shoyu and tamari are Japanese-type soy sauces. Shoyu contains soybeans, wheat, water, and salt. Tamari is a by-product of miso making and is saltier and more strongly flavored than shoyu, and it contains no wheat. It adds flavor and salt to soups, stews, sauces, and stir-fries. American, Japanese, and Chinese products are available in natural food stores, Asian groceries, and supermarkets.

Soy Yogurt   Cultured from soy milk and available in many flavors, soy yogurt is lactose- and cholesterol-free. It has the texture of dairy yogurt, but it does not taste the same.

Tempeh   This cultured soybean product is a fermented soybean cake with a nutty aroma and chewy texture that may remind you of meat. Marinate it in soy sauce, and then fry, grill, or steam it. Use it as a meat replacement in stir-fries or stews. Look for tempeh in most natural food stores either fresh or, more commonly, frozen. Thaw tempeh before using, but slice it while it's partially frozen to avoid crumbling.

Tofu   Tofu is a versatile food made by separating soy milk into curds and whey and pressing the curds into blocks. It has a unique custardlike consistency with little taste of its own. It readily absorbs the flavors from other ingredients, and the recipes in this book will help you turn tofu into one of your favorite fast foods. Tofu varies by firmness and texture.

Extra-firm tofu and *firm tofu* are dense and solid and are ideal for slicing, dicing, frying, and broiling. They hold up well in soups, lasagna, and spaghetti sauce. *Soft tofu* is creamy and useful for dressings, dips, shakes, and desserts.

Silken tofu has a fine, creamy consistency and is made from a slightly different process. Silken tofu is also available in extra-firm, firm, and soft. It can be used in the applications described earlier. In Japan, silken tofu is enjoyed as is with a touch of soy sauce and topped with chopped green onions.

Seasoned tofu is ready to eat straight from the package. It is a firm, dense tofu product produced by extracting the water under pressure and cooking the solids with soy sauce and spices. Use it in sandwiches and savory dishes.

Tofu is usually found in the produce section of the supermarket, although some stores sell tofu in the dairy or deli sections. It is most commonly sold in water-filled tubs, vacuum packs, or aseptic packages. Check the expiration date on the package, and buy tofu as far ahead of the expiration date as possible.

Store aseptic packages of tofu in a cool place or the refrigerator. Once an aseptic package is opened, refrigerate unused portions in an air-tight container, and use within 2 days.

Store water-filled tubs in the refrigerator. Opened water-packed tofu can be stored for a week if it is covered and the water changed daily. If tofu becomes slimy or sour, throw it away.

Store seasoned tofu in the refrigerator. *Do not rinse and cover seasoned tofu with water.*

Here's a chart to help you determine how best to keep your tofu fresh:

| | BEFORE OPENING | | AFTER OPENING | |
	Store in Refrigerator	Store in Cupboard	Rinse and Cover with Fresh Water	Store Covered in Refrigerator
Water-Filled Tubs	X		X	X
Vacuum Packs	X		X	X
Aseptic Packages		X		X
Seasoned Tofu	X			X

Depending on the dish you're making, you may want to make water-packed tofu firmer by pressing out some of the water. Pressed water-packed tofu grills beautifully and picks up more flavor in stir-fries. Strange as the pressing process may sound, give it a try. Sandwich the tofu between two plates. Weight the top plate with a heavy book. (Sometimes the top plate slides off during the pressing process, so keep the plates away from the edge of a counter or table.) After 15 to 30 minutes, remove the weight and top plate, and drain the water from the bottom plate. The tofu is now ready to slice and use.

Breads and Grains

Store whole grain bread, corn tortillas, whole wheat flour, brown rice, oatmeal, and most other grains in your refrigerator or freezer. They will last longer, and you won't find your supplies invaded by mold or insects. Single slices of frozen bread thaw in minutes, and if you're in a hurry, pop the bread into a toaster.

Shopping List

Shopping with a list can save you time and energy. Organize your list by type of item; this simplifies your path through the store. Keep a running list of basics; when you get low on an item, add it to the list. Here is a list of basic supplies to have on hand that will keep you cooking if there is a blizzard, you've got 2 days of nonstop exams, or you are sick and need to fend for yourself.

Breads and Grains

- ☐ Baked chips
- ☐ Brown rice
- ☐ Cornmeal
- ☐ Flour (whole grain and white)
- ☐ Oatmeal
- ☐ Rice cakes
- ☐ Tortillas
- ☐ Whole grain breads
- ☐ Whole grain pasta
- ☐ Whole grain pocket bread
- ☐ Whole grain, ready-to-eat cereal

Commercially Prepared Food

- ☐ Canned beans (black, garbanzo, kidney, pinto, refried)
- ☐ Canned whole tomatoes
- ☐ Chili
- ☐ Soup
- ☐ Pasta sauce

Fresh Produce

- ☐ Apples
- ☐ Bananas
- ☐ Bell peppers
- ☐ Carrots
- ☐ Garlic
- ☐ Lemons
- ☐ Lettuce
- ☐ Onions
- ☐ Oranges
- ☐ Potatoes
- ☐ Sweet potatoes
- ☐ Tomatoes
- ☐ Winter squash

Nuts, Seeds, Dried Beans, and Dried Fruit

- ☐ Dried beans (kidney and pinto)
- ☐ Dried split peas
- ☐ Figs
- ☐ Lentils
- ☐ Natural nut butters (refrigerate)

- [ ] Raisins
- [ ] Tahini (sesame seed butter; refrigerate)
- [ ] Unsalted nuts

Condiments
- [ ] Fruit spreads
- [ ] Maple syrup
- [ ] Mustard
- [ ] Salsa
- [ ] Soy sauce
- [ ] Tabasco
- [ ] Vinegar

Oil
- [ ] Canola oil
- [ ] Olive oil
- [ ] Toasted sesame oil

Refrigerated Items
- [ ] Cheese
- [ ] Eggs
- [ ] Lowfat yogurt
- [ ] Miso
- [ ] Soy milk or lowfat dairy milk
- [ ] Tofu

Frozen Foods
- [ ] Corn
- [ ] Peas

Beverages
- [ ] Coffee
- [ ] Juice
- [ ] Tea

CHAPTER 2

Tools, Techniques, and Terms

Secrets Revealed

Most people learn how to cook through trial and error. Don't let cooking intimidate you. It's really very simple: You just apply heat over time, and things cook. There's much more latitude in cooking than you might think, and numbers are fairly arbitrary. If you like carrots, add more. If you don't like mushrooms, use fewer. Taste as you go to learn how different ingredients add flavor to your cooking. As you become familiar with recipes, you won't feel the need to measure each 1/4 teaspoon of basil or 1/2 cup of chopped bell pepper. You will find many vegetarian recipes begin with cutting an onion, mincing a clove of garlic, or sautéing vegetables for 3 to 5 minutes. This simple process can make the difference between food that is disappointing or simply delicious. With a little experience, cooking will become more creative and faster. Finally, it's just food, and it can't bite back.

People have managed for centuries to put elaborate meals on the table with little more than one pot, a skillet, a bowl, a knife, a spoon, a spatula, and some source of heat. You can, too. You don't need fancy equipment to prepare delicious vegetarian meals.

A Few Helpful Tools

Knives You'll need a big knife (one that comfortably fits your hand) and a small paring knife for peeling and finer cuts. A good knife can be expensive, but it lasts a lifetime. (Sharpening knives is best done by hand rather than a machine. A few strokes across a steel—a metal rod with a finely ridged surface—keeps the edge sharp.)

Pans A 10-inch skillet is an ideal size to have on hand. Many chefs stand by indestructible cast iron pans and stainless steel skillets. Some cooks prefer nonstick cookware because it requires significantly less oil for cooking and makes cleaning up easier and faster. However, recent warnings about the possible danger of a chemical used in making nonstick cookware may persuade you not to use it.

Pots Buy a 3-quart or 4-quart pot with a lid. If you're a minimalist, this one pot is a suitable tool for performing most cooking functions. You may also need a larger pot if you're going to cook big batches of pasta or homemade chili. Get the best pots you can afford. Flimsy, thin-bottom cookware heats food unevenly and causes it to burn. Avoid aluminum pots because aluminum can leach into your food.

Miscellaneous Tools Here is a list of additional helpful items:

baking dish
colander
cutting board, wooden
dishcloths, two
dish towels, two
handheld can opener—not electric (The Swing-A-Way brand
    is a good bet at about $8.)
handheld grater

measuring spoons (If you don't have measuring spoons,
a regular teaspoon works fine. Three teaspoons equal
one tablespoon.)
mixing bowl
pot holders, two
potato masher
slotted long-handled spoon
slotted spatula
vegetable steamer basket or pot

Cutting Up Food

Knowing a few basic principles will help you cook efficiently
and make food taste great; good cooks soon attract hungry
spectators around their kitchen table.

To reduce preparation time and to wield your knife like
the cooks you see on TV, use a sharp knife. A knife is much
more likely to slip and cut you if it is dull, and the food may
turn out looking like it was run over by a bicycle tire.

For most cutting, hold the food in place with one hand,
curling your fingers slightly back so that no fingertips are left
sticking out for the knife to find. Hold the knife with your
thumb and first finger on either side of the blade.

Don't always cut things into tiny pieces. Cut larger
pieces, when possible, to save time. Use large chunks for stews
and smaller cuts for salads and stir-fries. Whenever appropri-
ate, use unpeeled fruits and vegetables. To make cutting
round food easy, first slice off a small portion to create a flat
surface. Place the cut side down, and begin slicing pieces.

Know Your Terms

Chiffonade   This is a way to cut large flat leaves like spinach
and kale. Crumple and rumple the leaves into a ball, and
hold them together with one hand while you cut with your

other hand. Another method is to roll the leaves from end to end and slice into thin strips.

Chop   Cut foods into pieces about 1/2-inch square.

Dice or Finely Chop   Cut slices crosswise in each direction to create cubes or pieces ranging in size from 1/8 inch to 1/4 inch. To speed things up, bundle slices together and cut through the pile.

Grate   Use a low-tech multisided grater to grate fresh vegetables and cheese for small salads and other meals. Grated foods add an interesting texture and lightness to dishes.

Mince   Garlic and gingerroot are commonly minced. Very small pieces tend to jump and scatter. Use the knife blade to push the pieces back into a heap to make cutting easier.

Slice   Make cuts about 1/2 inch apart for thick slices, 1/8 to 1/4 inch for thinner slices.

Cooking Terms

Baking and Roasting   What's the difference? There isn't any. Both terms describe preparing food with dry heat in an oven. Baking or roasting usually takes longer than most other cooking methods. Remember to preheat the oven so that it will be the right temperature when you are ready to begin cooking. This is especially important when baking cakes, breads, and cookies. Preheating also speeds up the cooking process.

Boiling and Simmering   Boiled foods cook in rapidly agitating liquid with bubbles breaking on the surface. Simmering involves more gently moving liquid, cooking just below the boiling point.

Braising This is simmering foods in a small amount of liquid. Use vegetable stock, wine, soy sauce, or juices as all or part of the liquid to increase the flavor of the finished dish. Add salt toward the end of cooking because salt concentrates as the liquids evaporate.

Broiling Broiling involves cooking in a preheated oven, with food approximately 3 to 4 inches from the heat. This method is fast and requires close attention because the heat is high and foods can quickly burn. Leave the oven door slightly ajar so you can see what's happening.

Microwaving Microwaves are good for reheating food and cooking a limited number of dishes. (For truly wonderful-tasting meals, use some other cooking method.) Never put metal items inside a microwave because they can cause dangerous sparking. If this happens, switch the oven off at once. Never turn the oven on when it is empty; microwaves may bounce off the walls and damage the cavity.

Sautéing Sautéing is a quick cooking method done on top of the stove. Food usually cooks in oil on medium or medium-high heat. Making sure the heat isn't too high can head off trouble. Heat the oil in the skillet before adding the food, and the food will absorb less of it. To *sauté until soft* means to cook until the food is tender but not browned. To *sauté until brown* means to cook gently until the food is golden. A flavorful sauté is what gives real body to different dishes. It may seem like the liquid and starchy ingredients form the "base" or "soul" of pot foods like stews, soups, and beans, but actually they are more the medium that holds the bright flavors of your sauté.

Steaming Hot vapor produced by simmering or boiling water in a tightly covered pot cooks the food. Use a two-piece steaming pot or stainless steel steaming basket inserted into a pot with a tight-fitting lid. Keep the water level lower than the bottom of the steamer to avoid sogginess. Let the water come to a boil, and then add the vegetables. Properly steamed vegetables are crisp and tender with good color.

Steaming times for vegetables will vary according to variety and cut sizes. Most vegetables cook in a matter of minutes. Brussels sprouts, cabbage, and cauliflower overcook quickly. You will know because your kitchen will start to stink. When preparing vegetables that require longer cooking, check the water level and add more water if it is boiling away. When you open the pot, tilt the lid so that the rising steam will move away from you.

Stir-Frying   Stir-frying is the Asian version of a hot, fast cooking technique. One of the advantages to this type of cooking is that you can cook a whole meal and use only one skillet or wok.

Chop and slice the vegetables and measure the seasoning before starting. Line up all of your ingredients near the stove. Heat a small amount of oil in a hot skillet, and then add the garlic, the seasonings for flavoring the whole dish, and vegetables a handful at a time. When cooking with garlic on high heat, keep an eye on it, because garlic burns easily. Avoid overcrowding the pan; otherwise you'll end up with soggy food. Begin by tossing in the hard vegetables first and progress to softer vegetables. Always keep the food in motion—stir and fry. The last things you add are liquid seasonings, like soy sauce. Remove the vegetables from the pan quickly to maintain crispness.

Never immerse a hot pan in cold water—this can warp the metal. Let the pan cool slightly, then add water.

Season to Taste

Research in the fields of chemistry and psychology suggests that specific aromas can increase brain power and the ability to concentrate. A study at the University of Cincinnati demonstrated that people in a room scented with peppermint had more correct answers to test questions than people taking the same test in unscented rooms. So take a deep breath when you season food in the kitchen. As you experiment, you'll learn how different seasonings and foods naturally go together. The more you use seasonings, the more your seasoning sense will become second nature.

Herbs and Spices

For starters, begin with a few basic dried herbs and spices: basil, cinnamon, cumin, curry, mint, oregano, rosemary, and thyme. It is best to buy herbs and spices in the smallest possible amounts, and store them in tightly closed bottles in a cool, dry spot out of direct light. Replace seasonings after 6 months to a year when their aroma and taste have faded. When substituting dried herbs for fresh ones, use about one-third the amount called for in the recipe. When increasing a recipe, don't increase the seasonings as drastically as the main ingredients. Make small changes, and taste. Sprinkle spices and herbs from your hand or a measuring spoon into a steaming pot, not from the bottle. Steam introduced into the bottle will hasten the loss of flavor and aroma.

Cilantro and parsley are two herbs that must be fresh. Dried parsley tastes like straw, and dried cilantro doesn't resemble the fresh version at all. Most people love fresh cilantro, but taste it before you toss a handful into something you're cooking. Substitute parsley if you don't like cilantro.

Sophisticated Tastes

Condiments from around the globe, once found only in expensive gourmet grocery stores, are now on the shelves of well-stocked supermarkets; they bring instant, striking flavor to meals. Use chutney to jazz up plain baked potatoes, winter squash, and bagels. If you like your food "hot 'n' spicy," Szechwan sauce and Vietnamese red chili sauce can perk up main dish meals. Hoisin sauce, often called the catsup of Asia, is a popular table condiment for a variety of dishes, including stir-fries. It is made from soy sauce, garlic, and chiles with the sweet flavor of anise. Hoisin sauce is a great marinade for tofu. A splash of vinegar gives oven-roasted potatoes, cooked vegetables, soup, and even a pot of beans a wonderful boost. Tahini, made from ground sesame seeds, adds interesting flavor to many dishes and dips. A few drops of toasted sesame oil gives stir-fries and cooked vegetables real character. It costs about $4, but its powerful flavor makes a small bottle last a long time. Don't forget the ever-popular salsa, Tabasco, catsup, and mustard for flavoring food.

CHAPTER 3

Breakfast Anytime

On most mornings, cold cereal or a bagel will do, but when you're ready for more, wake up to Overnight Oatmeal—it "cooks" while you sleep. Stir up a quick tofu scramble, or sdelight your friends with a Beer Pancake brunch. You will find ideas in this chapter that are satisfying any time of the day.

Open-Face Omelet

PREPARATION TIME: 15 minutes

This is so delicious! It's a great way to use up bits of vegetables. You need about 2 cups of vegetables for 2 eggs. The Sesame Sauce takes only minutes to prepare, and it's worth making to see the magic the cornstarch performs. Serve the omelet with a cup of hot tea and fragrant tangerine slices.

$1/2$ cup onions, thinly sliced (about $1/4$ medium onion)
1 tablespoon vegetable oil
1 cup bean sprouts (the white ones with the tiny pale
    yellow-green heads)
6 to 8 snow peas, thinly sliced (about $1/4$ cup)
$1/4$ cup celery, thinly sliced (about $1/4$ medium stalk)
2 eggs
$1/2$ teaspoon soy sauce
$1/2$ teaspoon fresh ginger, finely minced

Sesame Sauce
$1/2$ cup water
1 tablespoon soy sauce
$1/4$ teaspoon toasted sesame oil
1 green onion, finely chopped
2 teaspoons cornstarch
2 teaspoons cool water

1. In a medium skillet on medium-high heat, sauté the onion in the oil for 3 to 4 minutes, until translucent. Add bean sprouts, snow peas, and celery; continue to sauté for 3 to 4 minutes.

2. In a bowl, whisk together the eggs, soy sauce, and ginger.

3. When the vegetables are crisp-tender, pour the eggs over the vegetables. Cook on low heat until the egg mixture is golden on one side, about 3 minutes. Cut egg "pancake" in half with a spatula, and turn each piece. Cook until the undersides are golden and the eggs are set, about 3 minutes.

4. While the omelet cooks, make the sauce. In a small saucepan, bring $1/2$ cup water, soy sauce, sesame oil, and green onion to a boil. Dissolve the cornstarch in cool water, and stir it into the simmering sauce. Continue stirring until the sauce thickens. Remove from heat.

Serve omelet with a splash of Sesame Sauce, or if preferred, sprinkle with soy sauce and chopped green onions, or sprinkle with sesame seeds.

NOTE: You can substitute the following vegetables for the snow peas or celery: mushrooms, bok choy, broccoli, green peas, or bell pepper.

Makes two servings

Fried Egg Taco

This breakfast is ready to go in minutes. For a big meal, add a side dish of beans and a slice of melon.

$1/4$ cup commercial salsa
$1/2$ small tomato, chopped
1 teaspoon chopped fresh cilantro or parsley
1 egg
1 teaspoon vegetable oil
1 corn tortilla

Extras (Optional)
Black or green olives
Grated cheese
Green onion, chopped
Mild green chiles, canned

1. In a small saucepan, heat salsa, tomato, and cilantro until warm, but not simmering.
2. Fry the egg in a small, lightly oiled skillet on medium-high heat until well set on the bottom, about 1 minute; then cover the pan and cook until the egg is completely set (the white will no longer be clear).
3. Heat a corn tortilla in a heavy skillet on medium-high until just beginning to brown, about 30 seconds.
4. Place warm tortilla on a plate. Top with egg and salsa mixture. Sprinkle on your choice of extras; fold and eat.

Makes one serving

Fifteen-Minute
French Toast

PREPARATION TIME: 5 minutes

COOKING TIME: 3 to 4 minutes per pancake

If you're looking for a quick breakfast, soak the bread in the batter the night before, cover, and refrigerate until morning. They take just a few minutes to cook.

$1/2$ cup soy milk or dairy milk
1 egg
$1/4$ teaspoon vanilla
$1/4$ teaspoon ground cinnamon
1 teaspoon sugar (optional)
4 slices multigrain bread
2 teaspoons vegetable oil

1. In a shallow pan or bowl, whisk together the milk, egg, vanilla, cinnamon, and sugar.
2. Dip the slices of bread into the milk mixture one by one, turning to coat both sides.
3. Heat a lightly oiled, medium skillet on medium heat, and fry the bread until it is lightly browned on both sides. Serve topped with maple syrup, sliced fruit, applesauce, or your favorite fruit spread.

Makes two servings

Fluffy Vegan Pancakes

PREPARATION TIME: 4 minutes

COOKING TIME: 3 to 4 minutes per pancake

This eggless recipe makes light, fluffy pancakes due to whipping the liquid ingredients with a fork for 1 minute until frothy.

1 cup whole wheat flour
1 cup unbleached white flour
1 tablespoon baking powder
2 cups soy milk
1 tablespoon vegetable oil

1. Stir the flour and baking powder together in a large bowl. In a separate bowl, combine the soy milk and oil, and whip for about 1 minute. Pour the soy mixture into the flour mixture. Stir just to combine. Don't worry about lumps.

2. Lightly oil a medium skillet. Heat over medium heat. When a few drops of water sprinkled on the skillet sizzle or bead up, the pan is ready.

3. For each pancake, pour 1/2 cup of the batter onto the skillet. Cook until the pancakes begin to bubble, about 3 minutes. Turn with a spatula, and cook until the underside is lightly browned. Serve with maple syrup.

NOTE: If you like thin pancakes, add more soy milk a tablespoon at a time.

Makes two servings

Beer Pancakes

PREPARATION TIME: 5 minutes

COOKING TIME: About 3 minutes for each pancake

Eat these intriguing pancakes for breakfast or dessert.

1³/₄ cups whole wheat flour
1¹/₂ teaspoons baking powder
¹/₂ teaspoon baking soda
1 egg
3 tablespoons vegetable oil
1 tablespoon honey
1 can or bottle (12 ounces) beer

1. In a large bowl, combine the flour, baking powder, and baking soda, and mix well. In another bowl, whisk together the egg, oil, and honey with a fork.
2. Add the liquid mixture and the beer to the dry ingredients; stir just until a smooth batter is formed. The batter will be somewhat lumpy and slightly thick.
3. Lightly oil a medium skillet, and place it over medium heat until hot. Pour ¹/₂ cup of the batter at a time onto the skillet. Cook the pancakes until the bottoms are golden brown and the tops begin to bubble. Flip them over, and cook until the undersides are golden brown. Serve with maple syrup.

Makes two or three servings

Hot Stovetop Oatmeal

Preparation Time: 10 minutes

Steaming oatmeal properly prepared is a hearty, early morning meal. This version is sweetened with strawberry preserves and uses old-fashioned rolled oats.

$1/2$ cup rolled oats
1 cup water
$1/8$ to $1/4$ teaspoon salt
2 teaspoons strawberry preserves (or more if you like)
2 tablespoons chopped walnuts or almonds

Extras (Optional)
Sliced bananas
Fresh or frozen berries
Raisins, dates, currants
A dash of cinnamon, nutmeg, or cardamom
Warm Apple Slices (page 223)
Chopped walnuts or almonds

1. In a small pot with a tight-fitting lid, bring the oats, water, and salt to a boil. Lower heat to medium-low, and continue to cook, stirring for about 5 minutes.

2. Remove from heat and stir in the preserves. Cover and let sit for 2 to 3 minutes.

3. Serve the oatmeal sprinkled with nuts, along with any of the optional items listed. If you desire, top with a splash of soy or dairy milk.

Variation: Omit the preserves and substitute maple syrup or brown sugar when you serve the dish.

NOTE: Do not use "quick-cooking or "instant" oatmeal. It turns to glue. Fill the empty pot with water as soon as you serve the oatmeal, and let it soak while you eat. The oatmeal that sticks to the sides of the pot will slide right off when it's clean-up time.

Makes one serving

Overnight Oatmeal

PREPARATION TIME: 4 minutes

Watching the sugar melt on a bowl of hot oatmeal fresh off the stove is a heavenly sight, but on those mornings when you're too busy to cook, wake up to oatmeal ready and waiting in the refrigerator.

1 cup old-fashioned rolled oats
1 cup soy milk or dairy milk
1 tablespoon raisins
$1/2$ teaspoon ground cinnamon
$1/2$ to 1 cup chopped seasonal fruit (optional)

1. In a cereal bowl, combine the oats, milk, raisins, and cinnamon. Cover and refrigerate overnight.

2. In the morning stir in fresh fruit, if you desire, and breakfast is ready. Serve it chilled.

Makes one or two servings

Scrambled Tofu Curry

Preparation Time: 7 minutes

Tofu scrambles are quick and versatile. Serve this dish with a slice of whole grain toast and a glass of chilled orange juice for a great start to the day.

5 ounces firm or extra-firm tofu (packaged in tubs of water)
1 teaspoon vegetable oil
1 tablespoon finely sliced scallion
1 tablespoon diced green or red bell pepper
2 tablespoons diced carrot
$1/4$ teaspoon curry powder
Salt and pepper

1. In a shallow bowl or plate, lightly mash the tofu with a fork so that it resembles the texture of scrambled eggs. Set it aside.

2. Heat the oil in a small skillet over medium heat. Sauté the scallion, pepper, carrot, and curry for 2 to 3 minutes, or until the vegetables begin to soften. Reduce the heat to low, and stir in the tofu; cook for about 1 minute or until the mixture is hot. Serve immediately. Salt and pepper to taste.

Makes one serving

Greek-Style Scrambled Tofu

PREPARATION TIME: 7 minutes

Serve with hot coffee, a muffin, and crisp apple slices.

5 ounces firm or extra-firm tofu
1 teaspoon olive oil
1/4 cup chopped scallion (include green end, 1 large or
    2 small)
2 cloves garlic, minced
1/4 teaspoon dried oregano
1 cup tightly packed chopped fresh spinach
2 to 3 tablespoons crumbled feta cheese
Salt and pepper (optional)

1. In a shallow bowl or plate, lightly mash the tofu with a fork so that it resembles the texture of scrambled eggs. Set it aside.

2. Heat the oil in a medium skillet over medium heat. Sauté the scallion, garlic, and oregano for 30 seconds, and add the spinach. Cook, stirring until the spinach wilts, about 3 minutes. The water that remains on the spinach from washing will be enough to cook the spinach.

3. Reduce the heat to low. Add the tofu, and gently stir until the mixture is warm, about 1 minute. Stir in the feta cheese, and serve immediately. Season with salt and pepper, if you desire.

Makes one serving

Corn Cakes

Preparation Time: 3 minutes

Cooking Time: About 5 minutes per corn cake

Here is a delicious way to use leftover polenta. Serve these cakes for breakfast with maple syrup and fresh fruit, or for lunch with chunky salsa.

Cooked, cooled polenta
Vegetable oil

Cut the polenta into 1/2-inch-thick slices, about the size of your hand. Lightly oil a nonstick skillet with vegetable oil, and set it over medium-high heat until hot. Add the polenta and fry until it is warm and slightly crispy on both sides.

Makes one serving

CHAPTER 4

Dips, Spreads, and Snacks

The recipes in this chapter are premium formulas for fast food. Combine these dips and spreads with crusty bread, crackers, chips, and vegetables, and voilà, you have the makings for simple meals or great snacks. Whip up a bowl of hummus and have a feast! What could be more heavenly than guacamole scooped onto tortillas or toast? If you're in a hurry, take a moment to make one of the recipes in this chapter—it's worth it!

Salsa

This salsa makes a delicious topping for any bean and rice dish. Salsa over plain rice with slices of ripe avocado is irresistible. And baked chips dipped in salsa is a first-class snack. Use whole canned tomatoes in the winter when fresh supermarket tomatoes are expensive. (They may even taste better.)

3 cups chopped fresh tomatoes or whole canned tomatoes, drained and chopped
$1/2$ cup chopped cilantro
3 or 4 medium chopped green onions
1 medium jalapeño chile, minced
3 tablespoons fresh lemon or lime juice
1 clove garlic, minced
Salt to taste

In a medium bowl, mix all ingredients together. You're all set.

NOTE: For the kick in your salsa, cilantro is a must. Most of the heat in chiles comes from the seeds inside. If you want to lower the fire, cut the chile lengthwise, and remove the seeds and veins. Avoid touching your eyes when cutting and deseeding chiles.

Makes about 3 cups

Tsiziki Sauce and Dip

PREPARATION TIME: 6 minutes

Dip fresh vegetables and chunks of French bread into this garlicky sauce. Use it as a dressing for green salads, grain dishes, and pocket-bread sandwiches. Adjust the number of garlic cloves to suit your taste.

1 large cucumber, peeled and finely chopped
1 cup plain nonfat yogurt
1 teaspoon dried dill weed
4 large cloves garlic, minced
1 tablespoon fresh lemon juice
Salt

Combine all the ingredients in a bowl. If you can wait, let it stand at room temperature for 20 minutes. Dive in. Store leftover sauce in the refrigerator. It will keep for 3 to 4 days.

Makes about 1 1/2 cups

Tahini Sauce

Preparation Time: 5 minutes

Drizzle this luscious sauce over a platter of steamed vegetables, or spoon it over baked sweet potatoes and grain dishes. It will keep in the refrigerator for a week or longer.

1 cup nonfat yogurt
2 teaspoons tahini
1 clove garlic, minced
$1^{1}/_{2}$ teaspoons lemon juice
$1/_{8}$ teaspoon salt
Pepper

Whisk together all of the ingredients and store it in the refrigerator.

Makes 1 cup

Guacamole – The Real Thing

PREPARATION TIME: 5 minutes

Here is a recipe for transforming an ordinary fruit into one of the world's greatest dips. If you can use a fork, you can make guacamole ("avocado sauce"). Use it as a dip with chips or as a topping for burritos, tacos, and quesadillas.

1 avocado (slightly overripe works best)
1 tablespoon fresh lemon or lime juice (to prevent browning)
Tabasco
1/8 teaspoon salt (optional)

1. Slice the avocado in half lengthwise, and gently twist to remove the seed. Make lengthwise and crosswise cuts into the flesh every 1/2 inch. Scoop the avocado cubes into a bowl. Mash the avocado with a fork and stir in lemon or lime juice.
2. Add a splash of Tabasco, and salt to taste.

Makes about 1 cup

Eggplant and Garlic Spread

PREPARATION TIME: 10 minutes

COOKING TIME: About 20 minutes

Make this dish into a hearty meal surrounded with toasted pita bread and fresh vegetables for dipping, or spread it on crusty French bread for a creamy open-faced sandwich. Broiling an eggplant is as simple as deflating a balloon. It is done cooking when the eggplant is completely wrinkled, limp, and soft.

1 eggplant (about 1 pound)
2 tablespoons tahini
2 tablespoons fresh lemon juice
1 large clove garlic, finely minced
2 tablespoons minced onion
Salt and pepper
1 teaspoon olive oil (optional)
1 tablespoon minced fresh parsley (optional)

Preheat the broiler.

1. Prick the eggplant in several places with a fork, and cut off the stem end. Place the eggplant on a baking sheet, and broil for 20 minutes or until done, turning the vegetable several times so that the skin chars on all sides.

2. When the eggplant is cool enough to handle, cut it in half; scrape out the flesh into a bowl. Discard the skin, and mash the eggplant with a potato masher or fork. Add the tahini, lemon juice, garlic, onion, and salt and pepper to taste.

3. If you have time, cover the spread and refrigerate it for a few hours. Before serving, sprinkle it with oil and parsley if you desire.

Makes about 1 1/2 cups

Roasted Garlic

PREPARATION TIME: 4 minutes

COOKING TIME: About 60 minutes

Once cooked, garlic's strong smell disappears, and the flavor becomes sweet and buttery. Use it to replace mayonnaise on sandwiches, spread it on slices of crusty sourdough bread, or use it on baked potatoes and pizza. To eat it, gently squeeze the large end of the cooked clove, and the garlic will slip out of the shell.

3 heads of garlic

Preheat the oven to 350 degrees F.

1. Carefully remove the outer papery skin from the garlic heads. Leave the heads intact, and do not break them apart into cloves.

2. Carefully cut the top 1/4 inch off of each head. Arrange the garlic heads in a small baking dish without crowding.

3. Add enough water to cover the bottom of the dish with 1/4 inch of water. Cover with a lid or seal the dish with foil and bake for about 60 minutes until the cloves are soft to the touch. Roasted garlic will last for at least a week in a covered container in the refrigerator.

Makes about 1/8 cup

Hummus

PREPARATION TIME: 8 minutes

Hummus is a rich pâté made from garbanzo beans. If you've never eaten hummus, you're in for a classic treat. Spread it on whole grain bread to make a superior sandwich piled high with greens, tomatoes, and sliced red onions, or create an entire meal around a plateful of hummus with warm pocket bread for dipping, and a salad on the side. Hummus will keep for several days in a covered container in the refrigerator.

1 (15-ounce) can garbanzo beans, drained (about 1^1/$_2$ cups)
6 to 7 tablespoons fresh lemon juice (1 large or 2 small)
2 cloves garlic, minced
2 tablespoons tahini
2 tablespoons minced onion
Salt (optional)
2 tablespoons minced fresh parsley (optional)

1. Mash the garbanzo beans into a thick paste using a masher, fork, or blender. Add the lemon juice, garlic, tahini, onion, and parsley if you wish; stir.

2. Hummus should have a consistency similar to mayonnaise. If it seems too thick, add more lemon juice, 1 tablespoon at a time. Season with salt to taste and add parsley, if you desire.

Makes about 1^3/$_4$ cups

Toasted Nori

PREPARATION TIME: 1 minute

Nori is a sea vegetable best known as a wrapper for sushi. When you have a snack attack, here's a 1-minute fix. This chip is a delicacy that you won't eat by the handfuls, but will nibble and savor.

1 sheet nori
Toasted sesame oil
Salt

Heat a sheet of nori until it becomes fragrant, about 30 seconds, by waving it over, but not on, a burner on medium-high heat. Remove from the heat, and rub the sheet with a few drops of toasted sesame oil. Sprinkle with salt. You'll have a large, crisp "chip."

Makes one serving

Popping Ideas!

Store popcorn in an airtight container in a cool place, or refrigerate. Water inside the corn kernel is what helps popcorn explode when it's heated. If you have trouble with unpopped kernels when you make popcorn, put the popcorn in a jar and add water. Let it soak for a few minutes and drain. Shake the jar to moisten all the kernels. Put a lid on the jar. The popcorn will be ready to use the next day.

Popcorn Fundamentals

An air popper is the easiest method for making popcorn. If you don't have one, use a pot. In a 6-quart heavy-bottomed pot, heat 1 tablespoon of olive oil on medium heat with 1/2 cup of popcorn. Cover with a lid slightly ajar to allow steam to escape. When the corn begins to pop, shake the pot until the popping almost stops. Remove from heat and wait for the kernels to stop popping before removing the lid.

Flavoring

If you're a plain buttered-popcorn-with-salt sort of person, you know what to do next. If you want something different, try one of these flavors. Whatever you choose, the important thing to add is salt; it brings out the taste.

Parmesan Popcorn

Sauté two cloves of minced garlic in 1 to 2 tablespoons olive oil on medium-high heat for about 1 minute. Pour the oil and garlic over the popcorn, and add Parmesan cheese and salt. Mix thoroughly. Taste. Add more salt if necessary.

Hot Chili Popcorn

Sauté two cloves of minced garlic in 2 tablespoons of olive oil on medium-high heat for about 1 minute. Add 1 teaspoon cumin powder and 1 teaspoon chili powder to oil and stir for a few seconds to combine. Pour oil mixture over popcorn. Add salt, mix thoroughly, and enjoy.

CHAPTER 5

Soups and Stews

Forget the idea that homemade soup takes hours to prepare. Although opening a can of soup is convenient, the soups you will find here are surprisingly quick to make. Minute Miso Soup is good for breakfast and dinner. Impulse Minestrone is ready in 10 minutes, and if you like soup thick and creamy, you'll enjoy Corn and Potato Chowder. "A good soup gathers chairs," so invite your friends, and ask them to bring the bread.

Minute Miso Soup

Preparation Time: 6 minutes

Miso is a concentrated, fermented pâté made from soybeans, with the consistency of creamy peanut butter. It makes a delicate, clear soup in minutes. A cup of miso soup can be a satisfying one-bowl pick-me-up when you want something warm to take the chill out of a night of studying, or it can be a quick breakfast. In Japan, it's part of the traditional morning meal along with rice.

You will find miso in Japanese and Chinese markets, natural food stores, and some supermarkets. It keeps almost indefinitely in the refrigerator. Miso comes in many flavors. For starters try red miso, barley miso, or Hatcho miso.

Sip a modest cup of miso soup, or try an extravagant version with tofu and onions. The variations on this soup are endless. Just remember, for best results use vegetables in small amounts and cook them only slightly.

2 cups water
4 onion slices, cut into very thin half moons
$1/4$ cup carrots, cut into thin matchsticks
$1/4$ cup tofu, cut into small cubes
1 tablespoon miso
Dash of pepper
1 tablespoon chopped scallion (optional)

1. Combine the water, onion, and carrots in a small covered saucepan, and simmer for 3 to 5 minutes. Add the tofu.

2. Place the miso in a cup with about $1/4$ cup of the cooking liquid. Mix until all the miso is dissolved; add it to the soup. Do not boil after the miso is added. (High heat destroys miso's beneficial enzymes.) Season with pepper and garnish with scallions if you desire.

Makes two servings

Impulse Minestrone Soup

PREPARATION TIME: 15 minutes

This soup always turns out wonderfully, and it never needs to be the same. Start with one can each of tomatoes and beans and add from there. If you are using frozen vegetables, buy them in bags rather than boxes. It's easier to scoop out the amount you need.

1 teaspoon olive oil
1 large clove garlic, finely chopped
1/2 medium zucchini, sliced (about 1 cup)
1/2 teaspoon dried basil
1/8 teaspoon dried oregano
1 cup frozen mixed vegetables
1 cup canned kidney beans, drained
1 (141/2-ounce) can diced tomatoes, undrained
1 cup water
2 cups uncooked spiral pasta
Salt and pepper
Grated Parmesan (optional)

1. Heat the oil in a medium saucepan on medium heat. Sauté the garlic, zucchini, basil, and oregano, and cook, stirring, for 2 to 3 minutes. Add the mixed vegetables, beans, tomatoes, and water. Simmer for 10 minutes.

2. While the soup warms, cook the pasta in a small saucepan of boiling water for 7 to 9 minutes. Drain. Add the pasta to the soup.

3. Remove the soup from the heat and serve. Season with salt and pepper to taste. Sprinkle with grated Parmesan if you desire.

Makes two servings

Split Pea Soup

PREPARATION TIME: 18 minutes

COOKING TIME: About 40 minutes

Here chipotle chiles are used to add a hot, smoky flavor to the soup. You'll find chipotle chiles in cans packed in adobo sauce in the Mexican section of the supermarket. Wash your hands after cutting chiles because they can cause a burning sensation on your skin. Store leftover chiles in a container in the freezer.

2 teaspoons olive oil
1 cup chopped onion (1 small)
2 large cloves garlic, minced
2 medium carrots, sliced (about 2 cups)
4 cups water
1 cup dried, green split peas
2 chipotle chiles, chopped (optional)
1 large potato, cubed into $1/2$-inch pieces (about 2 cups)
$1/4$ teaspoon salt

1. Heat the oil in a 3- to 4-quart saucepan; sauté the onion and garlic on medium heat until the onion is tender, about 5 minutes, stirring occasionally. Add the carrots and continue cooking and stirring occasionally for another 3 to 5 minutes. Add the water, peas, and chipotles (if desired).

2. Cover the pot and bring it to a boil. Reduce the heat to low and simmer, covered, until the peas are tender (about 30 minutes), stirring occasionally.

3. When the peas are tender, add the potatoes to the pot and cook until they are tender, about 15 minutes. Add the salt. Serve with slices of crusty multigrain bread.

NOTE: Prepare the soup without the chipotle chiles, and it's still delicious—simply season to taste with salt and pepper.

Makes four servings

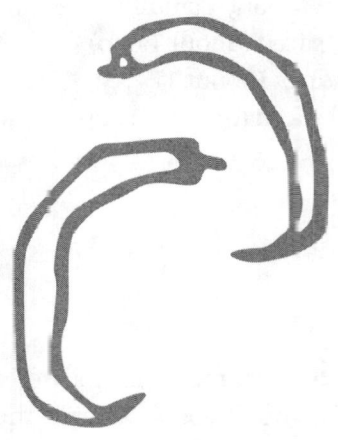

Barley Mushroom Soup

PREPARATION TIME: 20 minutes

COOKING TIME: About 45 minutes

This recipe turns water, barley, and a few vegetables into a satisfying, thick soup. It is amazing what a slow, 10-minute sauté can do to flavor the simplest ingredients. A pound of barley costs about $0.75 and can make four big pots of soup.

1 tablespoon chopped dried shiitake mushrooms (about 2)
1/2 cup hot water for soaking mushrooms
1 tablespoon olive oil
1 cup chopped onion (about 1 small)
4 fresh mushrooms, sliced (about 1 cup)
1 cup thinly sliced carrot (about 1)
1 stalk celery, thinly sliced (about 1/2 cup)
1/2 cup pearl barley
2 tablespoons flour
3 cups water
1/2 teaspoon salt
Pepper

1. Soften the shiitake mushrooms in hot water for 10 minutes, and then dice the mushrooms. Reserve the soaking liquid. Heat the oil in a 3- or 4-quart pot over medium heat. Add the shiitake mushrooms, onions, fresh mushrooms, carrot, celery, and barley. Sauté on medium-low heat for about 10 minutes, stirring frequently so the vegetables and barley do not burn. Keep an eye on the bottom of the pot and reduce the heat if the sauté is sticking or browning too quickly.

2. Add the flour, stirring continually for 1 minute. Immediately add 3 cups of water and the mushroom soaking liquid. Scrape the bottom of the pot with a big spoon to incorporate any flour that may stick to the bottom. This step is important because the flavor from the sauté is in the stuff that may be on the bottom of the pot. Continue scraping and stirring until the bottom of the pot feels smooth, about 1 minute.

3. Add the salt. Bring to a boil, then reduce the heat. Cover and simmer for about 45 minutes or until the barley is tender. Stir the pot occasionally as the soup cooks. Taste for seasoning, and add salt and pepper if necessary.

Makes two to three servings

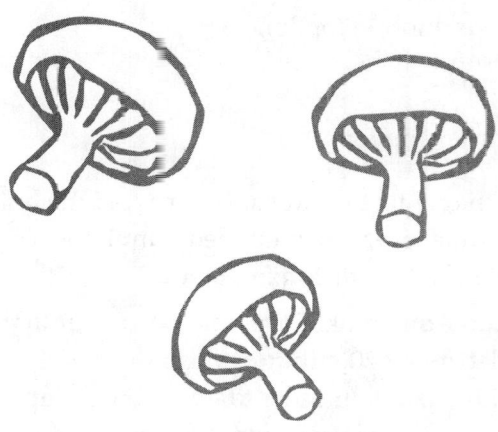

Corn and Potato Chowder

PREPARATION TIME: 10 minutes

COOKING TIME: About 20 minutes

This easy-to-prepare chowder has the richness of a creamed soup without the cream.

1 tablespoon olive oil
1 cup small onion, chopped (about 1 cup)
2 medium stalks celery, thinly sliced (about 1 cup)
2 to 3 medium russet potatoes, cut into $1/2$-inch cubes
  (about 4 cups)
$3^1/4$ cups soy milk or lowfat dairy milk
1 cup frozen corn kernels, thawed
$1/2$ cup frozen peas, thawed (optional)
$1/4$ teaspoon salt
Pepper
Minced fresh parsley (optional)

1. Heat the oil in a 3- to 4-quart saucepan. Add the onion and celery and sauté over medium heat until the vegetables soften, 7 to 8 minutes, stirring frequently.

2. Add the potatoes and milk. Cover and simmer until the potatoes are tender, about 20 minutes. Mash some of the potatoes in the pot with a potato masher to thicken the soup. Add the corn kernels. If you like peas, add them, too. Cook just until heated through, 1 to 2 minutes. Add the salt, and season with pepper to taste.

3. Ladle the soup into a bowl, and sprinkle with parsley if you desire.

Makes three servings

Tomato Ravioli Soup

PREPARATION TIME: 6 minutes

COOKING TIME: 45 minutes

Ladle this bright red soup over plump ravioli for a new taste. It will make you smile.

2 teaspoons olive oil
1/2 medium onion, finely chopped (about 1 cup)
2 cloves garlic, finely chopped
1/2 teaspoon dried thyme
2 (141/2-ounce) cans chopped tomatoes, undrained
1 medium fresh tomato, chopped
11/2 teaspoons honey
1/2 cup water
Salt and pepper
12 fresh or frozen cheese, spinach, or squash ravioli, cooked
1 tablespoon chopped fresh parsley (optional)

1. Heat the oil in a 3- to 4-quart pot over medium heat. Add the onion and garlic and sauté 5 to 8 minutes until the onion is soft, stirring frequently. Add thyme, canned tomatoes, fresh tomato, honey, and water. Stir.
2. Cover and simmer 45 minutes on low heat. Remove from the heat. Season to taste with salt and pepper.
3. Place 4 cooked ravioli in each serving bowl and ladle the soup over them.

NOTE: If you don't have ravioli, the soup is still delicious.

Makes three servings

Lentil Soup

PREPARATION TIME: 10 minutes

COOKING TIME: 30 minutes

Use the chop-and-toss method to make this colorful soup that serves three people for a total of about $1.00.

$1/2$ medium onion, chopped (about 1 cup)
1 tablespoon olive oil
1 medium unpeeled red or white potato
$1/2$ cup lentils
$2^1/2$ cups water
1 medium carrot, thinly sliced
$1/2$ cup fresh spinach or kale (washed and tightly packed into
    the cup
1 medium tomato, chopped
2 to 3 garlic cloves, finely chopped
1 teaspoon ground cumin

In a medium-size pot, sauté onion in the olive oil for about 5 minutes, until soft. Cut the potato into 1-inch cubes. Add all of the other ingredients. Cover and simmer for 30 to 35 minutes. What could be easier? Serve with a splash of Tabasco or lemon juice if you desire.

NOTE: For a quick fix, use 1 or 2 cups of frozen spinach instead of fresh spinach. Buy frozen spinach in bags for easy scooping.

Makes three servings

Beer Stew

PREPARATION TIME: 15 minutes

This is a flexible recipe. Adjust the amounts to suit your taste.

4 to 5 cups water
3 medium red potatoes cut into 1/2-inch pieces (about 3 cups)
2 teaspoons olive oil
1 medium carrot, cut into 1/4-inch slices (about 1 cup)
1/2 small onion, chopped (about 1/2 cup)
1 cup canned garbanzo beans, drained
1 teaspoon curry powder
1 cup dark ale or stout beer (about 1/2 bottle)
1/4 cup frozen peas
Salt and pepper

1. Bring the water to boil in a medium saucepan. Add the potatoes and cook until just tender, but not mushy, about 10 minutes. Drain.

2. While the potatoes cook, heat the oil in a skillet over medium heat. Add the carrot, onion, and garbanzo beans; sauté 5 to 7 minutes over medium heat, stirring frequently.

3. Drain the potatoes and add them to the vegetable mixture. Add the curry and 1/2 cup of the beer. Simmer, uncovered, for about 3 minutes. Add the remaining 1/2 cup beer and simmer another 3 minutes to allow the alcohol in the beer to boil off, leaving its flavor essence in the pot. Remove from heat and stir in the peas. Salt and pepper to taste. Serve immediately.

Makes two servings

Moroccan Stew

Preparation Time: 12 minutes

Cooking Time: 15 minutes

Serve this fragrant stew on a bed of warm couscous. If the ingredient list looks long, don't worry. The stew goes together in minutes.

2 teaspoons olive oil
3/4 cup chopped onion (about 1/2 medium)
1 1/2 cups thinly sliced cabbage
1/8 teaspoon salt
1/2 large green bell pepper or 1/2 cup zucchini, cut into strips
1/8 teaspoon ground cinnamon
1 (14-ounce) can tomatoes, undrained and chopped
3/4 cup canned garbanzo beans, drained (about 8 ounces)
1/4 cup raisins
2 teaspoons fresh lemon juice
Salt and pepper

1. Heat the oil in a medium skillet on medium heat and sauté the onion for 5 minutes. Add the cabbage and sprinkle with salt. Continue to sauté the vegetables for 5 to 6 minutes, stirring occasionally.

2. Add the bell pepper and cinnamon and sauté for 2 minutes. Stir in the tomatoes, garbanzos, and raisins. Cover and simmer for about 15 minutes.

3. Add the lemon juice. Salt and pepper to taste, and serve.

Makes two servings

CHAPTER 6

Salads and Dressings

You can practically live on salads, and there are plenty of substantial combinations to choose from here. When you mix greens, beans, and grains, you have the makings for one-dish meals. With very little preparation, you can reproduce the expensive salads found in supermarket deli cases at a fraction of the cost.

Orange Rice and Black Bean Salad combines oranges and walnuts for a surprising flavor. Pasta Salad with black beans and vegetables can easily fill the center of any plate. Middle Eastern Traditional Tabouli Salad is a must-have in your vegetarian repertoire.

Leafy green salads present a special problem. While washed lettuce is tempting, dirty lettuce shrivels in the refrigerator. If washing and drying lettuce puts a stop to your salad making, treat yourself to prewashed, packaged salad greens.

Pasta Salad

PREPARATION TIME: 10 minutes

Choose your favorite vegetables for this salad.

1 cup uncooked whole wheat spiral pasta
1 cup broccoli florets
$1/2$ cup frozen corn, thawed
1 cup canned black beans, washed and drained
1 small tomato, chopped (about $1/2$ cup)
Parmesan cheese, grated (optional)
Avocado slices (optional)

1. Cook the pasta, uncovered, in a pot of rapidly boiling water until it is al dente (cooked with a little "tooth" or crunch), 7 to 10 minutes. Just before you drain the pasta, toss in the broccoli and cook for no more than 1 minute. Drain the pot in a colander and rinse with cool water. This stops the cooking process and keeps the vegetables crisp-tender. (When making pasta salad, the noodles are rinsed, but do not rinse noodles when making hot pasta with sauce.)

2. Combine the pasta mixture with the remaining salad ingredients in a medium bowl.

3. Dress with your favorite Italian dressing, or try Bright Lemon Vinaigrette (page 84). Serve garnished with grated Parmesan cheese or avocado slices if you desire.

Makes two servings

One Potato, Two Potato Salad

PREPARATION TIME: 5 minutes

COOKING TIME: 12 minutes

This hearty salad sparkles with color and is a meal in itself.

4 cups water
1 cup red potato, cut into bite-size pieces
1 cup yam, peeled and cut into bite-size pieces
1 cup loosely packed, prewashed fresh spinach
6 peeled cucumber slices, about 1/8-inch thick
3 Greek olives
1 to 2 tablespoons fresh lemon juice or vinaigrette dressing
Salt and pepper

1. Bring the water to a boil in a medium saucepan. Add the potato and yam and cook in rapidly boiling water until tender but not mushy, about 7 minutes. Drain thoroughly.

2. Arrange the spinach on a plate. Top with the cooked potato and yam, cucumber slices, and olives. Squeeze fresh lemon juice over the salad, or dress with your favorite vinaigrette. Season to taste with salt and pepper.

Makes one serving

Fruit Salad

PREPARATION TIME: 6 minutes

If you are tired of chomping on apples, make a fruit salad. Once you get the hang of it, you can make a beautiful multifruit salad in minutes. Peel fruit only if necessary. Squeeze a little lemon juice onto the cut pieces—without the citrus, some fruit turns brown. Garnish with bananas just before serving; that way the bananas remain firm. You'll have a hard time keeping your housemates from snacking on fruit salad left in the refrigerator.

1 apple, cored
1 pear, cored
1 orange, peeled
1 tablespoon lemon juice
Banana slices
Yogurt (optional)
Nuts or raisins (optional)

1. Cut the apple, pear, and orange into bite-size pieces. Put the fruit into a medium bowl, drizzle with lemon juice, and gently stir.
2. Spoon fruit into a serving dish and garnish with slices of banana. If you desire, top the salad with yogurt and a sprinkle of nuts or raisins.

Makes three or four servings

Cabbage Slaw

PREPARATION TIME: 6 minutes

Humble cabbage is one of the most versatile and underrated salad ingredients. The tart yogurt is a nice contrast to the sweet fruit. This is a fine fall salad when apples and pears are luscious.

$^1/_2$ firm, ripe pear
$^1/_2$ apple
1 cup shredded green cabbage
$^1/_4$ cup raisins

Dressing
$^1/_4$ cup plain yogurt
1 teaspoon frozen orange juice concentrate
1 teaspoon honey or maple syrup

1. Core and cut the pear and apple into bite-size pieces.
2. In a medium bowl, combine the pear and apple with the cabbage and raisins.
3. In a small bowl, combine all the dressing ingredients. Pour the dressing over the cabbage mixture, and gently toss. Serve with a thick slice of multigrain bread if you wish.

Makes one serving

Green Salad with Oranges

Preparation Time: 6 minutes

This good-to-eat salad is especially satisfying in the winter when citrus fruit is less expensive and tomatoes cost a small fortune. It looks great and is a snap to prepare.

2 cups romaine lettuce, washed and dried
$1/2$ large orange, peeled and cut into bite-size pieces
1 tablespoon finely chopped red onion
Honey-Yogurt Dressing (page 85)
Salt and pepper

Tear the greens into bite-size pieces and arrange them on a plate. Top with the orange pieces, and sprinkle with the red onion. Splash with the dressing, and season with salt and pepper to taste.

Makes one serving

Radical Radish Salad

Preparation Time: 7 minutes

Don't let the simplicity of this recipe keep you from enjoying a crunchy, mildly sweet, refreshing salad.

1/4 green bell pepper
5 radishes
1 small carrot
1 teaspoon fresh parsley, chopped
Salt

Dressing
1 teaspoon honey
1 tablespoon apple cider vinegar

1. Slice the pepper lengthwise into 5 or 6 pieces, then crosswise into thin pieces. Slice radishes into rounds. Cut the carrot in half lengthwise and then thinly slice each half crosswise. Combine pepper, radishes, and carrot with parsley in a medium bowl.
2. Stir the honey into the vinegar to dissolve.
3. Toss the dressing with the salad. Add a pinch of salt.

Makes two servings

Traditional Tabouli Salad

PREPARATION TIME: 6 minutes

SOAKING TIME: 15 to 20 minutes

Bulgur wheat is grain that has already been partially cooked and cracked into small pieces. This salad begins by pouring boiling water over the grain and letting it stand. You'll find bulgur wheat in the supermarket shelved near the rice. This salad happily accepts variations. If you like carrots, grate some and toss them in. Are you passionate about broccoli? Steam a few florets until crisp-tender and add them to your salad. Do you love juicy cucumbers? Chop 1/4 cup and sprinkle it into the bowl, or pitch in a few garbanzo beans. If all that sounds like too much work, simply use the following recipe as is. It's delicious.

3/4 cup water
1/2 cup cracked bulgur wheat
1 tomato, finely chopped
2 scallions, finely chopped (use whole scallions, greens and all)
1 clove garlic, minced
1/4 cup finely chopped fresh parsley
1/4 teaspoon dried mint
2 tablespoons fresh lemon juice
1/2 teaspoon olive oil
Feta cheese (optional)
Salt and pepper

1. Bring the water to a boil in a medium saucepan. Add the cracked bulgur wheat, cover, and remove the pan from the heat. Let the pot stand for 15 to 20 minutes. The bulgur will become soft and fluffy.

2. When the bulgur has absorbed the water, spoon it into a medium bowl, and add the tomato, scallions, garlic, parsley, mint, lemon juice, and olive oil.

3. If you wish, sprinkle with feta cheese just before serving. Taste and season with salt and pepper. The salad will taste best if it sits in the refrigerator for 30 minutes before serving to let the flavors mingle. If you're too hungry to wait, go for it!

Makes two servings

Marinated Vegetables

Preparation Time: 7 minutes

Marinated vegetables make satisfying snacks. They're great tossed into salads, piled on slices of bread, or eaten straight from the jar. Before placing vegetables in a marinade, first lightly steam them. Mushrooms, red onions, cucumbers, and cooked beans do not need presteaming. Marinated vegetables need to relax in the sauce for several hours before they're ready to eat. They will keep up to a week refrigerated in a tightly closed container, but they'll probably disappear long before that.

2 cups vegetables (carrots, broccoli, cauliflower, green beans, bell peppers)
1/4 cup canned garbanzo or kidney beans, drained
1 to 2 teaspoons olive oil
1/4 cup apple cider vinegar, wine vinegar, or balsamic vinegar
1 clove garlic, minced
1/4 teaspoon dried basil

1. Place the vegetables in a steamer over boiling water. Cover and steam 1 to 1 1/2 minutes, or until the vegetables are crisp-tender but not mushy.

2. Remove from heat and quickly cool the vegetables under cold water for about 30 seconds.

3. Place the vegetables and beans in a container; add the oil, vinegar, garlic, and basil. Cover the container with a tight-fitting lid. Refrigerate. Rotate the container from time to time to evenly coat the vegetables.

Makes about 2 1/2 cups

Orange Rice and Black Bean Salad

PREPARATION TIME: 6 minutes

Here is a way to turn cooked rice and canned black beans into a light, elegant meal.

1/2 cup canned black beans, drained
3/4 cup cooked brown rice
1/2 cup finely chopped celery (about 1 stalk)
1/2 cup peeled and sliced orange (1 small or 1/2 large)
1 scallion, thinly sliced (about 1/4 cup)
1 tablespoon chopped fresh cilantro
Salt and pepper

Dressing
1/4 cup orange juice
1 tablespoon cider or balsamic vinegar
1/2 teaspoon olive oil
1/2 teaspoon ground cinnamon

1. In a medium bowl, combine the beans, rice, celery, orange, scallion, and cilantro.
2. In a small bowl, combine the orange juice, vinegar, oil, and cinnamon.
3. Pour the dressing over the rice salad and stir thoroughly. Season with salt and pepper.

Makes one serving

White Bean and Tomato Salad

PREPARATION TIME: 6 minutes

A rustic salad full of traditional flavor. The white beans give this salad a creamy, satisfying taste.

1 (15-ounce) can white beans
2 scallions, finely chopped
1 clove garlic, minced
1 celery stalk, thinly sliced
1 medium tomato, chopped
1 tablespoon fresh lemon juice
$1/4$ teaspoon dried basil
$1/2$ teaspoon olive oil
Salt and pepper
Pinch of red pepper flakes (optional)

1. Rinse the beans gently in a colander. Drain.
2. In a medium bowl, combine the beans, scallions, garlic, celery, tomato, lemon juice, basil, and olive oil. Gently mix.
3. Salt and pepper to taste. Sprinkle with red pepper flakes if you desire.

Makes two servings

Pineapple Banana Yogurt

PREPARATION TIME: 4 minutes

For the best flavor, use a well-ripened banana with brown "sugar" flecks on the skin.

1 small banana, peeled and sliced
1/2 cup canned pineapple chunks, drained
1 cup vanilla yogurt

Extras (Optional)
Sliced orange segments
Chopped nuts
Granola

Peel and slice banana. In a medium bowl, combine banana, pineapple, and yogurt. Add your choice of extras.

Makes one serving

Taco Salad

PREPARATION TIME: 8 minutes

COOKING TIME: 5 minutes

If you don't feel like washing lettuce, make the salad anyway and forget the greens. This salad is too good to miss. Don't let the long ingredient list scare you—the salad takes only minutes to prepare.

1 teaspoon vegetable oil
1 cup frozen corn
1 tablespoon water
1 teaspoon ground cumin
1 medium avocado
1 tablespoon lemon or lime juice
1/2 medium tomato, chopped
2 tablespoons chopped scallion (about 1 scallion with the
    green part)
2 cups salad greens, torn into bite-size pieces
Salt
Baked tortilla chips, crumbled
1 tablespoon chopped fresh cilantro
Tabasco (optional)

1. In a small saucepan combine the oil, corn, water, and cumin. Cover and cook on medium heat for 3 minutes. Uncover and cook for 1 or 2 minutes to evaporate the excess moisture. Set aside.
2. Slice the avocado in half lengthwise. Remove the seed. Cut lengthwise and crosswise slices in the flesh making a grid pattern. Scoop the avocado cubes out of the shells and into a medium bowl. Gently stir in the lemon juice. Add the corn mixture, tomato, and scallion.

3. Spoon the salad onto a bed of greens. Salt to taste. Crumble a handful of baked tortilla chips and sprinkle them on top of the salad. Toss on the cilantro and a shake of Tabasco if desired. Serve and enjoy!

Makes two servings

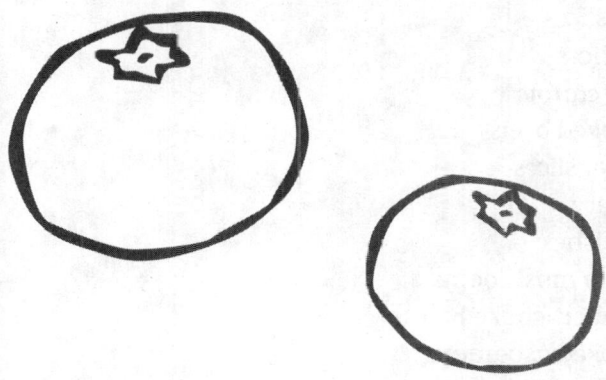

Savory Downtown Salad

PREPARATION TIME: 7 minutes

This salad couldn't be simpler.

Choose any of the following:
Romaine or Boston lettuce,
    washed, dried, and torn into bite-size pieces
Slivered red or green cabbage slices
Fresh spinach
Avocado slices
Tomato slices
Shredded carrots
Sliced cooked beets
Bell pepper slices
Sliced celery
Sliced radishes
Sliced fresh mushrooms
Quartered artichoke hearts
Sliced cooked asparagus
Snow peas
Sliced scallion or red onion rings
Sliced cucumbers

Frozen green peas. thawed
Cooked garbanzo, kidney, or white beans
Toasted nuts
Sautéed tofu
Sunflower seeds
Croutons
Grated cheese
Chopped fresh parsley
Minced fresh basil

Select your favorite ingredients from the list, and compose a salad on a big plate. Pour on your favorite dressing and dig in.

Make as much or little as you like

Avocado and Pear Salad

PREPARATION TIME: 6 minutes

This simple green salad makes a light meal served with a slice of multigrain bread.

Romaine lettuce (4 large leaves or 3 to 4 lightly filled cups)
1 ripe avocado
1 medium-ripe pear, cored, peeled, and diced
1 tablespoon fresh lemon juice
Salt

1. Wash and dry the lettuce. Tear it into bite-size pieces, and pile the lettuce onto individual plates.

2. Slice the avocado in half lengthwise, and gently twist to remove the seed. Make lengthwise and crosswise cuts into the flesh every 1/2 inch. Scoop the avocado cubes out of the shells. Place the avocado and pear in a medium bowl. Sprinkle with the lemon juice and gently stir.

3. Mound the pear and avocado mixture onto the lettuce leaves. Salt to taste.

Makes two servings

Salad Dressing with Savoir Faire

Many good bottled salad dressings are on the market. If you have the time, make your own— but don't think salad dressing is any old vegetable oil and a $1.25 bottle of vinegar. To make a salad worth eating, you absolutely need to have a good dressing. Choose quality oil such as extra-virgin olive oil. A good vinegar is also essential; balsamic vinegar, mellow wine vinegar, or mild rice vinegar are good choices. Pick balsamic vinegar carefully and try different brands. There can be a big difference in flavor between the taste of pricey brands and budget brands.

The Basics

For foolproof dressing, add a little salt and garlic to your basic oil and vinegar. Some people like a sweetener in the dressing: Honey always works (just don't overdo it), and the taste of pure maple syrup will amaze you.

Dried herbs are fine for cooked food, but they are not strong enough for dressings (unless the dressing sits at least several hours). With a little extra cost and effort, you can make dressing sublime with fresh herbs. You can't go wrong with basil. Other good flavors include the tart sweetness of lemon, orange, and berry juices, or a sharp hint of mustard or horseradish. If you love creamy dressing, add a small amount of lowfat soft cheese, pureed silken tofu, or nonfat plain yogurt. Dressings will keep at least a week in the refrigerator in a tightly sealed container or jar, and the taste improves as the flavors merge.

Bright Lemon Vinaigrette

This fresh dressing is lovely on lettuce salads. If you like, add a shake of Parmesan cheese when you toss the salad.

1/2 teaspoon lemon zest (paper-thin strips of the lemon skin)
3 tablespoons fresh lemon juice (about one medium lemon)
1/4 teaspoon salt
1 clove garlic, finely chopped
5 tablespoons olive oil

In a cup or small bowl, combine everything but the oil. Next, add the oil and whisk it in with a fork. Store in a covered jar in the refrigerator; it will keep for about 2 weeks.

Makes about 1/4 cup

Honey-Yogurt Dressing

PREPARATION TIME: 3 minutes

Use this sweet, creamy dressing on fruit salads.

1/3 cup plain yogurt
1 teaspoon honey
1/8 teaspoon vanilla
2 teaspoons orange juice concentrate (optional)

Combine the ingredients in a small bowl. If tightly covered and refrigerated, it will keep for about a week.

Makes about 1/2 cup

Creamy Garlic Dressing

PREPARATION TIME: 3 minutes

This dressing is delicious on lettuce salads, and it is also a tasty topping for baked or steamed potatoes.

$1/2$ cup plain yogurt
1 teaspoon Dijon mustard
2 cloves garlic, peeled and finely chopped
2 scallions, finely chopped
Salt and pepper

Whisk together the ingredients in a small bowl. If tightly covered and refrigerated, it will keep for about a week.

Makes about $1/2$ cup

Sweet Mustard
Vinaigrette

PREPARATION TIME: 3 minutes

This mildly sweet dressing is luscious on a winter or spring salad with lettuce and citrus.

2 tablespoons cider vinegar
2 tablespoons Dijon mustard
2 tablespoons maple syrup or honey
1/3 cup olive oil
Salt

In a small bowl, whisk together the vinegar and mustard. Continue stirring while drizzling in the maple syrup and then the oil, until well blended. Add salt to taste. If tightly covered and refrigerated, it will keep at least 2 weeks.

Makes about 2/3 cup

CHAPTER 7

Fast Foods, Vegetarian-Style

Sandwiches, Tortilla Wraps, Sushi Rolls, and Pizzas

Sandwiches are a reliable mainstay for quick meals, and broadly defined, you'll find them popping up from around the globe in a variety of forms. Enjoy a warm Middle Eastern falafel sandwich tucked into Greek pita bread, a Baked Eggplant Sandwich on crusty sourdough, or a Grilled Sandwich with Onions and Mushrooms. Make a creamy Green Chile Quesadilla on a crisp Mexican corn tortilla, or a versatile Italian pizza, or delight in one-bite sushi snacks.

Garden Variety Sandwich

PREPARATION TIME: 7 minutes

Combine these simple ingredients any time of the day, and you'll have a fantastic meal.

Crusty whole grain bread

Filling
Choose any of the following:
A leaf or two of fresh basil
Arugula
Avocado slices
Cucumber slices
Green pepper rings
Lettuce
Mustard
Olive slices
Pickles
Pickled peppers
Radish slices
Red onion rings
Roasted red pepper slices
Seasoned tofu
Tomato slices

Place two slices of bread on the work surface, and brush each slice lightly with mustard. Pile any of your favorite fillings on one of the slices, and top the sandwich with the second slice of bread. Enjoy.

Makes one serving

Absent Egg Salad Sandwich

PREPARATION TIME: 6 minutes

The texture of cubed Japanese-style silken tofu is very similar to that of boiled egg white in this sandwich. Spread the filling on toasted cracked-wheat bread. Tuck in a lettuce leaf or nutty-tasting arugula, and serve with juicy orange or tangerine slices.

$3/4$ cup Japanese silken firm tofu (about 6 ounces)
$1/2$ teaspoon fresh lemon juice
1 teaspoon prepared yellow mustard
$1/2$ teaspoon honey
$1/4$ teaspoon turmeric
1 tablespoon celery, diced
1 tablespoon onion, diced
1 teaspoon parsley, chopped
Dash of paprika
Salt and pepper to taste

Crumble the tofu in a mixing bowl with a fork. Add all of the remaining ingredients and stir to combine. Taste. If necessary add more salt and pepper. Refrigerated, it will keep for 2 or 3 days.

Makes two to three servings

Grilled Sandwich with Onion and Mushrooms

PREPARATION TIME: 15 minutes

A mushroom doesn't need to be psychedelic to expand your awareness. Pick your favorite whole grain bread or slices of crusty sourdough, and make the ultimate grilled sandwich. Add a crisp salad and a sliced apple, and you have a delicious lunch or dinner. This sandwich is too good to miss!

1/4 pound mushrooms, thinly sliced (about 3 cups)
1 tablespoon olive oil
1/2 medium onion, thinly sliced
1/4 teaspoon salt
Pepper
2 teaspoons chopped parsley
4 slices bread (whole grain or sourdough)
Dijon mustard
Cheese: mozzarella, Fontina, or Jack (optional)
Butter, softened

1. Gently dust off any soil that clings to the mushroom with a soft paper towel. (Do not wash the mushrooms.)

2. Heat 1/2 tablespoon of olive oil in a medium nonstick skillet. Add the onion and sauté over medium heat for about 5 minutes, until soft. Transfer to a bowl.

3. Heat the remaining oil in the skillet, add the mushrooms, salt, and a few pinches of pepper. Sauté the mushrooms over medium-high heat until golden and a little crisp on the edges, 5 to 6 minutes. Add 1/4 teaspoon water to the pan

to loosen the pan juices; stir for a moment. Add the mushrooms to the onions and stir together with the parsley.

4. Spread each slice of bread lightly with mustard. Pile the mushrooms and onions on two of the slices. Press the other two slices of bread on top of each sandwich. Lightly spread the top with butter. Place the sandwiches buttered side down on the skillet, and lightly spread the top side with butter. Cook over medium heat until golden, about 4 minutes, then turn and cook the underside. Serve immediately. Lean over your plate and take a juicy bite.

NOTE: If you desire, replace butter with olive oil. Lightly coat the pan with the oil.

Makes two servings

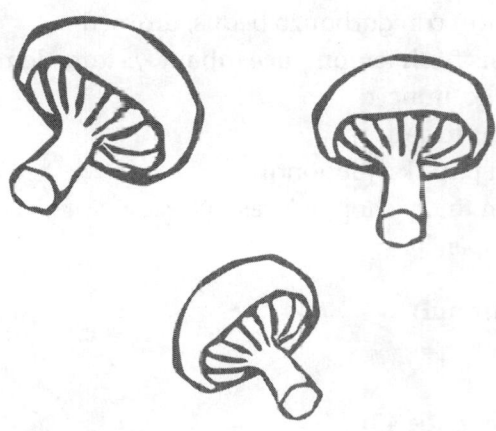

Falafel

Falafel is a spicy Middle Eastern pancake made from garbanzo beans. You can buy ready-made falafel mixes, but their taste or texture doesn't compare with falafel made from scratch. Stuff falafel into warm pocket bread with lettuce, tomato, and Tsiziki Sauce (page 43), a garlicky yogurt dressing. Here is a simple recipe for making these sumptuous pancakes without a mix. If there are extras, they won't last long. You don't need a food processor for this recipe— a masher or fork works fine.

$1/2$ medium red potato
2 teaspoons vegetable oil
1 small onion, finely chopped
1 ($15^{1}/_{2}$-ounce) can garbanzo beans, drained
3 tablespoons fresh lemon juice (about $1/2$ large lemon)
2 cloves garlic, minced
2 tablespoons tahini
$1/2$ teaspoon paprika (optional)
1 tablespoon finely chopped fresh parsley
Salt and pepper

Extras (Optional)
Lettuce
Tomato
Tsiziki Sauce (page 43)

Preheat the oven to 350 degrees F.

1. Cut the potato into 1-inch chunks. Place the potato in a small saucepan with enough water to cover; boil until it is

tender, about 10 minutes. Drain. While the potato cooks, heat the oil in a small skillet over medium or medium-low heat and slowly sauté the onion until it is soft, stirring frequently, 8 to 10 minutes.

3. In a medium bowl, mash the potato, garbanzo beans, and lemon juice. Add the onion, garlic, tahini, paprika, if using, parsley, and salt and pepper to taste; stir to combine. The mixture will have a consistency similar to cookie dough.

3. Lightly oil a baking sheet with vegetable oil. Spoon the mixture onto the baking sheet, forming 3-inch pancakes. Place in the oven and bake for 15 minutes. Serve the falafel in a warm pocket bread, garnished if you like with lettuce, tomato, and Tsiziki Sauce. Yum!

Makes six servings; 12 (3-inch) pancakes

Broiled Zucchini Parmesan

PREPARATION TIME: 10 minutes

What you see is what you get in this open-face sandwich.

2 teaspoons olive oil
$1/4$ cup minced onion
1 clove garlic, minced
1 cup grated or thinly sliced zucchini
$1/4$ teaspoon dried basil
$1/4$ teaspoon dried oregano
4 tomato slices
2 slices multigrain bread
1 tablespoon grated Parmesan cheese
Pepper

1. Heat the oil in a medium skillet over medium heat. Sauté the onion and garlic until the onion is soft, about 3 minutes. Add the zucchini, basil, and oregano and continue cooking until it softens, about 3 minutes.

2. Layer half of the vegetables and tomato slices on each slice of bread. Lightly sprinkle with Parmesan cheese.

3. Broil for 1 minute or until the cheese melts. Pepper to taste. Eat with a knife and fork.

Makes one serving

Curry in a Hurry

PREPARATION TIME: 10 minutes

This recipe makes enough filling for two pocket halves. Corn, sweet peppers, and curry deliver a delicious warm flavor.

1 teaspoon olive oil
$1/4$ cup chopped scallion (about 2 scallions)
$1/4$ cup thinly sliced green bell pepper
$1/4$ teaspoon curry powder
$1/3$ cup frozen corn
$1/2$ medium tomato, chopped
Salt and pepper
1 pocket bread, cut in half

1. Heat the oil in a small skillet on medium heat, and sauté the scallion and bell pepper for about 2 minutes. Stir in the curry, corn, and tomato and cook for 3 to 5 minutes, stirring. Remove from the heat; salt and pepper to taste.
2. Scoop the filling inside the warm pocket bread.

Makes two servings

Baked Eggplant Sandwich

PREPARATION TIME: 6 minutes

COOKING TIME: About 20 minutes

Filling, fast, and oh, so delicious—everything you could want in a sandwich.

4 1/2-inch eggplant rounds
2 teaspoons olive oil
Salt and pepper
2 teaspoons balsamic or red wine vinegar
4 slices bread, sourdough or whole grain
Dijon mustard or pesto
4 tomato slices
2 to 3 thinly sliced onion rounds
2 slices Monterey Jack or Fontina cheese
Softened butter or olive oil
Dijon mustard or pesto

Preheat oven to 350 degrees F.

1. Wash the eggplant and cut away any blemishes you find on the skin. Slice off four half-inch rounds. (This is enough to make two sandwiches.) Rub the eggplant rounds with olive oil, and sprinkle with salt and a pinch of pepper. Lay eggplant on oiled baking sheet, and bake for 15 to 20 minutes, or until the eggplant is soft. Remove from the oven, and rub each slice with a few drops of vinegar.

2. Spread the bread thinly with Dijon mustard or pesto. Pile the eggplant, tomato, onions, and cheese onto two slices of bread. Top each sandwich with a second slice of bread.

Spread soft butter on the top of each sandwich. Place buttered side down in a skillet on medium-high heat. Spread the tops of the sandwich thinly with butter. Cook until the underside is golden. Turn and cook the other side. Serve immediately.

NOTE: The eggplant skin is edible. Be careful when you slice the eggplant because the skin is slick, and the knife can slip. If you do not want to eat the skin, peel the eggplant before slicing. Cooked eggplant will keep covered in the refrigerator for 2 to 3 days. If you like mild, sweet-tasting onions, sauté them for 5 minutes in the skillet in a teaspoon of oil before you grill the sandwich.

Makes one or two servings

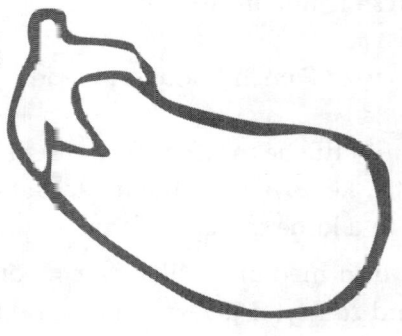

Crostini with a Bean and a Green

PREPARATION TIME: 15 minutes

Italian crostini, literally "toast," is best made with crusty Italian or French bread, but any toasted bread will work. This version of crostini is covered with a creamy white bean spread mixed with greens.

1 (16-ounce) can white beans (1 1/2 cups)
2 tablespoons water
2 teaspoons olive oil
1 large clove garlic, minced
2 1/2 cups washed, tightly packed kale leaves without stems, finely chopped
2 tablespoons fresh lemon juice
Salt and pepper
3 or 4 slices of toasted French or Italian bread

1. Wash and drain the beans and warm them in a saucepan with the water. Remove from the heat, and coarsely mash the beans with a large spoon.

2. Heat the oil in a medium skillet over medium heat. Add the garlic and sauté for a few seconds; add the kale and stir. Cook, stirring frequently until the kale is tender and bright green, 7 to 10 minutes. The water that clings to the kale from washing is usually sufficient moisture for cooking. If the kale appears to be too dry, add water to the skillet 1 tablespoon at a time as necessary and continue sautéing.

3. When the kale is done cooking, add it along with the lemon juice, salt, and pepper to the beans. Stir and taste. Add more salt and pepper if necessary. Spread the bean mixture onto the warm toasted bread for an open-faced sandwich, or use the toasted bread like you would chips, and eat the spread as a dip.

NOTE: If you like the sharp taste of uncooked garlic, add it to the beans when you add the lemon juice.

Makes two to three servings

Broiled Tofu

PREPARATION TIME: 5 minutes

TOFU PRESSING TIME: 30 minutes

COOKING TIME: About 10 minutes

Straight out of the box, tofu is a lot like pizza without a topping. But with a little planning, tofu might become your favorite fast food. Pressed tofu broils beautifully and tastes delicious. Pile broiled tofu onto a sandwich with your favorite toppings: mustard, relish, sliced onion, catsup, tomatoes, and crisp greens. It's so good you may find you've eaten it before there's time to build a sandwich. Make your own marinade or use hoisin sauce (available in well-stocked supermarkets and Asian markets). While the tofu is pressing, you'll have time to do a load of laundry.

1 block extra-firm or firm Chinese tofu (packaged in
    tubs of water)

Marinade
3 tablespoons balsamic vinegar
3 tablespoons soy sauce
2 teaspoons catsup

1. To press the tofu, sandwich the tofu between two plates. Weight the top plate with a heavy book, and let sit for 30 minutes. Remove the weight and top plate, and empty the water from the bottom plate. The tofu is now ready.

2. Preheat the broiler. Slice the pressed tofu into thirds, lengthwise. Place the tofu on a lightly oiled baking sheet and spread the tofu with the marinade.

3. Broil the tofu 3 to 4 inches from the heat for 5 to 7 minutes on each side, until browned and crisp on the edges. Serve it straight from the oven, or make a tofu sandwich on toasted multigrain bread topped with your favorite condiments.

Note: Prepared hoisin sauce can be substituted for the marinade.

Makes two servings

Pita with
Creamy Zucchini

PREPARATION TIME: 7 minutes

COOKING TIME: 5 minutes

Here is a simple shredded zucchini sandwich lightly flavored with yogurt and a hint of mint. Shredded vegetables have a wonderful texture and are great on top of pizza, inside tacos, or simply eaten straight from the pan. This version is tucked into a pita bread pocket.

1 medium zucchini
1 teaspoon olive oil
1 large clove garlic, minced
$1/4$ teaspoon dried mint
$1/2$ teaspoon dried oregano
1 tablespoon plain nonfat yogurt
Salt and pepper
1 whole wheat pita bread, cut in half

1. Shred the zucchini on the coarse side of a handheld grater with the largest holes.

2. In a medium skillet, heat the oil over medium heat. Sauté the zucchini, garlic, mint, and oregano, stirring often, until the zucchini is firm-tender and bright green, about 5 minutes.

3. Remove from the heat; stir in the yogurt. Season with salt and pepper. Scoop the filling into the warm pita bread halves. Mmm . . . this is a satisfying meal!

Makes one serving

Garlic Bread
with Attitude

PREPARATION TIME: 3 minutes

This method uses raw garlic, so the flavor will be sharp and biting.

1 or 2 slices bread
Olive oil
1 clove garlic, peeled

Preheat the broiler.

1. Lightly brush or drizzle the bread with olive oil and toast it under a broiler 3 to 4 inches from the heat. (It is good without the oil, too.) Watch closely because the bread will brown quickly.
2. Rub the toasted bread with the peeled garlic.

Makes one serving

Tortilla Wraps

Before you toss a package of tortillas into your shopping cart, read the nutrition label, because the ingredients vary greatly from brand to brand. The list for corn tortillas should be short: corn, lime, and water. Check out the number of fat grams on flour tortillas, and choose tortillas with the smallest number. (Some have zero fat, but their texture can be rubbery.) Also, look for refrigerated whole wheat tortillas free of preservatives. If you live in a community where freshly made tortillas are available, buy them—they're heavenly. Store all tortillas in the refrigerator or freezer. If you freeze them to use one at a time, let the tortilla thaw for a few minutes before cooking. Then, when the tortilla is warmed, it will toast and become crispy rather than steam and turn soggy. You can heat corn tortillas in a hot skillet with or without oil.

Green Chile Quesadilla

This quesadilla is delicious warmed on a dry skillet, but if you like the flavor of oil on your tortilla, add 1/4 teaspoon olive oil to the skillet before you warm it.

1/4 cup vegetarian canned refried beans
2 tablespoons canned, diced mild green chiles
2 (6-inch or 8-inch) wheat or corn tortillas
1/4 cup grated mozzarella cheese
1 tablespoon finely chopped fresh cilantro
Prepared salsa

1. Spread half of the beans and chiles on one half of each tortilla. Sprinkle the cheese and cilantro onto the filling.
2. Warm a dry skillet on medium heat. Heat each tortilla in the skillet. When the tortilla becomes pliable, fold the plain half of the tortilla over the filling and cook each side for about 2 minutes, or until the cheese melts.
3. Serve with prepared salsa.

Makes one serving (2 quesadillas)

Black Bean and
Yam Quesadilla

PREPARATION TIME: 20 minutes

Black beans and yams combine for striking flavor and color in this hearty tortilla wrap.

1 teaspoon vegetable oil
1/2 cup finely chopped onion (about 1/2 medium)
1 clove garlic, finely chopped
1 teaspoon ground cumin
2 teaspoons water
1 cup peeled grated yam (about 1/2 medium)
1/4 cup black beans, rinsed and drained
Salt and pepper
2 (8-inch or 10-inch) corn or wheat tortillas
1/4 cup grated Monterey Jack or mozzarella cheese
Prepared salsa

1. Heat the oil in a medium skillet over medium heat. Add the onion and garlic and sauté for 3 minutes or until the onion is soft. Add the cumin and water, and continue to sauté for 1 minute, stirring. Add the yam and beans, stir; cover and cook for about 6 minutes or until the yam is tender but not mushy.

2. Remove the skillet from the heat. Season the dish with salt and pepper, and put the yam mixture in a small bowl. In a minute or two, when the skillet is cool enough to handle, wipe it clean with a paper towel.

3. Place the quesadilla in the skillet on medium heat. Spoon on half of the yam mixture and sprinkle with half of the cheese. Cook the tortilla for about 30 seconds to soften, and then fold the tortilla in half and cook each side for about 2 minutes, until the cheese melts and the filling is warm. Repeat the process to make the second quesadilla. Serve with prepared salsa.

Makes one serving (2 quesadillas)

Tacos Monterrey

Preparation Time: 10 minutes

Cooking Time: 15 minutes

The distinctive smoky flavor in these unusual tacos comes from chipotle chiles. These chiles are tasty and very hot. You'll find small cans of chipotle chiles packed in adobo sauce in the Mexican section of the supermarket. (Mashed potatoes in a warm tortilla are delicious even without chipotle chiles. Add grated cheese and salsa to your taco instead.)

2 cups red or white potatoes, cut into 1/2-inch pieces
  (about 2 medium potatoes)
1/4 cup soy milk or dairy milk
1 canned chipotle chile, finely chopped
Salt
4 (6-inch) corn tortillas
1 teaspoon vegetable oil

1. Place the potatoes in a saucepan with enough water to cover; boil until tender, 10 to 15 minutes. Drain. Pour in the milk and mash the potatoes with a strong fork or masher until they are smooth and creamy. Add more milk if necessary. Stir in the chipotle chile. Taste. If you like food really hot, add one more chopped chipotle. Season with salt to taste.

2. Heat a tortilla on a hot, lightly oiled skillet over medium heat. The tortilla should be lightly toasted and flexible. Remove the tortilla from the skillet, and spread about 1/4 cup of the potato mixture down the center. Fold the tortilla around

the filling, and take a bite. Add more oil to the skillet if necessary, and cook the remaining tortillas.

Note: Freeze the remaining chipotle chiles for future meals. Spread the chiles out on a dinner plate so that they do not touch each other. Place the plate in the freezer for about 30 minutes. Next, put the frozen chiles into a plastic container, and store the container in the freezer. Now it will be easy to use the chiles one or two at a time.

Makes two servings

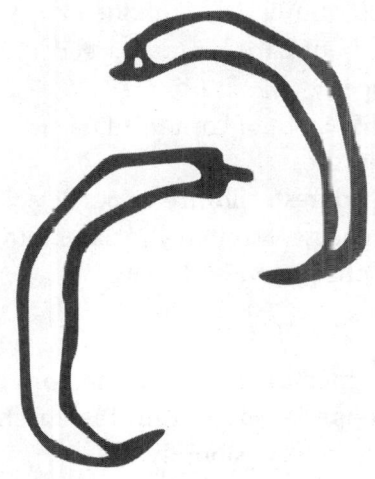

Spicy Zucchini Quesadilla

PREPARATION TIME: 8 minutes

Using jalapeño chiles is an inexpensive culinary trick that adds bright flavor to cooking. A little pepper costs about $0.05.

1 teaspoon olive oil
1/2 medium zucchini, thinly sliced (about 1 cup)
1/2 jalapeño chile (about 2 inches long), seeded, deveined, and finely chopped
2 (8-inch or 10-inch) wheat or corn tortillas
1 tomato (4 to 6 thin slices)
1 tablespoon chopped fresh cilantro or parsley
Grated mozzarella cheese, Monterey Jack, or feta cheese
(1 to 2 tablespoons per quesadilla)
Prepared salsa

1. Heat the oil in a medium skillet on medium heat. Add the zucchini and jalapeño; sauté until the zucchini is tender, about 5 minutes. Stir occasionally.

2. Layer the zucchini mixture on one half of each tortilla. Add the tomato slices, cilantro, and cheese on top of the zucchini. When the skillet is cool enough to handle, wipe it with a paper towel. Reheat the skillet on medium heat. Place the quesadilla in the skillet, and when the tortilla becomes pliable, fold the plain half of the tortilla over the filling. Cook each side for about 2 minutes or until the cheese melts and the filling is hot. Cook the remaining quesadilla. Before you take a big bite, add salsa.

Makes one serving (2 quesadillas)

Taco Mania

PREPARATION TIME: 5 minutes

Expand your taco horizon with a one-pan meal teaming with tasty tidbits.

1 (8-inch or 10-inch) corn tortilla

Filling
Choose any of the following:
Chopped fresh tomato
Fresh lettuce, torn into bite-size pieces
Sliced avocado
Cooked brown rice
Sliced olives
Chopped onions or scallions
Grated cheese: Monterey Jack, Cheddar
Plain yogurt
Chopped fresh cilantro
Chopped green bell peppers
Diced canned mild green chiles
Leftover sweet potato
Warm refried beans
Salsa

Heat a tortilla on a hot dry skillet; when it's pliable, in about 30 seconds, fold the shell in half. Lightly toast both sides and remove from the heat. Stuff the tortilla with your favorite fillings.

Makes one serving

Hot Lips Fajita

PREPARATION TIME: 10 minutes

Fold a warm tortilla around sizzling sautéed vegetables, and you have a fabulous fajita. Jalapeño chiles fire up this version.

2 teaspoons vegetable oil
1 medium zucchini, thinly sliced (about 1 cup)
1/2 cup broccoli (about 6 florets)
1/4 cup chopped and seeded red bell pepper
      (about 1/4 pepper)
1/2 jalapeño chile, seeded and minced (about 2 inches long)
1/4 cup corn kernels (frozen or fresh)
1/4 teaspoon ground cumin
2 (10-inch) flour tortillas
1/4 cup shredded Monterey Jack or soy cheese

1. Heat the oil in a medium skillet over medium heat. Add all of the ingredients except the tortillas and cheese. Sauté the vegetables and cumin for 2 to 3 minutes, until the vegetables begin to soften and are crisp-tender.

2. Spoon half of the vegetable mixture and half the cheese onto a warm tortilla. Sprinkle with chopped red onion if you desire. Fold up one edge of the tortilla and wrap the other sides of the tortilla around the vegetables and cheese. Take a bite from the open end. There is enough filling to make a second serving.

NOTE: Heat the tortilla in a warm skillet, or roll it up in a damp paper towel, and heat it in a microwave for 25 seconds on High.

Makes two servings

Sushi

There is nothing difficult about making sushi. It's a great snack, and once the rice is cooked, it takes less time to prepare than a taco or burrito. Sushi has three essential ingredients: sheets of edible seaweed (nori), rice, and various fillings.

Making sushi at home is *far less* expensive than eating at a sushi bar or buying ready-made packages. A tray of eight from a deli costs nearly $5.00 (about $0.63 each). A tray of eight made in your kitchen costs a total of $0.45 (about $0.06 each). Add a crisp green salad on the side, a cup of hot tea or cold Japanese beer, and celebrate.

Sushi-Making Tips

- Short-grain white sushi rice is much easier to work with because it's stickier than other rice. You'll find sushi rice in the Asian section of a well-stocked supermarket or in Asian specialty shops. If you prefer brown rice, choose short-grain rice, as it's stickier than the long grain.

- Let the cooked rice cool to near room temperature before scraping it out of the pot. If the rice is cool, it's easier to get out of the pot and will be ready to use. Do not put hot rice on the nori, because it softens the sheet and makes rolling the sushi difficult.

- Sushi is traditionally rolled with a bamboo mat, called a *sudore*, but it's not an essential prop. It's easy to roll many forms of sushi without a mat. As you roll the sushi, gently press it as you proceed, being careful not to cause the filling to bulge along the roll, because the nori may tear.

- Moisten your fingers with water to keep the rice from sticking to them when you spread and lightly press the rice onto the nori sheet.

- Flavoring the rice: Some people like sushi rice plain. Most people prefer the rice dressed with a sweet rice-vinegar dressing. Buy prepared sushi rice vinegar that's ready to use, or make your own (see page 120).

Perfect Sushi Rice

PREPARATION TIME: 5 minutes

COOKING TIME (FOR WHITE RICE): 15 minutes

COOKING TIME (FOR BROWN RICE): 35 to 40 minutes

The following recipe makes enough rice to fill two 7 × 8-inch sheets of nori, and it makes about 16 bite-size pieces. Choose either white sushi rice or short-grain brown rice.

White rice
3/4 cup sushi rice
1 cup water

Brown rice
3/4 cup brown rice
1 1/2 cups water

In a pot with a lid, bring rice and water to a boil over the highest heat. As soon as steam escapes from below the lid, turn off the heat for 5 minutes. Return to low heat and simmer until water is absorbed, 10 to 15 minutes for white rice, or 35 to 40 minutes for brown rice. Do not stir the rice while it cooks or it will become gummy.

Makes 2 cups

Sushi Wheels

PREPARATION TIME: 10 minutes

Sushi Wheels filled with rice and bright-colored vegetables are worth making just for their visual appeal. They make excellent everyday snacks or carry-along meals.

2 cups cooked sushi rice, near room temperature, *not* hot
1 to 2 tablespoons sushi-rice vinegar or Sweet Sushi-Rice
   Dressing (page 120)
2 sheets nori (7 × 8 inches)

Filling
Choose your favorites from (about 1 cup total):
Carrot
Green onion
Cucumber
Avocado
Pickle
Red radish
Daikon radish
Scrambled egg
Tofu
Arugula
Parsley

1. Sprinkle rice with dressing and gently stir to combine.
2. Put the nori, shiny side down, on a flat work surface, with the long edge of the rectangle nearest you. Spread a thin layer of sushi rice (1/8- to 1/4-inch thick, about 1 cup) on the sheet of nori. The process is similar to spreading refried beans onto a taco shell, but here you do it with your fingers.

Moisten your fingertips with water first, and it will be easier. Leave a half-inch of exposed nori on the end of the sheet farthest away from you. You'll use this to seal the roll.

3. Place small pieces of the filling (about 4 tablespoons) on the rice, in a line about $1^1/2$ inches from the edge nearest to you.

4. Carefully lift the edges of nori closest to you with both hands; gently fold the seaweed over the filling, capturing it in the first turn of the roll. Continue rolling away from you, gently pressing to create a well-shaped roll, like you were rolling up a sleeping bag. (Don't worry if a bit of rice and filling squeezes out of the two ends when you roll the sushi.)

5. When you're near the end of the nori, slightly moisten the exposed edge with water; continue rolling to the end of the sheet and lightly press to seal.

6. Place roll, seam side down, on the work surface. Cut into bite-size "wheels" (about 1-inch wide) with a sharp, wet knife. The first and last wheels on the roll may not be perfectly round or perfectly stuffed, but once you place them on a plate, cut side up, the problem disappears. Use soy sauce for dipping, if you wish.

NOTE: Sushi is usually filled with thinly sliced vegetables. For something different, try fruit-filled sushi. Choose among your favorites: apple, mango, kiwi, and pineapple. You want color and a bit of crunch. Have fun creating your own delightful masterpiece.

Makes 16 individual sushi wheels

Sweet Sushi-Rice Dressing

PREPARATION TIME: 3 minutes

Use about 1 tablespoon of dressing to flavor 1 cup of rice.

2 tablespoons rice vinegar or white vinegar
1 to 2 tablespoons sugar
Pinch of salt

Mix 2 tablespoons of vinegar with 1 tablespoon of sugar. Stir until the sugar dissolves. Taste. If you like, add more sugar.

Makes 2 tablepsoons, enough to flavor 2 cups rice

Pizza—There Are Many Paths to Pizza

Build pizza on a variety of foundations. Try English muffins, Italian focaccia, Boboli, bagels, French bread, or store-bought fresh or frozen pizza dough. Unless you love extra-thick pizza crust, cut Boboli bread in half to create two rounds of pizza, or buy thin-crust Boboli.

The following recipes are for mini-pizzas that use pita bread for the base. There is enough topping for two 6-inch pizzas. When you choose a larger pizza crust, increase the topping amounts.

Pita Pizza Crust

PREPARATION TIME: 3 minutes

Lightly toasted pita bread makes the perfect "crust" for a quick and easy pizza.

1 (6-inch) pita bread

Preheat the oven to 450 degrees F.

Lightly toast the pita bread for 3 minutes in the oven. Remove the pita from the oven. If you like thin-crust pizza, carefully split the pita bread around its outer edge to yield two equal rounds. If you like a thicker-crust pizza, use the pita whole.

Makes one or two 6-inch crusts

Pepper and Mushroom Pizza

PREPARATION TIME: 12 minutes

This straightforward combination is the essence of pizza.

2 teaspoons olive oil
1/4 cup chopped onion
1/2 cup chopped bell pepper
1 1/2 cups sliced mushrooms (about 6)
1/4 teaspoon dried basil
1 (6-inch) pita bread
6 thin tomato slices
Grated mozzarella cheese

Preheat the oven to 450 degrees F.

1. Heat the oil in a small skillet over medium heat. Add the onion, bell pepper, mushrooms, and basil; sauté stirring frequently for 3 minutes, or until the vegetables begin to soften. Remove from the heat.

2. Lightly toast the pita bread for 3 minutes in the oven. Remove the pita from the oven. Carefully split the pita bread around its outer edge to yield two equal rounds.

3. Spoon the filling onto the crust. Add tomato slices and lightly sprinkle with grated mozzarella cheese. Heat the pizza in the oven until the tomatoes are warm and the cheese begins to melt, about 2 minutes. Serve immediately.

Makes two servings

Vegan Farmhouse Pizza

PREPARATION TIME: 12 minutes

This gourmet pizza works without cheese.

2 teaspoons olive oil
1/4 cup diced onion
1/2 cup chopped apple
1 cup prewashed fresh spinach, tightly packed and then
  chopped
1 (6-inch) pita bread
1/2 teaspoon Dijon mustard
1 teaspoon chopped walnuts

Preheat the oven to 450 degrees F.

1. Heat the oil in a medium skillet on medium-high heat. Sauté the onion for 3 minutes. Add the apple and spinach; cook until the spinach wilts, 3 to 5 minutes. Press out excess moisture.

2. Lightly toast the pita in the oven for 3 minutes. Remove the pita from the oven and lower the heat to 350 degrees F. Carefully slice it in half around its outer edge to yield two equal rounds.

3. In a bowl, combine the spinach mixture and mustard. Spread the topping onto the toasted pita bread. Sprinkle with the walnuts, and warm in the oven for about 5 minutes.

Makes two servings

Roasted Vegetable Pizza

PREPARATION TIME: 7 minutes

COOKING TIME: 20 minutes

This pizza is full of luxurious flavor.

1 medium red potato, thinly sliced
1 small zucchini, cut into $1/4$-inch slices (about 1 cup)
$1/3$ medium bell pepper, coarsely chopped
$1/2$ cup coarsely chopped onion
1 large clove garlic, minced
1 teaspoon olive oil
$1/2$ teaspoon dried thyme
1 (6-inch) pita bread
Grated Parmesan cheese (optional)

Preheat the oven to 425 degrees F.

1. Place the potato, zucchini, bell pepper, onion, and garlic in a medium bowl. Add the oil and thyme and stir to evenly coat the vegetables with oil. Spread the vegetable mixture onto a baking sheet. Don't crowd them or they'll steam, not roast. Bake for about 20 minutes or until the potatoes are tender. Stir once or twice to ensure even cooking. Remove from the oven. Raise the oven heat to 450 degrees F.

2. Lightly toast the pita bread for 3 minutes in the oven. Remove the pita from the oven. Carefully split the pita bread around its outer edge to yield two equal rounds.

3. Spoon the filling onto the crust. If you desire, sprinkle each pizza with 1 or 2 teaspoons of grated Parmesan cheese and heat in the oven just until the cheese begins to melt. Enjoy.

Makes two servings

Zucchini and Cheese Pizza

PREPARATION TIME: 10 minutes

Halved pita bread makes a thin crust for lightly sautéed slivers of zucchini sprinkled with basil.

1 teaspoon olive oil
$1/4$ cup finely chopped onion
$1/4$ teaspoon dried basil
1 small zucchini, grated (about 1 cup)
$1/2$ cup chopped tomato
1 (6-inch) pita bread
Grated Monterey Jack cheese
Salt and pepper

Preheat the oven to 450 degrees F.

1. Heat the oil in a medium skillet over medium heat. Sauté the onion and basil for 3 minutes. Add the zucchini and cook, stirring frequently, for 2 minutes. Add the tomato, and cook for another minute. Remove from the heat.

2. Lightly toast the pita bread for 3 minutes in the oven. Remove the pita from the oven. Carefully split the pita bread around its outer edge to yield two equal rounds.

3. Spoon the filling onto the two crusts. Sprinkle with grated Monterey Jack cheese. Return the pizza to the oven and bake just until the cheese melts, 1 or 2 minutes. Season with salt and pepper.

Makes two servings

Pizza Party

One of the best parts about making party-size pizza at home is that you're freed from trying to recycle the unwieldy cardboard box that never fits into the trash bin. Traditional ungarnished Italian pizza is made with a crust, tomato sauce, and melted cheese, but you can toss on just about anything that will withstand a 400–degree F heat. To cut the cost, consider a potluck party, and ask your friends to bring toppings.

Eight Pizza-Making Tips

1. My main advice about homemade pizza is to have fun.

2. Pizza dough likes to be warm. If you store your flour and oil in the refrigerator, make sure they're at room temperature before you begin.

3. Some toppings need precooking (see the list on page 131). Mushrooms, for example, can release a lot of liquid if they are put on raw, which can make your pizza soggy. Cook them first in a lightly oiled nonstick skillet on medium high until they are soft.

4. If you like a tiny bit of crunch to your pizza, add a teaspoon of cornmeal to the dough, or sprinkle a teaspoon of cornmeal on the pizza pan before putting on the dough.

5. Put the topping out to the very edge so there is no crust to discard. This makes the pizza seem bigger.

6. Garnish the pizza with fresh herbs after baking. If fresh herbs are put on before baking, flavor is lost in the oven.

7. If you use Parmesan cheese, sprinkle it on after you take the pizza out of the oven. You'll get more flavor that way.

8. If you don't have a pizza cutter, use a silverware knife, and save the edge of your chef's knife for cutting vegetables.

Pizza Dough

MIXING AND KNEADING TIME: 10 minutes

DOUGH RISING TIME: 25 minutes

COOKING TIME: 12 to 15 minutes

Don't let the fact that pizza is made from a yeast dough scare you. It's easy! You won't need a rolling pin to form this soft dough; shape it right in the pan with your hands. Enjoy!

1/2 cup whole wheat flour
1 tablespoon active dry baking yeast (1 1/2 packages)
1/4 teaspoon sugar or honey
1/2 teaspoon salt
1/2 cup warm water
2 tablespoons olive oil
1/2 to 5/8 cup unbleached white flour

Preheat oven to 500 degrees F.

1. In a medium mixing bowl, combine the whole wheat flour, yeast, sugar, and salt. Mix.

2. In a small saucepan, warm the water and oil. Remove from stove. When water feels warm to your hand, but not hot, add it to the flour mixture. Beat with a spoon until almost smooth and the dough is the consistency of pancake batter. Stir in 1/2 cup white flour.

3. Turn the dough onto a lightly floured surface, and gradually add white flour, 1/2 teaspoon at a time, until you have a smooth dough and it is no longer tacky or sticks to your hands. Knead for several minutes until smooth and elastic.

4. Oil the mixing bowl. Pat the dough into a ball and place it in the bowl, turning to coat with oil. Set it aside to rise for 25 minutes in a warm place while you prepare toppings. If you're not ready for the dough after it rises, punch it down, and let it rise again for another 20 to 25 minutes.

5. Place the dough in the center of a greased 12-inch to 14-inch pan and push and pat the dough toward the edge, forming a 12-inch circle. If any holes or tears appear, repair by pinching the dough together. (Pizza doesn't have to be round. Make a rectangle, square, or free form.)

6. Add your favorite toppings. Bake on the top shelf of a very hot oven, 500 degrees, for 12 to 15 minutes.

NOTE: Mix the dough with your hands. At first, it will stick to your fingers, but as you add the additional flour, a teaspoon at a time, the dough will form into a lump.

Makes one (12-inch) pizza

Topping It Off

Some people like their pizza piled high with many toppings; some like a simple pizza with a few flavors. Make pizza with or without tomato sauce. Spread the topping mixed like confetti, or put different vegetables on single sections or in stripes across the pizza dough. Adding intense flavors like garlic makes a pizza interesting.

Sauce Possibilities

Commercial pizza sauce
Commercial pasta sauce
4-ounce can of tomato sauce flavored with
   1 teaspoon oregano

Topping Possibilities

These toppings are ready to use without precooking.

Artichoke hearts (commercial, packed in water, drained)
Bell peppers, red or green
Capers
Garlic
Green chiles
Green onions (add after baking)
Olives
Onions, red or yellow
Pineapple
Red chili
Roasted red peppers
Sun-dried tomatoes (Pour boiling water over dry-packed
   tomatoes, soak for 5 minutes, drain.)
Tomatoes

More Topping Possibilities

Precook these vegetables. Season with salt and pepper and a squeeze of lemon if you desire. (Add them before you bake the pizza even though they are precooked.)

Asparagus Snap off tough stem ends. Cut the spears in quarters. Simmer in water in a small saucepan until crisp-tender.

Broccoli Cook in lightly oiled skillet on medium high heat until crisp-tender.

Eggplant Slice into half-inch thick rounds, brush with oil, and bake at 350 degrees F until soft, or broil for 4 or 5 minutes on each side until lightly browned.

Mushrooms Cook in lightly oiled skillet on medium high heat until soft.

Spinach Sauté in lightly oiled skillet on medium high heat until soft.

Zucchini Sauté in lightly oiled skillet on medium high heat until crisp-tender.

Cheese Possibilities

Cheddar	Monterey Jack
Feta	Mozzarella
Gouda	Parmesan

Herb Possibilities (fresh or dried)

Basil	Parsley (fresh)
Cilantro (fresh)	Rosemary
Oregano	

CHAPTER 8

Bean Meals

Beans are just about the perfect food. Eat them straight from the pot, wrapped in tortillas, tossed into soup, or made into dips. The quick route to eating beans is to buy them in cans. When you have time for soaking and simmering dried beans, a thrifty meal becomes dirt cheap.

Spilling the Beans—Gut Instincts

If you avoid eating beans because of fear of flatulence (gas), there's good news. Beans contain sugars that humans cannot digest. When these sugars arrive in the large intestine, bacteria ferment them, producing gas. When beans become part of your regular diet, however, the body adapts and the intestinal problem disappears.

People react differently to beans. If someone you know complains of discomfort after eating them, don't assume that will happen to you. If beans are new to your diet, eat them more frequently in small portions, and avoid mixing beans in the same meal with other gas-producing vegetables, such as cabbage. There are products on the market sold in natural food stores that help prevent the gas that beans cause. Beano is one brand name. Just add a few drops to your first bite.

Buying the Best Beans

Look for unbroken dried beans with a deep vibrant color, and store them in airtight containers in a cool, dry, dark place.

Bean Cooking Chart

1 cup Dried Beans	Water (cups)	Cooking Time	Yield (cups)
Black	4	2 hours	2
Black-eyed peas	3	1 hour	2
Garbanzo	4	3 hours	4
Great Northern	$3^1/2$	2 hours	2
Kidney	3	$1^1/2$ hours	2
Lentils	3	45 minutes	$2^1/4$
Lima	3	$1^1/2$ hours	$1^1/4$
Navy	3	$2^1/2$ hours	2
Pinto	3	$2^1/2$ hours	2
Red	3	3 hours	2
Soy	4	$2^1/2$ hours	3
Split peas	3	45 minutes	$2^1/4$

Cooking Dried Beans

- Sort through dried beans. Pour the portion you are about to use onto a pan or dish. Run your fingers through them, and pick out any pebbles, twigs, or shriveled old beans you find. You will rarely find any, but it's worth looking. The last thing you want is a dentist's bill for a broken tooth from chomping on a rock. Pour the sorted beans into a colander and give them a quick rinse.

- Soak dried beans for 6 to 8 hours—overnight works well. Use plenty of water because beans swell during this process. (Lentils, split peas, and black-eyed peas do not need pre-soaking.)

- Drain the beans after soaking and they're ready to cook.

- Put the beans in a pot, and cover them with fresh water. Put a lid on the pot, and bring it to a boil. Then lower the heat and simmer until the beans are thoroughly cooked. Check periodically to see that the beans remain covered with water, and replenish if necessary.

Refried Pinto Beans

PREPARATION TIME: 15 minutes

Top this dish with salsa, add a side of rice, and you'll have a delicious, down-to-earth meal, or get out the chips and have a hearty snack. Of course they're great in tacos, too.

1 1/2 cups cooked pinto beans or (15-ounce canned pinto
  beans, rinsed and drained)
1 to 3 tablespoons water (use more if necessary)
1 tablespoon olive oil
1/4 cup onion, minced (about 1/4 medium onion)
1 to 2 cloves garlic, minced
1 1/2 teaspoons chili powder
1/2 teaspoon cumin powder
1/2 teaspoon dried oregano
2 tablespoons plain yogurt
2 tablespoons grated Cheddar or Monterey Jack cheese
1/4 teaspoon vinegar (apple cider vinegar or red wine vinegar)
Salt
2 tablespoons canned green chiles (optional)

1. In a medium bowl, mash the beans, adding as much water as necessary to make them creamy and thick; add a tablespoon of liquid at a time. Set mixture aside.

2. In a small skillet, heat oil on medium-high heat; add onion and cook for 2 to 3 minutes until the onion is translucent. Add garlic, chili powder, cumin, oregano, and stir. Continue cooking for another minute. Add the beans and cook for a minute or two over moderately low heat until warm. Stir in yogurt, cheese, and vinegar. Remove from heat and taste.

3. Adjust the seasoning, and salt to taste. Add more chili power if you like it hotter. Stir in chiles, if you desire.

NOTE: Mash the beans with a fork, spoon, or potato masher; the beans like to bounce around in the bowl when you begin, but once the skins break and you add a little water, it's easy.

Makes one or two servings

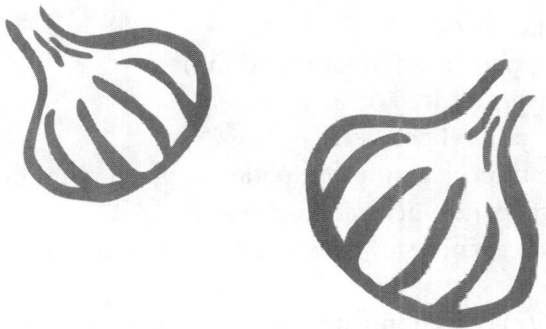

Chipotle–Black Bean Chili

PREPARATION TIME: 10 minutes

The chipotle chile pepper is the ingredient that gives this chili its deep flavor. You'll find chipotles in cans in the Mexican section of the supermarket. They come packed in adobo sauce, a very hot Mexican red sauce. A can of chipotle chiles goes a long way. It takes only 1 or 2 small chipotles to flavor a whole pot of chili.

1 teaspoon olive oil
1/2 cup chopped onion (about 1/2 small)
3 cloves garlic, minced
2 tablespoons chili powder
1 teaspoon minced canned chipotle pepper (1 chipotle)
2 (15-ounce) cans black beans, drained
2 (14 1/2-ounce) cans stewed whole tomatoes, undrained and chopped
1 (4 1/2-ounce) can chopped mild green chiles, drained
Salt and pepper

1. Heat the oil over medium heat in a large saucepan or skillet. Add the onion and garlic, and sauté 3 to 5 minutes until the onion is tender; stir frequently. Add the remaining ingredients. Bring to a boil.

2. Reduce the heat and simmer for 15 minutes. Ladle the chili into a bowl, and enjoy.

NOTE: Freeze remaining canned chipotle chiles for future meals.

Makes four servings

Chili Uno-Dos-Tres

<small>PREPARATION TIME:</small> 10 minutes

<small>COOKING TIME:</small> 35 minutes

This chili looks good and tastes great.

2 teaspoons olive oil
3/4 cup chopped onion (about 1 small)
3 cloves garlic, finely chopped
1/2 cup medium red or green bell pepper, diced
1 cup water
2 tablespoons chili powder
1 1/2 teaspoons ground cumin
1 (14 1/2-ounce) can ready-cut tomatoes, undrained
1 (15-ounce) can red kidney beans, drained
1 (15-ounce) can garbanzo beans, drained

1. Heat the oil in a medium skillet over medium heat. Add the onion, garlic, and bell pepper; sauté 5 to 7 minutes, stirring frequently.

2. Add the water, chili powder, cumin, tomatoes, kidney beans, and garbanzo beans. Bring to a boil. Reduce the heat; gently simmer, uncovered, for 30 minutes. Ladle into a bowl and serve with corn bread if you desire. ¡Olé!

Makes two or three servings

Black-Eyed Peas

PREPARATION TIME: 6 minutes

COOKING TIME: 45 to 55 minutes

Black-eyed peas are one of the few beans you can cook without pre-soaking. They cook in about 45 to 55 minutes and taste the same whether you soak them or not, but they won't look the same. When beans soak overnight, they slowly rehydrate and hold their shape throughout the cooking process. Without presoaking, a violent rehydration occurs, causing some of the skins to crack and separate from the beans. (It sounds more murderous than it really is.) If you're using the beans in a salad, consider soaking them first to improve their appearance. If looks don't matter, start cooking.

If you're out of onion and bell pepper, cooked black-eyed peas can stand on their own dressed with fresh lemon juice and a splash of olive oil. If you're in the mood for a simple-to-prepare, delicious meal, forget the soaking and start cooking.

2 cups dried black-eyed peas
1 small onion, finely chopped (about 1 cup)
1 medium bell pepper, chopped (about 1 cup)
1 teaspoon dried oregano

Toppings
Olive oil
Fresh lemon juice
Salt and pepper
Chopped tomato
Fresh cilantro

1. Cover the beans with fresh water; add the onion, bell pepper, and oregano. Bring the pot to a boil, and simmer until the beans are tender, 45 to 55 minutes. Keep the pot partially covered at all times. Check the beans occasionally, and add more water if needed.

2. Remove the beans from the pot with a slotted spoon; dress them with a drizzle of olive oil, lemon juice, and salt and pepper to taste. If you're a garlic fanatic, mince some and toss it on, too.

3. Garnish with chopped tomato and cilantro.

NOTE: For variety, garnish the black-eyed peas with salsa, a splash of Tabasco, or Vietnamese chili sauce. Black-eyed peas are also delicious spooned over cooked rice or added to soups.

If you choose to presoak the beans, here's how to do it: Cover the beans with twice their volume of water, and soak for 8 hours or overnight. Drain.

Makes four servings

Dal

PREPARATION TIME: 10 minutes

COOKING TIME: About 30 minutes

This souplike dish made with lentils is the Indian version of a stew. It's a robust one-pot meal for any time of the day. Garnish a bowl of dal with sliced avocado, chopped fresh tomato, a dollop of yogurt, or a spoonful of chutney. Pour yourself a cup of hot tea, and add a plate of sliced pineapple or mango on the side.

1 cup dried lentils
3 cups water
2 cups finely chopped onion (about 2 medium)
2 teaspoons olive oil
2 cloves garlic, finely chopped
1 teaspoon curry powder
Salt

1. In a medium saucepan, combine the lentils, water, and 1 cup of onion. Bring the ingredients to a boil; reduce the heat, cover the pan, and simmer until the lentils are tender, about 30 minutes.

2. While the lentils are cooking, heat the oil in a medium skillet; add the remaining 1 cup onion, garlic, and curry. Sauté the vegetables on medium or medium-low heat, stirring occasionally until the onions are golden, soft, and just beginning to brown, 10 to 15 minutes.

3. Add the onion mixture to the cooked lentils, stirring to combine. Heat the lentil mixture for a few minutes longer. Salt to
   taste.

NOTE: You'll find lentils in the supermarket near the dried beans.

Makes four servings

Easy Pot-o-Chili

PREPARATION TIME: 15 minutes

COOKING TIME: 60 to 90 minutes

Cook up a pot of chili and call your friends for a fiesta. Soak the beans for 6 to 8 hours before you plan to cook them, and allow about 1 hour for the beans to simmer. Serve with a big slice of hot corn bread, and top the beans with salsa and a dollop of yogurt if you desire.

2 teaspoons vegetable oil
1 cup chopped onion (about 1 medium)
2 cloves garlic, finely chopped
1 cup dried beans, presoaked (small red beans or
    kidney beans)
1 (14-ounce) can diced tomatoes
2 tablespoons canned diced green chiles
1 tablespoon chili powder
1 teaspoon powdered cumin
1 tablespoon cornmeal
Salt

1. In a large pot, heat the oil and sauté the onion and garlic on medium to medium-low heat for 6 to 10 minutes or until tender.

2. Drain the beans. Add the beans to the pot with enough fresh water to cover. Bring the pot to a boil, and then reduce the heat to low. Cover and simmer until the beans are tender, about 60 minutes. Check the pot occasionally to see that the beans remain covered with water.

3. When the beans are tender, add the tomatoes, green chiles, chili powder, cumin, and cornmeal. Taste and then season with salt. Gently simmer for another 10 to 15 minutes uncovered, stirring occasionally.

NOTE: If you like really thick chili, add more cornmeal a tablespoon at a time.

Makes four servings

White Bean Jumble

PREPARATION TIME: 12 minutes

COOKING TIME: 15 minutes

This tasty combination satisfies a hearty appetite. Don't let kale's stiff-looking leaves put you off; cooked, they become soft and delicious.

2 large white or red potatoes
1 cup chopped firmly packed kale leaves, with stems removed
2 teaspoons olive oil
1/2 cup chopped onion (about 1/2 small)
1 clove garlic, chopped
1/2 teaspoon dried thyme
1 small tomato, chopped
1/2 cup canned white beans, rinsed and drained
Salt and pepper

1. Wash the potatoes and cut them into 1/2-inch bite-size pieces. Add an inch of water to a steamer pot with a steamer basket. Cover the pot, and bring the water to a boil. Add the potatoes and steam for about 10 minutes, or until the potatoes are barely tender.

2. While the potatoes steam, wash the kale and remove stems; run a knife along each side of the stem to free the leaf. Discard the stems. Gather the leaves into a pile, and hold them together with one hand while you cut the kale into about 1-inch slices. When the potatoes are done, remove the pot from the heat and uncover it. Set the potatoes aside.

3. Heat the oil in a medium skillet over medium heat. Add the onion, garlic, and thyme; sauté, stirring frequently for about 3 minutes or until the onion softens and becomes translucent. Add the kale and tomato, and sauté for 1 to 2 minutes, stirring until the kale has wilted. Add the potatoes and beans and heat for a minute or two. Salt and pepper to taste. Serve immediately.

Makes one or two servings

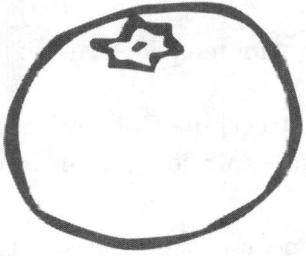

Pete's Harbor Special

PREPARATION TIME: 15 minutes

Prepared in a matter of minutes, this uncomplicated meal is full of flavor. It's the Monday night menu special from a fisherman's cafe on the San Francisco Bay.

1 medium zucchini
2 teaspoons olive oil
$1/2$ teaspoon dried thyme
1 cup canned vegetarian refried beans
1 clove garlic, minced
Salt and pepper
Prepared salsa
Grated mozzarella or Monterey Jack cheese (optional)

1. Wash and dry the zucchini. Cut off the ends. Next, cut the zucchini diagonally into long, oval-shaped $1/4$-inch-thick slices.

2. Heat the oil in a medium skillet on medium-high heat. Add the zucchini and sprinkle with thyme. Quickly fry the zucchini slices until they are golden-speckled on both sides, about 10 minutes. Remove the zucchini from the pan.

3. Heat the beans and garlic in a small saucepan. Spread the beans in a thin layer onto a warm plate. Arrange the zucchini slices on the beans. Season with salt and pepper. Add a splash of salsa and a sprinkle of grated mozzarella or Monterey Jack cheese, if desired. (Place the plate in a warm oven on low heat for a minute or two to melt the cheese if you desire.)

Makes one serving

Black Bean Quickie

PREPARATION TIME: 6 minutes

Here is a hearty meal without cooking. Eat this dish as a dip with baked tortilla chips, or pile it onto crusty sourdough bread.

1 (15-ounce) can black beans, drained
1 avocado
1/2 cup prepared Mexican-style red salsa
1 to 2 tablespoons chopped fresh parsley or cilantro
1/2 chopped medium tomato
Salt and pepper

1. In a medium bowl, roughly mash the beans with a fork or masher.

2. Halve the avocado lengthwise and gently twist to separate it from the pit. Make lengthwise and crosswise cuts about 1/2 inch apart in the flesh of each half. Scoop the avocado cubes out of the skin, and add them to the beans. Stir in the salsa, parsley, and chopped tomato. Salt and pepper to taste.

3. Serve as a dip or use as a sandwich spread.

Makes about 2 cups

Marinated Tempeh

PREPARATION TIME: 15 minutes

Tempeh is a favorite Indonesian soy food made from fermented soybeans. Think of it as tofu's sibling. It has a chunkier texture and a bit more flavor than tofu. Like tofu, tempeh acts as a sponge, soaking up the flavors that surround it. If you are still struggling with the idea of giving up meat, tempeh has a very "meaty" texture, and you can do anything to tempeh that you can do to meat. To keep tempeh fresh, store it in your refrigerator. It freezes well and keeps its flavor and texture for several months. You'll find tempeh widely available in natural food stores and even some supermarkets. If you notice a few dark spots on the tempeh when you open the package, that's normal. Eat this dish straight out of the frying pan or add it to soups, stews, salads, grains, chili, or filled tortillas.

2 ounces tempeh
1 tablespoon white or cider vinegar
1 tablespoon soy sauce
1 1/2 teaspoons water
1 large clove garlic, minced
1 teaspoon vegetable oil
Pepper

1. Cut the tempeh into about 1/4-inch-thick strips or cubes and set aside. In a shallow bowl, stir together the vinegar, soy sauce, water, and garlic.

2. Add the tempeh and stir it around a few times. Let it sit in the marinade for a few minutes to absorb the sauce.

3. In a medium skillet, heat oil on medium-high heat, and sauté the tempeh for about 8 minutes until it is golden and crisp. If necessary, add a little more oil to prevent sticking. Pepper to taste, and serve immediately.

NOTE: Tempeh can be easily cooked by broiling. Marinate the tempeh following the recipe directions. Lightly oil a baking dish, and broil the slices 3 to 4 inches from heat for 3 to 5 minutes on each side until lightly browned.

Makes one serving

CHAPTER 9

Grain Meals

Whole grain cooking is one of the most enjoyable discoveries a new vegetarian can make. Marketers design the ads you see for quick-cooking grains and rice cookers to make you think there is something mysterious and difficult about cooking grains. You'll soon see that cooking whole grains is as simple as boiling water. There are only two things that can go wrong: too much water or too little water, and that's easy to fix. If the grain is not tender at the end of the cooking time, add more water—just a little, 1/4 cup or less—and let the grain cook a little longer. If you added too much water, lift the cooked grain out of the pot with a slotted spoon, leaving the excess water behind. The grain may be soggy, but you can use less water next time.

Store uncooked grains, especially cornmeal, in the refrigerator or freezer. It doesn't take long for hungry insects to find a warm kitchen and begin feasting on your food supply. They know a good thing when they find it.

The Perfect Pot—of Grain, of Course

Here's a selection of favorite grains that are part of vegetarian cuisine. Rice, wheat, corn, oats, and buckwheat feed most of the world.

Bulgur Basic bulgur, or cracked wheat, is a wonderfully easy grain to prepare. Measure 1 cup of bulgur into a heat-proof bowl, and pour in 1 cup of boiling water. Cover the bowl, and set it aside for about 20 minutes. When the bulgur has absorbed the water, stir to fluff the grains. If it's still too chewy, add more hot water. (One cup of dry bulgur yields $2^1/2$ cups cooked.)

Couscous Part of its celebrated reputation is due to the fact that it's quick to prepare. Place equal amounts of boiling water and dry couscous in a heat-proof bowl. Cover and let sit for about 10 minutes. Stir to fluff the grain. If it's still crunchy, add a small amount of hot water. (One cup of dry couscous yields $2^1/3$ cups cooked.)

Kasha or Buckwheat Groats This eastern European dish has been a staple food for centuries. You'll find kasha at natural food stores and in the kosher section of many supermarkets. If the kasha you buy is dark brown, it's already been roasted; but if it's pale in color, pan-roast $1/2$ cup briefly on medium heat in a dry skillet until it begins to change color to bring out its hearty flavor. Boil 1 cup of water with a pinch of salt, pepper, and a splash of oil. Pour the liquid into the skillet with the kasha, cover, and simmer on very low heat for 15 minutes. (Yields $1^1/4$ cups.)

Noodles One of the most popular quick-cooking grains of all. Boil a pot of water; add noodles; cook until al dente. Drain the noodles immediately. (Al dente means "to the tooth"—chewy but not mushy.)

Old-Fashioned Rolled Oats   A bowl of hot oatmeal is delicious any time of the day and takes about 10 minutes to prepare. Its taste and texture are far superior to instant or quick-cooking oats.

Stove-top cooking: In a pot with a tight-fitting lid, bring 1 cup of water, 1/2 cup of old-fashioned rolled oats, and 1/4 to 1/2 teaspoon salt to a boil; then lower the heat to medium-low and continue cooking, stirring frequently, for 5 to 7 minutes or until the oatmeal is thick and creamy. Remove from heat, and let it stand for a few minutes before serving. Makes 1 cup.

Microwave cooking: Combine 1/2 cup of old-fashioned rolled oats and 1 cup of water in a big microwavable bowl. You need a lot of room in the bowl because the oatmeal bubbles and spurts. Cover the bowl with a glass plate while it cooks to avoid a big cleanup. Microwave on Medium for 2 minutes, stir, and heat for 2 minutes more or until the oats have thickened. Mix well before serving. Makes 1 cup.

Polenta (Cornmeal)   One of the best ways imaginable to eat corn. Serve the polenta while it's soft and warm, or pour it into a baking pan or onto a plate and refrigerate it to eat later. As polenta cools, it becomes firm and ready for slicing. When you're ready to eat, cut the polenta into slices and heat it in a skillet, the oven, or the broiler. It will keep refrigerated for several days.

Determining the amount of water used in cooking polenta is not an exact science and can vary slightly depending on how "stiff" you want the mixture to be. If it's too dry, add more water. Polenta is extremely elastic. Mixing the polenta with a little water before adding it to the boiling water keeps it from becoming lumpy.

Stove-top cooking: Combine ¹/₂ cup cornmeal and ¹/₂ cup water in a bowl. Bring 2 cups of water to a boil in a medium saucepan. Stir in the polenta mixture. Reduce heat to the lowest setting, stirring continuously to prevent the polenta from sticking. Simmer on low for 10 minutes or until the polenta is thick and creamy. If it becomes too stiff or dry while cooking, add a small amount of water (1 to 2 tablespoons at a time) and keep stirring. Makes 2 cups.

Microwave cooking: In a 1-quart microwavable bowl, whisk together ¹/₂ cup polenta and 2 cups water. Cook in microwave on High for 3 minutes. Stir, and then microwave on High for an additional 2 minutes. Remove the polenta from the microwave, and let it rest for 1 minute. The polenta should be the consistency of pudding. If it appears watery, microwave for an additional 1 to 2 minutes. Makes 2 cups.

Rice Whole grain brown rice is such a basic food that simply cooking it brings out its natural excellence for a satisfying meal. It takes about 40 to 45 minutes to prepare. That can be a problem when you're hungry and in a hurry. One solution is to create deliberate leftovers by cooking more rice than you need for one meal. Cooked rice will keep refrigerated for about 7 days, and you'll have a head start on future meals. One cup of raw brown rice yields 3 cups cooked.

Cook rice in a pot with a tight-fitting lid. Using a dented lid or one that is the wrong size lets too much water escape during cooking. Rinse 1 cup of rice and drain it, and then add 2 cups of fresh cool water to the pot. Cover and bring to a boil over the highest heat. When steam escapes from below the lid, turn off the heat for 5 minutes. Return to very low heat, and simmer for about 35 minutes or until the water has been absorbed. Remove from heat and let it sit, covered, for a few minutes before serving.

To cook white rice, use 1³/₄ cups water for each cup of rice and prepare as for brown rice. The water will be absorbed in

Grain Cooking Chart

1 cup Grain	Water (cups)	Cooking Time (minutes)	Yield (cups)
Barley	3	45	$3^1/2$
Brown rice	2	45	3
Buckwheat	2	15	$2^1/2$
Bulgur	2	15	$2^1/2$
Couscous	1	10	$2^1/3$
Kasha	2	15	$2^1/2$
Millet	$2^3/4$	40	$3^1/2$
Quinoa	2	15	$2^1/2$
White rice	$1^3/4$	15	2
Wild rice	3	60	$2^2/3$

15 to 20 minutes of cooking. One cup of white rice yields 2 cups cooked.

Use one of the following methods to reheat 1 cup of cooked rice.

On top of the stove: Heat rice in a covered saucepan on medium heat with 2 tablespoons of liquid for 4 to 5 minutes.

In the oven: Put rice in a baking dish. Add 2 tablespoons of liquid, and reheat in an oven set at 350 degrees F for 4 to 5 minutes.

In a microwave: Heat rice with 2 tablespoons of water. Cover the container; microwave on High 1 minute.

Steaming: Place the rice in a steamer basket over boiling water. Cover and steam for 2 minutes or until the rice is warm.

Cleaning the Pot

After removing cooked grains from the pot, you may notice a film that clings to the side of the saucepan. Fill the pot with water, and let it rest 30 minutes or overnight. When you wash the pot, the coating will practically slide off by itself.

Polenta with Mushroom Gravy

Preparation Time: 15 minutes

This recipe is a two-part process, but it's straightforward and uncomplicated. Make a lick-your-plate meal in 15 minutes.

Polenta
1/2 cup cornmeal
1 1/2 cups water

Gravy
1 tablespoon olive oil
1 cup chopped onions
1/2 teaspoon dried thyme
2 cups sliced fresh mushrooms (about 4 large)
1 tablespoon flour
2/3 cup water, or white wine, or red wine
1 tablespoon soy sauce
Pepper

1. In a 1-quart microwave-safe bowl, whisk together the cornmeal and water. Cook in the microwave on High for 3 minutes. Whisk carefully (mixture will be hot); return the mixture to the microwave and cook 1 minute on High or until the polenta is thick and creamy. Remove from the microwave, and let the polenta rest while you cook the gravy.

2. Heat the oil in a small skillet on medium or medium-low heat. Sauté the onion and thyme for 6 minutes; stir occasionally. Add the mushrooms and continue to sauté on

medium heat until the mushrooms soften, stirring often, for 3 to 5 minutes. If the skillet becomes dry before the mushrooms are soft, add 1 tablespoon of water and continue cooking.

3. When the mushrooms are soft, add the flour and stir for a moment; then add the water and soy sauce. Simmer on medium-high, stirring until the sauce thickens, about 30 seconds to 1 minute. Remove from the heat.

4. Serve the polenta topped with gravy. Pepper to taste.

NOTE: This gravy is delicious ladled on mashed potatoes, rice, or noodles. If you choose to use water rather than wine, add 1 clove of finely chopped garlic when you add the mushrooms. Believe it or not, the water makes as tasty a gravy as the wine; they're just different.

Makes two servings

Polenta with Black Beans

PREPARATION TIME: 15 minutes

A mixture of cornmeal and water cooked as a mush is native to the Americas. The Italians adopted it as a staple of their cuisine and called it polenta. If you like pasta, you'll love polenta. It's the ultimate comfort food, and it's versatile, nourishing, and cheap. Cooked polenta can be topped with pasta sauce, sautéed or steamed vegetables, or cooked beans. It is often used as a stuffing and can be broiled or fried. It's lovely sprinkled with grated cheese. Polenta makes a delicious alternative to potatoes or rice. In this recipe, polenta is made on the stove, but if you have a microwave, it's even faster. (See Polenta with Mushroom Gravy on page 158.)

Beans
1 teaspoon olive oil
1/2 cup chopped onion (about 1/2 small)
2 cloves garlic, minced
1 teaspoon dried thyme
1 (141/2-ounce) can diced or ready-cut tomatoes, undrained
1 (15-ounce) can black beans, rinsed and drained

Polenta
1/2 cup cornmeal
2 cups water

Grated Parmesan cheese
1 tablespoon chopped fresh parsley (optional)

1. Heat the oil in a medium skillet over medium heat. Add the onion, garlic, and thyme. Sauté on medium heat for 3 to 5 minutes, until the onion is tender. Add the tomatoes and beans. Reduce the heat to low and gently simmer the bean mixture while you prepare the polenta.

2. In a small bowl, combine the cornmeal and 1/2 cup water. Set aside. In a medium saucepan, bring 11/2 cups water to a boil; pour in the cornmeal mixture and stir; reduce the heat to its lowest setting. Cook, stirring frequently, until the mixture is thick and smooth, about 10 minutes. If the polenta sticks to the bottom of the pot, add more water, 1 tablespoon at a time.

3. Serve beans and polenta side by side. Sprinkle with Parmesan cheese and chopped parsley if you desire.

Makes two to three servings

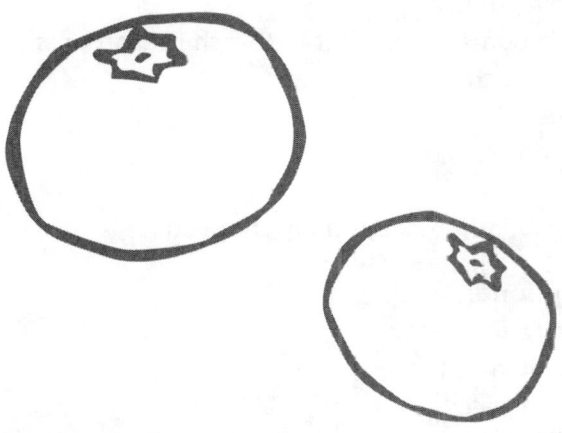

Kasha Pilaf

PREPARATION TIME: 10 minutes

COOKING TIME: 10 minutes

Kasha (or buckwheat groats) has a unique, earthy flavor, which you'll either like or you won't. There's not much middle ground between its fans and its detractors. Kasha can be a meal in itself, or it can be served as a side dish with steamed vegetables or baked tofu. It makes a tasty filling for baked squash and can take the place of rice or a potato on your plate. It's especially savory topped with gravy. The grain is ready to eat in 15 minutes.

1/4 cup kasha (buckwheat groats)
1 egg white, lightly beaten
1 tablespoon olive oil
1/4 cup onion, chopped
1 garlic clove, minced
1 cup mushrooms, chopped (two 3-inch mushrooms
    or four 2-inch)
1/2 cup water
1 1/2 teaspoons soy sauce (optional)
Pepper
1 to 2 tablespoons parsley, finely chopped

Extras (Optional)
Add with the mushrooms:
1/4 cup carrot, diced
1/4 cup celery, diced
1/4 cup bell pepper, diced

Add when the dish is finished cooking:
1/4 cup cooked bow-tie noodles or macaroni

1. In a small bowl, combine the egg white and kasha, and stir to coat the grain.

2. Heat oil on medium-high in small 8-inch skillet. Add the chopped onions and garlic, and sauté, stirring for 2 to 3 minutes until the onion is translucent. Add the mushrooms and one or two optional extras, if desired, and continue cooking, stirring until the mushrooms begin to give up their juice and look soft and shiny.

3. Add the kasha mixture to the skillet and stir well. Continue cooking for a minute or two on medium heat until the kasha kernels are separate and dry.

4. Mix the water and soy sauce together. Pour the mixture in the skillet. When the stock begins to simmer, cover and cook gently on low heat for about 10 to 15 minutes until the liquid is absorbed and the grain is soft. Adjust the seasoning; add pepper to taste and a splash of soy sauce if you desire. Garnish with fresh chopped parsley.

NOTE: The egg white creates a fluffier grain. Without it, the texture of the dish is more like porridge. You'll need a lid for the skillet in this recipe.

Makes one serving

Spontaneous Couscous

PREPARATION TIME: About 15 minutes

When liquid is added to this tiny mild-tasting grain, it magically puffs up and becomes tender in less than 10 minutes. Here couscous is energized with frozen green peas, tomatoes, and onions for a quick, light meal. If you desire, add Broiled Tofu (page 102) just before serving. Use about 2 cups of vegetables per serving and make substitutions at will. (Double the recipe, and chill leftovers for a ready-made salad for tomorrow, dressed with a vinaigrette dressing.)

1 teaspoon olive oil
1/2 medium onion, chopped (1 cup)
1/2 cup frozen peas
1/2 medium tomato, chopped
1/4 cup couscous
1/2 cup water
1 teaspoon finely chopped fresh parsley
Tabasco or fresh lemon juice (optional)

Salt and pepper

1. Heat the oil in a medium skillet. Sauté the onion on medium-low heat for 10 minutes or until the onions are lightly browned, stirring occasionally.

2. Add the peas, tomato, couscous, and water.

3. Cover and cook on low heat for 5 to 8 minutes, or until the peas are bright green, all the water is absorbed, and the couscous is soft. Add parsley.

4. Serve with a splash of Tabasco or fresh lemon juice, if desired. Salt and pepper to taste.

Makes one serving

Indian Rice

PREPARATION TIME: 12 minutes

Pineapple and banana make a perfect pair to flavor this sweet rice dish.

2 teaspoons vegetable oil
1/2 medium onion, chopped
1/2 medium carrot, thinly sliced on diagonal
1/4 green bell pepper, chopped
1/4 teaspoon curry powder
1/4 cup crushed pineapple
1 cup cooked rice
1/2 ripe banana, sliced
1 tablespoon raisins
Salt
1 tablespoon peanuts or cashews

1. Heat the oil in a large skillet over medium heat. Sauté the onion and carrot for 3 minutes. Add the bell pepper and curry, and sauté for another 2 minutes. Add the pineapple and rice; stir. Reduce the heat to low.
2. Gently stir in the banana and raisins, being careful not to mash the bananas. Cook until the bananas are warm, 1 or 2 minutes.
3. Salt to taste. Sprinkle with the peanuts. Serve.

Makes one serving

Beer and Aztec Rice

PREPARATION TIME: 7 minutes

COOKING TIME: About 40 minutes

The ingredient list may look long, but the recipe is super simple, and the taste is fantastic.

1 tablespoon minced jalapeño chile
1/2 cup finely chopped onion
3 large cloves garlic, minced
1 1/2 teaspoons olive oil
1 tablespoon finely chopped fresh cilantro
1 1/2 teaspoons ground coriander
1/2 teaspoon ground cumin
1 cup brown rice
1 cup water
1 cup dark beer, ale, or stout
1/4 teaspoon salt
1/2 cup frozen peas, thawed

1. If you like food really hot, leave a few of the seeds in the jalapeño. If you like a mild flavor, remove the seeds and vein. In a medium saucepan, sauté the jalapeño, onion, and garlic in olive oil until the onion softens, about 5 minutes. Add the cilantro, coriander, and cumin and sauté about 1 minute.

2. Add the rice, water, beer, and salt. Bring the pot to a boil. Reduce the heat and cover. Cook on low heat for 35 to 40 minutes, until the rice is tender. When the rice is nearly done and the liquid is almost gone, turn off the heat and let the rice sit on the burner for another 5 minutes.

3. Remove the pot from heat and stir in the peas. Re-cover the pot and let it sit for 5 minutes to warm the peas. Serve.

Makes three servings

Chinese Fried Rice

PREPARATION TIME: 10 minutes

MARINATING TIME: About 10 minutes

This recipe happily accepts substitutions. Use whatever vegetables you have on hand—broccoli, snow peas, or carrots are good choices.

2 tablespoons soy sauce
2 teaspoons sugar
1/4 block extra-firm tofu
1 teaspoon vegetable oil
1/4 medium green bell pepper, cut into thin strips (about 1/4 cup)
1 cup cooked rice
1/4 cup frozen peas
1 scallion, thinly sliced (about 1/4 cup)

1. In a shallow bowl, mix together the soy sauce and sugar. Cut the tofu into strips about 1/2 inch wide. Marinate for about 10 minutes in the soy and sugar mixture.

2. After the tofu has marinated, heat the oil in a large skillet over medium heat. Add the bell pepper, stir, and fry for 1 to 2 minutes. Remove the tofu from the marinade and add the tofu to the skillet. Stir for a moment. Add the rice and heat thoroughly, about 1 minute. Add the peas and scallion, and stir.

3. Taste. If you desire, top the dish with some of the remaining marinade. Serve immediately.

NOTE: If you have time, press the tofu to remove excess water for 15 minutes before you marinate it. See directions on page 16.

Makes one serving

Rice with Garbanzo Beans

PREPARATION TIME: 10 minutes

Traditional Mediterranean flavors give a cup of rice great taste.

1 teaspoon olive oil
1/2 cup finely chopped onion
1 clove garlic, finely chopped
1 cup tightly packed, washed, chopped spinach
1 tablespoon fresh lemon juice
1/4 cup garbanzo beans
1/2 medium tomato, chopped (about 1/2 cup)
1/2 teaspoon dried thyme
1 cup cooked rice
2 to 4 tablespoons crumbled feta cheese
Salt and pepper

1. Heat the oil in a medium skillet over medium heat. Add the onion and garlic and sauté for about 3 minutes, until the onion softens.

2. Stir in the spinach, lemon juice, garbanzo beans, tomato, and thyme. Add rice, cover, and cook for 2 to 3 minutes, stirring occasionally.

3. When the spinach has wilted and the rice is hot, serve topped with crumbled feta cheese. Salt and pepper to taste.

Makes one serving

Rice Vera Cruz

PREPARATION TIME: 6 minutes

COOKING TIME: About 8 minutes

This dish can be the center of your meal or complement a bowl of chili.

2 teaspoons vegetable oil
1/4 cup frozen corn
1 teaspoon seeded and minced jalapeño chile
1/2 teaspoon ground cumin
1/2 medium tomato, diced
2 scallions, finely chopped
1 tablespoon finely chopped fresh cilantro
2 cups cooked rice
Salt

1. In a medium skillet on medium heat, warm the oil. Add the corn, jalapeño, and cumin; cover and cook on low heat for 3 to 5 minutes, stirring occasionally.

2. Stir in the tomato, scallions, cilantro, and rice. Cook on low heat for 3 to 5 minutes until hot. Stir occasionally. Add a dash or two of water if needed to prevent the rice from sticking.

3. Salt to taste and serve.

Makes two servings

CHAPTER 10

Noodles

When you are busy and overworked, noodles can become one of your best friends; there are dozens of different kinds and shapes from which to choose (and don't forget full-bodied whole wheat varieties or delicate rice noodles). Ready-made pasta sauce straight from a jar is tasty, but it becomes boring as a steady diet. The following recipes will make you a versatile pasta cook, and you can prepare great toppings in the same amount of time it takes to cook the noodles. Add a fresh green salad with your pasta, and you'll have a whole meal.

Super-Excellent Pasta

To make one serving of pasta, use about 4 ounces of noodles. Bring 3 quarts of water to a rapid boil. Make sure you have enough water in the pot to allow the pasta to swim freely while it cooks. Add the pasta to the boiling water. Stir once with a long-handled wooden spoon to keep the pieces from sticking together; cover the pot so that the water will quickly return to a boil. (If you taste-test pasta dangling from a wooden spoon, you won't burn your lips or tongue on a hot metal utensil.) When the water boils, remove the lid and stir once again. The directions on packages of pasta usually overcook the noodles, so begin checking for doneness after about 5 minutes of cooking. For pasta served hot, cook it al dente, or just to the point where there is a slight resistance or "tooth" when you bite it. Drain cooked pasta immediately. Don't run cold water over it, because the outer layer of starch that remains helps the sauce stick. When you make pasta for cold salads, do rinse the cooked noodles.

Rice Noodles

You will find rice noodles in Asian markets and well-stocked supermarkets. They are great in clear soups, topped with your favorite pasta sauce, added to stir-fries, or in Thailand's best-known noodle dish—pad Thai. They're ready to eat in about 8 minutes.

To cook, place the noodles in boiling water and boil for 5 minutes; add salt and continue boiling for an additional 2 to 3 minutes or until translucent. Drain and rinse in cold water.

Whole Wheat Pasta
with Arugula

Preparation Time: 10 minutes

Arugula is a green with lots of pizzazz! It's a gourmet standard for salads, and here its sharp, peppery taste adds snap to pasta. Make a lot. It's great reheated in your microwave for lunch the next day or eaten cold from the container. The more often you make this recipe, the more arugula you'll find you want to toss into the bowl.

2 to $2^1/_2$ tablespoons olive oil
1 to 2 large cloves garlic, minced
$^1/_4$ pound uncooked whole wheat pasta (any shapes)
1 to 2 cups arugula (use more if you like)
$^1/_4$ cup black olives, pitted and sliced thin
1 large tomato, chopped in bite-size pieces
Salt and pepper
$^1/_4$ cup Parmesan cheese (optional)

1. Mix oil and garlic in a large bowl.

2. Wash arugula, spin or pat dry, cut off the larger stems, and discard; slice or chop the leaves into bite-size pieces.

3. Cook pasta al dente; begin checking for doneness after 5 minutes. Drain (don't rinse!), and add immediately to oil and garlic. Toss.

4. Add olives, tomato, and arugula. Salt and pepper to taste, and sprinkle with Parmesan, if desired. Lightly toss; serve immediately.

Makes one serving

Pasta with Green Beans and Feta Cheese

PREPARATION TIME: 12 minutes

The classic flavors of green beans and feta cheese combine in this dish to make a truly simple yet outstanding meal. Buy a bag of frozen green beans. It's easier to scoop out what you need from a bag than a cardboard box.

$1/4$ pound uncooked pasta
1 teaspoon olive oil
$1/4$ cup thinly sliced onion
1 large or 2 small cloves garlic, minced
$1/8$ teaspoon dried basil
$1^1/2$ cups frozen French-cut green beans
1 medium chopped tomato (about 1 cup)
1 tablespoon crumbled feta cheese
Salt and pepper

1. Bring a covered pot of water to a rapid boil, stir in the pasta, and cover until the water returns to a boil. Uncover the pot and cook the pasta until al dente, 8 to 10 minutes.

2. While the pasta cooks, heat the oil in a medium skillet over medium heat. Add the onion, garlic, and basil; sauté until the onion is soft, 3 to 4 minutes, stirring occasionally. Add the green beans and stir. Cover and cook on medium-low heat until the beans are hot and crisp-tender, about 5 minutes. Just before you serve the beans, stir in the fresh tomato.

3. When the pasta is al dente, drain and serve topped with the green bean sauce. Sprinkle generously with feta cheese and season with salt and pepper to taste.

Makes one serving

Pasta with Zucchini and Basil

PREPARATION TIME: 12 minutes

Zucchini is a vegetable that has an affinity for pasta.

$1/4$ pound uncooked spaghetti
1 teaspoon olive oil
2 to 3 cloves garlic, finely chopped
1 small or $1/2$ medium zucchini, sliced (about 1 cup)
$1/4$ teaspoon dried basil
Salt and pepper
2 teaspoons fresh lemon juice
Grated Parmesan cheese

1. Bring a covered pot of water to a rapid boil. Stir in the pasta, and cover the pot until the water returns to a boil. Uncover and cook until the pasta is al dente (begin checking for doneness after about 5 minutes of cooking).

2. While the pasta cooks, heat the oil in a medium skillet over medium-high heat. Add the garlic, zucchini, and basil. Quickly fry until the zucchini begins to brown, about 5 minutes, stirring occasionally. Add the lemon juice and stir. Remove from the heat.

3. When the pasta is al dente, drain it. Place the hot pasta on a warm plate; top with zucchini and grated Parmesan cheese. Lightly toss. Salt and pepper to taste.

Makes one serving

Farfalle and Peas

PREPARATION TIME: 20 minutes

Farfalle is the Italian name for bow-tie pasta. The nooks and crannies in the bow ties help hold the peas on your fork. The 15-minute onion sauté gives this simple dish great flavor.

2 teaspoons olive oil
1 small onion, chopped (about 1 cup)
1 cup frozen peas
Salt and pepper
2 cups uncooked bow-tie pasta
Grated Parmesan cheese (optional)

1. Bring a covered pot of water to a rapid boil. While the water comes to a boil, heat the oil in a medium skillet over medium heat. Add the onion, and lower the heat to medium-low; sauté for 10 to 15 minutes, stirring occasionally. (This long, slow sauté is what gives this dish its great flavor.) When the onion begins to turn brown, add the peas and salt and pepper to taste. Stir. Cook for 1 or 2 minutes. Cover and turn off the heat, leaving the skillet on the burner while the pasta finishes cooking.

2. When the pot of water boils, stir in the pasta, and re-cover the pot for a moment until the water returns to a boil. Uncover the pot. As soon as the pasta is cooked al dente (begin checking for doneness after about 5 minutes), drain it. Bow-tie pasta may take a few minutes longer to cook than spaghetti.

3. Serve the pasta topped with the onion and peas. Sprinkle with Parmesan cheese, if you desire.

Makes one serving

Pasta Primavera

Here is a pasta vegetable medley for two. Don't let the ingredient list scare you. It takes only 5 minutes to chop the vegetables.

$1/2$ pound uncooked spaghetti
1 tablespoon olive oil
$1/2$ medium onion, chopped (about 1/2 cup)
1 clove garlic, minced
$1/2$ medium carrot, thinly sliced
$1/4$ green bell pepper, chopped
4 mushrooms, sliced (about 1 cup)
1 medium zucchini, sliced (about 1 cup)
$1/4$ teaspoon dried basil
$1/8$ teaspoon dried oregano
$1/2$ medium tomato, chopped
2 tablespoons water
2 to 4 teaspoons fresh lemon juice (optional)
Grated Parmesan cheese
Salt and pepper

1. Bring a covered pot of water to a rapid boil, stir in the pasta, and cover until the water returns to a boil. Uncover the pot and cook the pasta until al dente; begin checking for doneness after 5 minutes.

2. While the pasta cooks, heat the oil in a medium skillet over medium heat. Add the onion, garlic, and carrot; sauté until the onion is soft, about 3 minutes. Add the bell pepper, mushrooms, zucchini, basil, and oregano; sauté, stirring occasionally until the vegetables begin to soften, about 3 min-

utes. Add the tomato and 2 tablespoons of water; cover and cook for 3 minutes or until the vegetables are just tender. Uncover, stir, and remove from the heat.

3. When the pasta is al dente, drain it. Serve the pasta topped with the vegetable mixture. Sprinkle each serving with a splash of fresh lemon juice, if desired, and grated Parmesan cheese. Salt and pepper to taste.

Makes two servings

Pasta with Garbanzo Beans

PREPARATION TIME: 15 minutes

The buttery flavor of garbanzo beans makes rich-tasting pasta. If you're out of spinach, use a chopped fresh tomato instead. Either way, it's delicious.

$1/4$ pound uncooked spaghetti
2 teaspoons olive oil
$1/2$ medium onion, chopped (about $1/2$ cup)
1 large clove garlic, minced
$1/2$ teaspoon dried dill
2 cups tightly packed, chopped spinach
$1/4$ cup canned garbanzo beans, rinsed and drained
2 tablespoon fresh lemon juice
Grated Parmesan cheese
Salt and pepper

1. Bring a covered pot of water to a rapid boil. When the water comes to a rolling boil, stir in the pasta; re-cover the pot, and return it to a boil. Uncover the pot and cook the pasta al dente (begin checking for doneness after about 5 minutes of cooking).

2. Heat the oil in a medium skillet on medium heat. Sauté the onion, garlic, and dill for about 5 minutes, stirring occasionally until the onion softens. Add the spinach and garbanzo beans and continue cooking, stirring until the spinach wilts, about 3 minutes.

3. When the pasta is al dente, drain it. Serve the pasta topped with the spinach mixture. Sprinkle with lemon juice and grated Parmesan cheese. Salt and pepper to taste.

Makes one serving

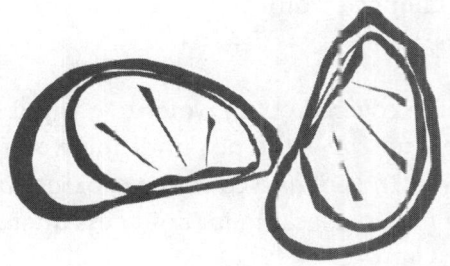

Pasta with Greens

Preparation Time: 10 minutes

Whip up this fabulous meal and enjoy the rich taste of tender greens and creamy cottage cheese tossed with pasta.

$1/4$ pound uncooked spaghetti
1 cup tightly packed kale or spinach
2 teaspoons vegetable oil
1 tablespoon water
$1/2$ cup nonfat cottage cheese
2 cloves garlic, minced
1 tablespoon chopped walnuts
Salt and pepper

1. Bring a large covered pot of water to a rapid boil. Add the pasta, stir, and cover the pot until the water returns to a boil. Uncover the pot and continue cooking until the pasta is al dente (begin checking for doneness after about 5 minutes of cooking).

2. Wash the kale and remove the tough center stems. Chop the leaves into bite-size pieces. Heat the oil in a medium skillet on medium-high heat; add the kale and sauté, stirring for 2 minutes. Add 1 tablespoon of water, cover, and cook until kale is wilted and still bright green, 3 to 5 minutes. Turn off the heat and stir in the cottage cheese and garlic.

3. When the pasta is al dente, drain it, and serve it tossed with the kale mixture. Sprinkle with walnuts. Salt and pepper to taste.

Makes one serving

Classic Tomato Sauce

PREPARATION TIME: 15 minutes

COOKING TIME: 15 minutes

Use this sauce for pasta, lasagna, or your favorite pizza. Commercial sauce is convenient when you're short on time, but it won't match the flavor of one you make yourself.

1/2 medium onion, finely chopped (about 1 cup)
3 cloves garlic, minced
2 teaspoons olive oil
1 (28-ounce) can whole tomatoes with juice (about 3 cups)
Salt and pepper

Extras (Optional)
2 teaspoons dried basil (3 tablespoons chopped fresh)
1/4 teaspoon dried oregano
1 tablespoon chopped fresh parsley

1. In a medium skillet, sauté onions and garlic in oil on medium heat until the onions are translucent, about 10 minutes.
2. Drain the tomato juice into the pan with the onions. Use your hands and gently squeeze the tomatoes into the skillet. Add one or more of the optional extras, if desired.
3. Simmer for 15 minutes uncovered, stirring occasionally. Salt and pepper to taste.

Makes 3 cups

Peanut Pasta

PREPARATION TIME: **12 minutes**

Boil up a pot of pasta and choose a sauce. Either one of these sauces can be ready in minutes without any cooking. Peanut sauce is also good served over cooked rice, baked sweet potatoes, and a variety of steamed vegetables.

$1/4$ pound uncooked spaghetti or linguini
1 cup broccoli florets
$1/2$ medium carrot, thinly sliced (about $1/2$ cup)
1 cup thinly sliced Chinese cabbage
1 scallion finely chopped (about 1 tablespoon)

Peanut Sauce with Tahini
1 tablespoon peanut butter
1 tablespoon tahini
1 tablespoon apple cider vinegar
1 to 2 tablespoons orange juice
1 teaspoon soy sauce

Peanut Sauce with Salsa
2 tablespoons peanut butter
2 tablespoons fresh lemon juice
2 tablespoons prepared Mexican red salsa
1 teaspoon brown sugar
Salt

1. Bring a covered pot of water to a rapid boil. While the water is heating, choose one of the sauces, and mix together the sauce ingredients in a small bowl until smooth and creamy. Add more juice if necessary.

2. When the water boils, stir in the pasta, cover the pot, and return it to a boil. Uncover the pot and cook until the noodles are al dente or just tender (begin checking for doneness after about 5 minutes of cooking).

3. While the noodles cook, steam the vegetables in a steamer basket placed in a pot or in a steamer. Add water to the pot and bring it to a boil, then add the broccoli and carrot; steam for $1^1/2$ to 2 minutes. Add the cabbage; steam for another 30 seconds or until the vegetables are crisp-tender. Make sure the water does not touch the vegetables while they cook.

4. When pasta is al dente, drain it, and serve it immediately tossed with the vegetables and sauce. Garnish with chopped scallion.

Makes one serving

Pad Thai

PREPARATION TIME: 20 minutes

Making pad Thai is easier than you might imagine. It's essentially a stir-fry with rice noodles. This recipe calls for mung bean sprouts. They are the sprouts you find in nearly every supermarket. The chile in this recipe is the ordinary little jalapeño chile. If you like your food hot, leave in some of the seeds, but look out! The hardest part of this recipe is hand-grating two carrots.

Noodles
2 quarts water
6 ounces rice noodles (1/4 inch wide)

Sauce
3 tablespoons fresh lemon or lime juice
3 tablespoons catsup
1 tablespoon sugar
1/2 cup soy sauce

Stir-Fry
1 to 2 tablespoons vegetable oil
4 large cloves garlic, minced
1 medium fresh green jalapeño chile, seeded and minced
2 medium carrots, grated (about 2 cups)
1/2 pound mung bean sprouts (about 11/2 cups)
4 scallions, finely chopped (about 3/4 cup)
2 tablespoons chopped peanuts
2 tablespoons finely chopped fresh cilantro or parsley
    (optional)

1. In a covered pan, bring the water to a rolling boil; stir in the rice noodles, and cook for 5 to 7 minutes. Drain the noodles, rinse them well under cool water, and set aside.
2. In a small bowl, combine the sauce ingredients; set aside.
3. Heat the oil in a medium skillet on medium-high heat. Add the garlic and jalapeño; stir and fry for a moment. Stir in the grated carrots. Stir and fry for 1 to 2 minutes. Add the sauce, noodles, bean sprouts, and scallions. Stir everything together. When the ingredients are warm, about 1 minute, remove to a platter. Garnish with the peanuts and cilantro, if you desire.

NOTE: Just before you're ready to add the noodles to the carrot mixture, check to see whether they're sticking together. If they are, quickly rinse and drain them again. They'll immediately come apart.

Makes two or three servings

CHAPTER 11

Various Vegetables and Stir-Fries

According to the book *Potatoes,* by Alvin and Virginia B. Silverstein, Frederick the Great of Prussia decreed in 1744 that anyone who refused to grow and eat potatoes would have their ears and nose cut off. You may not have time to grow potatoes, but you'll find delicious vegetable meals in this chapter, along with the how-to's of artichoke eating.

Deconstructed Artichoke

PREPARATION TIME: 5 minutes

COOKING TIME: 30 to 40 minutes

If you are looking for an entertaining meal and you like eating with your fingers, this strange-looking vegetable is for you. Cook the artichoke, and then just do what comes naturally. Pull off a leaf and dunk it in sauce. Put the leaf in your mouth and pull it through your teeth, scraping off the tender flesh. Discard what's left, and pull off another leaf. When you get to the center, scoop out and discard the thistle-like "choke." What's left under the choke is the soft "heart." It's the best part. Cut the heart into bite-size pieces and dunk it into the sauce. Tsiziki Sauce (page 43) and Tahini Sauce (page 44) are both excellent choices.

1 globe artichoke
2 tablespoons fresh lemon juice or wine vinegar
1 teaspoon olive oil
1 clove garlic

1. Cut off the stem of the artichoke so it will sit evenly on the bottom of a pot. Stand the artichoke up in the pot with 3 inches of water. Add the lemon juice or vinegar, oil, and garlic; cover the pot and bring it to a boil. Reduce the heat and simmer until the stem end is tender or a leaf can be removed with the slightest resistance (about 40 minutes). Check the pot from time to time to see whether the water has boiled away. Add more water if necessary.

2. When the artichoke is done, drain it well, and serve it hot, warm, or at room temperature. Most people enjoy dipping the leaves in sauce or melted butter, but it's tasty unadorned, too.

Makes one serving

Easy Asparagus

PREPARATION TIME: 5 minutes

COOKING TIME: About 20 minutes

Asparagus is a divine vegetable that arrives in the produce department in the spring. Eat it as a salad or as a side dish with a sandwich.

$1/2$ pound fresh asparagus
1 teaspoon olive oil
Salt
Lemon juice

Preheat the oven to 400 degrees F.

1. Wash the asparagus and snap off the tough ends of the stalks. Hold the stalk with the thumb and index finger of both hands, and the woody part will break off naturally in the right spot.

2. Place the asparagus on a baking sheet and drizzle the olive oil over the spears. Sprinkle with salt and roll the asparagus around until it is lightly coated with the oil.

3. Bake for about 10 minutes. When the stalks are slightly blistered, turn them over. Total roasting time will vary depending on the thickness of the stalks. Cook until tender, 10 to 15 minutes. Serve sprinkled with a few drops of lemon juice, or dip the spears in Tsiziki Sauce (page 43) if you desire.

NOTE: You can also cook asparagus by steaming it over boiling water for 3 to 6 minutes or by simmering it in water until it is tender.

Makes one or two servings

Steamed Vegetable Combo

PREPARATION TIME: 8 minutes

Enjoy steamed vegetables as a stand-alone one-bowl meal, or pair them with a variety of other dishes. The trick to making them taste good is to avoid overcooking. Begin checking for doneness in 2 minutes. The vegetables should be crisp-tender when done. Chilled and dressed with a vinaigrette dressing, a splash of balsamic vinegar, or a squeeze of lemon juice and seasoned to taste with salt and pepper, steamed vegetables make a salad, or serve them hot, topped with creamy Tsiziki Sauce (page 43) or Tahini Sauce (page 44) if you wish.

1/2 cup sliced carrots, cut 1/2-inch thick (1 carrot)
1/2 cup broccoli florets (1-inch pieces)
1/2 cup cauliflower florets (1-inch pieces)
Salt and pepper

1. Arrange the vegetables in a steamer over boiling water.
2. Cover and steam 4 to 5 minutes or until crisp-tender. Salt and pepper to taste.

Makes one serving

Roasted Red Bell Pepper

Red bell peppers take on a whole new personality when roasted or slowly sautéed. Each cooking method produces a special taste; both are delicious. Once you've discovered their sweet flavor, they'll become a mainstay in your vegetarian eating. They are cheapest in the fall. Use them on sandwiches, crackers, cooked pasta, green salads, baked potatoes, in stir-fries, and with cooked grains. Anywhere they land, they're luscious.

1 red bell pepper
2 teaspoons olive oil

Preheat the broiler.

To Roast
1. Cut the pepper in half lengthwise. Discard the seeds and membranes. Place the pepper on a baking sheet with its shiny skin side facing up. Broil 3 or 4 inches from the heat for 8 to 10 minutes or until the skin is blackened and charred.

2. Remove the pepper from the oven. Seal it in a paper bag to steam for 10 minutes. (It works even if you skip the paper bag trick.) Peel and discard the charred skin. Do not rinse; that will wash away the smoky taste. Slice roasted peppers into lengthwise strips. Drizzle with a little oil.

To Sauté

1. Cut the pepper in half lengthwise. Discard the seeds and membranes. Slice the pepper into lengthwise strips.

2. Heat oil in a small skillet on medium heat. Sauté the pepper on medium or medium-low heat for 15 minutes, stirring frequently until tender and lightly browned.

NOTE: Cooked peppers will keep for a week stored covered in the refrigerator.

Makes about 1/2 cup

Acorn Squash Bake (or Microwave)

PREPARATION TIME: 8 minutes

COOKING TIME: 40 to 45 minutes (or Microwave: 8 to 10 minutes)

Acorn squash is one of the tastiest in the fall harvest. Serve it as a side dish with baked tofu or refried beans. If you like squash extra-sweet, spoon on Orange Raisin Sauce (see recipe below).

1 acorn squash, split lengthwise and seeded
1 teaspoon olive oil

Orange Raisin Sauce
1/4 cup raisins
1/4 cup orange juice
1 tablespoon brown sugar
1/4 teaspoon cinnamon

Preheat oven to 350 degress F.

1. Place squash cut side down in an oiled baking dish. Bake 40 to 45 minutes or until tender.

2. In a small pan on medium-high heat, combine raisins, orange juice, sugar, and cinnamon. Warm the mixture until it just begins to simmer. Remove from heat and let it sit for 5 minutes. Spoon over the top of the cooked squash.

NOTE: To microwave instead of baking, place squash cut side down in a microwave-safe dish. Add 1/4 cup of water. Microwave on High 8 to 10 minutes or until tender

Makes two servings

Swee⊤ Potato Fries

PREPARATION TIME: 2 minutes

COOKING TIME: 10 to 15 minutes

The irresistible, rich flavor of sweet potatoes (often called yams) makes them great for broiling.

1 sweet potato or yam
1 to 2 tablespoons vegetable oil
Salt

1. Preheat oven to broiler setting. Cut the potato in half and then into French-fry shaped strips along the length of the potato. (No need to peel the potato, but wash the skin before you slice it.)
2. Place the fries in a large bowl. Add the olive oil, and stir to evenly coat the potatoes.
3. Spread the fries onto a baking sheet; avoid building a thick layer. If piled high the potatoes will steam, not broil. Place the potatoes in the broiler section of the oven on a shelf 3 to 4 inches from the top. Broil the potatoes 8 to 10 minutes, turning them once or twice until they are lightly browned.
4. Reset the oven to 400 degrees. Transfer the fries from the broiler portion of the oven to the center of the oven. Bake for 10 to 15 minutes. Sprinkle with salt and serve.

NOTE: Use this recipe to make "fries" from russet potatoes, white potatoes, and red potatoes.

Makes two servings

Gingered Chinese Greens Stir-Fry

Preparation Time: 15 minutes

Tofu Pressing Time: 15 to 20 minutes

Serve this simple, crisp stir-fry over warm rice or cooked noodles. (The chili oil in this recipe may also be labeled red oil, hot oil, or hot pepper oil.)

$1/2$ cake Chinese-style firm tofu (about 7 ounces)
2 cups packed shredded Chinese cabbage or bok choy
    (4 or 5 leaves)
2 teaspoons vegetable oil
$1/2$ teaspoon minced or grated gingerroot
1 to 2 teaspoons water
Splash of chili oil
1 tablespoon finely chopped fresh cilantro

Sauce
1 tablespoon soy sauce
3 tablespoons orange juice
1 tablespoon fresh lemon or lime juice
1 tablespoon water
1 teaspoon sugar
$1/2$ teaspoon cornstarch

1. Sandwich the tofu between two plates. Top with a heavy book. Let sit for 15 to 20 minutes. Remove the weight and top cover, and drain the water from the bottom plate. The tofu is now ready to use. Cut the tofu into $1/2$-inch cubes.

2. Wash and thinly slice the cabbage leaves and stems. Heat oil in a medium skillet over medium-high heat. Add ginger and cabbage. Stir and fry for about 2 minutes. Add water; cover and cook over medium heat until cabbage is soft, about 2 to 3 minutes.

3. In a small bowl, combine the sauce ingredients. Add the tofu and sauce to the skillet and gently stir until the sauce thickens, about 2 minutes. Serve immediately; splash with hot chili oil and cilantro.

NOTE: If you don't have chili oil, make this recipe anyway. (Substitute Tabasco for chili oil if you desire.)

Makes one serving

Tofu Cabbage Stir-Fry

PREPARATION TIME: 15 to 20 minutes

Here is a fast meal for breakfast, lunch, or dinner on a cold winter day. The pressed tofu becomes golden brown and crispy in this stir-fry. If you don't have sesame seeds, go for it anyway.

$1/3$ block (4 to 5 ounces) firm tofu
2 teaspoons toasted sesame oil or vegetable oil
1 large clove garlic, minced
1 teaspoon minced fresh ginger
2 cups shredded green or red cabbage (about $1/4$ small head)
Salt and pepper or soy sauce
1 teaspoon sesame seeds, toasted

1. Sandwich the tofu between two plates. Top with a heavy book. Let sit for 15 to 20 minutes. Remove the weight and top cover, and drain the water from the bottom plate. The tofu is now ready to use. Cut the tofu into $1/2$-inch cubes.

2. Heat 1 teaspoon of the oil in a medium skillet over medium-high heat. Add the tofu and stir and fry until lightly browned, 3 to 4 minutes. Add the garlic and ginger; sauté 1 minute longer. Remove the tofu from the skillet and set aside.

3. Re-oil the skillet with the remaining oil, and cook the cabbage over medium-high heat until soft, 3 to 5 minutes. Add the tofu. Remove the skillet from the heat. Season with salt and pepper or a splash of soy sauce. Serve when everything is hot. Sprinkle with toasted sesame seeds.

NOTE: To toast sesame seeds, place the seeds in a dry skillet on medium-high heat for 1 to 2 minutes. Watch the seeds carefully; they toast quickly. Stir the seeds and shake the pan frequently; when the seeds are golden, immediately remove them from the skillet.

Makes one serving

Assorted Vegetable Stir-Fry

PREPARATION TIME: 15 minutes

Have you ever wondered how Chinese restaurants get their stir-fries to glisten? The secret is in a sauce made with cornstarch. Choose one of the following sauce recipes, and serve the stir-fry over a bed of cooked rice, pasta, or noodles.

Sweet and Sour Sauce
1 tablespoon soy sauce
1 tablespoon white vinegar
1 tablespoon catsup
2 teaspoons sugar
$1/4$ cup water
1 teaspoon cornstarch

Tangy Sauce
1 tablespoon hoisin sauce
1 tablespoon white vinegar
1 tablespoon soy sauce
$1/4$ cup water
1 teaspoon cornstarch

Stir-Fry
2 teaspoons vegetable oil
1 clove garlic, minced
1 medium carrot diagonally sliced (about 1 cup)
$1/2$ bell pepper, seeded and chopped, or 12 snow peas
$1/2$ medium zucchini, diagonally sliced (about 1 cup)
1 tablespoon finely chopped scallion (optional)

1. Choose one of the sauces, and combine the sauce ingredients in a small bowl.

2. Heat the oil in a medium skillet over medium-high heat. Add the garlic and swirl it in the oil for a moment. Add the carrot, bell pepper, and zucchini; stir and fry for 3 to 4 minutes.

3. Stir the sauce and pour it over the vegetables; stir and simmer for about 30 seconds or until the sauce thickens and the vegetables become glazed. Serve immediately. Garnish with chopped scallion if you desire.

Makes one serving

Broccoli, Carrot, and Cashew Stir-Fry

PREPARATION TIME: 10 minutes

Almost any combination of vegetables works in a stir-fry. Figure on 2 to 2¹/₂ cups of cut, raw vegetables per serving. If that seems like a lot, remember that vegetables shrink from water loss during cooking. If you can't find extra-firm tofu, firm will work.

3 ounces extra-firm tofu
2 teaspoons vegetable oil
1 clove garlic, finely chopped
1 carrot, diagonally sliced (1 cup)
1¹/₂ cups broccoli florets
1 tablespoon soy sauce
2 tablespoons chopped scallion (1 small)
2 tablespoons coarsely chopped cashews

1. Blot the tofu between paper towels, and then cut it into ¹/₂-inch cubes.
2. Heat the oil in a medium skillet on medium-high heat. Add the garlic and swirl it in the oil for 30 seconds; add the tofu, carrot, and broccoli. Stir and fry for about 3 minutes. Add the soy sauce; stir and fry for about 30 seconds.
3. Serve immediately. Garnish with the scallion and cashews.

Makes one serving

Roasted Vegetable Rush

PREPARATION TIME: **12 minutes**

COOKING TIME: **15 minutes**

These brown and crispy potatoes take center stage, and the vegetables are sweet and caramelized.

3 medium red potatoes (cut into 1-inch cubes)
3 mushrooms, quartered (about 1 cup)
3/4 green bell pepper, cut into bite-size chunks
5 cloves garlic, coarsely chopped
1 tablespoon olive oil
1 teaspoon dried rosemary
1 tablespoon fresh lemon juice or balsamic vinegar
Salt and pepper

Preheat the broiler.

1. Cook the potato cubes in a pot of rapidly boiling water for 5 minutes. Drain thoroughly. Place the mushrooms, bell pepper, garlic and cooked potatoes in a large bowl. Add the olive oil and rosemary, and stir to evenly coat the vegetables with oil.

2. Spread the vegetables onto a baking sheet, but avoid building a thick layer; if piled high, the vegetables will steam not broil.

3. Broil vegetables for 10 minutes, until well cooked but not burned. Stir once or twice to ensure even cooking. Serve the vegetables with a splash of fresh lemon juice or balsamic vinegar. Salt and pepper to taste.

Makes one or two servings

Potato Skillet Hash

PREPARATION TIME: 10 minutes

COOKING TIME: 20 minutes

This meal turns heads in restaurants. If you didn't order it, it's the one you'll wish you had. Make the dish at home for breakfast, lunch, or dinner. Add more heat with a splash of Tabasco if you desire.

1 tablespoon olive oil
1 medium potato, diced (cut into $1/2$-inch cubes)
    (about 2 cups)
$1/3$ cup carrot, thinly sliced
$1/3$ cup medium green bell pepper, chopped
$3/4$ cup onion, chopped
 2 tablespoons water
$1/2$ teaspoon dried thyme
Salt and pepper

1. Heat the oil in a heavy skillet over medium-high heat. Add the potatoes, carrot, bell pepper, and onion; sauté for 5 to 7 minutes, stirring frequently.
2. Add the water. Reduce the heat to medium-low; cover and cook for 10 minutes or until the potatoes are tender.
3. Remove the lid. Add the thyme and stir. Continue cooking for 1 minute. If there is water in the pan, cook 1 minute longer or until the water evaporates. Remove from heat; salt and pepper to taste.

Makes one to two servings

Basic Baked Potatoes

PREPARATION TIME: 1 minute

COOKING TIME: 45 to 60 minutes

Turn a baked potato into a banquet. Top it with sautéed or roasted vegetables, chili, spaghetti sauce, a ladle of soup, or a dollop of non-fat plain yogurt. Just don't do it all at the same time.

1 or more russet potatoes
Vegetable oil (optional)

Preheat the oven to 400 degrees F.

Wash the potatoes, dry them, and rub with oil if you desire. Pierce the skin with a knife before baking to allow the steam that forms inside as they cook to escape. Otherwise, they may explode. Bake for about 60 minutes until fork-piercing tender. (If you want to speed up the process, cut the potato in half lengthwise and bake cut side down on a baking sheet for 45 minutes until soft.)

NOTE: Bake two potatoes at the same time and store the extra in the refrigerator. When you're in a hurry, you'll have one ready to go. Re-heat it in a microwave for a quick meal or snack, or moisten the potato and reheat it in an oven at 350 degrees F for 15 minutes.

Makes one serving

Five-Minute Microwave-Baked Potato

Preparation Time: 1 minute

Cooking Time: 5 minutes

If you are in a hurry and have a microwave, you can bake a potato in about 5 minutes.

1 potato

1. Wash and dry the potato and pierce the skin in several places.
2. Microwave on High for 5 minutes. Remove the potato from the microwave, and let rest, covered, for 5 minutes. Squeeze the skin to see if the potato is soft. If it is, it's ready to eat. If it feels hard, return it to the microwave and heat on High for another minute. (It's better to undercook the potato, test for doneness, and return it to the microwave if necessary, than to overcook it. Overcooked microwaved potatoes shrivel and become pasty.) Because of the size of the potato and the power of the microwave, cooking times may vary.

NOTE: You can also microwave a sweet potato or yam. Pierce the skin several times and cook on High for 4 to 6 minutes. Let it sit for 3 to 4 minutes before serving.

Makes one serving

Mashed Potatoes

PREPARATION TIME: 6 minutes

COOKING TIME: About 15 minutes

Here is a real comfort food. If you like mashed potatoes snowy white, peel them; if you like them with brown flecks, don't bother. (One-third of the potato's nutrients are just beneath the skin.) Do you like garlic? Add some when you mash the potatoes. Are you a potatoes and gravy person? See the gravy recipe on page 158, or skip the gravy and top a potato with grated cheese, sautéed vegetables, chopped cashews, or a handful of cooked corn or peas.

2 potatoes, washed
2 to 3 tablespoons soy milk or nonfat dairy milk
Salt and pepper

1. Cut the potatoes into thirds. Place the potatoes in a saucepan and cover them with water. Bring the pot to a boil; reduce the heat, cover, and simmer until tender, about 15 minutes.

2. Drain off the water. Mash the potatoes, mixing in the milk. Add more milk if the potatoes appear dry. Season with salt and pepper to taste.

NOTE: The water used for cooking the potatoes makes the beginning of a great soup.

Makes one serving

Colcannon

PREPARATION TIME: 10 minutes

COOKING TIME: About 15 minutes

This food favorite from Ireland and Scotland has only two main ingredients—potatoes and cabbage—and they're boiled together in one pot. It's a cheap, quick meal for a cold winter day.

2 medium russet or white potatoes, peeled
2 cups shredded green cabbage
1/2 cup chopped onion (about 1/2 medium)
1/4 cup soy milk or lowfat dairy milk
1 to 2 tablespoons grated Cheddar cheese or soy cheese
    (optional)
Salt and pepper

1. Cut the potatoes into 1-inch chunks. Place the potatoes in a medium pot, and cover them with water. Bring the water to a boil, and cook the potatoes until they are almost tender, about 10 minutes.

2. Add the cabbage and onion; continue cooking until the potatoes and cabbage are soft, about 5 minutes. Drain.

3. Add the milk and mash until the potatoes are smooth. Add cheese, if you desire. Taste; season with salt and pepper.

Makes two servings

Mashed Roots
with Horseradish

PREPARATION TIME: 5 minutes

COOKING TIME: About 20 minutes

If you've wondered what to do with a turnip, here's one answer. They're also good sliced and eaten raw.

2 red or white potatoes, cut into eighths
1 turnip, peeled and cut into eighths
1 carrot, cut into eighths
1 large clove garlic
2 to 4 tablespoons soy milk or dairy milk
Salt and pepper
1 to 2 teaspoons horseradish
1 tablespoon minced fresh parsley (optional)

1. Place the potatoes, turnip, carrot, and garlic in a saucepan, and cover with water. Bring the water to a boil, reduce the heat. Put a lid on the pot, and simmer for about 20 minutes or until the vegetables are tender.

2. Drain the pot and add the milk. Mash and whip the mixture together until smooth. If necessary, add more milk. Season with salt and pepper. Taste, add horseradish, and stir. Serve sprinkled with parsley if you desire.

NOTE: Avoid brands of horseradish made with egg yolk.

Makes two servings

Scalloped Potatoes Vegan-Style

PREPARATION TIME: 15 minutes

COOKING TIME: About 1 hour

This recipe tastes like old-fashioned scalloped potatoes, but without the milk and cheese. If you don't have a lid for your baking dish, cover it with foil.

1 teaspoon olive oil
1 white onion, finely chopped
4 cloves garlic, minced
1/4 cup tahini
2 tablespoons whole wheat flour
1/2 teaspoon salt
1 cup water
5 medium white or red potatoes

Preheat the oven to 400 degrees F.

1. Heat the oil in a skillet, and sauté the onion and garlic for 3 to 5 minutes on medium-high heat until the onion is soft and translucent.
2. In a blender or bowl, mix together the tahini, flour, salt, and water.

3. Thinly slice the potatoes. Don't bother to peel them. Arrange the potatoes in a lightly oiled 9-inch-square baking dish, overlapping them to cover the bottom of the dish. Spoon the onion and garlic mixture on top of the potato slices. Pour the tahini sauce over the top. Cover and bake for 1 hour. Uncover and bake another 5 to 10 minutes, until golden brown.

Makes two or three servings

Sweet Potato or Yam with Raisins and Pineapple

PREPARATION TIME: 6 minutes

COOKIING TIME: About 1 hour

Sweet potatoes are good enough to eat for dessert. The cooked texture of the light-skinned variety sweet potato will be dry and crumbly. The dark-skinned variety, sometimes labeled yam, is sweeter and more moist inside. Both are delicious.

1 sweet potato or yam
1 teaspoon raisins
$1/8$ teaspoon ground cinnamon
4 tablespoons canned unsweetened crushed pineapple, drained
1 tablespoon chopped walnuts

Preheat the oven to 375 degrees F.

1. Place potato on a baking sheet, and bake for 1 hour or until tender. Remove the potato from the oven and peel away the shell, or cut the potato in half and scoop out the inside.
2. Mash the potato with a fork in a small bowl. Add raisins, cinnamon, pineapple, and walnuts. If the potato mixture is dry, add pineapple liquid.

Makes two servings

CHAPTER 12

Desserts and Quick Breads

Here are sweet ideas for those times when you want to "boost your energy." If you're having a chocolate attack, Postmodern Chocolate Pudding is ready in 5 minutes, and Mountain High Chocolate Cake is made right in the baking pan so there's no mess to clean up. If you're not a chocoholic, there's plenty in this chapter for you, too.

Postmodern
Chocolate Pudding

PREPARATION TIME: **8 minutes**

If you're not home alone, double the recipe and make someone happy. (If you double the recipe, microwave on High for 3 minutes, stir, and microwave on High for another 2 minutes.)

2 tablespoons sugar
2 tablespoons unsweetened baking cocoa powder
2 teaspoons firmly packed cornstarch
3/4 cup soy milk or dairy milk
1/4 teaspoon vanilla

1. In a 1-quart glass microwavable bowl, combine the sugar, cocoa, and cornstarch. Add 1/4 cup of the milk and stir until mixture is smooth and creamy. Add the remaining 1/2 cup milk and stir.

2. Stir once just before you close the microwave door because cornstarch quickly settles to the bottom of the bowl. Microwave the mixture for 11/2 minutes on High. Remove the bowl from the microwave; stir carefully (the mixture will be hot). Return the pudding to the microwave, and cook for another 11/2 minutes on High. The pudding will begin to thicken.

3. Remove the bowl from the microwave and add the vanilla. Stir once. Let the pudding rest for 1 to 2 minutes. It will continue to thicken as it cools.

NOTE: Microwave cooking times can vary depending on the size of the cooking container, the power supply, and the temperature settings available on the oven. If you don't have a microwave, make the pudding in a small saucepan on top of the stove. Combine the ingredients in the pot. Cook over medium heat, stirring constantly, until the pudding comes to a boil. Lower the heat and gently simmer, stirring continuously until the pudding thickens, about 3 minutes. It is important to keep stirring to avoid burning or scorching.

Makes one serving

East Coast Custard

PREPARATION TIME: 12 minutes

COOKING TIME: About 1 1/2 hours

Stir up this recipe after dinner, and you'll have a marvelous late-night snack. It turns into smooth pudding as it cooks slowly in the oven. Serve it warm as is or topped with vanilla frozen yogurt.

1/2 teaspoon vegetable oil
2/3 cup cornmeal
1/4 teaspoon salt
1 teaspoon chopped fresh ginger or 1/2 teaspoon
    ground ginger
1/4 teaspoon nutmeg
2/3 cup raisins
4 cups soy milk or nonfat dairy milk
6 tablespoons maple syrup

Preheat the oven to 275 degrees F.

1. Lightly oil a 1 1/2- or 2-quart baking dish with vegetable oil. In a medium bowl, combine the cornmeal, salt, ginger, nutmeg, and raisins. Add 1 cup of the milk and the maple syrup. Stir to combine.

2. In a saucepan, heat 2 cups of milk to boiling. Gradually add the cornmeal mixture, stirring continuously. Reduce the heat to low and cook, stirring often, until the mixture is thick and smooth, about 10 minutes. Transfer to the prepared baking dish.

3. Pour the remaining 1 cup of milk on top of the cornmeal mixture. Bake until the milk is nearly all absorbed and the top of the pudding is golden brown. Begin checking for doneness in 1 hour. The baking time can vary 15 to 30 minutes depending on the coarseness of the cornmeal. It will be soft and creamy inside when done.

Makes six servings

Mountain-High Chocolate Cake

PREPARATION TIME: 7 minutes

BAKING TIME: 25 to 30 minutes

The best thing about this recipe is what it doesn't have. It doesn't have eggs, milk, cholesterol, a mixing bowl to clean, or a pan to oil. It does deliver a delicious, dark chocolate cake. Serve the cake topped with a dollop of applesauce, and call it a rustic version of the famous German Sacher torte.

1 1/2 cups unbleached white flour
1/3 cup unsweetened baking cocoa powder
1 teaspoon baking soda
1/2 teaspoon salt
1 cup sugar
1 1/4 cups water
1/4 cup vegetable oil
2 teaspoons vanilla extract
2 tablespoons plain red or white vinegar

Preheat the oven to 375 degrees F.

1. Combine the flour, cocoa, baking soda, salt, and sugar in a glass, ceramic, or stainless steel baking pan (9-inch round, 8-inch square, or 9 × 6-inch rectangle).

2. In a small bowl, combine the water, oil, and vanilla. Pour the liquid into the dry ingredients, and whisk with a fork to

combine. Add the vinegar, and stir just until the vinegar is distributed around the batter. (There will be color variations in the batter from the reaction between the vinegar and baking soda.)

3. Bake for 25 to 30 minutes. Remove from the oven, and call your friends.

Makes six or eight servings

Vanilla Tapioca Pudding

PREPARATION TIME: 15 minutes

Eaten warm off the stove or chilled from the refrigerator, this creamy pudding will make you smile. Be bold and add fresh fruit, such as raspberries, strawberries, blueberries, bananas, mangos, pineapple, or orange slices.

3 tablespoons instant or minute tapioca
2 tablespoons sugar
2 cups soy milk or nonfat dairy milk
1/2 teaspoon vanilla extract

1. Combine the tapioca, sugar, and milk in a saucepan, and let it sit for 10 minutes to begin thickening.
2. On medium heat, bring the tapioca mixture to a boil, stirring constantly to prevent lumps and sticking. Lower heat; continue stirring, and cook for about 2 minutes.
3. Remove from heat, and stir in vanilla. Let it sit for 5 minutes before serving.

The pudding thickens as it cools.

Makes three servings

Warm Apple Slices

PREPARATION TIME: 5 minutes

COOKING TIME: 10 minutes

These plumped apples are delightful right out of the pot or spooned on top of hot oatmeal. If you're not in the mood for oatmeal, there's always ice cream.

1 apple
1 teaspoon butter
$1/2$ teaspoon maple syrup or sugar
$1/4$ teaspoon cinnamon

1. Quarter, core, and cut the apple into $1/8$- to $1/4$-inch slices.

2. In a medium pot, combine the apples with the other ingredients, cover, and simmer on medium-low heat for about 10 minutes.

Makes one or two servings

Chocolate Chip Cookies

PREPARATION TIME: 10 minutes

COOKING TIME: 7 to 10 minutes per batch

If you're in a hurry, check out the nontraditional mixing option in this recipe.

1/2 cup butter, at room temperature
1 cup brown sugar or white sugar
1 egg
1 teaspoon vanilla
1/2 cup unbleached white all-purpose flour, plus
    2 tablespoons
1/2 cup whole wheat flour
1/2 teaspoon baking soda
1/2 teaspoon salt
1 cup chocolate chips
3/4 cup chopped walnuts (optional)

Preheat oven to 375 degrees.

Traditional Cookie Mixing
1. In a large bowl, cream together the butter and sugar until smooth. Beat in the egg and vanilla until well blended.

2. In a separate bowl, combine the white flour, whole wheat flour, baking soda, salt, chocolate chips, and nuts, if desired.

3. Stir the dry ingredients into the wet ingredients, mixing well.

4. Drop the batter by teaspoonfuls onto a greased cookie sheet about 2 inches apart. Bake 7 to 10 minutes until the bottoms are slightly browned. Check the oven after 7 minutes to avoid overbaking.

5. Remove the cookies with a spatula to a rack or dish to cool.

Nontraditional Cookie Mixing (It works!)
Dump everything into a large bowl and mush it together with your hands. Don't lick your fingers—raw batter with uncooked egg is a dangerous "treat" because of the risk of salmonella.

NOTE: Take the butter out of the refrigerator so that it can soften. If there's not time for that, put it in the microwave for a few seconds. It's much easier to cream butter when it's soft.

Makes about 2 1/2 dozen, 2-inch cookies

Cinnamon Oatmeal Raisin Cookies

PREPARATION TIME: 15 minutes

COOKING TIME: 10 to 15 minutes per batch

If you think only chocolate will do, you'll change your mind when you taste these cinnamon oatmeal cookies.

1/2 cup butter (at room temperature)
3/4 cup brown sugar
1 large egg
1 teaspoon vanilla
1 1/4 cup rolled oats
1 cup whole wheat flour
1 teaspoon ground cinnamon
1/2 teaspoon baking powder
1/2 teaspoon baking soda
1/4 teaspoon salt
3/4 cup raisins

Preheat oven to 350 degrees F.

1. In a large bowl, cream together the butter and sugar until smooth. Add the egg and vanilla, and mix until well blended.

2. Add remaining ingredients, and mix until well combined.

3. Drop the dough in 1/4-cup mounds about 3 inches apart onto a lightly oiled baking sheet. Bake for 10 to 15 minutes, until golden. Check after 10 minutes to avoid overbaking. Use a spatula to transfer the cookies to a rack or plate to cool.

Makes 12 to 18 cookies

Baked Bananas

PREPARATION TIME: 3 minutes

COOKING TIME: 10 to 15 minutes

These bananas are sure to cause a conversation with the way they change color when they bake.

1 banana
1 to 2 tablespoons yogurt
$1/8$ teaspoon ground cinnamon

Preheat the oven to 400 degrees F.

1. Lay the unpeeled banana on a baking sheet. Make a slit along the length of the banana. Bake the banana with the slit side up for 10 to 15 minutes, or until the skin turns black.
2. Remove the banana from the oven and split open the peel. Top with a dollop of yogurt and a sprinkle of cinnamon, and eat it with a spoon.

Makes one serving

Blueberry Tart

PREPARATION TIME: 6 minutes

COOKING TIME: 30 minutes

Enjoy nibbling on this warm berry tart along with a hot cup of green tea.

$2/3$ cup whole wheat flour
$1/2$ cup sugar
$1^1/2$ teaspoons baking powder
$1/4$ teaspoon salt
$2/3$ cup soy milk or lowfat dairy milk
$1/2$ teaspoon vanilla
2 tablespoons butter, melted
2 cups blueberries

1. In a medium bowl, combine the flour, sugar, baking powder, and salt. Add the milk and vanilla, and stir until the batter is smooth.
2. Swirl the melted butter over the bottom of a 6 × 10-inch glass, ceramic, or stainless steel baking pan.
3. Pour in the batter, and sprinkle the top with the blueberries. Bake for 30 minutes or until the tart is golden brown.

NOTE: If you use frozen berries, thaw them first. If you use fresh berries, wash them and pick off any stems.

Makes four servings

Corn Bread Country-Style

PREPARATION TIME: 7 minutes

This tasty corn bread is an excellent accompaniment to a bowl of chili, soup, or salad.

1 cup cornmeal
1 cup whole wheat or white flour
1/4 cup brown or white sugar
2 teaspoons baking powder
1/4 teaspoon salt
1 cup soy milk or dairy milk
1/4 cup vegetable oil
1 egg

Preheat the oven to 425 degrees F.

1. Lightly oil a 9 × 6-inch baking dish or loaf pan with vegetable oil. In a large bowl, combine the cornmeal, flour, sugar, baking powder, and salt.

2. In a medium bowl, combine the milk, vegetable oil, and egg.

3. Pour the liquid mixture into the dry ingredients and stir just to combine. Do not overmix. Pour the mixture into the baking pan. Bake for 15 to 20 minutes until a knife inserted in the center comes out clean. Serve warm with honey or fruit preserves, if you desire.

NOTE: Corn flour or cornmeal, sometimes called polenta, work in this recipe. Depending on the type of cornmeal you use, you may need to add more liquid.

Makes six servings

Sunday Morning Muffins

PREPARATION TIME: 10 minutes

COOKING TIME: 18 to 20 minutes

Set out a jar of honey or jam, and enjoy these muffins straight from the oven. The trick to making high-rising, tender muffins is in the blending. Too much stirring makes them tough. When you combine the flour mixture with the applesauce mixture, stir only until the dry ingredients become moist. If a few lumps remain, that's okay.

1 cup whole wheat flour
1 cup white flour
$1/4$ cup sugar
2 teaspoons baking powder
$3/4$ teaspoon baking soda
$1/2$ teaspoon ground cinnamon
$3/4$ cup raisins
2 cups unsweetened applesauce
$1/4$ cup vegetable oil

Preheat the oven to 375 degrees F.

1. In a large bowl, add the flours, sugar, baking powder, baking soda, cinnamon, and raisins. Stir to combine.

2. In a medium bowl, whisk the applesauce and oil together.

3. Add the applesauce mixture to the flour mixture, stirring just to moisten. Spoon the batter into a lightly oiled standard muffin tin. Bake for 18 to 20 minutes or until golden.

Makes 12 muffins

CHAPTER 13

Drinks

Be Fluid

Whether you choose bottled water from the supermarket or a glass of cold tap water with a slice of lemon, you'll be surprised by how much water you'll naturally drink when it's near at hand. Drink plenty of water, and also enjoy the recipes in this chapter for coffee, tea, and blender quenchers.

Take a Coffee Break

If coffee has become an integral part of your life during long nights of studying, here are some ideas to help you use it to your best advantage. Caffeine is similar to amphetamines but milder in its effects. It is a central nervous system stimulant that makes you feel more alert, temporarily relieves fatigue, and promotes quick thinking. It doesn't take much caffeine to accomplish this feeling of well-being. The amount in one or two ordinary cups of coffee is enough. However, at greater doses (five to six cups or more), caffeine can produce negative effects such as nervousness, anxiety, and panic attacks. Although coffee isn't a health food, recent research has turned up very little scientific evidence to indict a moderate intake of two cups daily.

Prepared coffee doesn't keep well. Warming it over a burner for only about 20 minutes can make the taste bitter. If you are making coffee for one person, the filter method is a good choice. It's simple to make only one or two cups at a time, and cleanup is easy. Measure 2 rounded tablespoons of ground coffee per cup into a filter-lined cone poised over your pot or cup. (In the world of coffee, a cup is 6 ounces, not the 8 ounces in a standard measuring cup. So if you are using a full measuring cup or a giant coffee mug to measure water, your coffee will probably be weak.) Rinse the pot and cup with hot water before you make the coffee, and the drink will remain hot longer. Heat cold fresh water just until it boils. Remove the water from the heat. Next, add just a few splashes of water to the coffee grounds to moisten them slightly. Let them absorb the water before pouring on the rest. This will prevent the water from going through the grounds too quickly without extracting maximum flavor.

Coffee Brazil

PREPARATION TIME: 5 minutes

This fragrant cup of coffee is a quick pick-me-up.

1 cup coffee
1 sliver lemon peel

Pour hot coffee into a cup. Twist the lemon peel to release its oils. Rub the yellow side of the peel around the rim of the cup for a citrus-flavored coffee.

Makes one serving

Café au Lait

PREPARATION TIME: 7minutes

This foamy mixture satisfies first thing in the morning or late at night. You will need a blender to foam the milk. It won't reach the heights of the steamed milk from an espresso bar, but it won't cost as much, either.

$1/2$ cup soy milk or dairy milk
1 teaspoon honey
$1/2$ cup freshly brewed strong coffee

Heat the milk and honey to a boil, and then whip it in a blender for 30 seconds. Next, pour the coffee into a cup and add the milk mixture.

Makes one serving

Coffee Alaska

PREPARATION TIME: 5 minutes

Here is the perfect drink for anytime you feel the impulse for something sweet.

1 cup freshly brewed coffee
1/4 cup soy ice cream, nonfat frozen yogurt, or dairy ice cream

Pour the hot coffee over vanilla or chocolate ice cream or frozen yogurt. If you drink the coffee quickly enough—before all the ice cream melts—you'll have a delicious warm puddle to sip from the bottom of your cup.

Makes one serving

Banana Express

PREPARATION TIME: 5 minutes

Here is a great way to use an over-ripe banana and whip up a cool coffee treat.

$1/2$ cup strong coffee
$1/4$ cup soy milk
$1/2$ ripe banana, peeled and sliced
1 ice cube

Whip the ingredients in a blender until smooth; while the blender is turning, add the ice cube through the small opening in the blender lid, and blend on high for about 30 seconds. Pour into a glass. Enjoy!

Makes one serving

Mocha Coffee

PREPARATION TIME: 5 minutes

Make this delicious coffee with equal parts ccffee and hot chocolate.

¹/₂ cup coffee
¹/₂ cup hot chocolate
Grated orange peel

Stir the hot coffee and hot chocolate together. Serve topped with grated orange peel.

Makes one serving

The Tea Zone

All tea varieties come from the same plant, *Camellia sinensis.* After they are harvested, different processing methods turn them into one of three basic types of tea: black, green, and oolong. Herbal "teas" do not come from the tea plant but are blends of other plant leaves, flowers, roots, and spices. Tea has about half the caffeine as a comparable cup of coffee. Make tea with fresh water; water that has been kept warm for a period of time will make flat-tasting tea. Rinse your cup with hot water before making tea so that the brew will stay warm longer. Allow the tea to steep 3 to 5 minutes to extract flavor and color. Serve immediately. Tea doesn't hold up well.

Chocolate Chai

PREPARATION TIME: 7 minutes

When you feel the impulse for something chocolate, make this simple duet.

1 cup hot water
1 commercial chai tea bag (without sugar)
1/3 cup dairy milk or soy milk
2 teaspoons cocoa
2 teaspoons sugar or honey

1. Pour hot water directly over tea bag in a preheated oversized mug.
2. While the tea steeps (3 to 5 minutes), heat milk, cocoa, and sugar in small saucepan, stirring to dissolve cocoa.
3. Remove tea bag. Pour the hot milk mixture into tea. Taste. If you like sweeter chai, add more sugar.

Makes one serving

Hot Apple Tea

PREPARATION TIME: 6 minutes

Relax with this warm, fragrant brew. Try Berry Zinger, Peppermint, Lemon Spice, or your favorite herbal tea.

1 cup apple juice
1 herbal tea bag

Bring apple juice to a boil in a small saucepan. Remove from heat and add tea bag. Steep for 5 minutes. Pour into a warmed mug.

NOTE: If the tea you choose is full of strong, sharp flavor like Berry Zinger, use half apple juice and half water.

Makes one serving

Blender Quenchers

Smoothies are a speedy way to give yourself a refreshing lift. They can be a fast meal or a relaxing drink for sipping. Inventing smoothies is simple. Ripe fruits blended with juices, yogurt, or milk and sweetened with honey or maple syrup make the base. Add a dash of vanilla, cinnamon, or nutmeg and you're ready to go. (Use ripe fruit, and you may not need to add sweetener.) If you want a savory veggie drink, try Pink Tomato Swirl (page 244).

When you're in the mood for a "chiller" drink and plan to add ice, crushed ice is the easiest to use. If you add ice cubes, make sure the blender is whizzing around at top speed, and that you add one cube at a time. Sweeten your drink before you chill it. Honey, for example, doesn't want to loosen up and mix once it's chilled. Ice dilutes the flavor of a drink, so taste-test as you go. You can also add sparkling water; add it after the drink is blended, because you'll lose the fizz if it's whirled in a blender. Enjoy!

Tofu Berry Shake

PREPARATION TIME: 4 minutes

This is an amazingly luxurious shake. You will never recognize tofu in this form. Honest, this is sooooo delicious.

1 (6-ounce) can pineapple juice
1 ripe banana
1/2 cup silken tofu (4 ounces)
1/2 to 1 cup fresh or frozen strawberries
1/2 teaspoon vanilla
1 to 2 tablespoons sugar or maple syrup (optional)

Combine all ingredients except the sugar in a blender and puree until smooth. Taste. Add sugar or maple syrup if you desire.

Makes two servings

Yogurt Fruit Shake

PREPARATION TIME: 4 minutes

Got a blender? Here's a fast way to start the day.

3/4 cup plain nonfat yogurt
1 cup chopped fruit (pear, pineapple, berries, banana—
    the riper the better)
1/2 teaspoon vanilla
1 teaspoon honey, sugar, or maple syrup (optional)

Place ingredients in blender, and process until smooth.

Makes two servings

Pink Tomato Swirl

If you like gazpacho, you will love this creamy tomato drink.

$^1/_4$ cup plain yogurt
1 cup tomato juice
1 clove garlic, chopped
$^1/_4$ cup peeled, chopped cucumber
1 teaspoon seeded, chopped jalapeño chile
Tabasco (optional)

Combine the ingredients in a blender. Add a dash of Tabasco, if you desire.

Makes one serving

CHAPTER 14

Beer and Vegetarianism

Jeff Byles

Beer and college are closely, and often notoriously, paired in popular imagination.

Movies like *Animal House* and *Revenge of the Nerds* stereotype college beer drinkers as brew-guzzling, hard-partying maniacs. Strange collegiate traditions routinely involve emptying beer kegs. Scenes of brew-induced mayhem around campus are, unfortunately, all too common in the real world. Beer's reputation has accordingly suffered.

The recent renaissance in microbrewing shows that beer has a tradition all its own. Microbrewers have revived centuries-old brewing traditions, making their beer in small batches with care and pride. A few years ago there were just a few brands of beer; today there are literally hundreds.

"Craft-brewed" beer has restored the dignity, quality, and pleasure to a pint of frothy ale or lager. Starting with fresh malted barley, seasoning the brew with extravagantly floral hop flowers, and fermenting with authentic yeast strains, craft brewers prize their ingredients much as vegetarians might prize a perfectly ripe avocado.

Actually, beer and vegetarianism have a lot in common. When people encounter a vegetarian, they often ask incredulously, "But what do you eat?" It is as if the world of food without meat amounted to a few heads of wilted iceberg lettuce and a pitiable stalk of broccoli. As any vegetarian knows, a little patient experimentation yields delicious meat-free rewards. What plump roast could ever compare with a tangy, succulent dish of pad thai?

Similarly, many beer consumers find it hard to believe that there is a vast world of beer beyond the pale-hued, mass-produced beers like Budweiser, Coors, and Miller. While those beers are not necessarily bad, drinking a mass-market "light" beer is like eating packaged macaroni and cheese when you could just as easily be dining on an elegant dish of Pasta al Pesto.

Like vegetarian cuisine, the world of beer is bursting with flavor. Try whatever comes your way: a nicely balanced pale ale, crisp with hops; a dark and roasty stout, thick and velvety as a milkshake; or real Belgian ale, tart and sweet with a delicately soft maltiness.

Besides increasing your gustatory pleasure, exploring beer is a way of educating your palate—much like exploring the unfamiliar territory of painting is how one learns to appreciate art.

This is not to say that there aren't other, more practical uses for beer. There are a variety of resourceful ways the steepings of malts can improve human morale. Should you find yourself in the possession of a quantity of beer that is, for whatever reasons, undrinkable, do not despair.

According to naturopaths, beer makes a wonderful shampoo, hydrating the hair while adding protein from the grains. Many home brewers claim that beer serves tolerably well as an insect barrier, and they dispense it liberally around their garden. Some other, perhaps unorthodox, uses for our wonderfully versatile malt beverage are as follows:

- Keep it in a sacred vessel and use sparingly for rituals honoring Ninkasi, the goddess of brewing.
- Freeze it for use in "beer-sicles."
- Age it carefully for a few months in a sealed container to make malt vinegar.
- Boil off most of the liquid to obtain "essence of beer," creating a captivating new perfume and cologne.

When William Blake wrote that the road of excess leads to the palace of wisdom, I do not believe he was talking about beer. Should you happen to venture that way, however, there are a few things to know about how beer affects the body. While cures for hangovers are prolific, beware: they are mostly the stuff of myth.

The liver needs only two essential aids to process the alcohol in beer—plenty of time and water. Because alcohol is a strong diuretic, it causes the body to lose water. Therefore, drinking water before and while you drink alcohol will help avoid that morning headache. Food also slows the rate of alcohol absorption from the stomach, so having a plate of falafel with a pitcher of ale will help ease the effects of alcohol on the body.

Researchers have found that women need to be particularly careful when drinking, because women's alcohol tolerance varies at different times of the month. A premenstrual woman will be most vulnerable to alcohol, because during this time enzyme action in the liver slows, causing more alcohol to accumulate in the bloodstream.

Beer can indeed be a profound part of anyone's education. Rich in tradition, robust in culture, and mellifluous in taste, beer offers a wealth of meaning unlike any other beverage. That luminous pint of ale can incite the intellect and soothe the soul.

Now that's beer for thought.

Resources

Good Books

Klein, Naomi. *No Logo: Taking Aim at the Brand Bullies*. New York: Picador, 2002.

Robbins, John. *Diet for a New America*. Walpole, NM: Stillpoint, 1987.

Schlosser, Eric. *Fast Food Nation: The Dark Side of the All-American Meal*. New York: HarperCollins, 2002

Good Group

EarthSave International
1509 Seabright Avenue, Suite B1
Santa Cruz, CA 95062
Phone: (800) 362-3648
Web site: www.earthsave.org

EarthSave International promotes the benefits of plant-based food choices for our health, our environment, and a more compassionate world. Contact them for information on volunteer opportunities, educational materials, or questions about Earth-Save's new projects.

Good Web Sites

Farm Animal Reform Movement
www.farmusa.org

Farm Sanctuary
www.farmsanctuary.org

Greenpeace
www.greenpeace.org

National Coalition Against the Misuse of Pesticides
www.beyondpesticides.org

North American Vegetarian Society
www.navs-online.org

Oxfam America
www.oxfamamerica.org

People for the Ethical Treatment of Animals (PETA)
www.peta.com

Tufts University Nutrition Navigator
www.navigator.tufts.edu

Vegan Action
www.vegan.org

Veggies Unite
www.vegweb.com

VegSource
www.vegsource.com

Youth for Environmental Sanity (YES)
www.yesworld.org

Index

50 SECRETS

OF THE WORLD'S

LONGEST LIVING PEOPLE

50 SECRETS

OF THE WORLD'S

LONGEST LIVING PEOPLE

SALLY BEARE

MARLOWE & COMPANY
NEW YORK

Published by
Marlowe & Company
An Imprint of Avalon Publishing Group Incorporated
245 West 17th Street • 11th floor
New York, NY 10011-5300

AVALON
publishing group incorporated

Originally published in the United Kingdom as *The Live Longer Diet* by Piatkus Books in 2003. This is a revised, expanded edition and published by arrangement.

Library of Congress Cataloging-in-Publication Data

Beare, Sally 1967–
    50 secrets of the world's longest living people / Sally Beare.—Rev., expanded ed.
        p. cm.
    "Originally published in the United Kingdom as The Live Longer Diet by Piatkus Books in 2003. This is a revised, expanded edition and published by arrangement."
    Includes bibliographical references and index.
    ISBN: 1-56924-348-4
    1. Longevity. 2. Aging—Prevention. 3. Diet Therapy. I. Title:
Fifty secrets of the world's longest living people. II. Beare, Sally, 1967– Live longer diet.
III. Title.
    RA776.75.B43 2006
    613.2—dc22

                                                            2005027068
ISBN-13: 978-1-56924-348-0

9 8 7 6 5 4 3
Designed by Maria E. Torres
Printed in the United States of America

For my parents,
for everything they have done for me and for eating their
greens

CONTENTS

PART THREE: **PUTTING IT ALL TOGETHER**

PREFACE

WHY I WROTE THIS BOOK

Five years ago I was sitting chatting in the back of my friend's car as she negotiated a tight parking spot. Glancing in the rear view mirror, she commented on the whiteness of my tongue. It was true—my tongue had been growing an increasingly thick white coating over the last two years or so, and, as three different G.P.s had been unable to offer any advice other than to take some aspirin and come back when I had a more concrete illness, I had started talking out of the corner of my mouth in public.

After the parallel parking incident, I knew it was time to do something. My friend suggested that I visit a nutritionist, and I duly made an appointment. The woman who opened the door to me radiated vibrant good health, energy, and mental well-being. She bounded up the stairs before me, and as she massaged my foot I explained to her that not only did I have this unpleasant fur on my tongue, but I also sneezed about twenty times a day; I had a pain somewhere down near my appendix; I frequently had a bloated, uncomfortable stomach; as soon as I was over one cold, I seemed to catch another; and I felt so lethargic it was often hard to get out of bed in the morning.

The nutritionist told me that all of my symptoms were related to a malfunctioning digestive system, and said that I needed to radically overhaul my diet, which was based mainly on pasta, sandwiches, wine, and inadequately sized salads. She didn't tell me what I couldn't eat—she just gave me a list of what I *could* eat, which included all kinds of delicious fruits and vegetables that I didn't normally bother with (avocados, asparagus, fennel, and papaya, for example), legumes, and wheat-free whole grains. I set off for the supermarket with my mouth watering.

Within a couple of months, I was bouncing out of bed in the mornings, the pains had gone, the sneezing had stopped, I hadn't had a cold, my mood was better, and my tongue was getting steadily pinker. I had also shed several pounds, despite enjoying my food more than ever and eating plenty of it. Friends were full of superlatives about the dramatically different "before" and "after" me, and started asking me for dietary advice. I began reading about nutrition; the books often contained testimonies of amazing recoveries from "incurable" illnesses through simple changes in diet.

At about this time, I had started work developing a television series about the process of aging and some of the most cutting edge work being done in this field. As I ate my salads of brown rice and lightly steamed sugar snap peas, seasoned with garlic and soy sauce, I read about the huge U.S. biotech companies eternally searching for expensive, complicated cures for aging and the diseases that accompany it. Meanwhile, it appeared, certain isolated pockets of people were already enjoying superb health and long life, in a way that the biotech companies can only dream of, simply through their dietary and lifestyle habits.

Soon afterward I gave up my television career and began training as a clinical nutritionist at the British College of Nutrition and Health. I found that the more I knew about nutrition from reading books and experimenting with my own health, the more friends sought my advice on the subject. Nutrition was clearly a valuable area of expertise that could be of great use to many people. Inspired by my findings on aging, I also started to write this book. I hope you will derive as much pleasure and satisfaction from the "secrets" described in it as I have. I firmly believe that the "secrets" described here should be shared with everyone who cares about health and quality of life.

INTRODUCTION

If I had known I was going to live so long, I'd have taken better
care of myself.

—Eubie Blake, celebrated ragtime pianist, 1883–1983

Scientists now agree that we could be living to around 120 years if
we achieved our maximum potential life spans. Living to 120
does not just mean that we could be around to meet our great-grand-
children and even our great-great-grandchildren. It also means that
we can feel and look thirty years old at forty, eighty years old at a hundred, and, most importantly, have more energy whatever age we are.
In short, we can stay younger for longer. The best news is that it is
never too late to start. Even those who are tired, ill, and getting on in
years can become biologically younger, reverse the damage, keep disease away, and add years, if not decades, to their lives.

So what are the "secrets" of living long and staying young?
Ancient wisdom, thousands of authoritative studies, and recent
groundbreaking research all indicate that the answer lies, above all,
in what we eat. We already know that eating the right food can help
us avoid some of the major killers, such as cancer and heart disease.
The U.S. surgeon general recently said that of the 2.2 million deaths
in America each year, 1.8 million are diet-related. Now, gerontologists have also discovered that we can actually slow down or even
reverse the aging process, appear and feel younger, and prevent most
aging-related diseases with the right diet, together with certain
other lifestyle habits such as regular exercise and avoiding stress.

It is amazing how reluctant some people are to accept these simple truths, especially when it is so much easier to eat well and take a little exercise than to find another way to slow aging. People have been trying, unsuccessfully, to find an instant, magical "cure" for aging since man has existed. Ancient myths derived from the Bible tell of a heavily armed archangel guarding a tree in the Garden of Eden—the Tree of Life—that holds just such a cure. More recently, in the 1930s, Russian physician Professor Serge Voronoff promised wealthy male patients that he could reverse aging by grafting thin slices of monkey testicle onto the insides of the scrotum, using silk stitches. There are no records of any of his patients living forever as a result, but some of them got VD, while Voronoff himself earned enough to live in immense luxury on the entire first floor of one of Paris's most expensive hotels.

Today, the pharmaceuticals companies are hopefully pumping millions of dollars into the search for an aging cure. None of their methods, which include injecting human brains with stem cells, developing "miracle" drugs, and trying to isolate the "gene for aging," has yet been proven to work. Isolating an aging gene seems a particularly simplistic approach, since studies show that genetic inheritance is influenced by environmental factors.[1] To date, no chemical or drug has been created that can slow aging any more effectively than the natural substances that are found in our food.

SAY NO TO THE TITHONUS OPTION

Living long does not have to mean existing in a world full of decrepit, senile people suffering from all sorts of age-related conditions. We do not want to be like the immortal Struldbruggs in Swift's novel *Gulliver's Travels*, who kept on growing older, more ill, and more miserable, and acquired "an additional Ghastliness in Proportion to their Number of Years." Nor would we want to go the same way as the unfortunate Greek mortal Tithonus, who was granted eternal life on the request of his goddess lover Eos. Unfortunately, Eos forgot to ask for eternal youth, and she eventually had to shut her increasingly frail, senile boyfriend in a room to gibber and babble away out of sight for eternity, until, out of pity, she turned him into a grasshopper.

Unlike Tithonus and the Struldbruggs, if we look after ourselves properly, we can enjoy not just an improved life span, but an improved "health span." This is important, because in developed countries such as the U.S.A., more and more people are living increasingly long lives, a phenomenon known as the "greying" of the world's population. There is a real danger that we are running out of younger generations to provide for the older people, with 77 million baby boomers looking forward to their impending retirement. If we are going to be active members of the community in our last years or decades, then it is important that we hold on to our health—and our marbles.

Living long in itself does not have to be the ultimate goal. Living to 120 may not sound so appealing if the last 20 or 30 years are spent in a nursing home, staggering about on a stick with a broken hip, forgetting what we came into the room for, and swallowing handfuls of drugs with every meal. The value of knowing that we are born with a "bank balance" of 120 years within us is that if we use it up slowly, we can be more active, healthier, and happier, whether we are children, thirty-somethings, or eighty, regardless of when we actually die.

THE WORLD'S LONGEVITY HOT SPOTS

In certain parts of the world, there are areas where the exceptionally healthy local populations prove that most of us grow old and ill unnecessarily fast, due to our diet and lifestyle habits. These "longevity hot spots" have extraordinarily good health records and unusually high numbers of sprightly, independent nonagenarians, centenarians, and supercentenarians. In Okinawa, for example, there are thirty-four centenarians per 100,000 people, as compared with ten per 100,000 in the U.S. Those in middle or old age behave and look like much younger people, and illness—*any* kind of illness, from headaches to cancer—is rare.

We know that it is environmental factors rather than good genes that are primarily responsible for the health and youthfulness of these people, because studies show that when they move to other countries and adopt the local diets, they also develop the local diseases and other signs of aging. The existence of such people also disproves the argument that the only reason for our current high rates of degenerative disease, such as heart disease and cancer, is that we are living longer.

The five longevity hot spots discussed in this book are:

- **Okinawa**, an island in Japan
- **Symi**, an island in Greece
- **Campodimele**, a village in southern Italy
- **Hunza**, a valley in northwest Pakistan
- **Bama**, a county in southern China

THE SECRETS OF LONGEVITY

This book reveals the "secrets" behind these populations' exceptional good health and longevity. In fact, there are really no secrets at all—common sense and some diet and lifestyle habits are all there is to it. Delicious, fresh, locally grown and caught foods, an active lifestyle, plenty of fresh air, and a positive approach to life's challenges are the factors that give these people their edge. With some extra effort, most of these elements can be incorporated into the lives of the rest of us. True, we cannot buy fresh air or a happy marriage in a supermarket, but we can all find ways to reduce stress, take more exercise, and look after ourselves if we really want to. As for the food, the ingredients for all of the recipes in this book, and more like them, are available from supermarkets and health-food shops.

ENJOY YOUR FOOD

The five longevity hot spots provide recipes that are not only nutritious but delicious. The rule is to obtain high-quality, fresh ingredients and then to interfere with them as little as possible, so that the flavors are allowed to come through. People complain that "health food" is bland, but health food does not have to mean a piece of apple and a rice cake. It can and should mean dishes of fresh vegetables and herbs, legumes, or fish, infused with the flavor of garlic and onions, ginger and soy sauce, a little red wine, or any other of the hundreds of ingredients involved in healthy cooking. The principles are simple: plenty of fresh fruit and vegetables, whole grains rather than refined foods, the right kinds of oils, not too much meat, and short cooking times.

We don't want to be eating a diet devised in a laboratory and tested on rats. We want usable, delicious recipes perfected over generations—not just because they give us health, but because they taste good. The recipes in this book and others like them will help you to forget about calories and willpower, and to serve the kind of food that you and your friends will love and appreciate. They will also help you to achieve optimum levels of energy and health each day, and to feel younger for longer. We all know Hippocrates's famous words: "Let food be your medicine and medicine be your food." The good news is that food doesn't have to taste like medicine for this to be true.

WHAT THIS BOOK CAN DO FOR YOU

In order to stave off degenerative diseases and enjoy optimum health, we have to get the full range of nutrients. These include at least seventeen to twenty minerals, thirteen vitamins, eleven essential amino acids, and two essential fatty acids ("essential" meaning that they cannot be made in the body, but they are also essential for health). At the absolute minimum, we should eat five portions (preferably ten) of fresh fruit and vegetables each day. We are made of food, and what we eat affects our minds, bodies, and spirits. Obesity is skyrocketing in developed countries, yet, increasingly, many people are starving to death—that is, they are starved of nutrients. Calorie-rich foods, such as pastries and sugary snacks, add the pounds but take out the things our bodies need to be healthy, such as vitamins and minerals.

In tandem with this, degenerative disease is on the rise. In 1988, the American surgeon general's *Report on Health and Nutrition* concluded that almost 75 percent of deaths in the United States involve nutritional deficiency. Despite all the technology, recent statistics from the World Health Organization rated the U.S. fifteenth out of twenty-five developed countries using basic health measures, and 2001 data show life expectancy in the U.S. to be a relatively low 77.2 years. On the whole, remedies and drugs can alleviate the symptoms of specific illnesses but cannot actually cure them. Many illnesses, and accelerated aging, are caused by one basic factor: a diet deficient in nutrients and excessive in toxins.

Too many of us are resigned to feeling lethargic, getting regular headaches, suffering from PMS (premenstrual syndrome), having mood swings and sugar cravings, and developing degenerative diseases as we age. Ulcers, indigestion, and allergies are all, quite wrongly, accepted as inevitable burdens of living and growing old. Anyone who has suffered from any of these and is skeptical about the immense power of diet to affect well-being has not tried eating truly healthily. The benefits commonly experienced by those on a high-nutrient diet include better skin, weight loss, increased energy, the disappearance of minor ailments, an ability to jump out of bed in the morning, improved libido, and a reduced risk of long-term illness. If, on top of that, we can live an extra ten or twenty years with good quality of life surely it is worth a try.

THE TOP THREE KILLER ILLNESSES ARE ALL PREVENTABLE

You have no need to fear the top killer illnesses in the U.S. With the exception of aging, which can be slowed down considerably, they are all largely preventable. The top three are:

1. Heart Disease

Heart disease is the number one cause of death in the U.S., with 696,947 people dying from it in 2002 [2] Stroke, which is related to heart disease, killed another 162,672. Heart disease is one of the most preventable diseases there is. Leading nutritionist Dr. Michael Colgan says, "Do not fear cardiovascular disease. It's the easiest of all man-made diseases to prevent and even to reverse, if only you follow the right nutrition, plus a little easy exercise to blow away the cobwebs."[3] By reducing your risk of heart attack, you also minimize the risk of getting diabetes, which is closely linked to it.

"Couch potato syndrome," obesity, smoking, and poor diet have been blamed in countless studies for the high rates of heart disease in the West. The world's longest-living people frequently reach their nineties and hundreds, yet medical researchers have found that they have extremely low rates of heart disease and exceptionally youthful arteries.

2. Cancer

Cancer affects one in three people in the U.S., with 57,947 people dying from the disease in 2002. Yet it is also highly avoidable. Three of the most common cancers in the West—breast, prostate, and bowel—are all strongly linked with diet and lifestyle habits. Even the ultraconservative American Cancer Society has said that 90 percent of colorectal cancer cases are preventable.[4] Cancer expert Dr. Patrick Quillin says in his book *Beating Cancer with Nutrition:* "The body is equipped to deal with cancer . . . but this process relies heavily on nutrition. . . . Proper nutrition could prevent 50–90 percent of all cancer."

3. Death by Doctoring

Around 250,000 people are killed in North America each year as a result of medical mistakes, a condition known as "iatrogenic" death. This figure—equivalent to several hundred jumbo jet crashes—is a conservative estimate, with real numbers thought to be nearer to 284,000. Research published in the *Journal of the American Medical Association* in 2000 showed that the causes of death break down as follows: 106,000 from the negative effects of prescribed drugs; 12,000 deaths from unnecessary surgery; 7,000 from drugs administered by error; 20,000 from other errors; and 80,000 from infections caught in the hospital.[5]

When functioning properly, doctors and modern medicine are a vital part of our healthcare system, as anyone who has been in a car accident or had any other life-threatening condition requiring immediate surgery will testify. However, drugs and surgery are often not the best solutions for chronic degenerative illnesses such as cancer, heart disease, or digestive diseases. Preventive medicine is best—according to the *New England Journal of Medicine*, "90 percent of patients who visit doctors have conditions that will either improve on their own or are out of reach of modern medicine's ability to solve."

SLOWING DOWN AGING

Until scientists find a way to make us immortal, and wake up all those people who have had their bodies frozen in anticipation of such a happy event, aging and death will be inescapable facts of life. In the 1960s, Dr. Leonard Hayflick discovered that the 50 trillion cells in the human body are only capable of dividing a certain number of times before they start to look old, reach their limit, and die out. This phenomenon, known as the "Hayflick Limit," shows that we are born with a kind of aging clock within us, which gives us a certain maximum allotted amount of time on earth—which is now known to be about 120 years.

The most common causes of death in the world today unfortunately do not include getting to the end of our Hayflick Limit; nearly all of us die while our cells are still dividing, as a result of disease or accelerated aging. In the U.S., the average person dies over 40 years earlier than the potential 120 years. Forty years! Following the advice of the world's healthiest and longest-lived people, not only can we slow the aging process, but we can also undo the damage already done, and transform aging bodies into more active, energetic, happy people.

PART ONE

The World's Five Longevity Hot Spots

This section describes five remarkable pockets of populations, where the people are bursting with health, live for record-breaking numbers of years, and are active and vigorous even past a hundred years of age. Each chapter provides a brief description of the population's lifestyle and habits that promote good health and long life. Nutrition and lifestyle are factors common to all five longevity hot spots, but as you'll see below, there are habits unique to each population that you will be able to incorporate into your own life with ease and pleasure.

The chapters in Part Two of this book describe the fifty secrets of longevity in more detail.

1

Okinawa—Island of World-Record Longevity

The Okinawan archipelago, a group of 161 coral islands in the East China Sea, is home to the people who, out of everyone in the world, can truly claim to possess the elixir of lasting youth. In this verdant, bountiful "Galapagos of the East," the people have beautiful skin, lustrous dark hair, and slim, agile bodies long past middle age. The main diseases of the West are at the lowest levels in the world here, suicide is almost unheard of, and the word "retirement" does not exist in the local dialect.

Okinawa's centenarians and supercentenarians do not spend their last years sitting in nursing homes but enjoy full, active lives. One local celebrity is a ninety-seven-year-old karate teacher, famous for recently defeating a boxing ex-champion in his thirties. When Okinawans do die, they die quickly, often without any known illness. With thirty-four centenarians per 100,000 people (compared with ten per 100,000 in the U.S.), and an unusually high number of people aged over 105, Okinawans are officially the longest-lived people on the planet.

Levels of heart disease, stroke, and cancer, so common in the West, are at their lowest in the world in Okinawa, and are only 60 percent of those of the rest of Japan, which itself has unusually low levels. Okinawans have 80 percent fewer heart attacks than Americans, and examinations by doctors have revealed unusually young arteries and low cholesterol levels. Breast cancer is so rare that mammograms are not needed, and most older men have not even heard of prostate cancer. Over all, there is 40 percent less cancer in Okinawa than in the West; when Okinawans do get cancer, they are over twice as likely to survive it.

Since 1975, a group of distinguished doctors has been studying the extraordinary health and longevity of the Okinawans, including four hundred centenarians and supercentenarians; their results have been published in their recent book, *The Okinawa Way*.[1] The Centenarian Study researchers found that the Okinawans are generally in "outstanding health."

The first person authors Dr. Bradley Willcox and Dr. Craig Willcox examined was a hundred-year-old man, whom they first took to be about seventy, and of whom they found that "after a hundred years of use, there was basically nothing wrong with his body." The doctors found that even in old age, Okinawans have youthful immune systems, very low rates of osteoporosis, fit, attractive bodies, high levels of sex hormones, and excellent mental health.

The study authors conclude that the "secrets" of these people are almost all replicable in the West, and primarily have to do with diet, as well as some other lifestyle factors such as regular exercise and a positive mental outlook. Unfortunately, the younger generations of Okinawans are abandoning the traditional diet and turning to the fast-food joints that surround the American air bases on the island. Their rates of "Western" diseases such as heart attack and cancer are going up accordingly, illustrating that genes only have a minor role to play in Okinawan longevity.

Below is a summary of some of the main factors influencing the good health and longevity of the Okinawans. These are all covered in more detail in Part Two of this book.

A HEALTHY DIET

The traditional Okinawan diet follows all the main rules of healthy, balanced eating, and as a result promotes good health and long life. The Okinawans have a saying, *Ishoku-dogen*, meaning, literally, "food and medicine from the same source." Their food is rich in anticancer, anti-aging antioxidants—the miracle molecules that neutralize age-promoting free radicals. The traditional diet is based mainly on sweet potatoes, leafy greens, and whole grains, supplemented with fish, rice, pork, and soy products. Okinawan food is unique to Japan in that it is influenced by both Chinese and Japanese cooking; with its pork and vegetable dishes from China as well as fish and seaweed dishes from Japan, the diet contains a wide range of nutrients. Only minimal amounts of age-promoting fat, meat, sugar, refined carbohydrates, and stimulants are consumed.

A Low-Calorie Diet

As is the case with all long-lived populations, the Okinawans also have a low-calorie diet. They eat plenty in terms of volume—in fact, the Centenarian Study researchers found that they actually eat more food by weight than North Americans—but they only eat around 1,500 calories daily. This is about 40 percent fewer calories than the average North American, although it has to be taken into account that Japanese people tend to be of slighter build than Americans.

In tests on laboratory animals, longevity scientists have shown that eating exactly what you need and no more—or eating a low-calorie, nutrient-dense diet, as the Okinawans do—is a possible method of extending the maximum human life span to beyond the known 120 years. See Secret 1, (page 49), for more on this, and on low-calorie nutrient-dense eating.

Plenty of Fresh Fruit and Vegetables

Over a third of the average Okinawan meal consists of fresh organic vegetables, packed with free-radical-quenching antioxidants and fiber. Okinawans grow their own organic vegetables, all year round, in nutrient-rich soil, and in Kijoka village, where islanders live the longest of all, the soil has been left particularly rich in minerals by the sea, which covered it 150 years ago. Okinawans also eat one or two pieces of fresh fruit daily. Part Two looks at the benefits of fresh fruit and vegetables in more detail.

Herbs are also a key ingredient to living longer. Around 460 varieties of herbs are grown in Okinawa, which are used for medicinal purposes as well as for flavoring foods. Secret 27 (page 146), will tell you more about the importance of herbs.

Fish

Fishermen as well as farmers, Okinawans regularly eat fish—around two or three times a week—caught fresh from clean seas. Oily fish such as tuna, mackerel, and salmon contain the omega-3 essential fatty acids that build our brains and nervous systems; are vital for the health of every cell in our bodies; and are thought to protect against cancer, heart disease, inflammatory disease, dry skin and hair, PMS, mental illness, and practically any other ailment you care to mention. Fish is also a complete protein, while being far more digestible than meat and much lower in saturated fats. See Secret 11 (page 91) for more on fish.

Soy

Soy is an Okinawan favorite. Studies show that it has many health benefits and may protect against heart disease and osteoporosis. The soy products eaten in Okinawa are made in the traditional way and are very different from the processed and genetically modified (GM) types found in Western foods. See Secret 24, page 138, for more on the health benefits of traditionally made soy.

Whole Grains

Around six to seven servings of grains, mainly whole grains, are eaten per day by Okinawans, making up about a third of the diet. Around three of these servings consist of white rice, which has started to replace the traditional sweet potato. This is just about the only area of the diet that could do with improvement, as brown rice is better for digestion and contains more nutrients. See Secret 3, page 59, for more information on whole grains.

Lean Meat Used Sparingly

Okinawans love pork, and they have it with many of their dishes. However, although meat is becoming increasingly common in the Okinawan diet (especially since Americans introduced Spam after their 1945 invasion), traditionally, meat such as pork and goat were eaten only a few times a year, or used in small amounts to flavor vegetable-based dishes. Meat has the fat trimmed off and is then usually boiled to make stock, which makes it comparatively lean and digestible. The Okinawans only derive 24 percent of their calories from fat, which is well under the Western dietary recommendation of 30 percent of calories; in addition, only a small amount of these come from unhealthy saturated fats. All of the people in this book eat limited amounts of meat; Secrets 6 and 7 (page 69 and 76, respectively), explain why this is an important aspect of longevity eating.

Low Salt Consumption

Okinawans traditionally had to extract their own salt from seawater, so it is not used in large quantities in Okinawan dishes. This factor is thought to be one reason for their low blood pressure and low incidence of stomach cancer (see Secret 28, page 148).

Longevity Drinks

Okinawans drink about three cups a day of green tea scented with jasmine flowers. They have also traditionally drunk plenty of local, calcium-rich water, which helps prevent osteoporosis and keeps the body slightly alkaline—how it needs to be for optimum health. Secrets 33 (page 168) and 34 (page 171) look at the health benefits of green tea and water, respectively.

Okinawans also consume *awamori*, a fermented rice wine much like sake that is used for cooking and seasoning as well as for drinking. See Secret 32 (page 165) on the benefits of moderate amounts of alcohol.

REGULAR PHYSICAL EXERCISE

Like all of the five long-lived populations in this book, traditional Okinawans get plenty of exercise every day, since most of them are fishermen and farmers, and they continue to work hard outdoors even in their eighties. Okinawans make a point of taking regular aerobic exercise, including martial arts and traditional dance, as well as gardening and walking. They also enjoy weekly matches of gateball, a game similar to bowling, which local doctors say keeps them out in the sunshine and allows them to vent stress. Okinawans are exceptionally fit and supple; even hundred-year-olds will sit cross-legged on the floor for long periods of time. See Secret 38 (page 192) on why exercise is as crucial a factor as diet in determining your health.

BUSY LIVES

The old and super-old Okinawans do not retire but keep busy, even in their nineties or hundreds, gardening, socializing, working in the fields, or maintaining cottage industries making handicrafts. The old and very old are revered and made to feel like an active and useful part of the community. When people attain lofty ages they are dressed in red and paraded through the streets, in a celebration of their achievement. This sense of purpose in later life is thought by gerontologists to maintain vigor and promote longevity. Staying active after retirement has been found to have a major impact on the rate of aging, and intricate work with the hands, such as weaving fabric, may stimulate the brain to keep it fresh.

LOW STRESS

High stress levels are thought to speed up the aging process and cause disease, so it is not surprising that the Okinawans have exceptionally low stress levels. People live at a relaxed pace, known locally as "Okinawa Time," and generally turn up late for everything. You do not see urgent or worried faces in Okinawa; instead, people sing as they walk through the streets or when they are working in the fields. It is not as if there have been no external stressors in Okinawa—the islanders suffered much poverty and loss during World War II, and of course they still experience death and some divorce. However, the Centenarian Study researchers

KIYOKO FUKUCHI, 102 YEARS OLD

At 102, Kiyoko Fukuchi is a typical Okinawan supercentenarian. Lively and enthusiastic for her age, she considers herself to be in good shape and has no complaints. With her smooth skin and supple body, she looks "very young," according to those who know her, and even her eyesight is good enough for her to see without glasses. Although she lives with her daughter, she is independent and capable, doing her own chores without any help, and going for walks whenever the weather permits. She also enjoys visiting friends and family, and attends local old people's get-togethers twice a month.

Kiyoko believes that the reason she is still in such good condition at this age is that she has always eaten well and stayed active. Her diet consists mainly of ample amounts of homegrown vegetables and locally caught fish. She also eats aloe with every meal; aloe is used in the East as an effective remedy for soothing and healing the digestive tract. She has never eaten much meat, and has never had access to junk foods or sweets.

found that Okinawans have a great deal of self-confidence and "unyieldingness," which helps them to cope with life's crises well. Okinawans live in close-knit communities, so have plenty of mutual support. They also practice meditation and have strong spiritual beliefs, both of which reduce stress levels—see Secrets 42 (page 205) and 43 (page 208) on how you can use these to slow your rate of aging.

OKINAWAN DOS AND DON'TS

Okinawans Do:

- Eat a high-nutrient, low-calorie diet
- Plan a well-balanced, varied diet
- Consume plenty of fresh vegetables and fruit, grown organically and locally
- Ingest plenty of essential fatty acids, mainly from fish
- Eat soy regularly, which balances hormones and provides vegetable protein
- Choose whole grains rather than refined carbohydrates
- Moderate their alcohol intake
- Drink green tea and calcium-rich water
- Exercise regularly
- Encourage mental activity throughout their lives
- Maintain a healthy psycho-spiritual outlook and low stress
- Live in happy, close-knit communities

Okinawans Don't:

- Overeat
- Overcook their food
- Eat refined sugar
- Consume much salt
- Eat refined or processed foods
- Eat much meat or dairy
- Smoke
- Drink black tea or coffee
- Drink alcohol in excess

2

Symi—Home of Truly Ancient Greeks

The fish-laden Mediterranean diet, so well known for its wonderful health benefits, is perhaps best exemplified on the Greek island of Symi. Greece is famous for the good health of its population, especially in Crete, but it is in Symi that you will find the most truly ancient Greeks, although of course young and old all mix together happily on the island. Even when they are old, Symiots are young—men in their seventies and eighties, well toned and vigorous, flirt openly with any woman who catches their eye, which is hardly surprising, as the women on Symi are also well toned and vigorous, with beautiful skin and hair.

Right up to their nineties, men and women can be found chasing after their herds, collecting herbs, making yogurt, and gardening. Everyone in Symi knows someone who has passed the age of one hundred, and a traditional birthday greeting is "may you live to be one hundred and more!" The population of Symi is small, at a mere 2,700, and the number of centenarians and ninety-year-olds varies from year to year. However, epidemiologists have found that Symi has the best health records and highest life expectancy for the region.[1]

The rocky outcrops of the island are softened by clear blue water full of fish, and the welcoming sea breeze is scented with pine, sage, and eucalyptus. In the main village, neoclassical houses painted in blues and creams rise steeply above one another, each looking out over the harbor and the spectacular Turkish coastline a few miles away across the Aegean Sea.

Each morning, a flotilla of brightly painted fishing boats sets off from the harbor, returning in the evening to deliver delicacies such as squid, lobster, giant sardines, and prawns to the restaurants along the harbor and the houses up above. Ropes of garlic and bunches of herbs picked from the hillside hang everywhere along the seafront. The bottles of extra-virgin olive oil are flavored with herbs, and there are also bars of olive oil soap. Everything is kept swept, scrubbed, and free of litter, and thanks to the islanders' dedication to avoiding pollution, even the water in the harbor is pristine.

THE CLASSIC MEDITERRANEAN DIET

The most important ingredient in the long and healthy lives of the Symiots is their diet. Symi has its own unique style of cooking, although it has much in common with the classic heart-friendly Cretan menu. The Symiot fare is delicious, fulfilling, and wonderfully undietlike.

Not for the Symiots the sad and lonely lettuce of the abstainer's plate—they enjoy olive oil, fish, succulent tomato sauces, goat's cheese, Greek yogurt, and a little meat with their vegetables and salads, all washed down with moderate quantities of wine. The basics, however, still conform to the ideal diet for longevity as outlined in this book, with raw or lightly cooked fruit and vegetables forming the bulk of meals, plenty of the right kinds of fats, few saturated fats, and an absence of refined or processed foods.

Olive Oil

Extra-virgin olive oil is consumed with everything and is thought to be an important factor in the low rates of cardiovascular disease in Symi, and in the Symiots' efficient digestion. Olive oil is safe for cooking, as it is more stable than polyunsaturated oils, and is even better used raw in salad dressings. See Secret 13 (page 104) for more information.

Mediterranean Fruits and Vegetables

Plenty of fruits and vegetables, both grown organically on the island and brought from nearby islands, are an essential part of the Symi diet. See Secret 2 (page 53)on the importance of eating plenty of fruits and vegetables. Tomatoes, used in salads and sauces, have their own special properties and are covered in Secret 19 (page 120).

Garlic, Capers, and Herbs

These are used to flavor dishes, and each has valuable health-giving properties. They are discussed in Secrets 15 (page 110), 23 (page 134), and 27 (page 146).

Fish

Most Symiots eat fish at least twice or three times a week, including oily fish such as fresh, locally caught sardines. See Secret 11 (page 91) on why this is such a significant factor in their good looks and vitality.

Homemade Whole-Wheat Bread

Fresh, homemade bread from whole-wheat flour is a dietary staple. It is dipped in olive oil and accompanies feta cheese, soups, stews, fish, and salads, or eaten on its own for breakfast. Bread made with whole wheat and sesame seeds is a Symi specialty (see recipes section, page 243). Whole-wheat bread contains fiber, B vitamins, iron, magnesium, zinc, and vitamin E. Wheat, especially the adulterated wheat used in sliced supermarket bread, is not always an ideal food source, however, and is discussed more in Secret 3 (page 59).

Vegetable Protein from Beans

Symiots make stews with beans, tomatoes, garlic, herbs, and a little lamb if available. Secret 9 (page 86) explores the benefits of eating beans, a high-fiber, nutrient-rich food that is a healthy alternative to meat.

Lean Meat Used Sparingly

Meat is eaten only in small quantities in Symi. Organ meats, rabbit, goat, and lamb are all used in stews or roasted with garlic and herbs such as rosemary. Meat has traditionally been available only from local herds, and there are no supermarkets in Symi with stacks of cheap, factory-farmed meat, as there are in our cities. Hence, meat is reserved for special occasions only, such as a Sunday dinner. The sheep and goats all wander around the hilltops of Symi freely, and are not treated with antibiotics or hormones, so are lean and organic. Wild animals contain fewer saturated fats and higher levels of essential fats than their factory-farmed equivalents. See Secrets 6 (page 69) and 7 (page 76) on the importance of eating only small amounts of lean, good-quality meat.

Organic Feta Cheese and Yogurt

Feta cheese from ewe's milk and live yogurt are enjoyed in moderate quantities in Symi. See Secrets 8 (page 79) and 22 (page 128).

Wine

Meals in Symi are usually taken with a little red or white wine, or local variations on ordinary wine such as *ouzo, raki,* and *retsina.* Retsina, flavored with pine resin, is enjoyed by locals, as it makes a good accompaniment to the strong flavors used in Greek peasant cooking, such as capers, herbs, and salty feta cheese. Wine drinking is partly credited by cardiologists for the low rates of heart attack in Mediterranean areas, and is discussed in more detail in Secret 32 (page 165).

REGULAR EXERCISE

Symiots are kept fit by the 387 wide stone steps leading up through the village, which people go up and down several times a day to do their errands (although someone has had the foresight to build a bar at the 375th step, where people can rest and chat). Traditionally, fishermen have had the additional benefits of using oars rather than outboard motors, while herders and farmers are obliged to run about the hillside after their herds and tend their crops. Taking regular exercise is an important part of the Symi formula for long life and good health. See Secret 38 (page 192).

LOW STRESS AND HAPPY FAMILIES

Symiots thrive on living, loving, and eating, but they do not gorge themselves on anything. They bask in the sense of well-being that comes from living in a beautiful environment with fresh air and clean soil. Most of them are happy, relaxed, and serene, and keep themselves busy and fulfilled, although many of the older ones have had to work very hard during their lives. This lifestyle is a common factor among the people described in this book.

Symiots live in a close-knit community, and families are large and loving, so that members benefit from knowing they have an unconditional support system. Additionally, unlike men in many other cultures, Mediterranean men such as Greeks and Italians are able to express their feelings, argue, cry, and be physical with each other, all of which lower stress and are thought to benefit heart health.

GEORGIOS KOKKINOS, NINETY-SIX YEARS OLD

Georgios Kokkinos, ninety-six, still walks down and back up the eighty village steps to do his shopping each month. He describes himself as being in "a good state of mind" and enjoys an active life, waking at sunrise to do housework and tend the fava beans, onions, and garlic in his garden. Georgios believes that the secret of his longevity is that he has worked hard and kept busy. He also believes in God, and feels that close family bonds are a necessary component of long life. "My favorite time is when my family is all together," he says.

Georgios loves meat, especially tripe, brain, and entrails, but only eats it once a week. He also eats fish two or three times a week, and he loves salted fish. He used to eat homemade pasta and homemade bread several times a week. He has yogurt every night and a little feta or goat's cheese every day. He has always eaten a lot of vegetables and salads, although he is not so fond of them anymore. He drinks about one and a half liters of water daily, and he used to drink tea with cloves, sage, cinnamon, and rosemary. He has a glass of ouzo every day, and used to have wine on special occasions.

SYMIOT DOS AND DON'TS

Symiots Do:

- Eat a diet high in nutrients and moderate in calories
- Consume plenty of fresh fruit and vegetables from local sources
- Ingest plenty of essential fatty acids from fish
- Use olive oil regularly
- Choose whole grains rather than refined carbohydrates
- Eat vegetable protein
- Moderate their alcohol intake
- Exercise regularly
- Maintain busy but mainly stress-free lives
- Live in a loving, close-knit community

ESMERALDA STAVRA, 107 YEARS OLD

Esmeralda Stavra was 107 when she died. Her son and daughter-in-law, Manoles and Maria, say: "Her house was at the top of the village steps, and even when she was 100 years old she went up and down them three or four times a day so that she could sell the feta cheese and yogurt she made." Esmeralda was never sick during her lifetime and never went for a checkup with the doctor. Maria says, "When she died, my mother thought she had just gone to sleep—that's how quietly she went."

Manoles and Maria believe that Esmeralda's health was due to hard work and not too much food. "I think the food has to do with this," says Maria. "There's no sugar, and they don't have diabetes like they do where they eat a lot of rubbish. She had fish about twice a week, but not much meat. She preferred not to eat meat at all. She ate mostly vegetables and salads, with bread, olives, cheese, and tomatoes. The vegetables were never sprayed. They don't use butter, only olive oil. She also drank a little bit. She was also a very spiritual person—they had less worries than we do now."

Symiots Don't:

- Overeat
- Overcook their food
- Eat refined sugar
- Eat refined or processed foods
- Eat too much meat or dairy
- Smoke
- Drink much tea or coffee
- Drink alcohol in excess

3

Campodimele—Village of Eternal Youth

It is not unusual to see a ninety-year-old whizzing about on a Vespa among the teenagers or rising at dawn to work in the fields in Campodimele, otherwise known as Europe's "village of eternal youth." Campodimele (literally, "meadow of honey"), a serene hilltop village halfway between Rome and Naples in southern Italy, seems to breed unusually high numbers of death-defying inhabitants.

It is rare for anyone to die before the age of eighty-five, and Campodimelani often reach their nineties and even sail past a hundred without ever having to visit a doctor. At the last count in 1995, there were forty-eight 90-year-olds, three 99-year-olds and a 104-year-old among the 840-strong population. Yet this is not an old people's resort, but a family-based community where people ranging from one to one hundred years old gather daily in the cobbled piazza to enjoy each other's company. For some unknown reason, men often live longer than women. The oldest man, currently, is 102 years old—an age that passes without particular comment in this haven of health and happiness.

The village, a labyrinth of cobbled streets and stone-walled houses surrounded by a medieval fortified wall, enjoys a panoramic view of the valley below and is blown with clean mountain air and fresh sea breezes. Growing below are endless olive groves, orchards of fruit and nut trees, and terraces sprouting vegetables and grains as well as grazing areas for cows, goats, and sheep. Outside the houses are trellises of grapevines and decorative pots of basil, oregano, rosemary, and bright orange chili peppers. Each household has its own plot of land, and work traditionally consists of tending the crops and helping each other bring in the harvests to make olive oil, Parma ham, and generous quantities of red and white wine.

For a decade, experts have been studying the villagers in an attempt to find the secrets of their longevity. Their findings indicate that it is due to fresh mountain air, plenty of outdoor exercise, low stress, and above all a diet containing large amounts of fresh vegetables. In short, there has not yet been a modernization, or *Americanizzazione*, as they call it, of lifestyle. In addition, a combination of good diet and healthy living through each generation is thought to have contributed to robust genes, giving newborn Campodimelani a useful head start. The number one killer in the West, heart disease, is not a problem for Campodimelani. According to a study conducted by the World Health Organization in 1985, even villagers in their eighties have extremely low blood pressure, and a 1995 University of Rome study showed that cholesterol levels at all ages are equivalent to those of infants.[1]

CAMPODIMELE COOKING

Campodimelani relish their food, and during the day they discuss forthcoming meals with interest and happy anticipation. Porcini mushrooms and snails in garlic and white wine, artichoke in season with lemon and olive oil, fresh handmade cannelloni with tomato and wild boar sauce, and salads of freshly picked arugula and lettuce with a morsel of delectable homemade goat's cheese are all typical fare for the gourmet Campodimelani. Campodimele cuisine has its origins in simple Italian peasant food which, low in salt and high in life-prolonging antioxidants, was pounced upon in the 1960s by American nutritionists for being exceptionally healthy, and is now revered by professional chefs all over the world.

Dishes are based around whole-wheat bread and pasta, legumes, and large amounts of fresh fruit, olive oil, and vegetables grown in fertile, organic soil rich in vitamins and minerals. According to the Campodimelani, the particular essence of their diet is that food is home grown and homemade, uncontaminated by additives, pesticides, or artificial substances of any kind. Soil kept fertile with organic manure ensures that the villagers enjoy top-quality fresh ingredients that are full of vitamins and minerals as well as flavor.

A Perfectly Balanced Diet

The University of Rome study showed that the Campodimele diet is "perfectly balanced."[2] It has a good ratio of protein, fats, and carbohydrates, although it has higher amounts of all of these than the diets of some of the other people featured in this book, with around 100 grams of protein, 70 grams of fats, and 300 grams of carbohydrates eaten daily. Protein tends to come from vegetable sources such as legumes, rather than animal protein, and requirements for all eight essential amino acids are perfectly satisfied. As a result of low meat intake and high consumption of olive oil and plant foods, the diet is low in harmful saturated fats but high in beneficial monounsaturated fats and essential polyunsaturated fats. Cholesterol intake is not particularly low in the diet, but, crucially, blood cholesterol levels are low due to a diet that induces high HDL ("good" cholesterol) levels and low LDL ("bad" cholesterol) levels. According to study leader Dr. Pietro Cugini, Campodimelani also possess a particular enzyme that keeps blood cholesterol levels down.

Campodimelani say that they like to eat and drink "a little of everything." The wide variety of produce grown and eaten ensures consumption of the full spectrum of vitamins and minerals, enabling these nutrients to work together as they must. The University of Rome researchers found that the vitamins and minerals essential for good health are provided in abundance in the local diet.

Campodimelani Eat Just Enough

There are no supermarkets in Campodimele—any food eaten has to be grown at home—so eating is not done to excess. The University of Rome study showed that women eat an average of 2,200 calories a day and men 2,650 calories, which seems to be an acceptable amount for those who exercise as hard as the Campodimelani, and they are not overweight. Campodimelani also give their digestive systems an easy time by eating in a relaxed setting—they sit down together for dinner, taking the time to linger over their food and enjoy their delicious cooking.

Homegrown Fruit and Vegetables

Fruit and vegetables are grown and eaten in great abundance and variety, with greens, salad vegetables, root vegetables, garlic and onions, herbs, and tomatoes all being staples of the diet. The wide range of plant foods gives everyone the full quota of fiber and antioxidants required for optimum health. Villagers are wary of fruit and vegetables offered for sale from outside, lest they contain artificial chemicals, and people claim proudly that the best food is to be found at home. Because produce is collected in season from a very short distance away, the vitamins do not have a chance to disappear by the time it is eaten, and maximum flavor is retained. Vegetables are eaten as salads, or boiled and served alongside other dishes, and are of such good quality that they are delicious just on their own. Some Campodimelani drink the water they have cooked their vegetables in, believing that it purifies the blood.

Olive Oil

Olive oil, used ubiquitously in cooking and on salads, is harvested from the olive groves all around the hill. It is organic, extra-virgin, and unrefined, so that it is green and cloudy in the bottle, and full of flavor.

Whole Grains

Fresh whole-wheat bread is baked at home from homegrown whole wheat, full of fiber, B vitamins, and minerals such as magnesium, zinc, and iron. As with Symi bread, it is not contaminated with the hydrogenated vegetable oils or extra rising agents used in "plastic" supermarket bread to make it squishy and quick to rise. Homemade pasta called *laina* is made into various shapes cut from a sheet and is cooked fresh with tomato sauce and olive oil or put in vegetable soup with legumes. See Secret 3 (page 59) for more on wheat, which is not easily digested by all people.

Another grain, corn, is eaten on the cob with olive oil, salt, and pepper, or ground into maize (polenta). The recipes section in this book (page 243) contains recipes for homemade bread and polenta.

Vegetable Protein from Beans and Nuts

Cicerchie beans, which look like a cross between a chickpea and a large kernel of corn, and *fagioli* beans are used to make substantial soups, added to stews, or put in salads with olive oil, herbs, and garlic. Cicerchie beans are not available outside of Campodimele, but can be replaced with any of the large beans, such as borlotti or butter beans, available in our supermarkets and health-food shops. Beans are a good source of protein and fiber, and provide some of the essential amino acids we need for growth and immunity (see Secret 9).

Another useful source of vegetable protein is almonds, full of essential fats and vitamin E, which grow on trees around the village and are eaten straight from the shell.

Fish

Anchovies and sardines, an excellent source of youth-promoting omega-3 essential fatty acids, are caught on the coast twelve miles away and eaten once or twice a week, which is the amount recommended by nutritionists (see Secret 11, page 91).

Lean Meat Used Sparingly

Any meat used has to be taken from a household's own stock and is therefore only enjoyed as a treat around once a week, or is used in small quantities to flavor stews and soups. Meat is lean, because it comes from roaming animals that are not stuffed with food and hormones to make them fat, as is done in factory farms. Chicken is the most readily available meat, and chickens fed on seeds also provide free-range eggs containing some omega-3 essential fats (you can buy omega-3 eggs in some supermarkets). Other animals include goats, lambs, cows, rabbits, snails, and wild boar, which is hunted—by local men, even in their seventies and eighties—to make delicious wild boar sausages and pasta sauce.

Organic, free-range pig meat is made into sausages or delectable Parma ham. Cured meat is not a healthy source of food, but it is not eaten here often, as it is in short supply. Campodimele hams and salamis are, in any case, a very distant relation of the tasteless, antibiotic-filled, fatty variety found in supermarkets in the West. Because meat consumption is low and the meat itself is not fatty, diseases related to the consumption of animal fat, such as heart disease and cancer, are almost nonexistent in Campodimele.

Cheese

Milk taken from sheep, goats, and cows is sometimes drunk or made into cheese, which is allowed to mature for maximum flavor and is eaten on its own or grated over pasta. Sheep's cheese is the most often eaten; sheep's and goat's milk are easier to digest than cow's milk, and the Campodimelani only have moderate quantities. Parmesan is not indigenous to Campodimele, and butter is not used—bread is dipped in olive oil instead. The milk is fresh, organic, unpasteurized, and free of pesticides, antibiotics, or artificial hormones. (As explained in Secret 8, page 79, cheese is not a health food; if you do want to eat it, it is probably best to confine yourself to a limited intake of organic sheep's and goat's cheese.)

Wine

Grapevines grow on trellises outside every house in the village, and each household makes around three to four hundred liters each of white and red wine every year (this is shared with large families, so does not mean that everyone is drunk on two bottles a day). Wine, which contains the powerful antioxidants known as proanthocyanidins, is taken in moderate quantities, always with food, and sometimes diluted with water. Spirits are drunk only very rarely.

Malt Drink

Coffee is drunk by only around one third of the population, and then in small quantities. Some villagers prefer a malt drink, made with barley and milk in the morning, which is full of B vitamins and considered locally to be better for health.

Water

Recent development has brought water into the village from some distance away, but traditionally villagers drank pure mountain spring water, piped down from nearby Mount Faggeta, source of the local brand of bottled water.

REGULAR PHYSICAL EXERCISE

Villagers keep fit by walking up and down the hill, digging crops, and chopping wood. Some villagers, even one or two in their nineties, use bicycles to get up and down, which is very hard work and excellent for heart and lung health. Men, including the octogenarians among them, go out hunting wild boars occasionally, and everyone enjoys a game of soccer.

In Campodimele, which is 650 meters above sea level, you can almost taste the clear mountain air, and there is a noticeable absence of cars in the village. Fresh sea breezes from the coast keep the climate temperate, which seems to be a common factor among the homes of very long-lived populations. Those of us living in cities do not have such benefits, but even walking in an urban park and taking in some deep breaths will help dissipate some of the sludge from the lungs.

LOW STRESS

The visitor to Campodimele is instantly given a sense of deep, penetrating calm. Villagers keep their blood pressure down with a relaxed and positive attitude toward life and an ability to live in the moment. They also take a two-hour siesta in the afternoons, and the University of Rome study found that they sleep eight hours a night on average. The study also found that villagers are remarkably in touch with their natural body clocks, traditionally going to bed soon after dusk and rising at dawn.

ACTIVE SOCIAL LIVES

Campodimele is a small, close-knit community where people can be as independent as they like, but they also have access to friends and relatives whenever they want to socialize. For entertainment, the village has its own tiny amphitheater, cut into the side of the hill, with a spectacular valley view, and there is also a piazza and a bar where people gather in the evenings. There is a sense of reciprocity within the community, with everyone joining in to help each other with the harvest, and when people are short of something, or old and infirm, their neighbors and family make sure they are provided for.

GIUSEPPE SEPE, 102 YEARS OLD

Giuseppe Sepe is 102 years old, but looks decades younger. Always smiling and cheerful, he has clear, alert eyes and smooth skin, which he keeps shaven for the purpose of "kissing the ladies." Until very recently, he would walk up the hill himself to collect his pension; for a month now, he has been walking with a stick. According to his daughter Filomena, he eats a lot and enjoys his food.

"I don't know why I've lived so long—you have to ask the God up in the air," he says. "Five years ago, I was sick with sore bones, but that's the only time I've been to the doctor." About his diet, he reveals, "I eat what there is—corn one day, pasta the next, beans the next. I've never smoked, and I used to drink wine. I couldn't eat the modern food we have here today. We've always grown and eaten our own vegetables. There would be one big plate in the middle of the table at meal times, and everyone got just enough—when it was finished, it was finished."

QUIRINO DE PAROLIS, NINETY-FOUR YEARS OLD

Quirino De Parolis, ninety-four, stands at his front door, joking and chatting with visitors. "I don't feel too bad today," he laughs. "I live each day as it comes—I am a joyful man." Quirino lives by himself and is completely self-sufficient, although he usually eats with relatives. "When I eat I have a glass of wine and sometimes I'll have a glass of beer," he says. "I eat everything—I like meat and I have it twice a week, and fish when someone can get it for me. I like figs. I get up each day and have coffee and two biscuits, then I'll walk to the bar and have a talk with my friends. I used to ride my bicycle until I was ninety-two but I had to stop when I fell, but it wasn't my fault—there were stones in the road."

CAMPODIMELE DOS AND DON'TS

Campodimelani Do:

- Plan a well-balanced, varied diet
- Consume plenty of fresh vegetables and fruit, grown organically and locally in nutrient-rich soil
- Get their essential fatty acids, mainly from fish and nuts
- Use olive oil regularly
- Choose whole grains rather than refined carbohydrates
- Eat vegetable protein
- Moderate their wine intake
- Exercise regularly
- Enjoy a stress-free environment
- Live in supportive families and have an active social life

Campodimelani Don't:

- Overeat
- Overcook their food
- Eat refined sugar
- Consume much salt
- Eat refined or processed foods
- Eat much meat or dairy
- Smoke
- Drink much tea or coffee
- Drink alcohol in excess

4

Hunza—"Happy Land of Just Enough"

Hunza is a sublimely beautiful valley high up on the old Silk Route in the mountains of northeast Pakistan, where the great Karakorams meet the Hindu Kush and the Himalayas. Home to about twenty thousand people, the Hunza valley forms an unexpected lush green cleft among stark glacial peaks and precipitous rocky cliffs. A glance up and down takes in what appears to be the entire height and depth of the planet's surface: the 7,790-meter, snow-covered Mount Rakaposhi towering overhead, bare walls of rock sweeping downward, green terraced fields on the slopes beneath, and the glacial-blue Hunza River carving its way through the valley floor.

The Hunzakuts who live in the valley are famous for their extraordinary longevity and freedom from illness. They are widely believed to have been the inspiration for the original Shangri-La, a fictional land described in James Hilton's novel *Lost Horizon*, whose inhabitants enjoy an idyllic life and everlasting youth. During the 1960s and 1970s, a sudden flurry of media interest in Hunza led to exaggerated reports of Hunzakuts attaining such great ages as 140, 150, or even 160 years.

When it was discovered that birth dates were measured against calendar events, such as the invasion of the British in 1892 or the birthday of the Hunza ruler, the Mir, rather than being determined by birth certificates, the myth was debunked and interest in Hunza faded away. Unfortunately, the baby was thrown out with the bathwater, because the myths are firmly rooted in fact. Hunzakuts may not live to 140, but a respectable body of research shows that they certainly enjoy levels of health and longevity comparable to those of the other people featured in this book, and their diet and lifestyle accord with the same principles.

Before the Karakoram Highway was completed in the 1980s, the occasional visitors to this almost impenetrable land were invariably struck by the long life, good looks, and virility of the Hunzakuts. When the eminent physician Sir Robert McCarrison was posted to Hunza in the 1920s, he asked, after a seven-year study, "How is it that man can be such a magnificent physical creature as the Hunza . . . ?" He wrote, "These people are long lived, vigorous in youth and age, capable of great endurance and enjoy a remarkable freedom from disease in general."[1]

Hunzakuts of all ages apparently thought nothing of walking rapidly to the nearest town, sixty miles away, scarcely pausing for breath, while men of eighty were observed playing brutal, vigorous games of polo alongside "young" men of forty or fifty, and ninety-year-olds were even reported to be fathering children. Visitors particularly noted the cheerful dispositions of the Hunzakuts. In 1960, Dr. Jay M. Hoffman wrote, "Here is a land where people do not have our common diseases. . . . Moreover, there are no hospitals, no insane asylums, no drug stores . . . no police, no jails, no crimes, no murders, and no beggars."[2]

The few doctors to work in Hunza have often been Western researchers trying to uncover the secrets of the Hunzakuts' good health. Physicians visiting in the twentieth century found that cancer rates were zero, serious illnesses were virtually unknown, and digestive disorders such as ulcers, appendicitis, and colitis did not exist.[3]

When cardiologists Dr. Paul Dudley White and Dr. Edward G. Toomey visited in 1964, they reported in the *American Heart Journal* that among their sample of twenty-five Hunzakut men, who were "on fairly good evidence, between 90 and 110 years old," not one showed a single sign of coronary heart disease, high blood pressure, or high cholesterol.[4]

Doctors working in Hunza today agree that the main cause of premature death has traditionally been by accident, from landslides or falls from the treacherous rock faces. There has been some infant mortality and death from infectious diseases such as tuberculosis and smallpox, but otherwise, the average person lives to be over eighty, in good health, and many live into their nineties and past one hundred.

EXPERIMENTS USING THE HUNZA DIET

Doctors have been studying the Hunza diet for decades, but the most famous research was done in 1927 by Dr. Robert McCarrison, who carried out some dramatic experiments on 1,189 rats in order to discover the Hunzakuts' secrets of long life. He gave the rats a typical Hunza diet consisting of everything apart from the fruit—whole-grain chapattis with a little butter, sprouted legumes, fresh raw carrots, fresh raw cabbage, unpasteurized whole milk, a little meat once a week, and plenty of water for washing and drinking. The rats also had plenty of air and sunlight, and some opportunity for exercise, although far less than the equivalent for Hunzakuts.

When the rats reached the age of twenty-seven months (the equivalent of fifty-five years in human beings), they were examined. Even McCarrison himself was amazed by the results: the rats had no diseases that he could detect, and there had been no infant mortality other than the occasional accidental death. McCarrison also noted that during their lifetimes the rats were alert and cheerful of temperament, and lived harmoniously together.

McCarrison then compared his Hunza rats with rats fed on other national diets. First he fed a group of "Bengali" rats a diet consisting of white rice, legumes, vegetables, and spices. The rats soon developed diseases of the lungs, nose, ears, eyes, gastrointestinal tract, urinary system, reproductive system, skin, blood, lymphatic system, nervous system, and heart—in short, of every organ in the rat anatomy. They also suffered from hair loss, weakness, ulcers, boils, and bad teeth, and in addition they became vicious and irritable.

McCarrison fed an even more unfortunate group of rats a typical lower-class English diet of white bread, margarine, sugared tea, boiled vegetables, canned meats, and cheap jams. According to McCarrison, these rats duly contracted "diseases of the lungs, diseases of the stomach and intestines, and diseases of the nerves—diseases from which one in every three sick persons among the insured classes in England and Wales suffers." Additionally, he wrote, "They were nervous and apt to bite their attendants; they lived unhappily together, and by the sixteenth day of the experiment they began to kill and eat the weaker ones among them."

A TRADITIONAL WAY OF LIFE

The health-giving diet and lifestyle of the Hunzakuts is part of a traditional way of life that, until the building of the Karakoram Highway in the 1980s, was untouched by the modern world. Traditionally, Hunzakuts have eaten only what they can grow themselves, natural food unadulterated by additives, sugar, or processing methods. There has been no pollution from traffic or heavy industry, and no artificial Western products. The Hunzakuts use glacier water to wash and apricot kernel oil to moisturize their skin, and so avoid soaking their bodies with the harmful chemicals that are in modern personal care products.

With the building of the new road, however, convenience foods such as white flour, refined sugar, and cheap cooking oils are starting to penetrate Hunza, along with the increased levels of stress that come with a changing way of life. Now, men of sixty-five remark on their grey hairs and wonder why they are getting them so much earlier than their fathers did, and some heart disease and hypertension cases are starting to appear. Cancer has also come to Hunza—local doctors have estimated that rates are at one in a thousand, low by our standards, but doctors agree that rates are rising and cannot be wholly explained by better diagnostic techniques.

The "Happy Land of Just Enough"

Hunzakuts do not make themselves ill with overeating; they get just the right amount of nutrients to keep their systems running perfectly. In her book *Hunza Health Secrets*, Renee Taylor quotes the Hunza ruler, the Mir, who summed it up by describing Hunza as the "happy land of just enough."[5] In other words, they eat a high-nutrient, low-calorie diet. When Dr. Alexander Leaf studied the Hunzakuts, he found that they ate around 1,900 calories daily, including 50 grams of protein, 36 grams of fat (mainly essential fats of vegetable origin), and 354 grams of carbohydrates.[6]

As a rule, nothing is eaten between rising and doing an initial two or three hours' work in the fields, which gives the digestive system a good chance to wake up before being put to work. Eating breakfast immediately on rising, as most of us do, is not a healthy way to start the day—it is much better to wait for half an hour first, while sipping a drink of hot water and lemon to cleanse the system.

Just after the winter, before the new crops are in, the Hunzakuts traditionally had a lean period during which there was very little food for a few weeks. As a result, they had to skip meals, which gave their bodies a chance to break down and expel any undesirable matter such as diseased cells or cholesterol. Fasting practitioners who have studied the Hunzakuts believe that this annual "spring cleaning" has been an important component of their excellent health (see Secret 36, page 177). Hunzakuts have the additional advantage that they do not load their bodies with extra toxins from an unhealthy diet or exposure to chemicals, as we do.

Life-Enhancing Compost

Historically, the Hunzakuts have been an isolated pocket of healthy people, surrounded on all sides by undernourished, diseased, and crime-ridden populations. In farming, they distinguish themselves from their less healthy neighbors by avoiding pesticides and religiously fertilizing their otherwise barren soil with carefully nurtured organic compost. As J. I. Rodale wrote in *The Healthy Hunzas*, "The magnificent health of the Hunza is due to one factor, the way in which his food is raised. Of that there can be no doubt."[7]

Every scrap of organic plant and animal waste is collected and lovingly nurtured into a rich compost teeming with life-giving vitamins and minerals. The Hunzakuts even put their own feces back into the land, creating an extra-fertile organic manure. The result is that the land is continually replenished with what it has lost and produces healthy plants full of essential micronutrients— plants that are not only full of health, but also full of flavor.

Hunza is famous for its apricots, which have often been cited as an important reason for the legendary longevity of the Hunzakuts. Apricots and the kernels inside them, full of essential fatty acids, are discussed in Secret 20 (page 123).

Cherries, Mulberries, and Walnuts

High fruit intake, especially during the summer, is a major characteristic of the Hunza diet; there is so much of it around that even the animals eat it. Apart from the apricot trees, every family has mulberry trees, and most also have cherry, apple, peach, and pear trees. Grapevines also grow everywhere, with grapes being eaten fresh or made into antioxidant-rich wine. Whichever fruit is in season at the time is eaten in large quantities, fresh, ripe, and raw, thus enabling maximum intake of vitamins and minerals and the enzymes needed for their proper absorption.

Walnuts are also a dietary staple, a significant factor in the Hunza diet, since these are one of the best plant sources of omega-3 essential fatty acids. Walnuts are eaten straight from the shell or ground up to make walnut paste to spread on chapattis along with apricot kernel oil. In winter, they are mixed with dried fruit to make a satisfying fruit and nut cake called *sultan coq*.

A Vegetable-Based Diet

Organic vegetables, lovingly grown in nutrient-rich soil, form a major part of the Hunza diet and are eaten raw or boiled in a little water. They provide the Hunzakuts with anti-aging antioxidants, vitamins, minerals, enzymes, and fiber, and they keep the system alkaline. Tending the terraced fields on the steep hills also provides the hardy Hunzakuts with plenty of exercise. See Secret 2 (page 53) on why the long-lived populations in this book all eat large amounts of vegetables, raw or lightly cooked.

Whole-Wheat Chapattis with Everything

Chapattis are eaten at almost every meal in Hunza, and every self-respecting Hunzakut knows how to slap the dough between the palms until it is a perfect round circle of just the right thickness. The wheat, harvested from the lush green wheat fields in the Hunza valley, is ground up by hand into whole-wheat flour.

As will be discussed in Secret 3 (page 59), wheat can be a problematic grain. However, the Hunza chapattis do not contain additives or yeast, and because the germ and husk of the wheat stay in the flour, the chapattis are an excellent source of fiber, minerals, and B vitamins. Chapattis are cooked for just a couple of minutes on each side, thus preserving most of the nutrients.

Sprouted-wheat bread, which is easy to digest and very high in nutrients, is also eaten in Hunza and can be eaten in the West by people with gluten intolerance—see Secret 4 (page 66).

Other whole grains used are millet, barley, and maize, which are often ground into flour for chapattis. Those who are ill are often given bread made from buckwheat, which is a rich source of vitamin B_{17} and is thought by local doctors to prevent cancer.

Vegetable Protein from Beans and Legumes

Hunzakuts eat around 50 grams of protein daily, mainly from vegetable sources such as beans and legumes. Lentils are made into dhal, while black and white pealike beans similar to fava beans are used to make flour or added to curries. Chickpeas are sometimes ground into flour to make chapattis. Beans and legumes are a useful source of B vitamins, protein, and fiber, and are filling without being fattening. Because of fuel scarcity in summer, Hunzakuts commonly sprout their beans to use in salads, rather than cooking them. Sprouting can double and even triple the content of certain vitamins and minerals, and it also increases the vitamin B_{17} content (see Secret 25, page 141, on sprouting).

Small Amounts of Organic Meat and Dairy Products

Hunzakuts love meat, and keep cows, yaks, sheep, and goats for their meat and milk. However, these animals are skinny, small, and few in number. As a result, meat is eaten in small amounts, and only rarely; thus, the Hunza diet is short on harmful saturated fats and the toxins from meat that are linked with bowel cancer and other diseases. Meat is boiled, which is the healthiest way to eat it. Hunzakuts also eat small amounts of cheese, fermented butter, and ghee (clarified butter).

Glacier Water

The Hunzakuts, being engineers par excellence, have a very sophisticated, ancient system of irrigation channels. These cut through the near-vertical rock faces to bring icy, pale blue water full of beneficial minerals and silt down from the high Ultar glacier to the valley, for irrigation and drinking. In the absence of soft or caffeinated drinks, the Hunzakuts drink up to ten or fifteen glasses of water daily, thus keeping their systems cleansed and hydrated. Secret 34 (page 171) contains more information about water—how much, and what type, you should be drinking.

Herb teas and locally made red wine are other beverages commonly drunk in Hunza, and there are more details on these later in this book.

PLENTY OF AEROBIC EXERCISE

Apart from leaping nimbly about the mountains all day and moving large boulders from landslides off the roads, the Hunzakuts enjoy various leisure activities that involve vigorous exercise. Their most popular traditional sport is polo, although nowadays this is mainly played in Gilgit, the town just outside the Hunza valley. Theirs is a fast and brutal version of the game, originally using a goat's head instead of a ball, in which the horses gallop at extreme speed, there are no rules, and blood is likely to be shed. The party-loving Hunzakuts also consider themselves to be superior dancers, and young and old love to perform their fast and furious dances at every possible opportunity.

LIVING FOR THE MOMENT

The Hunzakuts are not innocent natives living in a state of ignorant bliss. They embrace their own liberal form of Islam and, thanks to their ruler, the Mir, have traditionally enjoyed superior levels of education. However, their traditional lifestyle means they are concerned mainly with matters of the present, such as digging the fields, cooking supper, playing, praying, or just contentedly existing in their magical surroundings. They keep themselves busy, but such stressful matters as mortgages, bills, and taxes have never been a problem for them. Stress is a major cause of aging, and the later secrets in this book explain some ways of reducing the stress levels in our lives.

Hunzakuts live in extended families that provide a loving, accepting environment. The responsibility for crying babies and other family

JANNAT GUL, NINETY-SIX TO ONE HUNDRED YEARS OLD

Jannat Gul ("flower of paradise") is aged somewhere between ninety-six and one hundred years old. She measures her age according to the 1922 visit of the Aga Khan III's brother, when, she says, she was in her late teens or older. The most striking thing about Jannat is her infectious spirit. She laughs, jokes, and punches her great-niece playfully. "When I want to go out my son tries to stop me, fearing that I might get hit by a car," she says. "I say to him, 'Why should you worry when my vision is perfect, and I have no problem with my legs or knees?' I don't even get headaches."

When asked how she has kept in such good health, Jannat replies, "I used to drink a lot of apricot oil. I eat bread at most meals, and in summer I eat a lot of fruit—mulberries, apricots, peaches, and grapes. We only eat meat in winter. We never used to have tea, only hot apricot juice. We also used to have a lot of lassi. My husband was about eighty-six or eighty-seven when he died—he used to eat sprouted wheat, and apricot kernel oil." Jannat stops talking to burst into fits of giggles, and high-fives everyone. "In my opinion, the secret of my longevity is God's kindness, but I've worked hard and eaten well."

members is shared out among everybody, so that everyone gives a little and everyone gets plenty. The elderly are respected rather than sidelined, and so have a strong sense of purpose in life. They look particularly dignified, wearing their hair curled up at the back and sporting big moustaches, and anyone passing them is expected to be first to offer a greeting. In Hunza, the later years are something to look forward to, and are referred to as the "rich" years.

HUNZA DOS AND DON'TS

Hunzakuts Do:

- Eat moderate portions that are naturally low in calories
- Consume fresh, organic, local produce grown in nutrient-rich soil
- Eat large amounts of raw fruit, especially apricots
- Ingest essential fatty acids from apricot kernel oil and nuts
- Choose whole grains rather than refined carbohydrates
- Moderate their wine intake
- Drink herb tea
- Exercise regularly
- Enjoy living for the moment and remain mentally active throughout their lives
- Live in loving extended families

Hunzakuts Don't:

- Overeat
- Overcook their food, which would result in lost nutrients
- Eat refined sugar
- Consume much salt
- Eat refined or processed foods
- Eat much meat or dairy
- Smoke
- Drink tea or coffee
- Drink alcohol in excess

5

Bama—Where Longevity Medicine Grows

Bama County, otherwise known as Wangang (literally "hundreds of mountains"), is an untouched land high up in semitropical Guangxi, southwest China. Cut off by the mountains surrounding them on all sides, the people of Bama have no cars, no industrial plants, no supermarkets, and no fast-food joints—just the sparkling clear Panyang River flowing down from the green peaks into the tranquil valley below.

Here, the exceptionally long-lived, vibrant Yao people till the fields and terraces, climbing up and down the mountains to cultivate the crops that provide them with their own special brand of Chinese medicine for long life. Even the horses grazing the nutrient-rich mountain grass are known to live extra-long lives here. The World Health Organization recently named Bama an official "hometown of longevity," and a research institute has been established in order to discover the reasons for its people's exceptional good health.

Octogenarians in Bama have the dubious pleasure of looking up to their elders, the nonagenarians, who in turn defer to those aged a hundred and over, of which the area typically has about seventy-four in total, or thirty-four per 100,000 (at times, the number tops even Okinawa's supposed world record). Up to five generations of people often live under one roof, with the oldest joining in the chores and social activities; hundred-year-olds have even been known to climb the mountains each day to work the fields, despite the protestations of younger family members. Spirited centenarians can also be found competing against their juniors at the popular folk-singing contests that are held along the banks of the Panyang River every week.

The people of Bama have an exceptionally low incidence of heart disease and cancer, along with low blood cholesterol and robust immune systems. There is no sudden steep increase in the rates of killer diseases after the age of forty, as there is in the West—rather, the people enjoy prolonged youth and vitality to the end. Only 10 percent of those over ninety suffer from coronary heart disease, while a mere 4 percent have been found to have excess blood lipids.[1] In one study, not a single malignant tumor could be found among the population, while in another, the rate was just 4.4 per 10,000 people.[2] The life expectancy in Bama has increased over the last few decades as a result of improved healthcare, which has reduced infant deaths and deaths from infectious diseases such as tuberculosis.

A NATURAL DIET

Bama air is fresh, the water is pure, and the people are kept fit by trekking around the rugged terrain every day. Bama people have happy family lives and a positive outlook on life, and some centenarians have cited "doing good deeds" and "close relationships" as the reasons for their longevity. Researchers have also found a slight genetic element, as there tends to be longevity in certain families, with 37 percent of centenarians having parents over eighty years old.[3] However, genes are thought to be only a minor factor, and genetic inheritance is, in any case, influenced by the diet and lifestyle of previous generations.[4]

In general, diet is considered by researchers to be the most important "secret" of longevity in Bama. Three vegetable-based meals are eaten daily, using homegrown, unrefined, organic produce. The diet is low in calories, low in fat, low in animal protein, and low in salt, while being high in fiber, complex carbohydrates, vegetable proteins, and antioxidants. The diet also contains the necessary quota of the all-important omega-3 and omega-6 essential fatty acids, derived from the seeds of the hemp plant.

Bama villagers are cultivators rather than herders, and there is therefore little danger of suffering from colon cancer or any of the other unpleasant ailments caused by a colon clogged with meat. In short, the Bama diet is ideally balanced for optimum health.

When researchers studied the feces of Bama elders aged between 80 and 109, they found that levels of beneficial *bifidobacterium* were higher than those of other elderly populations.[5] Intestines blooming with friendly flora are a reliable indicator of good general health and diet, and this utopian intestinal environment is brought about by eating plenty of whole foods—and by avoiding popular Western foods, such as meat, sugar, and processed foods, which ferment improperly in the colon and feed disease-causing organisms.

Nutrient-Rich Soil for Nutrient-Rich People

The soil in Bama is full of all the minerals and trace elements we need for optimum health, which find their way through the crops into the people who eat them. When researchers analyzed the soil in Bama, they found it contained high levels of manganese and zinc, both of which are essential for breaking food down into the nutrients the body needs.[6] Manganese also helps make the powerful antioxidant enzyme superoxide dismutase (SOD), which protects our bodies from dangerous superoxide free radicals.

Soil analysts also found that the soil contains the right balance of trace elements such as chromium, copper, and iron, which are needed in small amounts for such life-lengthening functions as regulating blood sugar, making SOD, and building red blood cells, respectively. Hair analysis tests in the same study found that villagers who were still fit and well in their nineties had correspondingly good levels of trace elements.

Needless to say, the farming in Bama is organic and devoid of GM strains or artificial fertilizers and pesticides, which leach the soil of nutrients and cause toxins to accumulate in our cells. The climate is subtropical, so there is bounteous fresh produce available year-round for the locals. As with all the long-lived people in this book, Bama people pick their food and eat it soon afterward, before the vitamins have a chance to deteriorate.

Appetizing Food

There are certain rules in Chinese cooking: the dishes must be colorful, the aroma must be appealing, and the taste must be delicious. When food is lovingly tended and hand-picked so that it is naturally bursting with flavor and beauty, a certain respect is inevitably given to it.

In China, a few extra seconds are always devoted to presenting the food in such a way that just looking at it gets the digestive juices going. This ensures not only enhanced pleasure but also proper absorption and assimilation of the food. It doesn't matter how simple the food is (in Bama, it often consists of nothing more than cornmeal simmered with vegetables); it can always be presented in an appetizing way, for instance by arranging colors around the plate. In Bama, herbs are used both to flavor cooking and to aid the digestion.

Fruit and Vegetables

Bama people eat large amounts of a wide range of homegrown organic vegetables, including pumpkins, tomatoes, a green leafy vegetable called amaranth, and peppers. Nutrients in these vegetables are high because of the quality of the soil, and they are kept high with minimal cooking. Fresh bananas, guavas, grapes, and pears, all bursting with vitality and straight off the tree or vine, are also an important part of the diet.

Hemp, Corn, and Brown Rice

Hemp is an important staple of the diet and a highly nutritious, delicious food that is available in the West in various forms—see Secret 5 (page 67). Corn is another staple crop in Bama, and the ground-up maize is eaten as porridge for breakfast and as a main meal. Brown rice, full of fiber and vitamins and minerals, is also eaten. Secret 3 (page 59) explains more about corn and brown rice.

Fresh Fish and Small Amounts of Animal Protein

Fresh fish is caught from the Panyang River and provides locals with a healthy source of protein. The diet also contains some animal protein in the form of eggs and meat, but only in moderate quantities, and all from the lean, organically raised animals that roam the mountainside.

Vegetable Protein from Beans

The Bama diet also contains ample amounts of fibrous, nutrient-rich vegetable protein from beans and legumes. Bean varieties include lima beans, mung beans, and soy beans, which are used to make tofu.

Drinks

The people of Bama are partial to a drop of snake wine—fermented rice or corn wine bottled with real snakes preserved in the alcohol. Water for cooking and drinking comes from the pure, clear Panyang River, which flows into the valley. Secrets 32 (page 165) and 34 (page 171) have more detail about these.

LIFELONG PHYSICAL ACTIVITY

Thanks to the mountains surrounding them on four sides and the fact that they have no cars, the people of Bama get plenty of aerobic activity. The fact that they live 4,500 feet up in clean, oxygen-rich mountain air enhances the experience, of course. Couch potato syndrome is unknown in Bama—children have to climb the mountains to get to school, adults have to climb up and down them all day to tend their crops, and men enjoy hunting and archery even when they are in their eighties. The hard physical work involved in everyday life gives the people strong bones and muscles, including the heart muscle, and is no doubt an important factor behind their excellent health.

FOLK SINGING AND OTHER MENTAL GYMNASTICS

Bama people do not have hurried, stressful lives, but they always have a reason to get up in the morning. Nobody, young or old, is ever made to feel useless. Mahjong, chess, and calligraphy are included in the leisure activities, and there are always household chores to be done. The favorite pastime is folk singing, which has been enjoyed in Bama for the last thousand years, and is thought to be an important contributor to the good health of its people (see Secret 40, page 200).

HAPPY FAMILIES

Bama people live harmoniously together in extended families, which helps reduce stress and gives a sense of fulfillment. Studies found that most of the very old were happy and contented, barring those who had recently lost a close relative.

HUANG BUXIN, 101 YEARS OLD

Huang Buxin, 101, is typical of many Bama supercentenarians. He says that he is very happy and contented, and considers himself to be in excellent health. Having stayed fit from walking over the mountains all his life, he still does housework every day and goes on daily outings.

> Although he lives with his family, he bathes, dresses, goes to the toilet, and eats without any help. He has brown rice with almost every meal, accompanied by tofu and other beans, as well as small amounts of fish, meat, and eggs. He also has fresh fruit almost every day. He rarely eats sugar or salt, and he avoids smoking and drinking.[7]

BAMA DOS AND DON'TS

Bama People Do:

- Plan a diet that is high in nutrients and low in calories
- Consume plenty of fresh vegetables and fruit, grown organically and locally in mineral-rich soil
- Ingest essential fatty acids
- Choose whole grains rather than refined carbohydrates
- Eat vegetable protein
- Moderate their alcohol intake
- Drink plenty of water
- Exercise regularly
- Encourage mental activity throughout their lives
- Maintain low stress levels
- Live harmoniously in extended families

Bama People Don't:

- Overeat
- Overcook their food
- Eat refined sugar
- Consume much salt
- Eat refined or processed foods
- Eat animal products
- Smoke
- Drink tea or coffee
- Drink alcohol in excess

PART TWO

The Fifty Secrets

This section describes fifty secrets of living long—and staying young—that the five longevity hot spots in the world have in common. Each secret explores a specific dietary or lifestyle habit and explains how you can incorporate it into your own life.

Eat Until You Are Only Eight Parts Full

T he long-lived people discussed earlier in this book all have one very important factor in common: they eat *just enough and no more*. This is largely because they have to catch or grow most of their food themselves, so it is not available in excess. The health-conscious Okinawans are aware of the health benefits this brings, and they even have a saying, *hara hachi bu*, which means "eat until you are only eight parts full."

Crucially, the diet of all these people is *low in calories* and *rich in nutrients*. Their food consists of moderate amounts of fresh produce in its natural, unaltered state, such as fruit, vegetables, fish, and whole grains. It is therefore full of vitamins, minerals, protein, fiber, and beneficial fats. It is low in saturated fats (from meat and cheese) and refined carbohydrates (such as white flour and rice), which are both devoid of nutrients and high in calories. These people do not go hungry, because their high-vegetable diet is rich in nutrients and bulky fiber, which make for a perfectly satisfying meal.

GETTING YOUNGER BY EATING LESS

The wisdom of this way of eating was demonstrated in the 1500s by a Venetian nobleman named Louis Cornaro. Cornaro enjoyed a hedonistic lifestyle and an overindulgence in food and drink until the age of forty, by which time he looked like an old man. His doctors told Cornaro, who was afflicted with gout, colic, and a continual fever, that he only had months to live. Cornaro immediately simplified his diet to include only foods that he found easily digestible, and he reduced his food intake to a mere 350 grams daily. He died at 102, sitting up in a chair, and without pain. At ninety-five he wrote, "O, how glorious is this life of mine, replete with all the felicities which man can enjoy on this side of the grave! How different from the lives of most old men, full of aches and pains and foreboding, while mine is a life of real pleasure, and I seem to spend my days in a perpetual round of amusements."

EXTENDING LIFESPAN WITH A HIGH-NUTRIENT, LOW-CALORIE DIET

The science behind Cornaro's findings has been studied by experts interested in extending the maximum life span of human beings. Our natural maximum life span is considered to be about 120 years, with the longest life ever recorded being that of Frenchwoman Jeanne Calment, who was born in 1875 and died in 1997, aged 122. Dramatic tests on laboratory animals indicate that our time on Earth could be extended even further than this, to 130 or even 140 years.

Dr. Roy Walford has fed a "high-nutrient, low-calorie" diet to various species in thousands of tests, with extraordinary findings. Three-year-old mice, which would normally be grey, arthritic, and shriveled, look and test as healthy and agile as one-year-old mice. Rats live 60 percent longer than usual, and fish enjoy (if only they knew it) a life extension of 300 percent.

In 1991 and 1992, Dr. Walford tested the diet on himself and six other men and women at Biosphere 2, a closed ecological space in Arizona. For two years, the Biospherians ate approximately 2,200 calories daily, with their diet consisting of nothing but fruits; organic, whole cereal grains; nineteen types of vegetables; legumes; and small amounts of lean meat, eggs, fish, and dairy. The result was a spectacular and rapid drop in blood pressure, blood cholesterol, and blood sugar levels for all of them. In addition, their skin cleared up, they lost weight, and they had more energy. This does not necessarily mean that the Biospherians would have lived to 140 if they had continued. However, it showed that by eating a high-nutrient, low-calorie diet we can become *biologically younger*—at thirty-five we can look and feel thirty, rather than forty, for example.

HOW A LOW-CALORIE, HIGH-NUTRIENT DIET WORKS

When you eat, a by-product of toxic waste is generated, containing millions of atoms known as "free radicals" that can potentially wreak havoc in your body, laying the foundations for serious diseases and causing aging of cells. The high-nutrient, low-calorie diet both limits the amount of free radicals generated *and* provides antioxidants to neutralize the effects of free radicals. Researchers have found that Okinawans have wonderfully low blood levels of free radicals, with hundred-year-olds measuring just over half the level of the free radical lipid peroxide that is present in the average seventy-year-old.[1]

Low-calorie, high-nutrient food also protects your health in many other ways. It improves the liver's ability to detoxify, it enhances hormone function, it helps the kidneys' blood-clearing functions, and it inhibits osteoporosis, just for a start. If you need proof that overeating kills, ask yourself, "How many obese over-seventies do I know?" One 1995 study published in the *New England Journal of Medicine* found that overweight women died earlier than underweight women, particularly from cancer or heart disease, and that the lowest mortality rates were among women 15 percent below the average U.S. weight.[2]

HOW MUCH SHOULD I EAT?

If you currently overeat, cutting your calorie intake by up to 10–20 percent should bring you benefits. If you don't want to count calories, then eat until you are only just full, as the people in this book do, and then push your plate away, even if there is still something on it. You should feel neither overly hungry nor overly full. Roy Walford recommends an upper limit of 2,200 calories daily; the people in this book eat around 1,600–2,700 calories on average, which compares with 3,300 calories for the typical American. Remember to make allowances for your height and how active you are, and be sure to consult your health practitioner before embarking on any new health regimen.

You should always eat plenty of high-nutrient foods, which will keep you healthy, energetic, and satisfied while being low in calories. Do not go on a crash diet. Crash dieting is bad for health, rarely works, and speeds up the aging process. One model has recently revealed that after she kept her weight down by living for seventeen years on a diet of cigarettes, coffee, mineral water, and the occasional chocolate croissant, her hair became completely white and she had to have surgery to mend three holes in her heart.[3]

A note of caution: Calorie restriction is not for children, who are still growing. For optimum benefits, Roy Walford recommends beginning at twenty years of age.

WHAT SHOULD I EAT?

A low-calorie, nutrient-dense diet includes plenty of fresh fruit and vegetables, some whole grains, beneficial fats (from oily fish and fresh nuts and seeds), and sufficient protein, derived from high-quality sources such as fish and beans. There are more details about all of these later on in this book. If you need to lose weight, eating this way will help you to lose weight permanently, but without ever going hungry or getting food cravings. It should also help you to look good, feel good, and age slowly, just like the long-lived people featured in this book.

🦋 2 🦋

Consume Five to Seven Servings of Fresh Fruits and Vegetables a Day

Fruits and vegetables are the Cinderellas of our diet—crucial, delectable, but so often neglected. Yet one of the most conspicuous things about the diets of the five longest-lived populations is that they all include large amounts of fresh fruits and vegetables. These people love their juicy apples and pears, roasted red peppers, seaweed, and other fruits and vegetables. (Who doesn't love a green bean or a carrot they've grown themselves?) Current anti-cancer recommendations are that we eat a minimum of five servings of fruits and vegetables daily. Most of us have less, while the people in this book have up to ten servings, with vegetables often forming the bulk of the meal.

In Symi, classic Mediterranean vegetables such as artichokes, green beans, stuffed vine leaves, potatoes, and Greek salads are all popular staples, and are made into mouthwatering dishes with the use of olive oil, lemon, herbs, and garlic. Artichokes are an excellent tonic for digestion and liver function, and have been found to lower cholesterol levels. Symiots also enjoy their fruit, much of which is still homegrown, with fig and pomegranate trees decorating the streets and squares, and vines full of sweet bunches of grapes shading the courtyards and doorways.

Fruits and vegetables are the pride and joy of the Campodimelani, who grow and eat them in great abundance and variety. *Verdura* (greens) are considered to be especially important for health. Favorite vegetables include artichokes, eggplant, cabbage, asparagus, green beans, fennel, cauliflower, arugula, lettuce, peppers, chili peppers, zucchini, celery, peas, and carrots. Wild porcini mushrooms are gathered from the mountainside and used in pasta and gnocchi sauces. Campodimelani also eat plenty of tomatoes, full of the potent anti-aging antioxidant lycopene, in pasta sauces, stews, and soup dishes. As far as fruit goes, Campodimelani enjoy fresh-picked apples, pears, oranges, and lemons from their orchards, and grapes from the vines growing in trellises in their gardens.

Over a third of the average Okinawan meal consists of fresh organic vegetables grown in nutrient-rich soil. Carrots, sweet potatoes, cabbage, watercress, white radish, and oriental greens are all used frequently. *Goya*, a bitter squashlike vegetable resembling a cactus, is ubiquitous in stir-fries and celebratory dishes. Goya contains high levels of vitamin C, even when cooked; is used as a folk remedy for various ailments; and is thought to be a male aphrodisiac. Goya is available in the West in Asian supermarkets; alternatively, you can substitute zucchini or summer squash.

An important vegetable commonly used in Okinawa is seaweed, which is used to flavor dishes and make stocks. Sea vegetables contain almost ninety-two nutritional elements in a highly bio-available (easily assimilated by the body) form, including essential fatty acids, protein, antioxidants, and crucial minerals such as calcium, magnesium, zinc, and iodine. Seaweed also contains alginic acid, which chelates (binds to and removes) heavy metals such as lead and cadmium from the body. According to the Japanese, seaweed prevents grey hair and baldness, which is why it is added to Japanese hair products. Popular types of seaweed are *kombu*, *nori*, *hijiki*, and *wakame*, all of which are available in Asian and health-food shops in the West and are increasingly available in local super-markets.

Some of the fruits most commonly eaten in Okinawa are papayas, watermelons, bananas, pineapples, and tangerines. Fruit is eaten raw, and so provides revitalizing digestive enzymes—papaya and pineapple contain the enzymes papain and bromelain, respectively, which are excellent digestive aids and help relieve constipation. Papain and bromelain are available in supplement form, but you can also try eating one to two servings of these fruits daily as a digestive aid.

The Hunzakuts also thrive on large amounts of fruits and vegetables. Anticancer cauliflower and cabbage are staples, along with root vegetables such as yams and a dark red variety of carrot. Salads are made with radishes, lettuces, cucumber, and sprouted seeds. Spinach, high in vitamins, minerals, protein, calcium, and magnesium, is eaten almost every day with potatoes or chapattis. Spinach and other dark green leafy vegetables, such as broccoli and amaranth (see page 56), are an essential part of any anti-aging diet, as they are rich in beta carotene and another powerful antioxidant called lutein, which protects against age-related macular degeneration in the eye, the leading cause of blindness in the elderly. Dark green leafy vegetables are also a source of the "miracle" anti-aging nutrient alpha lipoic acid (see also Secret 37, page 182, on supplements).

Fruit trees fill the beautiful Hunza valley with their pink and white blossoms in spring, yielding apricots, mulberries, cherries, apples, peaches, and pears. When the Hunzakut wants a snack, he doesn't grab a bag of chips—he climbs a tree. Grapevines also grow everywhere, and grapes are either eaten fresh or made into antioxidant-rich wine.

In Bama, sweet potatoes and pumpkins, their orange flesh packed with anticancer beta carotene, are often eaten with corn to provide flavor and texture, as well as color. Tomatoes and peppers, also full of beta carotene, are frequently used in Bama. The Bama equivalent of spinach is amaranth, a green leafy plant high in calcium, magnesium, and other minerals, as well as antioxidants. Amaranth seeds, which have a nutty, malty flavor, are now available in health-food shops in the West in the form of bread, pasta, and other flour products.

THE ANTI-AGING PROPERTIES OF FRUITS AND VEGETABLES

The most important anti-aging aspect of fruits and vegetables is their high levels of antioxidants, which come from certain vitamins and minerals. Antioxidants are the molecules that stop free radicals in their tracks and prevent them from doing damage to our cells. They protect the DNA inside cells and the cell membranes outside them, thus helping to prevent cancer. Antioxidants also protect the heart by preventing the oxidation of LDL cholesterol. They protect tissues from cross-linking, a process that causes arteries to stiffen and skin to wrinkle. To test your cross-linking, put your hand flat on a table surface. Take a pinch of skin from the back of your hand and pull it upward. If it springs back, your cross-linking damage is minimal. The longer it stays raised, the more cross-linking damage you have.

Antioxidants are such an excellent safeguard against disease that renowned anti-aging authority Dr. Richard Cutler has said,

"The amount of antioxidants that you maintain in your body is directly proportional to how long you will live." However, most people do not eat nearly enough antioxidant-rich fruits and vegetables. You could say that one of the commonest causes of aging is a fruit and vegetable deficiency.

Fruits and vegetables contain other substances that keep us healthy, some of which are known about and some of which are still being discovered. Most contain at least five different vitamins and minerals that our bodies need in order to perform their biochemical reactions. A healthy head of broccoli, for example, contains calcium, magnesium, phosphorus, B vitamins, beta carotene, and vitamin C. When raw or lightly cooked, fruits and vegetables are also high in fiber, which helps remove toxins and excess fats from the body and "sweeps" the colon clean.

Phytochemicals are biologically active compounds found in plant foods that boost our immune and endocrine systems and stimulate our enzyme systems. Some of the substances found in plant foods that can be of great importance to health, but are beyond the scope of this book, are sterols and sterolins, enzymes, indoles, sulforaphane, phytoestrogens, and lignans, to name but a few. It is thought that many of these work together, which is why vitamin and mineral supplements, while useful, should be used to supplement a healthy diet rather than to replace it.

HOW MUCH?

In order to get enough fruits and vegetables, aim for seven to ten servings a day. That way, if you don't hit your target, you may at least reach government recommendations of five servings. In fact, the U.S. government's recently revamped guidelines recommend a minimum of $2^1/2$ cups of vegetables and 2 cups of fruit per day for people who consume 2,000 calories a day. One serving is equal to one-half to one cup, so it should be easy to get enough. A piece of fruit, half a cup of broccoli, and one large carrot each equal one serving. You should aim for a higher ratio of vegetables to fruit; one or two pieces of fruit and five to seven servings of vegetables is best, since fruit, especially sweet fruits such as grapes and bananas, are high in fructose, which is turned into glucose in the body and can exacerbate existing blood sugar imbalances. The Okinawans eat around six servings of vegetables and one of fruit, which is a good ratio.

Try to eat organic, locally grown produce if you can, as the populations described here do, as this is highest in flavor and nutrients. When fruit and vegetables are organic, you can also get the benefits of eating the pesticide-free peel, which is where most of the antioxidants tend to be—hence the color—as well as extra fiber. The thrifty, long-lived peoples of this book would never dream of throwing their peel away, while the Okinawans prize it so much that they make special dishes such as radish-peel salad.

COOKING METHODS

Avoid deep-frying, overboiling, or otherwise overcooking your fruit and vegetables, as this destroys up to 100 percent of nutrients and enzymes. In Hunza, because of the scarcity of fuel, vegetables are either eaten raw or cooked in only small amounts of water for a short time. The leftover juice is drunk, so that any minerals that have leached out into the water are regained. In Bama, vegetables are simmered for a short time in hemp-seed broth, which ensures that they retain most of their nutrients.

Fruit should always be eaten raw, while vegetables are best eaten as salads or lightly steamed. You can also lightly stir-fry vegetables in olive oil or canola oil, as the Okinawans do; alternatively, you can steam-fry by adding a little stock or water and putting the lid on. Add taste to salads by adding olives; herbs such as basil, coriander, or dill; and a dressing using olive oil and garlic. Steamed greens can be tossed in olive oil or a small knob of butter with some lemon juice, or in soy sauce, ginger, and garlic.

Make your salad and vegetable dishes appealing by using plenty of color. Where you find color and flavor in a fruit or vegetable, you will also find the most antioxidants—notice how excessive cooking removes color, as well as flavor. Combining colors also means you are combining different antioxidants, which is how they work best. Creating attractive vegetable dishes will have the additional advantage of galvanizing your digestive juices into action, which will greatly enhance nutrient absorption by your body.

It is easy to avoid a fruit and vegetable deficiency, yet it is probably one of the primary reasons for premature death. If you have previously ignored vegetables or found them boring, you may find that by making them taste and look good, you start to look at them anew, and that a meal no longer seems complete without them.

3

Choose Buckwheat, Brown Rice, and Other Whole Grains

Whole grains such as buckwheat and brown rice have suffered in popularity lately because of the fashion for low-carbohydrate diets, but they are eaten regularly by the people featured in this book and should not be ignored. Whole grains are very different from refined carbohydrates such as white rice and white bread, since they are high in fiber, lower on the glycemic index, and rich in nutrients.

Refined carbohydrates, which are mainly devoid of nutrients, cause many health problems, especially blood sugar imbalances (see Secret 31, page 160, on the hazards of the pastry counter).

Some grains, especially wheat, are not easily digested by everybody and are best eaten in moderate amounts only. Whether you are eating a protein meal or a grain meal, vegetables should always form the bulk of the menu, in any case, for fiber and nutrients. Your blood type may influence whether you digest grains well and which types of grain you can tolerate. I recommend that you consult Dr. Peter J. D'Adamo's book *Eat Right 4 Your Type* for more on this subject.

Another reason not to go overboard on grain consumption is that grains contain phytic acid, a substance that binds to minerals and proteins and prevents them from being properly absorbed by the body. Calcium, iron, and zinc are the minerals that most commonly bind to phytic acid. Eating grains as part of a balanced, nutrient-rich diet should mean that you get an overall sufficiency of minerals. The long-lived people in this book use whole grains as a staple, and they have very good nutrient levels in their bodies.

Unlike white flour and rice, whole grains contain the B vitamins we need for energy and metabolism, and which are a crucial part of any anti-aging plan. Many people are low in B vitamins, because when we eat refined grains, the body has to "borrow" from its stores of B vitamins in order to digest them. B vitamin deficiency is implicated in diseases of the nervous system such as multiple sclerosis, and in mental disorders such as loss of memory, dementia, and depression. When white rice was introduced to Asia, it brought an epidemic of beriberi, a disease of the brain and nervous system. A vitamin B_6 deficiency may also cause heart disease, as B_6 is needed to metabolize the amino acid homocysteine, elevated concentrations of which are thought to increase the risk of heart disease by damaging the lining of blood vessels and enhancing blood clotting.

Whole grains also contain a large range of other crucial vitamins and minerals. Zinc is an antioxidant that rejuvenates the powerhouse of the immune system, the thymus. Magnesium is essential for heart health and bone density. Vitamin E keeps the heart young by protecting blood vessels from oxidized cholesterol and keeping blood fluid. Chromium keeps insulin levels down and boosts levels of the "youth hormone," DHEA. Potassium is required for water balance in the body and the correct function of cells, and is used in cancer therapy. Whole grains also contain other beneficial nutrients such as iron, beta carotene, manganese, and phosphorus.

GUIDE TO GRAINS

Whole Wheat

Fresh, homemade bread from whole-wheat flour is always found on the table at mealtimes in Symi and Campodimele. Campodimelani pasta, known as *laina*, made from durum semolina wheat, is made into various shapes cut from a sheet and cooked fresh with tomato sauce and olive oil, or put in vegetable soup with legumes. In Hunza, whole-wheat chapattis are everywhere—people are either rolling them out, slapping them between their palms, cooking them on a hot-stone fire, or eating them. Like other whole grains, wheat contains fiber, B vitamins, and minerals. Wheat germ also contains vitamin E, which may explain why the Hunzakuts believe chapattis to be good for reproductive vigor.

Wheat is high in gluten, which a great many people, especially those with celiac disease, have difficulties digesting, whether they realize it or not. According to the Celiac Disease Foundation (www.celiac.org), 1 in 133 people in the U.S. have the disease. If you feel lethargic, are constipated, or develop stomach pains any time during the two days after eating wheat, whether white or brown, it is likely that you are intolerant of wheat and that you should avoid it. Its inclusion in the diets of the people described in this book does not necessarily mean that whole wheat should be eaten by all. It may be that other factors among these populations, such as chewing well, being relaxed over mealtimes, the quality of the wheat, or not overeating it may also play a part; it is also possible that not all of them tolerate wheat well.

If you do feel that you can tolerate wheat, then buy quality whole-wheat bread from a good bakery or make your own, and avoid the squishy, white, sliced supermarket loaves, which are full of such joys as hydrogenated vegetable oils, extra gluten, pesticides, and rising agents—and are high on the glycemic index.

Spelt and kamut are ancient forms of wheat that are much more easily digestible; breads and pastas made from these grains are supplied in health-food shops. You can also try sprouted wheat bread—see Secret 4 (page 66).

Buckwheat

In Hunza, those who are ill are often given bread or pancakes made from buckwheat. Buckwheat is thought by local doctors to prevent cancer, as it contains vitamin B_{17} (see Secret 3, page 59). Okinawans also eat buckwheat regularly, in the form of delicious soba noodles.

Buckwheat is very effective in reducing high blood pressure, as it contains capillary-strengthening rutin. Another heart-friendly property of buckwheat is its high fiber content, which helps remove excess cholesterol from the body. Buckwheat contains choline, a B vitamin that helps the liver deal with excess alcohol, which is why soba noodle soup and soba water are served in soba shops in Japan to hung-over businessmen. Buckwheat is also a good source of protein. It is gluten-free, so suitable for celiacs and gluten-intolerant people.

Brown Rice

Okinawans have unfortunately started eating white rice, but when Japanese mainlanders are ill, they often turn to brown rice. Brown rice contains magnesium, iron, and B vitamins. It has both insoluble and soluble fiber, both of which are essential for ridding the digestive tract of disease-causing toxins. In Bama, brown rice is grown in the bottom of the valley by the river, which may explain why a majority of the centenarians (62 percent of them) are found in this part of Bama, since the dietary intake may be higher where the rice is grown. It lowers cholesterol levels, and is thought to boost the reproductive system and to promote sexual and mental vigor. A serving of brown rice with legumes such as chickpeas, beans, or lentils provides the body with all eight essential amino acids (see Secret 6 on protein needs). Brown rice is also gluten-free.

Corn

In Campodimele, corn is eaten on the cob with olive oil, salt, and pepper, or ground into maize (polenta). Corn is the staple crop in Bama and can be found everywhere, either growing on the mountainside, hanging up to dry in the sun, or being hand-milled into maize. Every day a large iron pot is hung up by the fire, and the maize is stirred into it with a big wooden pole and turned into the Bama equivalent of polenta. Extra corn is also fermented and made into corn wine.

Corn is not a superfood, but it seems to work for the people of Bama, as part of a balanced diet that is generally rich in nutrients. The fact that the corn comes from nutrient-rich soil helps, of course. Cooking corn increases its antioxidant content and also releases ferulic acid, a phytochemical that is thought to have anti-cancer properties. Additionally, the soluble fiber in corn helps stall the aging process by regulating blood sugar levels and lowering cholesterol.

However, intolerance to corn has been found to be quite common in the U.S., as tends to be the case in places where one grain is eaten frequently. Possibly this is also the case in Bama, but research has not brought it to light yet. Another disadvantage of corn is that it can contain aflatoxins, which are harmful to the liver. As with everything, buy from a good source, eat in moderation, and watch for foods that disagree with you.

Corn is gluten-free.

Oats

Oats are easily digestible, and soothing to the stomach and intestines. They aid heart health by lowering LDL and raising HDL levels; the soluble fiber removes bile acids from the colon which are otherwise turned into cholesterol. Oats have a good effect on blood sugar: Dr. James Anderson of the Veterans Administration Hospital of Kentucky, who has been studying fiber for decades, found that eleven out of twenty diabetic men eating 100 grams of oat bran daily stopped needing insulin shots. Oats are a much better option than supermarket breakfast cereals, which are often high in sugar and hard on digestion. Oats contain gluten, but of a type that is more easily digestible than that in other grains—oats can even be eaten by those with celiac disease in remission.

Barley

Full of B vitamins, barley water is a traditional remedy for illness and is drunk by Campodimelani in place of coffee. Barley is also ground up by the Hunzakuts and used to make chapattis. It is full of minerals, especially calcium and potassium. There are two kinds of barley—beige and white. Use beige grains rather than white pearl barley.

Millet

Millet, which is also used by the Hunzakuts, is a good protein grain, as it contains all eight essential amino acids. Millet is also easily digested, unlike some starches, and is the only alkaline-forming grain, which makes it agreeable to the digestive system.

Millet contains silicon, a part of collagen, the connective tissue that gives us elasticity. There are various flours, breads, and pastas made from millet available in health-food shops. Millet is gluten-free.

Amaranth

Amaranth is a spinachlike vegetable that is grown in Bama. Its seeds have recently become popular among health-food enthusiasts in the West, since they are rich in nutrients, including protein, fiber, vitamins, and minerals. They can be cooked to make a sticky, highly digestible grain with a nutty, malty flavor, or ground into flour to make pasta, biscuits, or bread. Amaranth seeds combined with brown rice or corn make a complete protein meal. The seeds can also be sprouted and used in salads. Amaranth products are available from health-food shops in the West and are growing in popularity, especially among those with wheat intolerance who want an alternative whole grain. Amaranth is gluten-free.

Hemp

Hemp, or *Cannabis sativa*, a cousin of the more well known *Cannabis indica* plant, is a highly nutritious seed or grain (it is treated as both) with a wonderful flavor, and it is becoming increasingly popular as a health food. Secret 5 (page 67) is devoted to the subject of hemp and how you can use it.

Quinoa

Quinoa is not eaten by any of the populations in this book, but is an ancient grain from the Andes, and such a healthful grain that it is worth including here. It is an excellent source of protein, as it contains all eight essential amino acids our bodies need. It also contains omega-6 essential fatty acids, and is a good source of calcium, phosphorus, and iron. Unlike some grains, quinoa is very easy to digest. It can be used in salads, in casseroles, with pasta sauce, or just on the side. Quinoa is also gluten-free.

❧ 4 ❧

Eat Sprouted Wheat Bread

If you love bread but you pay for it with gas and bloating, then it is wise to find an alternative. Intolerance to wheat is very common, and it is thought that such food intolerances may lead to more sinister health problems, including autoimmune diseases (such as lupus, rheumatoid arthritis, or multiple sclerosis). A good indication that you cannot tolerate wheat is that you feel you couldn't tolerate life without it. This may mean that the gluten in bread is not broken down properly in your intestines, causing particles called gliadorphins to escape through a damaged intestinal lining into your bloodstream. These can penetrate your brain, where they act like a drug, making you feel first good, then bad, and leaving you wanting more.

Good wheat-free breads are widely available now, but for those who don't digest grains well, especially grains containing gluten (such as rye and barley, as well as wheat), sprouted wheat bread may be the answer. This revered bread, known in the West as Essene bread, is made by the Hunzakuts for very special occasions such as the winter equinox. They sprout their wheat and then grind it between two rocks for hours; you can make your dough in a blender in a matter of minutes. Sprouted wheat bread is also available in good health-food shops.

This wonder-bread is low in starch and easily digestible, even for the gluten-intolerant, as the gluten is largely broken down in the sprouting process. Sprouting also liberates vitamins and minerals and increases enzyme content, making the bread extremely rich in nutrients. Sprouted wheat contains essential fatty acids, B vitamins, vitamin E, high-quality fiber, and very little fat. Because of the slow cooking time, most of the nutrients are preserved. The bread is also deliciously moist, sweet, and filling. No wonder the Hunzakuts consider *diram phitti*, as they call it, to be the "seed of life."

Another benefit of this bread is that all you need to make it is wheat and water—it contains no yeast, which those with candida should avoid, or baking soda, which can be high in aluminum. To make your own sprouted wheat bread, please see the recipe section at the back of this book (page 243).

5

Use Hemp

One of the main ingredients for long life in Bama is the seed of the hemp, or *Cannabis sativa* plant, a cousin of the better-known *Cannabis indica* plant. Unlike its relative, the hemp grown in Bama does not have any psychoactive properties—the villagers get those from their sake and snake wine, instead. Far from being harmful to health, hemp is packed with vitamins, minerals, protein, and the essential fatty acids that are needed by every cell in our bodies and are common in the diets of the long-lived populations discussed in this book. For thousands of years, hemp has been used as a folk remedy in Asia, Russia, and Eastern Europe.

This delicious, nutty-tasting product is a subject of much interest among nutrition scientists, and it is now viewed as a superfood with an almost perfect nutrient content. Hemp is very adept at soaking up vitamins, such as B vitamins, and minerals, such as magnesium, calcium, iron, and zinc, from the soil. Hemp grain is also high in protein (25 percent of its content) and is a complete protein, containing all eight essential amino acids. Hemp is also full of fiber, which is why it is used to make ropes, sails, and clothes.

One of the most valuable properties of the hemp seed is its high content of essential fatty acids in a perfect balance of three times as much omega-6 as omega-3 (see Secrets 11, page 91, and 12, page 97). Hemp also contains ready-made gamma-linoleic acid (GLA), a metabolite of omega-6, which spares our bodies the energy needed to metabolize it themselves.

The hemp that grows all over the slopes of the Bama mountains is harvested for its seeds, which are then sun-dried, ground into a paste, and stirred into a pot of clear mountain water. This creates a nutritious milky emulsion, which is used as a kind of oily broth in which to cook vegetables, or it is made into *houmayou*, a soup that is eaten once or twice daily. The seeds are also eaten just as they are, thus preserving the essential fats in their purest, most raw state.

Western hemp products include pastas, breads, cold-pressed oils, and seed bars. Hemp pasta is quick and easy to make; it's full-flavored and goes with most pasta sauces. It is gluten-free, so ideal for those with gluten intolerance or celiac disease, and it is also lower on the glycemic index than ordinary pasta. You can also get hemp flour, so you can make "cannabis cookies," which are safe for your own children to eat. The oil, cold-pressed and available from health-food shops, is an excellent alternative to olive oil for making salad dressings. The oil is also sold as a beauty product and is said to improve the elasticity and luster of the skin.

It is currently illegal to grow hemp in the U.S. due to some mistaken beliefs about the psychoactive substance tetrahydrocannabinol (THC), which is actually not present in hemp food products. However, the crop is grown in Canada, and hemp products are sold across the U.S. Negative publicity has adversely affected hemp food product sales in this country, but wrongly so. It seems ironic that hemp cannot be cultivated, while GM crops, which some research has shown to harm health, are grown so extensively. By buying and using hemp products, you can help promote this nutritious crop, at the same time benefiting your own health, so go ahead and use hemp freely.

🎕 6 🎕

Eat Meat as a Treat

The people featured in this book love meat, but they don't eat much of it. Cows, lambs, goats, sheep, wild boar, pigs, snails, chickens—all of these are savored, but they have to be either caught or taken from a household's own stock. These people cannot go to the supermarket and choose from rows and rows of cheap, plentiful meat every day. As a result, meat is eaten only as a special treat around once a week, or in small amounts to flavor vegetable-based dishes. This no doubt benefits these people's health, because, while we do need protein, animal meat in excess can be a very problematic source.

It is a myth that human beings need to eat large amounts of animal protein in order to gain sufficient bulk and muscle. The eight-hundred-pound adult male gorilla thrives very happily on a vegan diet of vegetables, fruit, and nuts. True, the gorilla is only a close relative of ours, but the latest research in sports nutrition shows that our top athletes not only build sufficient muscle, but do best in terms of endurance and stamina, when following a vegetarian diet. Animal protein does help us grow, but it also lays the foundations for disease when eaten in excess. One study showed that when laboratory animals are fed with animal protein, they mature and grow more quickly than those on a vegetarian diet, but they also die earlier.[1] Another study has shown that, on average, vegetarians develop degenerative diseases ten years later than meat eaters, and that they visit the doctor half as often.[2]

We do not have carnivorous bodies, as lions and tigers do, so we are not designed to eat large amounts of meat. For a start, we have much longer intestinal tracts and colons. The products of meat digestion have a long way to travel and tend to linger in the intestines for days or weeks, smearing themselves stickily (and stinkily, even if we are oblivious to the fact) over the colon wall and impacting themselves in any cavities they can find. They are broken down by putrefactive bacteria, which create toxic byproducts such as ammonia, phenols, amines, and fecal bile acids. These linger in the intestines and can be reabsorbed by the body, especially if there is a lack of plant fiber present to escort them out via the stool.

If you were to try biting into the side of a cow, you would see that your teeth are not well suited to eating meat. Even our "canine" teeth are better adapted to biting into the side of an apple. We chew from side to side with our large, flat, molars, shaped for grinding grains and grasses, and any meat we eat has to be tenderized first by cooking, marinating, or bashing it with a hammer. It is then broken down to some extent by the hydrochloric acid in our stomachs, but ours is much weaker than that of true carnivores. Cats, for example, secrete ten times more hydrochloric acid than we do.

Dr. T. Colin Campbell of Cornell University, cochairman of

the World Cancer Research Fund, was raised on a dairy farm and milked cows from the age of five to twenty-one. He now believes that "animal protein is one of the most toxic nutrients there is." His view is based on his findings from the China Project, an ongoing study he has led, which is the biggest study of population and diet that has ever been undertaken. The study data show clearly that mainly vegetarian Chinese from rural areas have far lower rates of heart disease, stroke, osteoporosis, diabetes, and cancer than urban Chinese eating a meat-based diet. The data also show that the rural Chinese have only 6 percent of the amount of heart disease seen in North Americans.

The link between meat intake and cancer is well established. Back in 1976, John Morgan, the president of Riverside Meat Packers, attempted to counteract the damage done to the meat industry by publicity over a very strong link between meat eating and colon cancer.[3] He said, "Beef is the backbone of the American diet and it always has been. To think that meat of all things causes cancer is ridiculous." Six years later, he died of colon cancer.[4]

The populations in this book all have exceptionally low levels of cancer, and one important reason for this is likely to be their relatively low intake of meat, with the bulk of their meals being made up by antioxidant- and fiber-rich plant foods, instead. Meat is devoid of fiber, and its carcinogenic by-products can linger and build up in the intestine. Dr. Campbell has said, "In my view, no chemical carcinogen is nearly so important in causing human cancer as animal protein."[5] Meat is also high in saturated fat, which can raise levels of estrogen in the body and therefore lead to estrogen-related cancers such as breast, prostate, and colon cancer. The next secret explains more about saturated fat in meat and how to reduce it, while still having meat, if you really feel you can't live without it.

HOW MUCH PROTEIN?

Protein is needed for many essential functions, including growth and repair, hormone function, and immune system function. Digested more slowly than starches, protein helps prevent the blood sugar imbalances that can be caused by diets high in carbohydrates (especially refined carbohydrates).

The World Health Organization recommends a minimum of 35 grams of protein daily, while the U.S. recommended daily allowance (RDA) is 0.36 grams of protein per pound of body weight, which is slightly higher. Some experts recommend an average of 50 grams daily, although, within this figure, women need less than men. Some groups, such as infants, pregnant women, athletes, and growing teenagers, need more protein than others, but not necessarily much more. For specific guidelines, you may want to consult a nutritionist.

We certainly need a lot less protein than we eat: the average American eats around 151 grams daily. The people described in this book tend to eat no more than 50 grams of protein daily, most of which is from a vegetarian source such as legumes or nuts. They also eat fish, which can be an excellent source of protein (see Secret 11, page 91). A table showing the protein content of different foods appears on page 75.

WHICH PROTEIN?

You must get enough amino acids from your food, which come from protein and are used for growth and repair of cells. There are twenty-five amino acids, eight of which are "essential," meaning that they are essential for life but you cannot make them in the body. Certain types of protein are complete proteins, meaning that they contain all eight essential amino acids. These are meat, fish, eggs (see Secret 10, page 87, for more on eggs), dairy products, and a few types of vegetable protein, such as quinoa and avocado. Good sources of vegetable protein include legumes, nuts, and seeds. Dairy products are not ideal because they are high in fat and can be hard to digest (see Secret 8, page 79). Limiting your meat and dairy intake while eating fish and vegetable protein regularly should ensure that you get your essential amino acids.

The table below shows how you can combine different types of vegetable protein in order to get all eight essential amino acids. If you get all eight over the course of the day, they will link up with each other in the "amino acid pool" in your body.

PROTEIN SOURCES CONTAINING ALL EIGHT ESSENTIAL AMINO ACIDS

Meat	Hemp
Dairy products	Quinoa
Fish	Avocado
Eggs	Millet
Soy	

Spirulina (freshwater algae available in supplement form)
Chlorella (freshwater algae available in supplement form)

VEGETABLE PROTEIN COMBINATIONS CONTAINING ALL EIGHT ESSENTIAL AMINO ACIDS

Whole grains (e.g., brown rice, brown bread, chapatti) + lentils (e.g., dhal)

Whole grains + nuts

Whole grains + beans (e.g., kidney beans, soy beans)

Beans + nuts or seeds

Hummus + brown bread/brown-rice cake

WHAT ABOUT IRON?

There are some nutrients that vegans and vegetarians may become deficient in, if they do not take care of their diet. Iron is commonly thought to be one of these, but iron deficiency rates for the meat-eating North Americans and British are relatively high, while subjects of the China Project and the people studied in this book have good iron levels. One reason for this is that vegetarians tend to consume more vitamin C, from fresh fruit and vegetables, which is needed for proper absorption of iron.

There are just two nutrients that you can get from meat but cannot get from plant foods: vitamin D and vitamin B_{12}. Vitamin D is manufactured by the action of sunlight on skin, but strict vegetarians may need to take vitamin D supplements, particularly if they don't live in a sunny climate (see Secret 39, page 197). The best food source of vitamin D is oily fish. Vitamin B_{12} is obtained from meat, fish, or tofu, and it is also made by "friendly" bacteria in the intestines. It is needed only in small amounts, and deficiency is rare. However, it is an important nutrient, and it is wise to make sure you have enough. If you are a vegan or have been a strict vegetarian for some time, it is a good idea to check levels of vitamin B_{12} and to take supplements if you are deficient.

Some experts believe that a little animal protein is necessary for the correct balance of intestinal flora. Vegetarians eating a high-carbohydrate diet can have excess levels of fermentative bacteria, which cause gas and bloating and can be detrimental to health. A little animal protein encourages putrefactive bacteria, which help keep fermentation from becoming excessive. The populations shown in this book may well have it right with their moderate meat-eating habits.

If you like meat, then have it. The key is to avoid having it too often, or to change the ratios around, so that plant foods form the main part of the meal, and meat is used more for flavor than bulk. Less can be more, and by limiting the amount of meat you eat, you will appreciate it more; you will also be justifying the expense of buying really good, organic lean cuts. The next secret describes the healthiest ways of cooking your meat so that you can still enjoy it, while at the same time greatly reducing the damage to your body.

PROTEIN CONTENT OF COMMONLY EATEN FOODS

Please note that some of these amounts may be approximate, due to variations between samples.

Food	Protein Content (g)
100g steak	30
100g chicken	25
100g cheddar cheese	25
100g mixed nuts	23
100g cod	21
100g quinoa	16
100g kidney beans	12.5
100g tofu	12
100g lentils	9
240 ml (1 cup) milk	8
2 tablespoons peanut butter	8
100g Greek cow's yogurt	6.4
100g oatmeal	6
100g pasta	6
1 egg	6
100g low-fat yogurt	5
1 baked potato	4
100g brown rice	2.25
1 slice brown bread	2

❧ 7 ❧

Prepare Your Meat Right

One of the main problems with meat, especially Western factory-farmed meat, is its high saturated fat content. Saturated fats, or "hard fats" (solid at room temperature), are found in animal products, especially meat and full-fat dairy products. These fats are the white, greasy substance you find in your roasting pan after the gravy has cooled, and that remain in your blood after you have eaten them.

If you eat meat from an ordinary supermarket twice a day, you are likely to be consuming unhealthy amounts of saturated fat. High saturated fat consumption, a common feature of the SAD (Standard American Diet), is linked with many degenerative diseases of the West. It raises levels of testosterone and estrogen in the body, which increase the risk of prostate and breast cancer.[1] It also contains arachidonic acid, which feeds cancer cells.

Saturated fat promotes inflammatory conditions such as PMS, asthma, and rheumatoid arthritis. It prevents healthy functioning of cell membranes, so that nutrients cannot be transported into, or wastes out of, cells properly. It also prevents the proper use of insulin by cells, which can cause insulin resistance, resulting in accelerated aging caused by high levels of insulin and glucose in the blood.

The animals used by the people discussed in this book are very different from the fattened, overgrown livestock pumped full of chemicals, whose meat is sold in our supermarkets today. The animals eaten by the longest-living populations keep lean and wholesome by roaming the mountainsides and pastures, grazing on organic, nutrient-rich grasses. Luckily, we can now buy organic, free-range meat, which is more like theirs.

If you buy fatty meat, removing the fat before cooking can reduce its fat content by up to half; you should also avoid eating the skin of chicken and poultry, which is high in fat. Cooking methods also affect the amount of saturated fat you get from your meat. Stewing and boiling meat reduces its fat content if the fat is skimmed off the surface of the soup or casserole. Grilling, braising, and roasting are all lower-fat methods of cooking than frying. Red meat is fattier than white meat, so choose chicken over beef and lamb.

Cholesterol is a waxy, fatty substance found in both plants and animals, and necessary in small amounts for health. Meat that is high in saturated fat and cholesterol may raise blood cholesterol levels in some people, leading to atherosclerosis, although this is a controversial subject. Udo Erasmus, expert on fats, and author of *Fats That Heal, Fats That Kill*, states that only 30 percent of people will have increased blood cholesterol levels as a result of eating dietary cholesterol. Other factors also come into play, such as the higher ratio of plant foods in a low-meat diet, which provide fiber and antioxidants. Fiber helps keep the intestines free and clear of toxins and excess fats, while antioxidants prevent the oxidation of LDL cholesterol, which is how it does its damage.

Of all types of meat, processed meats such as hot dogs, bacon, and salami appear to be the worst culprits.[2] Hot dogs and other cured meats are treated with nitrites and nitrates, which form highly carcinogenic nitrosamines in the stomach (these are also found in much higher levels, in cigarette smoke). If you really want to eat meats cured with nitrites from time to time, eat them with tomatoes, which contain substances that block the formation of nitrosamines. The bacteria in live yogurt also help to deactivate nitrites. Incidentally, nonorganic vegetables that have been treated with nitrate-containing fertilizers are one of the main sources of nitrates in our diet, so eat organic vegetables if possible.

Cooking meat on a high heat—by frying or barbecuing, for example—creates very dangerous carcinogenic substances called heterocyclic aromatic amines (known as HAAs or HCAs) and polycyclic aromatic hydrocarbons (PAHs), which are also found in cigarette smoke and diesel fumes. These develop in the cooked meat, even where it isn't browned, so you cannot scrape them off. Oven roasting and baking produce fewer of these molecules, while boiling, stewing, or poaching generate hardly any.

The people described in this book do not barbecue or fry their meat. In Symi, meat is used in stews or roasted with garlic and herbs on special occasions, such as for Sunday dinner. In Campodimele, it is used in small quantities to flavor stews and soups. Occasionally, wild boar are also hunted to make delicious sausages and pasta sauce, but these boar are lean and lower in fat than our supermarket counterparts. The Hunzakuts boil their meat, rather than frying it, with goat stew being a specialty served to visitors. The Okinawans love pork and have it with many of their dishes, but again, the pork is often boiled.

Of course, these people all eat their meat with plenty of vegetables. Eating broccoli and other cruciferous vegetables aids the liver in converting these to less toxic substances, so if you have to have a barbecue, eat lots of broccoli or cauliflower with the meat (see also Secret 16, page 112). Green tea, onions, and garlic also help the liver to detoxify. Antioxidants neutralize the formation of HAAs, so you can also eat a large salad with your meat. Fish is a better option than meat, as it produces only around one-fifth of the amount of HAAs as meat, even when cooked at high temperatures.

While excess saturated fat may be damaging to health, low-fat diets are not necessarily any better. We do need fats, but it is best if the majority of these consist of essential fatty acids and monounsaturated fats. These come from oily fish, nuts and seeds and their cold-pressed oils, and olive oil, and are discussed elsewhere in this book. It is also true to say that trans fats from heated polyunsaturated oils and hydrogenated fats are almost certainly a greater cause of degenerative diseases than saturated fats, as is explained in Secret 14 (page 106).

If you eat meat, choose lean meat over fatty meat, and prepare it in the ways described above so as to limit the potentially damaging effects. Buy organic, free-range meat, and use it in small to moderate amounts only. This will negate the extra cost and make it something to really look forward to.

❧ 8 ❧

Choose Organic Goat's and Sheep's Cheese

The Symiots, Campodimelani, and Hunzakuts make their own organic, traditionally fermented cheeses from the milk of their cows, goats, and sheep. Cheese is not an ideal food, as it is high in saturated fats and, as with wheat, cheese, and other dairy products such as milk and cream, can cause digestive problems for some people. However, the people studied in this book eat cheese in limited quantities, since they have to do their own milking and churning.

In addition, their organic, traditionally fermented cheeses are very different from the processed cheese you might find on a cheeseburger. Being a fermented product, cheese, like yogurt and other fermented foods, does contain some beneficial bacteria that aid in its digestion and enhance the bioavailability of the vitamins and minerals it contains. If you love cheese, this secret will help you to choose the right dairy products so that you can find a place for them in a healthy diet.

In Symi, Greek feta cheese is traditionally homemade from organic, unpasteurized ewe's or goat's milk, and is sliced up and eaten with bread or a Greek salad. In Campodimele, milk taken from sheep, goats, and cows is sometimes drunk or made into cheese, which is allowed to mature for maximum flavor and is eaten on its own or grated over pasta. Butter is not used—bread is dipped in olive oil, instead.

In Hunza, a delicious soft cheese called *burus*, made from cow's, yak's, or goat's milk, is mixed with herbs and spread over chapattis or sprinkled over dhal or lamb stew. Burus is similar to cottage cheese, which is one of the more easily digested cheeses (see page 81). The Hunzakuts also eat a fermented butter that has been buried in the ground for some time (they claim up to a hundred years), making it a little like a rancid, pungent cheese. Hunzakuts also use traditional ghee in cooking (see page 83).

Cheese made from goat's milk and sheep's milk may be more easily digested by those who cannot tolerate cow's milk products, the reasons for which are explained below. Bear in mind, however, that full-fat dairy products are high in saturated fat, so whichever animal they are from, they should be eaten in moderate amounts only.

LACTOSE INTOLERANCE

Dairy products contain a sugar called lactose. In order to digest lactose, we need an enzyme called lactase. We are all born with this enzyme, but in many people it is lost after two or three years of age. This suggests that we evolved to digest breast milk, but that after we are weaned there is no need to consume dairy products.

Whether or not you are lactose intolerant can depend on your racial origin. Populations that have been herding dairy animals for thousands of years have evolved to some extent to be able to digest milk and milk products. About 90 percent of Asians, 65 percent of Mediterraneans, and 10–15 percent of Caucasians are estimated to be lactose intolerant, and it is estimated that between 30 and 50 million North Americans are affected.

Lactase is produced at the tips of little hairlike protrusions in the intestinal lining called microvilli. The microvilli can easily become damaged by a modern diet and lifestyle, and some people may therefore lose the ability to digest lactose as a result. People with celiac disease, whose villi have been damaged by gluten, are especially likely to have a problem with dairy products.

If a person without sufficient lactase eats milk or dairy products, undigested lactose will go into the colon and ferment, causing gas. Typical symptoms of lactose intolerance include constipation, diarrhea, excess mucus production, and gas. Some dairy products are higher in lactose than others, as shown by the table below.

LACTOSE CONTENT OF SELECTED DAIRY PRODUCTS

High	Medium	Low
Cow's milk (especially skimmed milk)	Cottage cheese	Hard cheese
	Ricotta cheese	Soft cheese
Goat's milk	Crème fraiche	Butter (has negligible amounts)
Sheep's milk	Greek yogurt	
Yogurt (some brands)	Yogurt containing live bacteria	

As this list shows, yogurt and cheese contain less lactose than milk, and are therefore more digestible. This is because they are fermented with bacteria that produce lactase and partially digest the milk. The bacteria also digest some of the proteins in yogurt, which can cause allergies and intolerances, as is explained below.

DAIRY ALLERGY

Some people are either intolerant of or allergic to certain proteins in dairy products, and some are both allergic to and intolerant of them. An allergy is different from an intolerance. With an allergy, the immune system is involved, as it produces antibodies to the milk proteins called immunoglobulin E (IgE) and/or immunoglobulin G (IgG), with IgE antibodies being produced for more severe reactions, and IgG antibodies for delayed and less severe reactions.

It is thought that around 2–3 percent of infants are allergic to proteins in cow's milk. There are five main allergenic proteins in cow's milk; children may be allergic to one or more of these. Eighty percent of these children have grown out of the allergy by age six. However, it can cause havoc in the meantime, if milk is not removed from the diet. Children who are sensitive to dairy products frequently develop atopic allergies (asthma and eczema) later in childhood. Childhood-onset diabetes has also been linked to the consumption of cow's milk before one year of age, since proteins in the milk can escape through the intestinal lining and cause an autoimmune reaction that results in destruction of the pancreatic cells responsible for making insulin. Infants should never be given cow's milk before one year of age, since they have a permeable intestine in the first year of life, which predisposes them to sensitivity.

Although cow's milk allergy mainly affects infants, it can also occur later in life. Symptoms of allergy in adults and children include skin, respiratory, and gastrointestinal problems, and migraine. Research shows that cow's milk can also cause anemia in babies, and rheumatoid arthritis, estrogen dominance, athero-sclerosis, and other illnesses in adults.[1] If you suspect an allergy to dairy or other foods, you can have your blood tested for anti-bodies. At the end of this section, there is information on how to test for intolerance to dairy products.

Cow's milk is the dairy product most likely to cause an allergic reaction or intolerance. Milk contains proteins called whey and casein, both of which can cause problems. The protein composi-tion in goat's and sheep's milk is slightly different to that in cow's milk, and some people find that they can digest these better. Goat's and sheep's milk are lower in casein than cow's milk, which is why they are popular alternatives. However, since the proteins are similar, some people cannot eat dairy products from any animal. Mare's milk, like human breast milk, is very low in casein and is the least likely to cause problems.

Ghee, or clarified butter, contains only negligible amounts of lactose and casein. It is made in Hunza by gently heating butter to separate the solid whey and casein from the fat, which can then be used for cooking or to spread on bread. If you cannot tolerate butter, try making your own clarified butter at home by putting a pat of unsalted, organic butter on a very low heat in the oven. Pour off the clear liquid and store it in the refrigerator. It makes a solid, sweet-tasting, yellow type of butter that you can use for cooking and spreading.

Cheese also contains another potentially problematic sub-stance called histamine, made by the presence of bacteria. Histamine is a substance we make in our bodies as part of an allergic reaction. Histamine tends to be highest in very ripe cheeses; it is also found in fish and wine. The liver has to detoxi-fy it, and those who cannot break it down properly may suffer from nausea or headaches as a result. Increased intestinal perme-ability, or "leaky gut syndrome," will also decrease tolerance to histamine.

WHERE DO I GET MY CALCIUM?

We are frequently told that we should eat dairy products so as to avoid osteoporosis. Yet those countries where most dairy products are eaten, such as the United Kingdom, the United States, Finland, and Sweden, have the highest rates of the disease, whereas Asians eating a traditional diet, and the people in this book, have very low rates.[2] According to the authors of *The Okinawa Way*, Okinawans' risk of hip fractures is about half that of North Americans.

It seems dairy products are not the perfect source of calcium, after all. This may be because, with the exception of yogurt and unpasteurized milk, dairy products are acid-forming in the body and may therefore cause alkaline calcium to be leached out of bones, in order to "buffer" the acid in the blood. The calcium in milk is also not particularly well absorbed by the body. The calcium in yogurt and cheese is more available to the body, due to the actions of bacteria used to ferment these products.

Alternative sources of calcium are kale, kelp, fish with soft bones (e.g., salmon, sardines), nuts, tofu, kelp, and molasses. These should be eaten with sources of vitamin D (dietary sources include eggs and liver; see also Secret 39, page 197, on sunlight) and magnesium (kelp, whole grains, nuts, molasses) in order for the calcium to be absorbed into bones.

Unpasteurized milk is not easily available in the West due to the fear of infection by bacteria, especially the bacteria that cause tuberculosis. However, it is worth mentioning that unpasteurized dairy products, as consumed by the Symiots, Campodimelani, and Hunzakuts, retain their original vitamins and enzymes, which make them easier to digest and richer in nutrients than pasteurized milk products.

If you want to include dairy products in your diet, yogurt and small amounts of cheese are more digestible than milk and, therefore, a better option. You may be able to digest goat's and sheep's milk products—and, if you can get them, mare's milk products—more easily than cow's milk products. Buy organic yogurt and cheese to avoid ingesting the antibiotics and pesticide residues that are likely to be present otherwise. It is also best to buy traditionally made yogurts and cheeses, from health-food shops and specialist suppliers, since these are likely to have been fermented using superior methods and to contain larger amounts of beneficial bacteria than mass-produced varieties.

ARE YOU INTOLERANT TO DAIRY PRODUCTS?

The most common test used for lactose intolerance is the lactose hydrogen breath test. Undigested lactose will create excess hydrogen, which will find its way into the lungs and show up in the breath test. If you do decide to have this test, be aware that it is not 100 percent reliable and should be used in conjunction with a study of any symptoms you might have.

Another test you can do at home is to avoid having any dairy products for two weeks. After that time, choose a quiet hour, then sit down and measure your pulse. Have some milk or cheese and then take your resting pulse after ten, thirty, and sixty minutes. If your pulse rises by more than ten beats, this is a good indication of dairy intolerance. You may also experience other symptoms over the next one to three days. If you find you are intolerant to dairy products, these are best avoided or severely limited in your diet.

🌿 **9** 🌿

Be Full of Beans

Beans and the seeds they contain (such as lentils and peas), called legumes, are the mainstay of many a vegetarian diet. Often maligned due to their gas-causing reputation, beans were once known as "poor man's meat." However, they should perhaps be renamed "long-lived person's meat," because beans and legumes are an important component of the diets of the people described in this book. Embrace the humble bean, because it is a versatile, tasty, satisfying food that can provide you with many valuable anti-aging nutrients.

Beans and legumes can be used in a wide variety of dishes. The Hunzakuts eat dhal with lemon and coriander almost daily, and they grind chickpeas into a flour we know as "gram flour" to make chapattis. The Symiots make rich, filling stews with beans, tomatoes, garlic, and herbs, sometimes flavored with a little lamb. Campodimelani can't live without their local variety, the revered cicerchie bean, which is made into a delicious bean and pasta soup (see the recipes section in this book, page 243). Fagioli beans are used to make soups and stews or put in salads with olive oil, herbs, and garlic. Okinawans eat fermented soy beans, or tofu, regularly, while the people of Bama use tofu as well as lima beans and mung beans (see Secret 24, page 138, for more about soy).

Beans and legumes are an excellent source of protein, while being low in fat, and therefore make a healthy substitute for meat. Soy beans, for example, contain around 29 grams of protein per 120 grams, over half the daily protein requirement for the average person. Soy beans are the only bean that is a "complete protein," one containing all the eight essential amino acids we need, but other beans do make a complete protein when combined with whole grains such as buckwheat, brown rice, or whole wheat flour. Beans and grains can be combined either at the same meal or over the course of twenty-four hours in order for our amino acid pools to be restocked with everything they need.

Fiber, one of the most powerful anti-aging tools there is, is abundant in both its insoluble and soluble forms in beans and legumes. Fiber ensures that we rid the body of undesirables such as excess fats, "bad" cholesterol, used hormones, and toxic material, and it also keeps blood sugar levels—and therefore pro-aging insulin levels—low, and aids weight loss. In other words, fiber helps prevent heart disease, cancer, diabetes, and other diseases of aging.

Beans contain antioxidant flavonoids, found also in fruit and vegetables, which protect cells from the ravages of aging. Beans also have a wide range of vitamins and minerals, including B vitamins, potassium, zinc, calcium, and magnesium. Many beans, including pinto, kidney, and soy beans, also contain anticancer agents such as protease inhibitors and genistein. In short, they have most of the things we need; bean fans might call them a perfect food. Eating just beans, however, would not be a good idea, quite apart from being boring. Beans are at their most valuable when eaten as part of the diet described in this book.

❧ 10 ❧

Have a Good Egg

Eggs can be an excellent addition to your diet, especially if you eat the right kind. The Campodimelani, Okinawans, and people of Bama all eat eggs from quality sources, which provides them with many of the nutrients required for optimal health.

Eggs are one of the best sources of protein available. They are a "complete" protein, meaning they contain all eight essential amino acids we need to obtain from our diet on a daily basis (these are leucine, lysine, isoleucine, valine, methionine, phenylalanine, threonine, and tryptophan). One egg contains about 6 grams of protein, so this makes up a good part of the 35–50 grams or so of protein we need daily (see Secret 6, page 69).

It is a myth that eggs raise cholesterol levels. It has been known for a long time that even if a food is high in cholesterol, as eggs are, that does not mean that it will raise levels of "bad" cholesterol in the body. It is the ratio of "bad" LDL cholesterol to "good" HDL cholesterol that matters, and including moderate amounts of eggs in your diet will not affect this. One egg contains around 250 grams of cholesterol, so eating four or five eggs a week is fine. In addition, eggs contain lecithin, which emulsifies fats to enable our bodies to digest them.

The yolk of an egg consists of about 30 percent fats and oils by weight. Some of this consists of saturated fats, and some essential fatty acids—the fats that are vitally important for our good health and that we must obtain from our diet every day (see also Secrets 11, page 91, and 12, page 97). This is where the difference between "good" eggs and factory-farm eggs becomes crucially important. Eggs contain both omega-6 and omega-3 fatty acids, both of which we need, in a ratio of about 2:1. Most North Americans have an imbalanced ratio of about 20:1, at the same time as generally being deficient in both types of fatty acid. An egg laid by a factory-farmed chicken will add to this problem, as it contains around twenty times more omega-6 fatty acids than omega-3s.

However, high-quality, free-range, organic eggs have recently come on the market, which are laid by chickens fed a diet enriched in omega-3 essential fats, from sources such as flax oil. These eggs contain essential fatty acids in a much better ratio, nearer to 2:1 or 1:1, depending on the egg production methods. In a high-quality egg, around a third of the total fats in the egg should consist of essential fats, with one egg providing you with around a quarter of your daily omega-3 needs. So don't order an egg-white omelet, as is fashionable—eat the whole egg from a high-quality source instead.

Another advantage of the omega-3 fats in free-range, organic, omega-3 supplemented eggs is that much of the omega-3 fats have already been turned into their desired end products, EPA (eicosapentaenoic acid) and DHA (docosahexaenoic acid), the hormonelike substances our bodies make from omega-3 fats in order to perform many important functions. DHA is particularly important for brain development in fetuses and infants.

Egg yolks also contain lutein and zeaxanthin, powerful antioxidants from the yellow/orange-colored carotenoid family, of which carrots are also a member (spinach and broccoli also contain lutein and zeaxanthin). These are thought to reduce the risk of cataracts in the eye by preventing oxidative damage.

There are many other vitamins and minerals in eggs. According to data from a large U.S. study, the *National Health and Nutritional Examination Survey (NHANES III 1998–94),* people including eggs in their diet have higher levels of most nutrients than those not eating them. Eggs contain several minerals, including zinc and iron, and thirteen vitamins, including the fat-soluble vitamins A, D, and E. One of the B vitamins they contain is choline, a substance that aids normal cell function and is a significant provider of methyl groups, which are needed for liver detoxification. Choline is required by fetuses for brain development, and is especially important during pregnancy. Studies on animals showed that the offspring of mothers who had choline in their diet had significantly better memories, even as adults, making them genuine "eggheads."

Free-range, organic, omega-3 eggs currently constitute around 5 percent of the U.S. market. However, when consumers were asked whether they were willing to pay more for better-quality eggs, around half said they would; so hopefully factory-farmed eggs will start to decline in popularity. Chickens are designed by nature to roam around outside, eating grains, live insects, and plants. Yet factory-farmed chickens are trapped in tiny cages indoors all day, are fed low-quality feed, and regularly receive antibiotics because of the susceptibility to infection caused by their dirty, crowded conditions. Essential fatty acids are removed from their feed to protect it from spoiling, since these fats are fragile and go rancid easily. Beneficial plant sterols are also removed from their diet. The eggs produced, which are sterile, are colorless and tasteless compared to high-quality eggs, which have a full flavor and a rich orangey-yellow yoke. It is hardly surprising—wouldn't our eggs be healthier, if we roamed around outside in the sunshine and ate healthy natural food, than if we lived in small cages eating waste products from food industries?

When buying eggs, read the labels carefully and beware of deceptive packaging. Chicken-factory farmers, eager to get on the natural-foods bandwagon, depict carefree chickens on their egg boxes and use attractive but empty terms such as "farm fresh." The best way to be sure that you are getting good eggs is to buy them from a reputable health-food shop, and don't be afraid to ask questions about the source. Make sure they are labeled "omega-3 enriched" and that they are organic, as nonorganic eggs may contain residues from grains contaminated with pesticides. "Pasture-fed" is a good label, meaning that the chickens have been given grains and allowed to forage outside for insects and grass. "Cage-free" also means that the bird has been given a fair amount of freedom, whereas "free range" can mean that a meager two to five square feet is allocated for each chicken. Expect to find more quality eggs in summer, as chickens lay seasonally.

Eggs can be allergenic, so avoid eating too many, and watch out for any adverse reactions. This is particularly important when weaning infants, who should not be given eggs before one year of age. Raw eggs, however, are not thought to pose a problem, as it is cooking that alters the protein structures in eggs to make them allergenic. Raw eggs are also an excellent source of nutrients, which is why the film character Rocky drank them for breakfast. They have a higher risk of salmonella, but to get this in perspective, only around one in thirty thousand eggs is thought to be contaminated. Organic, cage-free, omega-3 fed chickens lay much healthier eggs than factory-farmed chickens, and the risk of infection from their raw eggs is much lower. If you do eat raw eggs, make sure they are fresh—the yolk should be firm when the egg is opened, and of course there should be no odor. Remember also that if you have a healthy diet and lifestyle, your immune system is much more able to protect you from bacteria such as salmonella.

Eggs, raw or cooked, are very versatile. If you have them raw, you can eat them like Rocky, by tipping one down your throat, or you can make delicious homemade mayonnaise with raw eggs and olive oil. If you cook them, you can have them in a Spanish omelet with vegetables and herbs, in a quiche, or as huevos rancheros. Boiling or poaching is less damaging for the essential fats, however, so enjoy them regularly boiled, in a tuna or bean salad or just poached on toast.

🌿 11 🌿

Find Good Fats in Fish

THE IMPORTANCE OF FISH OILS

As you may know, there are good fats and bad fats, and whichever ones you include in your diet are likely to affect your health quite considerably. As Udo Erasmus has explained in his authoritative book on the subject, *Fats That Heal, Fats That Kill*, the good fats heal, and the bad ones kill.

The bad fats come from heated and processed vegetable oils, as found in supermarket vegetable oils and fried and processed foods (see Secret 14, page 106), and the saturated fats in meat and dairy products. Monounsaturated oil, as found in extra-virgin olive oil, is a "good fat" (see Secret 13, page 104 on olive oil).

Then, crucially, there are the *essential,* page 104, fats. These cannot be made in the body and must be obtained from the diet on a daily basis, and they are absolutely essential for health. These essential fatty acids (EFAs) come mainly from the *fresh, unspoiled* polyunsaturated oils found in nuts and seeds and in oily fish. The EFAs from nuts and seeds and their oils are mostly omega-6 fats (or linoleic acid), and the EFAs from oily fish are omega-3 fats (or alpha linolenic acid).

The longest-living people in the world have all been noted for their velvety skin, glossy hair, high IQs, and low rates of degenerative disease, and it seems very likely that their intake of EFAs is a good reason for this. EFAs, both omega-3 and omega-6, help make up the structure of cell membranes, keeping them flexible, as they need to be to allow nutrients in and toxins out. This shows on the surface of the body as supple skin and shiny hair, and underneath as healthy tissues and organs. In various ways, EFAs affect virtually every aspect of health, from immunity to cancer, as well as keeping your cells—and therefore you—young.

It can be no coincidence that most of the people featured in this book live on or near the sea, so that their diet includes plenty of omega-3 fats from fish. The Okinawans and Symiots, being islanders, are fishermen and eat fish at least two or three times a week. The Okinawans usually grill theirs, while the Symiots have theirs either gently sautéed in olive oil, roasted in the oven, or made into a succulent soup. Large, fresh sardines, which are high in omega-3 fats, are a particular Symi favorite. In Campodimele, two types of oily fish, anchovies and sardines, are caught from the coast twelve miles away and eaten once or twice a week. In Bama, fresh fish is caught from the Panyang River. Only the Hunzakuts eat no fish, but they obtain omega-3 fats from walnuts and linseeds, which are two good vegan sources.

If you have PMS, rheumatoid arthritis, or eczema, you may well be deficient in omega-3 fats, since they are very useful anti-inflammatories. They also protect the heart by helping to transport cholesterol from the blood, lowering blood pressure and preventing blood from clotting. They decrease tumor formation and the metastasis of cancer, and can even kill cancer cells.[1] They boost metabolism, and so can help with weight loss, despite the fact that they are a "fat." They allow friendly bacteria to adhere to the intestinal wall, which has enormous implications for health (see Secret 22, page 128, on yogurt).

What can't omega-3 fats do? They can even make you more intelligent—in fact, if anyone ever calls you a fathead, you can thank them for the compliment. Around 60 percent of our brains are, or should be, made of docosahexaeroic acid, or DHA, which is converted from omega-3 and found in oily fish. DHA is essential for proper thinking, feeling, seeing, and motor coordination. The last trimester of fetal development and the first twelve months of life are the most important for brain development, with our brains tripling in size by our first birthday, so it is vital that we get a good intake of DHA during that time, from our mother's supplies and from breast milk. Research shows that breast-fed children have IQs several points higher than formula-fed children; DHA is now added to some formulas to make up for this.

Pregnant and lactating women should therefore eat oily fish at least twice a week or supplement with 200–400 milligrams daily of DHA. Capsules must come either from marine algae, which is where the fish gets its DHA from, or from fish body oil, rather than fish-liver oil capsules, since fish livers contain high amounts of vitamin A, which can be toxic to a developing fetus. If you are pregnant or lactating, you should use fish oil capsules that have been purified to remove toxins, which are often found at high levels in fish, due to our polluted seas. Fish oil should also not be fed directly to infants, as it has been shown in some studies to impair mental development, for reasons that are not yet clear, although one might speculate that this was a result of the quality of the oils used in the studies.

DHA is necessary for proper neurotransmitter function. For example, attention-deficit hyperactivity disorder (ADHD) is characterized by low levels of the neurotransmitter dopamine, which relies on DHA for production. In an Oxford University study, it was found that children with ADHD had essential fatty acid deficiency. After the children were given fish-oil supplements for three months, DHA levels in their brains recovered, and the researchers found "stark" differences in markers such as ability to pay attention, relaxation, and emotional volatility. DHA also raises levels of serotonin, the antidepressive neurotransmitter. In a UK study, when fish oil was given to patients with manic-depression, the researchers saw "dramatic differences" in their subjects; improvements were so striking the study was ended several months early.[2]

HOW MUCH?

Udo Erasmus recommends that we have 2 grams of omega-3 fats daily as a minimum maintenance dose, 6 grams daily as an optimum maintenance dose, and up to 70 grams daily to correct a severe deficiency, with no known toxic dose. In practical terms, you should aim for around one to two teaspoons daily, or one to three capsules of a high-quality fish oil daily, and/or oily fish up to three times weekly. Options for vegans are explained in the next secret.

Omega-3 and omega-6 fats compete with each other for space in the cell membrane, so it is important to get them in the right ratios. This is thought to be somewhere between 1:3 and 1:5 (i.e., three to five times as many omega-6 fats as omega-3 fats). Experts differ in their opinions, and there is no blanket amount that is correct for everybody. The best way to find out how much you need is by experimenting and closely monitoring how you feel. Most North Americans, while being deficient in both fats, have a ratio of around 1:20, which is damaging to health and will cause symptoms of omega-3 deficiency. Excess omega-6 fats are implicated in blood clotting, inflammatory disease, and some cancers.[3] The next secret explains more about omega-6 fats and what you should be getting.

Deficiency symptoms of omega-3 fats include:

Growth retardation
Weakness
Learning difficulties
Motor incoordination
Tingling in arms and legs
Behavioral changes
Dry skin and hair

HOW TO GET YOUR FISH OILS

The best sources of oily fish are mackerel, herring, wild or organic salmon, and sardines. Tuna has a small amount of oil, but intake should be limited, especially by pregnant women, to one small can of light tuna weekly, maximum, since it is very high in mercury. Try to get your fish from the cleanest waters possible, to avoid pollutants such as dioxins; arctic fish in particular seem to be high in these, and Inuit women have been found to have high levels of dioxins in their breast milk. Farmed salmon is best avoided, as it can contain high levels of carcinogenic PCBs (poly-chlorinated biphenyls), growth enhancers, and pesticides. Large fish such as shark and tuna are the highest in mercury and should only be eaten occasionally.

You can also buy fish-oil capsules, but make sure you buy a good brand that is made from fish from clean waters, purified of toxins, and regularly checked for freshness. For vegans, omega-3 fats can be obtained from certain plant sources such as linseeds and walnuts, as explained in the following secret. Fish oils are a more useful source, however, since the fish has already metabo-lized the omega-3 fats into two of the products we need, EPA and DHA. An alternative source of DHA is supplements of marine algae, which is where the fish get it in the first place, but remember you also need EPA.

Our bodies convert omega-3 fats to EPA and DHA, which in turn are converted to another essential end product called series 3 prostaglandins. In order for this to happen, we need certain vitamins and minerals. These are vitamins B_3 and B_6, biotin, vitamin C, magnesium, and calcium, so it is important to get these in the diet and from a good multivitamin and mineral supplement. We also need the fat-soluble antioxidants, vitamins E and beta carotene (which the body converts to vitamin A), so as to protect the fats once they are in the body and prevent them from becoming rancid and generating free radicals, which pro-mote aging.

Our DHA-rich brain cells are especially vulnerable to free rad-ical damage. Green tea, which contains the fat-soluble antioxi-dant epigallocatechin gallate (EGCG), is thought to be even more effective than vitamin E at protecting brain cells, while the antioxidant proanthocyanidins, which are found in red wine and red berries, also protect brain cells from free radical damage.

Fish is an excellent source of protein and it can be very quick and easy to prepare. Gentle cooking by poaching or oven-baking limits the damage done to the fats by cooking; fresh sushi is of course ideal in terms of fatty acid content. Poached organic salmon, or good old sardines on toast, with a salad of avocado, carrots, baby spinach leaves, and a vitamin-E-rich olive oil and garlic dressing is a good omega-3 meal that also contains antioxidant vitamins. Follow with a cup of green tea and a bowl of mixed berries. Who says you have to suffer to be healthy and beautiful?

≈ 12 ≈

Have a Handful of Nuts and Seeds Daily

The last secret explained why fish oils and nut and seed oils are so important if you want to stay healthy and young, and focused specifically on fish oils. This secret looks at nuts and seeds and their oils, and at what exactly you should include in your diet. Whereas fish oils contain omega-3 fats, nuts and seeds and their oils contain mainly omega-6 fats, although some are also good omega-3 sources. The two work together and should be taken in balance.

The people featured in this book do not necessarily get their essential fats in the exact "perfect" balance, which is thought to be somewhere around three times as much omega-6 as omega-3, although this varies slightly from person to person. However, they do get both types of fat in their diet roughly in balance, and they all get their omega-6 fats from sources such as nuts, seeds, plant foods, wheat germ, and soy beans (see the list on page 102 for essential fat content of these).

Of all the people in this book, the Hunzakuts are the most enthusiastic nut eaters. They do not have access to oily fish, but they get omega-3 oils from certain nuts and seeds, which is good news for vegans. Linseed paste, high in omega-3 fats, is spread over chapattis, while walnuts, also a good source of omega-3, are ground up and either put into tea or mixed with apricot kernels and mulberries to make a fulfilling, sweet cake called sultan coq (see recipes section, page 243).

The Hunzakuts get their omega-6 fats from apricot kernels, which they crack open in order to eat the almondlike nuts they contain. These are sometimes crushed and mixed with chopped onions and herbs to make a spread for chapattis. The marzipan-flavored, cloudy oil is also extracted from these nuts and kept in bottles to drink, spread on chapattis, or put on the skin and hair to keep it supple and shiny. Apricot kernel oil and almond oil, which is similar, also contain a powerful anticancer substance called vitamin B_{17} (see Secret 20, page 123).

Another very useful vegan source of both omega-3 and omega-6 fats, in the right balance, is hemp seed, which is eaten in large quantities in Bama. This versatile and delicious seed is now becoming a major commodity in health-food outlets in the West and is covered in more detail in Secret 5 (page 167).

As well as eating nuts and seeds, these long-lived people also have limited amounts of saturated fats and no or almost no trans fats or hydrogenated fats from heated and processed polyunsaturated oils. These interfere with essential fatty acid use by taking up space in the cell membrane, which means that those with a lot of bad fats in their diets need extra essential fats to compensate. In addition, the animals eaten by the long-lived people, being mainly wild game or free-range animals feeding on plant foods, contain a higher percentage of essential fats in their meat than factory-farmed animals. Essential fats should make up a minimum of one-third of your total fat intake.

We need a minimum of approximately 4 percent of total calories from omega-6 fats, which is about a tablespoon daily. You can achieve this by having either a handful of omega-6-rich nuts and seeds, or a tablespoon of their cold-pressed oils. A handful of nuts and seeds also makes a good high-protein, blood-sugar-balancing snack to have in the middle of the afternoon or with breakfast. If you choose nuts and seeds, make sure you buy them as fresh as possible, preferably in their shell, since these volatile oils go rancid quickly; old nuts are also apt to have a lot of mold on their surfaces. If you buy oils, they should come in dark, refrigerated bottles from health-food suppliers; they should not be common supermarket oils. Supplements containing both kinds of EFA are also available; consult your health practitioner or a good health-food store. The best oil you can use is almost certainly Udo's Choice Blend (see page 102).

Most North Americans eating the SAD. (Standard American Diet) have bodies that are crying out for essential fats, and will need more as an initial therapeutic dose. Udo Erasmus, expert on fats and author of *Fats That Heal, Fats That Kill*, recommends 3 grams of omega-6 fats as a minimum daily maintenance dose, 9 grams as an optimum daily maintenance dose, and up to 60 grams as a therapeutic dose where there is major deficiency. There is no known toxic dose, but you must make sure that you are not taking a lot more omega-6 fats than omega-3 fats—remember, the ratio of omega-3 to omega-6 should be 1:3. However, most North Americans have not only a deficiency in both fats but also a very imbalanced ratio of around 1:20. This means that taking more omega-3 fats for a while is likely to be necessary to correct the balance.

If you are taking both types of fat but have an imbalance, you may have symptoms of deficiency of one or the other. The previous secret lists symptoms of omega-3 deficiency. Symptoms of omega-6 deficiency include:

Dry skin and acne
Hair loss
Liver degeneration
Behavioral disturbances
Kidney disease
Water loss through skin
Drying up of glands
Male infertility
Female miscarriage
Heart problems
Poor circulation
PMS

All of these symptoms, some of which may lead eventually to serious illness, can be reversed by taking omega-6 fats.

PROTECT YOUR FATS

Once the omega-6 fats are in your body, they can cause damage unless you are eating them in conjunction with a generally healthy diet. First of all, you must make sure you get enough vitamin E and beta carotene, which are fat-soluble and will protect the omega-6 fats from going rancid and generating free radicals. You also need to make sure that your body can create the right end products from its omega-6 fats. These are hormonelike substances called type 1 prostaglandins (PGE1s), which issue instructions in the body and have an anti-inflammatory effect. In order to metabolize omega-6 fats into PGE1s, your body needs to make enzymes using certain vitamins and minerals. These are vitamin C, vitamin B_3, vitamin B_6, biotin, zinc, and magnesium.

By eating a healthy diet rich in whole plant foods and taking a multivitamin and mineral supplement, you should be able to ensure that your body uses omega-6 fats properly. If your body does not make enough PGE1s, a substance called arachidonic acid can be released in excess from cell membranes. This acts as fuel for cancer cells and creates other types of prostaglandins, called PGE2s, which promote inflammation and can therefore cause harm when present in excess.

TAKING A SHORTCUT

Some people are not good at metabolizing essential fatty acids to their desired end products. Diet should help, but there may also be other factors involved. For these people, there are certain oils on the market that provide omega-6 fats containing a high proportion of gamma-linoleic acid (GLA), so that the body does not have to make the conversion to GLA itself. These oils can therefore be of great benefit to those who cannot metabolize their essential fatty acids well. They are:

> Evening primrose oil, containing 9 percent GLA
> Black currant oil, containing 18 percent GLA
> Borage oil, containing 24 percent GLA

Many women find that taking these oils is a highly effective method of preventing symptoms of PMS. The best way for you to discover whether or not you can metabolize omega-6 fats is to try different products and see which works best for you.

The table on page 102 is a list of nuts and seeds, as well as a few other plants, with their omega-6 and omega-3 content.

GUIDE TO NUTS AND SEEDS AND THEIR OMEGA-6 AND OMEGA-3 ESSENTIAL FATTY ACIDS

Omega-3 and Omega-6 Sources:

Udo's Choice: This is a mixture of nuts and seeds containing both omega-6 and omega-3 fats in the perfect balance for the long term (but see the previous secret for why fish oils may be a better choice for omega-3 fats).

Linseed oil (otherwise known as flax oil): This oil contains four times as much omega-3 as omega-6, and is therefore useful for short-term use to correct imbalances, and in conjunction with some other nuts and seeds/oils thereafter. Having it without extra omega-6 sources can lead to symptoms of omega-6 deficiency in the long term.

Hemp: Hemp seeds and their oil contain omega-6 and omega-3 in a 3:1 ratio, which is ideal for a healthy person.

Olive oil: This oil also contains a very small amount of omega-6 and omega-3 fats (but mainly contains monounsaturated fats).

Omega-3 Sources:

Walnuts and their cold-pressed oil

Soy beans and their oil

YOUR OVERALL FAT CONSUMPTION

Your omega-6 fat consumption is part of a wider picture that is covered in various sections in this book. In summary, in order to have the right kind of fats in your body, you should aim to:

- Limit saturated fats from meat and dairy products
- Avoid trans fats and hydrogenated fats from heated vegetable

Omega-6 Sources:

Almonds
Apricot kernels
Pumpkin seeds and their cold-pressed oil
Sesame seeds and their cold-pressed oil
Sunflower seeds and their cold-pressed oil
Safflower seeds and their cold-pressed oil
Wheat germ and its cold-pressed oil
Cashews
Peanuts
Pistachios
Hazelnuts
Almond butter
Peanut butter
Hazelnut butter
Evening primrose oil
Black currant oil
Borage oil

NOTE: If you have a nut allergy, you will obviously not be able to have many of these products, so great care should be taken in choosing the ones that you can use.

oils and processed foods (such as cookies, chips, crackers and ready-made meals)
- Include monounsaturated fats from extra-virgin olive oil
- Include fish oils regularly
- Include nut and seed oils regularly
- Get omega-3 oils (mainly from fish) and omega-6 oils (mainly from nuts and seeds) in the right balance

🌿 13 🌿

Choose the Wonder Oil— Extra-Virgin Olive Oil

For people living in the Mediterranean, olive oil is a staple part of almost every meal. It is also cited by some, such as the Campodimelani and the Symiots, as their most precious health commodity. In Symi, bread is dipped in it, vegetables are cooked in it, salads are drizzled with it—even coffee is drunk with it. In Campodimele, it is poured liberally over salads and used daily in cooking by every household; soups have a dribble of olive oil poured on at the end. The oil, harvested from the olive groves all around the hill, is organic, extra-virgin, and unrefined, so that it is green and cloudy in the bottle, and full of flavor.

Extra-virgin, unrefined olive oil is unlike most vegetable oils you can buy in the supermarket because it has not been stripped of its nutrients, bleached, and heated to very high temperatures. This is because olive oil contains mainly monounsaturated fats and only a small amount of polyunsaturated fats, which gives it a long shelf life without needing to be processed. Monounsaturated fats, while not being *essential* for health like the omega-6 fats found in polyunsaturated oils, are certainly very useful in many ways.

Olive oil is your heart's friend. It carries fat-soluble vitamins E and A around the body, preventing cholesterol from oxidizing and damaging the arteries, and it raises levels of "good" HDL cholesterol, which scours excess fats out of the bloodstream. It is a "good" fat that you can eat without guilt: When cardiologist Serge

Renaud put three hundred heart-attack patients on a low-fat diet and three hundred on a traditional olive-oil-rich Cretan diet, within two years the latter group had a 75 percent lower incidence of heart attack and death than the low-fat group.

People on no-fat diets have been found to have a higher risk of cancer than others, partly because fats such as olive oil are needed to transport fat-soluble antioxidants to cells. Olive oil has some other specific anticancer properties. It promotes cell health by improving membrane development, cell formation, and cell differentiation. New research has also found that a substance called oleic acid in olive oil dramatically reduces levels of a gene called HER-2/neu, which is thought to trigger breast cancer.

Olive oil aids digestion by prompting the gall bladder to release bile, clearing undigested food particles, and lubricating the intestines. Do not worry about the calories in olive oil, because these properties will help you to eliminate excess fats, as well as toxins, from your body. Your intestines will also benefit from the antifungal properties in olive oil, which help eliminate candida overgrowth and protect "friendly" intestinal flora. Olive oil also protects the intestinal lining from harm—Symiots drink a spoonful of it neat if they are planning to go out for a boozy evening.

Your love life may even be given a boost by olive oil, as it keeps the circulation going to those all-important areas of the body. It is considered by the Greeks to be an aphrodisiac, and newlyweds traditionally ate bread soaked in the first olive oil of the year. As they say in Greece: "Eat butter and sleep tight, eat olive oil and come alive at night."

When you buy olive oil, make sure you buy the cold-pressed, extra-virgin type, which will taste best and retains most of the original nutrients of the olive. Olive oil that is not extra-virgin has been stripped of its vitamin E, which is then sold to supplements companies, who will sell it back to you in an expensive capsule.

Olive oil is one of the safest oils to use in cooking, since monounsaturated fats are less easily damaged in cooking than polyunsaturated oils. However, it is best to keep it on a low heat and add a little water or stock to keep the temperature down. The healthful properties of olive oil are best preserved when it is used raw in salad dressings, so it makes a perfect accompaniment to your anti-aging daily salad.

🦋 14 🦋

Beware of Fats in Disguise

A common thread in the diets of the long-lived populations in this book is an absence of killing fats and an abundance of healing fats. In the typical Western diet, it is the other way around, and yet many people are happily oblivious to this fact, since these fats are often "hidden" in our foods, even some foods masquerading as "healthy" foods. This is no doubt a very significant factor in the high rates of degenerative diseases we now have. With a little awareness, you can avoid these killing fats and enjoy greater health and prolonged youth.

Healing fats are the essential fatty acids from fish oils and unprocessed nut and seed oils, described in earlier secrets, as well as monounsaturated fats such as olive oil. Killing fats are saturated fats, the hard fats found in meat and dairy products, which are described in Secret 7 (page 76), and altered fats, the most sinister kind of all. These altered fats, otherwise known as trans fats and hydrogenated fats, come from processed polyunsaturated oils and make their way into many commonly eaten foods.

THE DESTRUCTION OF VEGETABLE OILS

Today's vegetable oils are so unlike food, they may as well be used as car fuel. In fact, they are—one website, www.greasecar.com, provides instructions for locating and converting waste vegetable oil to use as fuel (called biodiesel), while there are people who have converted their cars to run on free waste vegetable oil from restaurant fryers. What has happened to our oil?

Traditionally, in Europe, vegetable and nut and seed oils were extracted by using a manually operated press that did not heat or damage the volatile polyunsaturated omega-3 and omega-6 fats they contain. These oils were then delivered to local villagers fresh every few days, in small bottles, and they were used up before they had a chance to go bad. This is the way apricot kernel oil is still made in Hunza, and also how cold-pressed vegetable oils, which you can get from a health-food shop, are made.

The cheap polyunsaturated oils such as corn oil and sunflower oil sold in supermarkets today are heated to very high temperatures, refined, and even bleached, to give them a longer shelf life. The exposure to excessive amounts of heat and oxygen they undergo turns them into trans fats, which have an unnatural molecular structure in which the molecules have become twisted and rigid. This gives the oil a long shelf life, which is useful for manufacturers, but these molecules also get into our cells and sabotage their structure. These oils are also high in the free radicals we now know to cause accelerated aging and degenerative diseases such as cancer and heart disease.

Polyunsaturated oils are bad fats in disguise. They have been touted as being good for cholesterol levels, yet the steep rise in heart disease in the last century corresponded with the increased use of these cheap cooking oils. These oils would be good for heart health, if only they had not been destroyed by processing. Beware of any supermarket oil you see other than cold-pressed extra-virgin olive oil, because it has been processed in this way, and beware of these oils hidden in products such as mayonnaise or foods canned in oil.

HYDROGENATED FATS

If you do not already avoid hydrogenated fats, take a look at the labels on the packages in your pantry. You will see that "hydrogenated vegetable oils" and "partially hydrogenated vegetable oils" are in most cookies, almost all cereals aimed at your children, most chocolate, cakes, crackers, margarine, frozen meals, and ice cream. The dangers of these damaging, unnatural products are now so well known that the Food and Drug Administration is coming under pressure to ban them, although they are still waiting for more solid "evidence." The health of a few million more people may have to suffer before a ban takes effect, so make sure you are not one of those people by boycotting these products now.

Hydrogenated fats are created by adding hydrogen atoms to polyunsaturated fat molecules to make them stiffer and similar to saturated fats. They are solid or semisolid at room temperature, which makes them useful for maintaining shelf life and giving that satisfying texture to "foods" such as chewy cookies, chocolate, margarine, and ice cream. "Partially hydrogenated" vegetable oils have been put through a similar process to become trans fats. If you want to eat products such as ice cream and cookies sometimes, read the labels carefully, because you can get higher-quality brands made without these dangerous altered fats, which taste just as good, if not better. Oatmeal is one of the few cereals you can buy in the supermarket that does not contain altered fats.

You don't die from eating one french fry or bowl of ice cream, but after years of eating these and other products containing altered fats, your bodily foundations start to become shaky and vulnerable to collapse. Altered fats can also damage the DNA in our cells, which means they can harm our genes, which we then pass down to our children. Trans fats and hydrogenated fats also contribute to heart disease by promoting blood clotting and raising LDL cholesterol levels.[1] These altered fats cannot be digested or metabolized properly, and the body needs to call on its extra reserves of nutrients to process them, which depletes the vitamins and minerals we need to ward off illness.

Trans fats and hydrogenated fats are prohibited in baby foods. What does this tell you about them? They can find their way into babies just the same, through their mothers, during pregnancy and breast feeding. According to Udo Erasmus, altered fats have many harmful effects on cell membranes, brain development, the cardiovascular system, the liver, and the immune system of fetus and child.

OILS YOU CAN USE

It is important that you do include the right oils in your diet, as they are essential for good health. These oils, from fish's, nut's and seed's, and apricot kernel's oil, are described elsewhere in this book. If you must cook with oils, use monounsaturated oils such as olive oil, avocado oil, and canola oil, as these are more stable than polyunsaturated oils and are not as easily damaged by heat. Canola oil, which is popular in the U.S. and is also used in Okinawa, is probably less useful for cooking than olive oil, since it is relatively high in polyunsaturated fats and therefore more susceptible to damage from heat.

🌿 15 🌿

Use Garlic and Onions— Nature's Healers

Garlic and onions are powerful healing foods with a long history of use for all kinds of ailments. It is said that Hippocrates used garlic fumes to treat ovarian cancer, while monks in the Middle Ages chewed garlic cloves to ward off the plague. Once known as "the stinking rose," garlic is an incredible superfood that deserves all the praise it gets, and onions have very similar properties.

Health-promoting diets such as those eaten by the people featured in this book often include liberal amounts of garlic and onions, both cooked and raw. The Symiots eat garlic with everything—*tsatsiki* (a yogurt dish), fish, Greek salad, meat, and vegetables are all infused with its potent, uplifting flavor. Campodimelani use garlic to flavor every kind of dish from salad to snails, while the *scalogna*, a local variety of onion thought to be especially high in nutrients, is another favorite. The Hunzakuts use onions and garlic as a base for their stews and dhal; they also chop up raw onions and mix them with apricot kernel paste or cheese and spread them over their chapattis for a bit of extra bite.

Garlic is an all-round medicine that has been used to treat asthma, candida, colds, diabetes, high cholesterol, and high blood pressure. It is an immune-system-boosting food containing at least twelve different antioxidants, including two of the most important ones, selenium and zinc. Garlic contains a sulfur compound called S-allylmercaptocysteine, which has been found to slow the growth of prostate cancer cells in vitro. Animal studies have also shown that garlic inhibits cancerous tumors. One anticancer property of garlic is its ability to stimulate the body's own production of natural killer cells, which destroy the cancer cells we all make daily in our bodies.

Garlic and onions have antibacterial, antiviral, antifungal, and anti-inflammatory properties; garlic was used to prevent wound infections by the ancient Romans and in World War II by the Russian army. If you are suffering from any kind of infection of the digestive tract, swallowing one to four cloves of raw garlic daily is an excellent way of ridding the intestines of pathogens while leaving friendly bacteria unharmed. Studies also show that eating garlic cuts the risk of colorectal and stomach cancer by up to half.[1]

Onions help protect the heart by lowering blood pressure and preventing blood clots, and they boost the immune system. They also have powerful anticancer properties. They are rich in quercetin, an antioxidant flavonoid which blocks cancer cell promoters, and they are also high in the cancer-fighting antioxidant selenium. One study published in the *Journal of the National Cancer Institute* showed that Chinese people eating the most onions had significantly lower rates of stomach cancer than those not eating onions, with onion intake being isolated as the main difference in the diets of the two groups.[2]

Garlic and onions are a cheap and easy way to add flavor to foods that might otherwise be bland, so use them liberally. Use them for casseroles, stews, and any dish you cook with olive oil, keeping the heat low so as not to destroy the antioxidants. Use them raw in salads, salad dressings, and sandwiches. If you feel deprived without having a grilled cheese sandwich, add plenty of chopped garlic and tomatoes to make it a healthier meal. Toss your steamed vegetables in garlic and a little soy sauce or olive oil, make onion soup in winter, and add chopped onions and garlic to buckwheat noodles. Alternatively, if you feel a cold coming on or just want to give your body a boost, you can swallow a clove of raw garlic daily, chopped up.

🌿 16 🌿

Discover the Power of Crunchy Vegetables

The amazing power of cabbage came to light in the 1950s during the Cold War, when scientists, wary of nuclear attack, fed animals either beets or cabbage, and then exposed them to radiation. They found that the animals given cabbage had significantly lower death rates. At the time, it was thought that something in the beets was exacerbating the effects of the radiation. Now we know that it is actually something in cabbages that gives protection against cancer-causing agents.

That "something" consists of several compounds that are also found in other crunchy or cruciferous vegetables, otherwise known as the brassica family. The brassica family members include cabbage, broccoli, cauliflower, bok choy, kale, and Brussels sprouts. When scientists at Johns Hopkins University fed these vegetables to animals and then exposed them to a powerful carcinogen, aflatoxin, they found that the animals had a 90 percent reduction in cancer rate, as compared to the control group.[1] When we inhale, eat, or drink potential carcinogens such as cigarette smoke, exhaust fumes, barbecued meat, drugs, or alcohol, it falls to the liver to neutralize these toxins so that they cannot do harm to the body. First the liver turns them into highly reactive, even more toxic carcinogens during "phase I" of detoxification, and then it links these molecules with other molecules during "phase II" of detoxification, so that they can be safely escorted from the body in the feces or urine. The system goes wrong in many people because there are such high amounts of these toxins coming into the liver for processing. Excessive amounts of molecules created during phase I, known as "intermediate metabolites," build up in the liver, and, because the liver is too overworked to deal with them immediately, they damage the liver and also escape into the bloodstream to cause havoc in the rest of the body.

This is where crunchy vegetables come to the rescue. Compounds they contain, such as indole-3-carbinol and sulforaphane, enhance the liver's ability to deal with toxins during both phase I and phase II of detoxification. Sulforaphane also helps activate immune cells called helper T-cells to order the extermination of cancer cells by other immune cells called natural killer cells.

Brassica family vegetables also increase levels of glutathione, a vital agent of detoxification used in the liver to neutralize free radicals produced during phase I, and to render carcinogens harmless during phase II. Heavy metals such as mercury and lead, for example, depend upon glutathione in order to be eliminated from the body. Glutathione is a vitally important part of our detoxification systems; low levels are associated with accelerated aging and death.

If you react very strongly to gas and paint fumes and other chemicals, this may well be a sign that you are an "imbalanced detoxifier," meaning that your phase I of detoxification is being speeded up by these toxins, while your phase II is too slow to cope with them (phase I can be speeded up by toxins as well as by certain nutrients such as cruciferous vegetables). If this is the case, rather than eating cruciferous vegetables, try eating foods cooked with curcumin (found in the yellow-colored spice turmeric), as curcumin has the interesting property of slowing down phase I of detoxification while enhancing phase II.

You can discover how your phases I and II of liver detoxification are working by having a functional liver detoxification profile measured at a laboratory via a nutritionally aware healthcare practitioner. Your liver will be challenged with caffeine, aspirin, and acetaminophen in safe oral doses in an easy-to-do test at home. You will then be provided with comprehensive information about your liver detoxification ability as well as advice on which substances to avoid and which nutrients to include in your diet.

Crunchy vegetables, as well as enhancing liver detoxification, have many other benefits. They contain calcium and magnesium, which work together to maintain bone density and prevent osteoporosis. When kept crunchy by not overcooking, they are high in fiber, which binds with toxins and excess fats, cleanses the colon, satisfies the appetite, and helps keep the glycemic index of a meal low. When eaten raw or lightly steamed, these vegetables also provide other vitamins and minerals, including vitamin C. If you have an underactive thyroid gland, avoid eating very large amounts of raw cruciferous vegetables, since they are goitrogens, meaning that they can block uptake of iodine by the thyroid gland.

Cruciferous vegetables are grown and eaten regularly by the people described in this book, and the Okinawans, Campodimelani, and Hunzakuts all eat cabbage and cauliflower regularly in salads, lightly steamed, or in stir-fries. Buy them fresh and organic, and try steaming them and then tossing them in garlic, olive oil, and sesame seeds; incorporating them into stews; eating them raw or lightly steamed in salads; or chopping cauliflower and broccoli up and using them as crudités for dips. They should be a part of the diet of everyone who wishes to be protected from the many carcinogens in today's toxic world.

❧ 17 ❧

Keep Aging Away with a Salad a Day

The people featured in this book are all very fond of their salads. The classic Greek salad, with tomatoes, lettuce, cucumber, olives, feta cheese, onions, garlic, herbs, and capers, all drizzled with extra-virgin olive oil, appears at almost every Symiot meal. The Hunzakuts eat a large part of their diet raw, either in a salad with their famous apricot kernel oil or rinsed in a bit of glacier water and eaten on the spot. The inclusion of raw vegetables in the diets of these people is an important factor in their remarkable health and longevity. It is also practical: Why cook, when cooking removes flavor and nutrients and wastes time and fuel?

Raw vegetables are high in vitamins and minerals, as well as a very important anti-aging substance, superoxide dismutase (or SOD), all of which are depleted with cooking. Seventy-five percent of the vitamin C content of a cabbage is destroyed in boiling, and cooking plant foods in water causes important minerals such as calcium and magnesium to leach out and be lost.

Certain vitamins and minerals provide antioxidants, substances that protect us from free radicals, the rogue molecules that go rampaging through the body, damaging other molecules by oxidizing them. Medical science now accepts that free radicals are a primary cause of at least 70 percent of degenerative disease such as stroke and cardiovascular disease, as well as the process of aging itself. Eating a salad a day will help keep these diseases away.

The top five antioxidants we need are vitamin A, vitamin C,

vitamin E, selenium, and zinc. Vitamin A is made in the body from beta carotene, which is found in red and yellow fruit and vegetables, so include red and yellow peppers, carrots, and tomatoes in your salads. Beta carotene is also provided by dark green leafy vegetables such as spinach and watercress. Vitamin C is plentiful in raw cabbage, red peppers, and green salad leaves. Vitamin E is found in avocadoes and in extra-virgin olive oil. Selenium and zinc are in pumpkin seeds and sesame seeds, so use these liberally to add texture and flavor to your salads. Different colors indicate different antioxidants, and since antioxidants work best together, try to eat a range of colors in your salads.

Raw produce contains the highest-quality fiber, both soluble and insoluble. Fiber acts like a broom to sweep out the intestines, ensuring that food does not putrefy in the digestive tract. Fiber also makes you feel fuller for longer, regulates blood sugar levels, dilutes harmful substances, encourages friendly bacteria, removes carcinogens such as excess bile acids, and causes less fat to be absorbed by the body.

Raw vegetables are also rich in enzymes, the "spark plugs" that initiate every one of the millions of biochemical reactions in the body that keep us alive. We make our own enzymes from the vitamins and minerals we eat, but not enough to keep us in a state of optimum health, so we also need to get ready-made enzymes from food. Our own enzyme production drops with age, which means that the amount of enzymes each one of us has is a measure of how fast we are aging. Up to 100 percent of the enzymes in food are killed by heating.

People changing to raw food diets (including fruit and nuts and seeds, besides vegetables) have reported finding that their skin looks tighter, puffiness is removed, their eyes become clearer, and grey hair starts to grow back dark—the result of improved circulation of nutrients and removal of toxins from cells. Collagen, responsible for the elasticity of our skin, is kept in production by the vitamin C that comes with a raw food diet. Cellulite has also been found to disappear on a raw food diet, partly because raw food helps to eliminate the toxins that are linked with cellulite.

Studies show that salads and other raw food can help you to lose weight, without suffering any of the agonies and failures of going on a diet. Raw food expert Dr. John Douglass has said, "For many years I struggled with obesity and was frustrated in treating patients because nothing ever seemed to work. . . . Then I discovered the potential of uncooked foods and found that the more uncooked foods patients used, the less they wanted to eat. These foods are more satisfying for patients and they lose weight on them."[1]

Salads are quick and easy to make, and they can also be taken to the office. You can make them more satisfying by adding quinoa, brown rice, or a sweet potato. You can also add lightly steamed beans, broccoli, or asparagus for variety. In terms of antioxidant scores, some of the highest-scoring salad foods are baby leaf spinach, broccoli, beets, alfalfa sprouts, and avocado, which happen to make a delicious salad when used together. Make a dressing of extra-virgin olive oil, apple cider vinegar, and garlic. Apple cider vinegar contains many vitamins and minerals, while garlic has antifungal and antibacterial properties, and at least twelve different antioxidants, including selenium and zinc.

Try finely shredding vegetables such as cabbage, carrots, or radishes, as the Okinawans do, and serving them alongside your main meal. Or you can do as the Hunzakuts do, and make raw canapés a dietary staple. If you are having a predinner drink, instead of chips try eating chopped carrots, cauliflower, and broccoli dipped in hummus or guacamole.

🌿 18 🌿

Give Thanks for Sweet Potatoes

Sweet potatoes, also known as yams, are one of the most nutrient-packed vegetables there are. They are rich in a wide spectrum of vitamins and minerals, especially beta carotene, the antioxidant that gives them their vivid orange color. Traditionally eaten at Thanksgiving, sweet potatoes have an important place in the history of the Americas. Twenty-thousand-year-old remnants of them have been found in caves in Peru, they were grown by Native Americans, and they were farmed by George Washington. A staple crop of the southern United States, they can be baked, grilled, roasted, fried, sautéed, and used to make sweet potato pie. During the Civil War, when coffee ran out, they were even brewed to make a hot drink.

The sweet potato is eaten regularly in Bama, while its Okinawan version, a reddish-skinned vegetable called the *imo*, is revered on the island. They are so important in Okinawa that there is even an old local greeting, *nmu kamatooin*, meaning "Are you getting enough sweet potato?" There is a statue of the man, known as the Imo King, who introduced them to Okinawa from China in the 1600s, and up until World War II they were the main carbohydrate eaten. Today, white rice is starting to replace the sweet potato, and the Okinawan diet will be the poorer for it.

Sweet potatoes, with their juicy orange flesh, are not potatoes at all, but a root vegetable like the carrot. They are lower in carbohydrates than potatoes and are "allowed" on low-carbohydrate diets. They are also relatively low in calories and lower on the glycemic index than potatoes, especially when eaten with the fibrous skin.

Sweet potatoes are recommended by the National Cancer Society as an anticancer food, since they contain antioxidants including beta carotene, alpha carotene, vitamin C, lycopene, and vitamin E. They are also a valuable source of B vitamins, potassium, manganese, zinc, copper, magnesium, iron, and phosphorus.

Sweet potatoes make an excellent component of your five to seven recommended servings of fruit and vegetables daily (see Secret 2, page 53). When combined with differently colored vegetables, such as beets, baby leaf spinach, green and red peppers, tomatoes, and lettuce, they help provide the full range of antioxidants, which need to work together in order to be most effective.

Sweet potatoes are thought to aid the treatment of many illnesses, including HIV, diverticulitis, stomach and muscle cramps, asthma, vascular disease, menopausal symptoms, gallstones, and arthritis. They are higher in beta carotene than any other vegetable, with 10 milligrams per sweet potato; nutrition experts recommend an intake of 10–30 milligrams daily. Beta carotene protects cells from aging and is especially effective at preventing free radical damage from one of the more harmful free radicals, singlet oxygen. Beta carotene converts to vitamin A in the body, which helps boost immunity and protect the mucous membranes of the respiratory and digestive tracts; studies have shown that people with a high beta carotene intake are at a much lower risk of getting cancers of the mouth, throat, lung, and stomach.

Beta carotene is also found in other yellow and orange fruits and vegetables such as carrots and pumpkins, as well as dark green leafy vegetables such as spinach and watercress. The Hunzakuts do not grow sweet potatoes, but they get plenty of beta carotene from their pumpkins, carrots, and spinach. If you dislike sweet potatoes, you can substitute these or other orange and dark green vegetables instead.

The best time to get sweet potatoes is from August to October when the harvest is fresh, but try to get imported ones at other times of the year if you can. Choose organic ones so that you can eat the skin, which is rich in vitamins and minerals as well as fiber. Sweet potatoes can be used in all kinds of dishes, including salads, meat dishes, casseroles, and soups. An extra advantage the sweet potato has over the ordinary potato is that it does not act like an unquenchable sponge for soaking up butter, and it is easy to mash without having to add anything. Some sweet potato recipes are given at the back of this book.

❦ 19 ❦

Enjoy Pizza . . . Guilt Free

Some researchers believe it could be the humble tomato that is at the center of the famed good health of Mediterranean peoples such as the Greeks and Italians. Tomatoes are very popular among the Symiots and the Campodimelani, and are used in pasta sauces, stews, and soup dishes, as well as the classic Greek salad. Tomatoes are the best food source of lycopene, a powerful antioxidant which gives tomatoes their red color. It is the subject of much interest among longevity scientists, as it is an even more potent antioxidant than either beta carotene or vitamin E.

Tomatoes are perhaps best known for helping prevent prostate cancer, the most common cancer affecting men in the U.S., with more than 200,000 new cases being diagnosed each year. It usually affects men over the age of sixty-five—in other words, it is a disease of aging. Prostate cancer is, however, much less common in Mediterranean countries where a lot of tomatoes are eaten.

In a Harvard University study of almost 48,000 men, it was found that those eating ten or more servings weekly of tomatoes, tomato sauce, or pizza more were 45 percent less likely to get prostate cancer than those eating none. Pizzas appeared to be the most protective; this is thought to be because lycopene is a fat-soluble antioxidant, and the oil and cheese in pizza help transport it to our cells. Cooking tomatoes also enhances the absorption of lycopene by breaking down the cell walls in tomatoes; tomato ketchup and tomato paste are also good sources of lycopene. For some reason, in this study at least, tomato juice did not appear to be protective.[1]

The study leader, Dr. Edward Giovanucci, concluded that it is the lycopene in tomatoes that has this protective effect, since the men without prostate cancer had more lycopene than beta carotene in their blood, and it is known to be more powerful than beta carotene as an antioxidant. It is also thought that lycopene may be preferentially deposited in the prostate gland. Incidentally, it is also deposited in the liver, lung, colon, and skin, and ongoing research indicates that lycopene does indeed protect against cancers of the lung and gastrointestinal tract. One study has also shown that it protects against cervical cancer in women.[2]

Lycopene may also have other anti-aging benefits. It is thought to protect against heart disease, as it prevents cholesterol from oxidizing and damaging arteries. It may also protect the brain from aging. In the 1986 "Nun Study" led by Dr. David Snowden at the University of Kentucky, it was found that elderly women with the lowest levels of lycopene in their blood were the least able to perform mental and physical tasks, such as getting dressed and using the bathroom, without help.

Tomatoes are the only reliable source of lycopene, although it can also be found in other red and pink fruits and vegetables, such as guava, watermelon, pink grapefruit, and red peppers. However, if you do not eat tomatoes regularly, you are unlikely to be getting protective levels of lycopene. Within just one day of eating tomato products, your blood levels of lycopene will rise considerably, although lycopene cannot be stored for long periods of time, so you need to eat them regularly.

Lycopene is available in supplement form, but it is thought that supplements probably do not have the protective effect of tomatoes. This may be because tomato contains other nutrients, such as the antioxidants vitamin C and glutathione, or it could have to do with the way tomatoes are cooked. Tomatoes also contain *p*-coumaric acid and chlorogenic acid, which block the formation of carcinogenic nitrosamines. These nitrosamines are made in the body from nitrites, common preservatives found in many foods, and nitrates, natural chemicals found in food. Preserved meats such as salami are especially high in nitrites, but if you love ham and salami, eating tomatoes with them will help limit the damage.

Tomatoes are a member of the nightshade family, along with peppers, eggplant, and potatoes, and may not be suitable for those with arthritis, since they contain a substance called solanine, which can aggravate pain in the joints. If you can eat tomatoes, however, have them regularly in the form of tomato sauce, casseroles, tomato soup, tomato salad with an olive oil dressing, tarts, and, occasionally, a guilt-free pizza. You can also make your own healthy version of pizza at home, using a whole-wheat or other whole-grain base and plenty of vegetables, herbs, and olive oil, along with tomatoes and tomato paste—and go easy on the cheese.

❧ 20 ❧

Snack on
Apricots and Apricot Kernels

Hunza would not be Hunza without its apricots, which is why it is sometimes called "the land where the apricot is king." Apricot trees grow everywhere, filling the valley with pink blossoms in the summer. Every family owns several apricot trees, and when a girl gets married, she is often given a tree as a gift by her parents. During the harvest, thousands of apricots are spread out over the flat roofs to dry, adding bright orange patches to the pink and green landscape.

Apricots often form a meal of their own, and apricot-eating competitions are frequently held, with, it is claimed, up to a hundred being eaten at once. In the summer, during apricot season, apricots are eaten as they are, cooked in soup, or pureed with glacier water to make apricot smoothies. They are also made into jam, which is spread on whole-wheat bread and eaten for breakfast. Apricots are stored over the winter so that people can carry on eating them with everything—even pureed with snow to make ice cream.

Fresh apricots are a rich source of copper, iron, potassium, fiber, and anticancer beta carotene, and when they are dried the nutrient level is even greater. However, it may be in the apricot kernel, rather than the fruit itself, that the real secret of Hunzakut longevity lies. Resembling and tasting like small almonds, the kernels are a rich source of essential fatty acids. They are eaten by the handful or ground up with other nuts to make a delicious nut spread or a paste for curries. Hunzakuts also crack them open to extract the oil, which has a delectable marzipan-like taste and is used to make salad dressings, spread over cooked chapattis, or drunk on its own. The women also put it on their hair and skin to keep them shiny and soft.

Apricot kernels are the best known source of vitamin B_{17}, otherwise known as laetrile, which some speculate to be an effective anticancer agent. However, laetrile's healthful properties are very controversial and it should be treated with caution.

While it is used in alternative clinics today as a treatment for cancer, Laetrile currently is banned for use by the Food and Drug Administration due to many controversial beliefs about possible toxicity, since one of the active anticancer compounds in laetrile is cyanide. There are as yet no large-scale studies of the effects of laetrile on human beings, which is thought by its supporters to be due to anti-laetrile information from the chemotherapy industry.

Vitamin B_{17} is in fact present in small amounts in many commonlyeaten plant foods including macadamia nuts, walnuts, pecans, lima beans, kidney beans, sweet potatoes, yams, linseed, buckwheat, brown rice, millet, maize, sprouted beans, alfalfa sprouts, bamboo shoots, beet tops, cashews, fava beans, garbanzo beans, lentils, huckleberries, strawberries, blackberries, cranberries, spinach, and watercress. These, along with apricots, contain many anti-aging substances including fiber as well as vitamins and minerals, and are in all ways excellent foods to include in your anti-aging diet.

Make apricots a regular snack to enjoy between meals instead of chocolate or chips. The bright orange apricots available in the West have usually been treated with preservatives, but fleshy, dark orange, organic apricots, with a wonderful texture and flavor, are now also sold. Apricot kernels are also sold in some health food outlets, and either these or fresh almonds can be eaten with a handful of apricots to add protein and essential fats. Dried apricots can also be chopped up and added to porridge or muesli, or you can blend them in a smoothie or eat them fresh when in season.

❧ 21 ❧

Find Long Life in a Bowl of Berries

One of the best ways to keep aging away is to eat food that is high in antioxidants, and one of the most powerful foods in this respect is the blueberry. Blueberries, like other highly colored berries (e.g., cranberries, bilberries, blackberries, strawberries, cherries, raspberries, mulberries, and boysenberries, as well as red grapes) contain very superior antioxidants called anthocyanins and proanthocyanidins. These are eighteen times more effective even than vitamin C at scavenging pro-aging free radicals, and fifty times more potent than vitamin E. They are also capable of acting both as water-soluble antioxidants, like vitamin C, and fat-soluble ones, like vitamin E, thus protecting both fatty and watery parts of the body.

Members of the bioflavonoid family, anthocyanins and proanthocyanidins give certain foods their blue and red color—the richer the color, the more antioxidant protection you are getting. Blueberries come third on the ORAC (Oxygen Radical Absorbance Capacity) score, a measure of antioxidant power devised by researchers at Tufts University.

The Tufts researchers recommend that we aim for 3,500–6,000

THE TOP SEVEN ANTIOXIDANT FOODS
AND THEIR ORAC SCORES ARE:

Food	ORAC score per 100g (approx. 4 oz)
Prunes	5,770
Raisins	2,830
Blueberries	2,234
Blackberries	2,036
Kale	1,770
Cranberries	1,750
Strawberries	1,536

units daily, so if you eat a cup of blueberries and a few prunes plus your five to seven servings of vegetables, you are getting an excellent dose of anti-aging antioxidants for the day. In one USDA study, rats fed a few blueberries daily showed fewer signs of mental or physical aging than the control group.

A remarkable effect of proanthocyanidins is that, unlike most other antioxidants, they are able to cross the blood-brain barrier so as to protect cells in the brain and nervous system from free-radical damage. It is thought that proanthocyanidins may be an exciting way forward in the treatment of Parkinson's and diseases of the nervous system such as multiple sclerosis.

Proanthocyanidins also strengthen blood vessel walls so that nutrients can be taken to cells. They are excellent for eye health because of the tiny blood vessels in our eyes; it is said that World War II pilots in Britain prepared themselves for night flights by eating bilberry jam the night before, for good night vision. If you bruise easily or your gums bleed when you brush your teeth, try eating berries.

Berries (including cranberries and blueberries) and cherries also contain a compound called ellagic acid, which causes cancer cells to self-destruct, in a process called apoptosis. In one study, Japanese researchers gave rats a powerful carcinogen to induce tongue cancer, and then gave the rats either polyphenols (a class of plant substances to which proanthocyanidins and anthocyanins belong), ellagic acid, or no protection. The first group had a much lower rate of cancer than the rats given nothing, but the rats given ellagic acid *got no cancer at all*. In another study conducted at Harvard University, it was found that men who eat the most strawberries are at the lowest risk of developing prostate cancer. In berries and cherries you get not only both ellagic acid and proanthocyanidins but also vitamin C and fiber, and possibly some as yet unknown anticancer compounds.

The Hunzakuts get their daily dose of all these from a dense cake called sultan coq (see recipes section, page 243) made out of ground mulberries and walnuts, both of which contain ellagic acid. Hunza has always been famous for its absence of cancer, and it may well be that sultan coq deserves part of the credit for this. Grape seeds, found in the grapes grown in Campodimele and Symi, also contain proanthocyanidins. Grape seed extract is sold in the West in health-food shops, but if you don't mind eating a few grape seeds, then you know now that there is no need to spit them out or to buy the seedless variety of grape.

It is best to buy berries when they are in season; try to buy locally grown berries if you can, since these are less likely to have been picked when they are unripe, which lowers their antioxidant value. You can buy them the rest of the year as well, or stock up on seasonal ones and keep them in the freezer. Organic berries are also best since they tend to be higher in nutrients, as well as having fewer or no pesticide residues. Eat them on their own by the handful, with your breakfast, in a yogurt smoothie, in a fruit salad, in baking, or even, as is fashionable today, in a blueberry burger, and treat yourself every day.

🌿 22 🌿

Have Yogurt for Very Friendly Bacteria

Yogurt is a common remedy for diarrhea, and it's good in a smoothie. But did you know it may also help prevent rheumatoid arthritis, multiple sclerosis, mental illness, cancer, and accelerated aging? Live yogurt is teeming with beneficial bacteria which it is essential to have in your digestive tract; otherwise, toxicity and illness become almost inevitable. Good health starts in the intestines, and good intestinal health starts with good bacteria, otherwise known as probiotics ("for life").

Most people are familiar with *Lactobacillus acidophilus* and *bifidobacterium*, the "friendly" bacteria found in live yogurt, although many other strains exist, all with their own beneficial properties. *Lactobacillus bulgaricus* was named by Dr. Ilya Metchnikoff, a Russian scientist and 1908 Nobel Prize winner credited with linking yogurt consumption with longevity after studying long-lived, yogurt-loving Bulgarian peasants. Metchnikoff found that yogurt can prevent bacterial infection and reduce levels of toxins produced by our own bodies.

Live yogurt is part of the traditional Symi diet. One resident of Symi, who died at 107, was still going up and down the 387 steep steps of the village selling her yogurt when she was 100 years old. Made from organic local cow's milk, Symi yogurt is not low-fat, but it is free of sugar, thickeners, and additives. It is eaten either on its own or blended with cucumber and plenty of raw garlic to make tsatsiki. (To make your own tsatsiki, see the recipes section, page 243.)

Yogurt is also eaten in Hunza, either as it is or blended with water to make a yogurt drink called *diltar*, otherwise known as lassi or buttermilk. Traditionally, lassi was prepared by filling a goatskin container with the milk, then rolling the container on the ground to make butter and a watery buttermilk, which was then poured off for drinking. You, however, can put yogurt and water in a blender, which will have a similar effect.

When the stools of Bama elders aged 80 to 109 years old were analyzed by Zhang Yan et al. in 1994, it was found that *bifidobacterium* constituted 53 to 87 percent of the total stool bacteria—significantly more than in the elderly population of other nearby districts. The Bama people's healthy *bifidobacterium* populations are encouraged by a diet high in fibrous foods such as grains, fruit, and vegetables, as these provide fuel for such bacteria (see page 132).

Almost half of our immune cells reside in our intestines, so the good intestinal health that beneficial bacteria provide helps give us immunity against all kinds of illness, including infectious diseases and autoimmune illnesses (such as multiple sclerosis and rheumatoid arthritis). If all your intestinal bacteria, good and bad, died today, you would lose a few pounds, since we have a huge amount—we have the same number of intestinal bacteria as body cells.

Beneficial bacteria perform the following functions:

- Manufacture B vitamins and vitamin K
- Produce enzymes to digest milk products
- Extract calcium from milk
- Aid digestion of proteins, sugars, and fibers
- Aid absorption of nutrients such as vitamins and minerals
- Lower intestinal pH so as to deter putrefactive bacteria
- Produce substances such as hydrogen peroxide to kill pathogens
- Aid detoxification and digest endotoxins produced in the body

- Deactivate nitrites in the digestive tract before they can become carcinogenic
- Produce antibiotics that selectively harm only pathogens
- Kill the *Shigella* bacteria, which cause dysentery
- Rid the intestinal tract of salmonella
- Act as an antifungal; reduce levels of candida
- Help prevent allergies
- Aid intestinal motility to prevent constipation
- Help rid the body of excess cholesterol
- Manufacture essential fatty acids
- Help prevent vaginal and urinary tract infections
- Establish good health and digestion in babies
- Produce butyric acid, which is used as fuel for the colon
- Produce lactic acid, which inhibits pathogens
- Some strains have antitumor effects

Many of us living a Western lifestyle have an imbalance in our intestinal flora, known as "dysbiosis." Dysbiosis means that levels of friendly bacteria are low, leaving space for pathogens and yeasts to take over. These create toxins and damage the intestinal lining, causing the syndrome known as "leaky gut," in which improperly digested food particles escape into the bloodstream, causing allergic reactions and toxicity. Leaky gut is linked with Crohn's disease, colitis, and irritable bowel syndrome. Signs of possible dysbiosis include food intolerance, immune dysfunction, constipation, diarrhea, eczema, allergies, arthritis, and migraine. Even mental illness, including autism, has been linked to dysbiosis.

Candida is a yeast that, when levels of good bacteria are low, overpopulates the intestinal tract and produces toxins that cause shakiness, exhaustion, and depression. Candida infection is thought by some doctors to be extremely common. When levels of good bacteria are low, it is also much easier for pathogenic bacteria from food to cause gastrointestinal upsets—if you get stomach problems easily when traveling abroad, this may indicate dysbiosis.

Diet and lifestyle factors that kill beneficial bacteria and encourage harmful bacteria will cause dysbiosis. Causes of intestinal dysbiosis include:

- Antibiotics, which devastate good bacteria
- Infant formula (although some now contain probiotics)
- A high-sugar/high-alcohol diet, which encourages candida
- A high-animal-protein, fatty diet, as this encourages putrefactive (bad) bacteria
- Long-distance air travel
- Stress

INFANTS AND PROBIOTICS

The time to start populating your intestinal tract is in infancy. A breast-fed baby should have good levels of friendly bacteria, although this is less the case today than it was several decades ago, due to the high levels of toxins in our environment. If you are pregnant or lactating, eating a probiotic-promoting diet and taking a good probiotic supplement may be necessary.

The strains of bacteria that are ideally at high levels in the infant's digestive tract are *Bifidus infantum* and *B. bifidum*, both of which can be taken by the mother as supplements (see page 132). *Bifidus infantum* can also be dusted onto the nipples before a feed. Bottle-fed babies have much lower levels of beneficial bacteria in their intestines and their diet should be supplemented with *Bifidus infantum*; this is best done with the advice of a nutrition practitioner who is experienced in infant care. The state of an infant's intestinal ecology has been found in studies to be a reliable predictor of whether or not it will develop allergies as a child.

YOGURT

Yogurt is easier to digest than other dairy products, since the bacteria help to digest lactose, the milk sugar that can cause digestive problems. Yogurt is also the only dairy product that is not acid-forming in the body. This makes it a better source of calcium than other dairy products, since acid-forming foods can cause the bones to release calcium in order to buffer acidic blood. The best live yogurt is made with *Streptococcus thermophilus* and *Lactobacillus bulgaricus* in a ratio of seven to one, which makes a smooth creamy yogurt, but there are other beneficial yogurts available. Avoid those containing sugar, and choose those that specify the use of live bacteria on the label. The yogurt should not contain stabilizers or additives, and avoid any which have been pasteurized after the addition of live cultures, since pasteurization kills the friendly bacteria.

FEEDING YOUR FRIENDLY BACTERIA

To promote friendly bacteria in your digestive tract, you need to feed them their favorite food. They like fructooligosaccharides (FOS) and inulin, types of fiber found in bananas, Jerusalem artichokes, asparagus, onions, chicory, garlic, leeks, fruit, soybeans, whole wheat, and rye. Keep to a diet low on the glycemic index (see Secret 31, page 160) and high in fiber, since friendly bacteria also thrive in a world of fast-moving stools. They also need essential fatty acids from fish oils and nut and seed oils, since these enable them to cling to the intestinal mucosa. Avoid excessive amounts of animal protein, saturated fats, and sugar, which feed harmful, putrefactive bacteria and create toxicity in the body.

SUPPLEMENTS

Yogurt and FOS will maintain good levels of bacteria in an already healthy digestive tract, but if you have dysbiosis, as many people do, probiotic supplements are the best way to redress the balance. A good one will contain around a billion *Lactobacilli acidophilus* and *bifidobacteria* per capsule, will not be centrifuged, and will have a guaranteed potency date. These are quite powerful and may be best taken with the advice of a nutrition practitioner—there is such a thing as too much "good bacteria," which can cause excessive fermentation and gas. Probiotic supplements are particularly useful for getting rid of candida. You can also take them for a short period when traveling abroad, when stomach upsets are more likely.

WHICH STRAINS?

The best yogurts contain a mixture of *Streptococcus thermophilus* and *Lactobacillus bulgaricus*, as mentioned earlier. Other superior strains found in supplements and yogurts are *Lactobacillus acidophilus*, *Lactobacillus bulgaricus*, and *bifidobacterium bifidum*. *Lactobacillus acidophilus* and *Lactobacillus bulgaricus* fight for space within a product, with the acidophilus losing, so should not be used together. The intestine of a healthy infant will contain high levels of *Bifidobacterium infantis*, which is also found in the human vagina and should be swallowed by the baby on its way down the birth canal.

OTHER BACTERIA-CONTAINING FOODS

Other fermented foods, such as sauerkraut, miso, and pickled vegetables, also provide a variety of strains of beneficial bacteria and can form a valuable part of the anti-aging diet; these are discussed in the next secret.

🌾 23 🌿

Eat Fermented Foods

In the days before sterilization and refrigeration, one of the ways to preserve food was to put some nice friendly bacteria in it, such as the lactoacidophilus found in yogurt, in order to ward off any invading putrefactive bacteria that might rot the food. This technique not only allows the food to keep for months or years, but it also has the side benefits of enhancing flavor and greatly increasing the nutrient content of foods.

Dairy products such as yogurt and cheese are examples of fermented foods, but there are also many nondairy fermented foods. Sauerkraut and miso are two of the best known of these. Sauerkraut, or pickled cabbage, is thought to have been made in China as far back as six thousand years ago. The thirteenth-century Mongol leader Genghis Khan is said to have fed fermented vegetables to his plundering hordes to keep them strong. Captain Cook gave them to his sailors, thus protecting them from scurvy, a deadly disease that could ruin a round-the-world voyage in those days. Pickled vegetables are commonly eaten in Asian and Central European countries today, and cheeses and yogurts are popular in Western Europe.

The traditional diets of many long-lived people contain fermented foods. The mainland Japanese and the Okinawans eat them on a daily basis. Fermented soy products such as miso, tempeh, and soy sauce are common, and it is rare that you will find a meal without a pickled delicacy such as an *umeboshi* (pickled plum) accompanying it. The Okinawans are one-up on the rest of the Japanese in that they also eat special fermented tofu, which is easier to digest and higher in nutrients than ordinary tofu (see Secret 24, page 138). Fermented soy products are especially rich in the isoflavone aglycones, genistein, and daidzein, natural plant compounds that are thought to prevent cancer and are the subject of much interest amongst anticancer researchers today.

Capers are an important part of the Symiot version of the Greek salad. The sharp piquant taste of capers is an excellent addition to salads, olives, and rabbit and fish dishes; Symiots also sometimes eat them on their own, including the little stalk and leaves. Capers are used as a folk remedy for stomach ailments in Greece and are thought to promote longevity. Agapios Monachos, a Cretan monk writing in the fifteenth century, wrote of the caper, "It cures the spleen, destroys vermin, heals the hemorrhoids, increases the vitality of the sperm, cures liver ailments and cramps, mobilizes the urinary bladder, facilitates menstruation, and prevents rheumatism," and recommended eating one before each meal.

The Hunzakuts include fermented food products in their diet, since they do not have refrigeration or supermarkets. As well as ripened cheese, they also make *maltash*, a butter that is churned from milk and then carefully wrapped in birch bark and buried in a hole in the ground. Locals claim that they leave it there for decades or even a hundred years, until the head of the family (who was presumably around when it was first buried and can remember where it was put) decides the time is ripe to dig it out. Maltash is a much-prized commodity that was once used as currency and is still used for taxes; it is also given as a gift at weddings, funerals, and births. The nearest food to maltash in the West is probably an aged French cheese, so you don't have to travel to the Karakoram mountains of Pakistan to eat this pungent, smelly food.

Today in the West, traditionally fermented foods are making a comeback, since they are so helpful for treating common digestive disorders such as bloating, constipation, diarrhea, and irritable bowel syndrome. The beneficial bacteria in yogurt and fermented foods are crucial to the health of our digestive systems and, hence, to us.

Fermented foods are produced by adding bacteria, yeasts, or molds to the foods. These can be produced in laboratories, but are also found in the environment—the ancient Bulgarians put their milk in lambskin bags in order to introduce friendly bacteria, and today's Bulgarian scientists obtain their national pride, a bacterium called *bulgaricus*, from soil, tree bark, and anthills.

These organisms partially digest the proteins, carbohydrates, and fats in the food, thus making them much easier for us to assimilate. The fermenting process also greatly enhances the bioavailability of vitamins (especially vitamins C and B_{12}), minerals (such as calcium), and essential fatty acids in the food. This may be one reason that the Hunzakuts seem to get adequate omega-3 fatty acids from their diet, despite their lack of oily fish. Fermented foods can therefore be a good addition to a vegetarian or vegan diet.

The bacteria in these foods also help us to colonize our own intestines with the "friendly bacteria" that are so essential to our own health. These bacteria protect the intestinal lining, boost the immune system, produce enzymes to digest foods, produce anti-tumor, antibiotic, and antiviral substances, and help prevent gastrointestinal disorders such as diarrhea. Fermented foods also contain powerful anticancer substances called isothiocyanates.

If you suffer from digestive problems, eating fermented foods will help to heal your digestive tract, and if you don't, eating them will still benefit your health. On page 137 is a list of common fermented foods. Make sure that you buy traditionally lacto-fermented varieties, such as the marinated vegetables found in specialist delicatessens and in the refrigerated sections of health-food shops. Some pickled foods are mass-produced and will not contain the beneficial bacteria you need—for example, traditional marinated Greek olives from a delicatessen will be different from the cheaper kind bought in a jar. If in doubt, consult your retailer about the manufacturing process used.

Common Fermented Foods:

- Sauerkraut
- Yogurt
- Kefir (a fermented milk drink)
- Tempeh
- Miso
- Aged cheese
- Aged, seasoned French sausages
- Salt-pickled sea urchins (from Japan)
- Marinated artichokes
- Marinated peppers
- Capers
- Marinated mushrooms
- Marinated olives—the traditional Greek kind
- Crème fraiche
- Pickles
- Sourdough bread
- Umeboshi plums
- Traditionally brewed soy sauce
- Traditionally brewed vinegar
- Nam-pla (Thai fish sauce)
- Wine, beer

CONTRAINDICATIONS

If you suffer from candida (an overgrowth of yeast), fermented foods are best avoided, since they can contain yeasts and molds. It is not known whether eating fermented foods will make the candida worse, but your body may have become sensitive to yeast or mold, and you may experience a mild allergic reaction.

Many fermented and pickled foods are also high in salt, so are best avoided by those who have high blood pressure or cannot have salt for other reasons. It is thought that highly salted foods may raise the risk of stomach cancer, which is much more common in Asia than in the West. However, the Okinawans have a low incidence of stomach cancer, and they eat fermented foods. Bear in mind that fermented foods have a place in a generally nutritious diet, and it is best to choose the less salty ones.

🌿 24 🌿

Choose Soy—
the Traditional Way

Soy—the celebrated bean, and the subject of some controversial press. Should we be eating it or not, and if so, how much and in what form? The people of Bama eat soy regularly, in the form of tofu, while the Okinawans eat a lot of soy—around three ounces a day, which means they are probably the biggest soy eaters in the world. The Okinawans are also the longest-lived, healthiest people in the world. Is there a link? The majority of scientific evidence suggests that there is.

Soy is available in several forms: tofu (bean curd), miso, soy sauce, tempeh, edamame, and soy milk. Miso is a fermented soy product that is extra-high in beneficial nutrients due to the fermentation process, as noted in the previous secret. Unlike other

Japanese, the Okinawans also eat *tofu-yo*, a Chinese-style delicacy made from tofu fermented for three to four months in alcoholic *awamori*. Tofu-yo was originally consumed only by the upper classes, who guarded their recipe closely. However, when the ladies of Tsuji, the red-light district, discovered how to make it, tofu-yo's popularity spread across the rest of the islands. Now it is used as a side dish, with a single treasured cube being placed on a small plate and nibbled at with chopsticks. Tofu-yo has a mellow flavor and a melt-in-the-mouth texture, and it is thought to have medicinal properties.

Soy is largely credited with the extremely low rates of breast cancer in soy-eating Asian populations. Breast cancer is very common in Western populations, and the incidence is also increasing among men. One reason for this is that many of us have a lot of excess estrogen circulating in our bodies as a result of a high-fat, low-fiber diet. Soy contains plant estrogens called phytoestrogens that bind to our estrogen receptors to stop our own much stronger estrogen from taking effect. As some breast cancers use estrogen to grow, this would partly explain the anti-cancer effect of soy. Women who eat soy regularly also have fewer other hormone-related problems such as PMS and polycystic ovarian syndrome.[1]

Soy keeps your heart young in several ways. It contains antioxidants that protect blood vessels by preventing the oxidation of "bad" LDL cholesterol; it also lowers LDL cholesterol levels.[2] Isoflavones in soy strengthen blood vessels and inhibit the development of atherosclerosis.[3] Soy also contains vitamin E, which prevents blood from clotting, as well as lecithin, the fat-digesting enzyme. Two of the amino acids in soy, glycine and arginine, keep the heart and blood vessels young by regulating pro-aging blood sugar and insulin levels. Soy also contains heart-friendly omega-3 and omega-6 fatty acids.

Soy seems to protect against osteoporosis, of which there is a very low incidence in Okinawa, Bama, and other soy-eating areas. The phytoestrogens in soy help to counteract the lack of estrogen that is responsible for the sudden loss of bone density in postmenopausal women. Soy also contains both calcium and magnesium, which are needed together for good bone density.[4]

Soy occasionally gets some bad press. It contains phytates, which block the uptake of certain minerals such as calcium and magnesium. However, eating soy with seaweed and fish reduces the phytate effect as well as increasing the amount of minerals eaten. Eating fermented soy products should not be a problem, as these are much lower in phytates. Other studies have shown that soy beans have some toxic properties and may be harmful when eaten in large amounts. However, these findings were based on tests in which rats were given large amounts of soy and little or nothing else, whereas Okinawans and people in Bama eat moderate amounts *as part of a nutrient-rich, well-balanced diet.*

One recent study found that Japanese men in Hawaii who ate two or more servings of tofu per week experienced more brain aging than those who did not. However, elderly Okinawan men have been found to have exceptionally able brains; perhaps, again, more studies need to be done on soy within the context of the rest of the diet. Another possible problem with soy is that when consumed in amounts over 30 grams daily (just over an ounce) it may weaken thyroid function, according to some studies.

Finally, soy is a relatively common allergen, especially in the West, possibly because non-Asian Westerners have not evolved with it as part of their diet. Soy formula for babies and soy products for children should be used with caution, partly because of the risk of allergies, and also because there is currently some speculation that if soy is eaten in large amounts, the phytoestrogens it contains may affect the sexual development of children.

Soy, therefore, may have some possible drawbacks, although the balance would seem to swing heavily in its favor. The drawbacks may depend on what type of soy you are eating. There is a big difference between the processed, chemically enhanced GM soy products used in ready-made meals in the U.S. and traditional types of soy used in China and Japan. Fermented soy products, which include miso, natto, tempeh, and fermented soy milk, are especially beneficial, since the fermenting process greatly enhances their digestibility. The fermenting process also converts the isoflavone precursors, genistein and daidzein, to their active, anticancer forms.

When buying soy sauce, choose the traditionally brewed kind, which contains beneficial microbes such as acidophilus and usually has less salt. Ordinary unfermented tofu and soy milk also have their benefits, and are easy to use in cooking. Add organic, GM-free tofu to stir fries and rice or noodle dishes; soy milk can be used with breakfast oats or in a smoothie with fruit and yogurt. As with all foods, remember that soy should be enjoyed in moderation and within the context of an overall balanced diet.

❧ 25 ☙

Sprout Your Own Superfoods

Sprouted beans and seeds are a favorite of health food enthusiasts and long-lived people alike. Sprouts are plants at their most nutritionally rich, since they contain everything a seed needs in order to grow into a healthy plant. The sprout is a little powerhouse of living vitality, and when you eat it, that vitality goes into you.

When sprouted, the nutrient content of beans and seeds increases several-fold to enable germination to take place. The resulting plant is very rich in enzymes, vitamins, minerals, trace minerals, amino acids, protein, essential fatty acids, and other nutrients. Some micronutrients, such as vitamin B2, are multiplied by up to 2,000 percent. Because enzymes are released in the soaking process, nutrients are partially broken down into their constituent parts, such as amino acids from protein, so our bodies absorb high levels of nutrients with minimum effort. We also get a good dose of important enzymes such as superoxide dismutase, the powerful anti-aging antioxidant enzyme.

Sprouts are almost a complete food. The list of micronutrients they contain resembles the label on a multivitamin jar: beta carotene, vitamin C, vitamin E, B complex vitamins, vitamin K, vitamin B_{17}, calcium, magnesium, potassium, phosphorus, selenium, manganese, chromium, iron, zinc, and germanium are all in there. The sprouting process also reduces levels of phytic acid, a substance that in unsprouted grains and beans can inhibit our absorption of certain minerals such as zinc.

Sprouts have anticancer properties, including their antioxidant and chlorophyll content. When Dr. Chiu-Nan Lai at the University of Texas Systems Cancer Center exposed bacteria to carcinogens, cancer was inhibited by 99 percent if extracts from wheat, mung bean, and lentil sprouts were used. Sprouts also contain RNA and DNA, nucleic acids that are necessary for proper cell division. In addition, they are high in fiber, to keep the digestive tract toxin-free, and they increase levels of lecithin to break down fats in the body.

Sprouting is traditionally an important part of the Hunza diet. Sprouting requires no fuel, and makes a fulfilling salad with very little preparation. Seeds and legumes used for sprouting are soy beans, alfalfa seeds, lentils, green peas, lima beans, and barley. Wheat is also sprouted to make a special type of bread (see Secret 4, page 66). Sprouting is also acceptable on the hunter-gatherer diet, thought to be the most compatible with our body chemistry, since sprouts are foods that occur in nature and can be gathered and eaten as they are.

As with most foods, sprouts should not be overeaten, but should form part of a balanced diet in which a little of everything is eaten. Do not eat more than one or two cups of sprouts a day, as some contain a substance called L-canavanine, an amino acid that can suppress the immune system. If you have cancer or suppressed immunity, avoid alfalfa sprouts in particular because of their L-canavanine content. Alfalfa sprouts can also cause joint pain, and have been implicated in causing arthritis.

Sprouting is extremely cheap and it is easy to do at home, or you can buy sprouts from the refrigerator section in a supermarket or health-food store. To make your own, just soak your chosen seeds in mineral water or distilled water overnight, rinse them, and put them in a sprouting tray or sieve. Place them in a well-lit spot, ideally at a temperature between 64 and 72°F (18 and 22°C). Rinse them twice a day by dousing with water or by putting them in a bowl of water then draining them. After three to five days, the sprouts will be long enough to harvest and eat in a salad with your favorite dressing, or to throw into a stir-fry or curry.

🌿 26 🌿

Eat Magical Mushrooms

Would you like some *Grifola frondosa*, full of D-fraction, in your stir-fry? Say yes, because this mushroom, commonly known as the maitake, adds some powerful anticancer substances, as well as a subtle, distinctive flavor, to your dinner. Maitake and other similar Asian mushrooms, such as shiitake and reishi mushrooms, are used extensively in Chinese and Japanese cooking. They have been used for centuries to treat a range of illnesses, and are the subject of much interest among Japanese scientists due to their ability to dramatically reduce tumor growth.

The Japanese word *maitake* literally means "dancing mushroom," supposedly because people would dance for joy when they found one growing on the hillside. The mushrooms were greatly valued for their taste as well as their medicinal properties, and they could be exchanged for silver. Maitake mushrooms contain polysaccharides called beta-glucans, which give a profound, long-term boost to the immune system. When D-fraction, a combination of two types of beta-glucan, was given to cancer patients, their natural killer cells, which kill tumor cells, were increased for a year. The same researchers found that D-fraction "markedly" suppressed the growth of tumors in mice, and that natural killer cells were still being activated three weeks after the treatment was given.[1] D-fraction has also been found to alleviate the unpleasant side effects of chemotherapy.

Maitake mushrooms also contain a polysaccharide known as X-fraction, which can reduce insulin resistance, a part of the diabetic profile; this means that maitake can reduce levels of pro-aging insulin and glucose that are circulating in the bloodstream, and enable them to be properly used by our cells. Maitake has other health benefits, too: Japanese doctors use it to lower blood pressure and blood lipids, thus improving heart health, and it is also used to treat stomach ailments, since it improves digestion.

The shiitake mushroom, used for centuries in China and Japan, has a long history of use as folk medicine. In Okinawa, it is used to treat coughs and heart disease, since it contains an amino acid that helps reduce cholesterol levels. Shiitake mushrooms are also high in anticancer vitamin D, with 840 IU (international units) per 100 grams.

Like maitake, shiitake mushrooms contain beneficial polysaccharides, in particular one called lentinan. Lentinan is a very powerful immune booster, and is used widely in Japan as a highly effective antitumor medicine. It boosts the power of macrophages, the "Pac-men" of our immune systems, which circulate in our bloodstreams gobbling unwanted bodies such as cancer cells. The immunity-enhancing properties of shiitake have also made it the cause of much excitement among AIDS researchers, and there have been some positive results so far in studies on AIDS patients. It is thought that shiitake may be as effective in reducing HIV-infected cells as the commonly used drug AZT, only without the side effects.

Shiitake literally means "oak mushroom," since it was traditionally hand-harvested from fallen oak logs. Today, the mushroom is widely cultivated in Japan due to a high demand. It is also grown in North America, and you can buy organic shiitake mushrooms in many health-food shops. Alternatively, if you feel ambitious, you can buy a "shiitake grow-log" and grow your own.

The reishi mushroom is a Chinese mushroom otherwise known as "the plant of immortality" and the "Elixir of Life." Like maitake and shiitake mushrooms, reishi mushrooms have been known to boost immunity and aid cardiovascular health. They can also be used as an effective treatment for asthma and respiratory complaints as well as liver disorders and arthritis. Reishi mushrooms increase the level of T-helper cells, the immune cells that are targeted by the AIDS virus. Reishi has antiallergic, antiinflammatory, antiviral, antibacterial, and antioxidant properties.

Use these mushrooms in soups, broths, teas, or in stir-fries and noodle dishes. They can easily be made into an exotic broth with kombu seaweed to flavor Japanese dishes, or eaten on their own with olive oil and garlic. You can also get them in capsule form; the nutrients are kept most intact this way and are most easily absorbed by the body, giving your anti-aging immune system a powerful boost.

🌿 27 🌿

Remember Your Herbs

Herbs make all the difference to the flavor and nutrient value of a dish. We sprinkle basil over our tomato salads without really thinking about it, but how many people know that basil is an effective remedy for stomach cramps, vomiting, and constipation? Many herbs, like basil, enhance our ability to absorb the goodness in our food by aiding digestion. Others have more specific medicinal properties. Many pharmaceutical drugs are derived from culinary herbs, but when you eat the real thing, so long as you use them sensibly, you do not have to worry about side effects.

The people described in this book all use herbs in cooking and as home remedies. All over Symi, the breeze carries a cocktail of herbal smells to greet the nostrils and remind one of dinner. Thyme bushes, with their mauve and lilac flowers, dot the hillsides, while basil, sage, peppermint, and spearmint grow in pots on doorsteps. Their essential oils waft up in summer, and their leaves are pungent and fresh in the winter rain. Marjoram goes into Greek salads and marinades, rosemary is steeped in wine and olive oil, and mint, a great digestive aid, is used to flavor cheese and lamb dishes. Thyme is used with ham and as a preservative for dried fruits. Sage tea is considered to help cure colds and bronchitis, settle the stomach, improve the memory, and prevent women's ailments. Basil is grown outside houses to keep evil spirits away, and lemon balm is used to make a home remedy for angina, as well as hysteria and other nervous disorders.

Basil, oregano, thyme, parsley, and rosemary grow in pots outside every house in Campodimele, so that handfuls of fresh herbs can be used liberally in cooking. The Campodimelani are gourmets, and their soups, casseroles, salads, and roast vegetable dishes would not be the same without the addition of herbs. Parsley aids digestion and relieves gas, while oregano helps balance intestinal flora with its antifungal properties.

In Okinawa, around 460 varieties of herbs are grown. Mugwort, drunk in tea or awamori (the local version of sake), is thought to reduce a range of problems, particularly respiratory illnesses such as tuberculosis and the common cold. Turmeric, technically a spice, which is used to enhance soups and fish and chicken dishes, contains curcumin, which boosts the immune system, is antioxidant, is anti-inflammatory, aids digestion, helps prevent blood clotting, and helps the liver to neutralize toxins. Ginger, used in many local dishes, has antiviral properties and helps alleviate morning sickness and nausea.

Two popular herbs used in Bama are ginseng and astragalus, both of which can be obtained in health-food shops. Ginseng is very popular in the Far East as a general tonic for weakness and fatigue, and it also has anti-inflammatory properties, making it useful for treating conditions such as rheumatoid arthritis. Astragalus increases metabolism, combats fatigue, and is an excellent tonic for the immune system.

If feeling a little under the weather, Hunzakuts drink an herb collected from the mountainside called *tumuru*, which we know as wild thyme. Tumuru tea was once misnamed "tomorrow tea" by the Western media in their quest for the fountain of eternal youth. Tumuru is also used to make *tumurotze doudo,* or thyme soup. Tumuru is said to relieve headache, calm nerves, soothe sore throats, and bring color to the face.

Hunzakuts also use other herbs, such as mint, coriander, and parsley, to flavor their food, rather than the salt and spices used in the rest of Pakistan, which can be damaging to health.

Herbal remedies sold in health-food shops can be very beneficial to health, but these are best used with the advice of a good herbalist. However, ordinary culinary herbs, such as most of those described in this secret, can be easily used at home, so don't forget to include them regularly in your cooking. You can buy dried herbs in jars or, better still, buy them fresh or grow them in pots. Sprinkle dill, cilantro, or basil over your salads, use ginger in stir-fries, cook fish and rice with dill or cilantro, and use sage, thyme, or marjoram for meat dishes. Drink them as herb teas after a meal to aid digestion, or any time of day instead of tea or coffee.

🌿 28 🌿

Don't Pass the Salt

It's shaken over restaurant foods, it's poured into fast foods, it's in processed food by the bucketload, pickled foods are almost swimming in it, and we keep it on the table to sprinkle over our home-cooked food. It's in the mines and the oceans, and it's in your body. Salt has been a prized culinary commodity for thousands of years. It has even been used in the past as currency, with the word *salary* coming from the Latin root *sal*, meaning salt.

Yet it is now known that excessive salt consumption—which applies to the majority of us—causes high blood pressure, stroke, kidney disease, osteoporosis, stomach cancer, migraine, and many other diseases commonly found in the Western world.

We do need some sodium, which comes from salt, otherwise known as sodium chloride. Sodium is used for nerve transmission and to regulate blood pressure, while sodium chloride provides the chloride ions with which we make stomach acid. However, we only need a very small amount of sodium. The National Research Council of the National Academy of Sciences in Washington, D.C., recommends a salt intake of 500 milligrams minimum, which is about half a teaspoon daily, and an upper limit of 2,400 milligrams. As sodium is naturally present in plant and animal foods, it should not be necessary to add any extra to our cooking. Most Americans have 6,000 milligrams or more of salt daily. This obviously poses a hazard to health—more than 50 million Americans have high blood pressure, and high salt consumption is very likely to be an important contributing factor, as there is a well-established link between the two.

Excess salt disrupts the sodium-potassium balance crucial to healthy cells. Cells should have potassium inside them and sodium outside them, but excess salt causes the invasion of cells by sodium and the loss of potassium. As potassium is required to make enzymes in cells, while sodium inhibits enzyme production, the result is malfunctioning cells. Sodium also draws in water, causing fluid retention. The movement of fluids in and around cells stagnates, so that toxins cannot drain properly from cells and nutrients cannot get in. This causes a condition called tissue damage syndrome, or TDS. This is why salt is completely banned in anticancer nutritional regimes such as the Gerson Therapy. When cancer patients first start the Gerson Therapy, they often find that their swollen ankles and faces become normal as the excess sodium is rapidly excreted from their bodies and their body chemistry normalizes.

Dr. Max Gerson, who founded the Gerson Clinic, found that all patients with chronic degenerative illness have low potassium and high sodium levels. As a medical student, he had cured his own chronic migraines with a salt-free diet. By correcting the sodium-potassium ratio by removing salt from the diet and introducing high-potassium fruit and vegetable juices, he achieved amazing success at curing all kinds of illness such as arthritis, diabetes, multiple sclerosis, cardiovascular disease, autoimmune diseases, and chronic fatigue syndrome.

It is well known that excess salt causes high blood pressure, although the exact mechanism is unknown. It may be because the kidneys, which are responsible for excreting excess sodium, become overwhelmed and unable to regulate blood pressure properly. It is also thought that too much sodium causes the muscles to put extra pressure on the arteries (as though squeezing a hose). Needless to say, high blood pressure significantly increases the risk of heart attack and stroke.

High salt intake is also linked with osteoporosis, since excess sodium causes the loss of calcium from bones. It raises the insulin response, causing blood sugar imbalances and increasing the risk of diabetes. It contributes to the fast growth of tumors. It also significantly increases the risk of stomach cancer.[1] Excess salt can cause kidney disease, which is why salty foods should not be given to children, whose kidneys cannot deal with the load.

Traditional health-promoting diets, such as those of the people featured in this book, are invariably low in salt. Salt tends not to be readily available; for example, the Okinawans traditionally had to extract theirs from sea water. Their food is full of flavor, and does not require extra salt. One of the most prominent features of these healthy populations is low blood pressure, even in old age. There are also other health benefits of their low-salt diet. The Okinawans, for example, have lower stomach cancer rates than mainland Japanese, who have relatively high rates. This is thought to be due to lower salt consumption, as salt encourages infection from *Helicobacter pylori*, a type of bacteria common in Asia that is linked with stomach cancer and stomach ulcers.

If you are used to eating a high-salt diet, it is not too late to reverse much of the damage that may have been done. In the early twentieth century, the famous professor Dr. Albert Schweitzer found that African people in Gabon had adopted a modern high-salt diet and were developing kidney disease and other illnesses as a result. Yet as soon as they stopped eating salt, the kidneys recovered. As well as cutting down on salt, it is a good idea to improve your potassium-sodium ratio by drinking plenty of vegetable juices. Potassium is found in its most absorbable form in fruits, vegetables, and whole grains; another reason to switch to a diet high in these foods.

If you have adrenal fatigue, you may need some salt in your diet, since adrenal fatigue can cause excessively low blood pressure. If you feel dizzy on standing, this is a sign of possible adrenal fatigue. Those with diarrhea or who sweat a lot may also need some salt, as too much sodium may be lost from the body.

However, for most people, it would be very beneficial to their health to reeducate the palate to go without salt. When people who are used to eating a lot of salt stop using it, they generally find that their food seems to taste bland to start with. After a week or two, however, their taste buds sharpen, and they start to discern the real flavors of the food. If you are used to eating a lot of salt, try making your food without salt and really chewing and savoring the food while it is in your mouth, to taste the natural flavors.

Most processed foods and fast foods are extremely high in sodium, probably because they would have no flavor otherwise.

These foods are best avoided. Sliced bread, processed meats, cheese, pickles, and canned vegetables are all high in salt. If you use soy sauce or miso, find a low-sodium variety. The sodium content of foods has to be marked on the packaging by law; to calculate the salt content, multiply this by 2.5. The fresh counterparts of these foods are, conversely, high in potassium and low in sodium. Fresh fruits, vegetables, fish, and meat all have good potassium-sodium ratios. Do not add salt when cooking these, as this will upset the ratio. Use herbs, low-salt stocks, and lemon juice as flavor instead, and taste and feel the difference—you may be pleasantly surprised.

29

Go Organic and Avoid "Frankenfoods"

The long-lived people described in this book are organic farmers par excellence. They do not use pesticides, artificial fertilizers, or GM crops. Yet their yields are abundant, their crops are healthy, their soil is rich, and they do not have problems with insect "pests," because these are eaten by other insects and birds. The Hunzakuts in particular are famous for their skillful manure making and other farming methods, and their health has been attributed by some researchers to the high quality of their soil. When soil is healthy and rich in minerals, the plants that grow on it are also healthy and rich in minerals, as are the human beings who then eat those plants.

WHY FARM ORGANIC?

The use of artificial fertilizers and pesticides has been very seductive to commercial farmers, as they increase the quantity of crops in the short term. However, in the long term, they cause the soil and crops to become dependent upon them, much as people given medicine may become dependent on it and need more and more of it, while their health continues to decline. Artificial fertilizers drain the soil of valuable minerals such as calcium and magnesium, so the food that is grown in it can no longer provide us with them. They also leach nitrates into drinking water, and these are converted into carcinogens in our bodies.

It is true that when pesticides are first introduced into a farming environment, insects literally drop from the crops, and yields increase as a result. Over time, however, while the weaker breeds of insect die out, the hardier ones adapt and evolve pesticide-resistant strains, which are stronger and worse than the original strains. According to John Robbins, author of *Diet for a New America*, the percentage of U.S. crops lost to insects doubled between 1950 and 1974, mostly because pesticides disturbed the ecological balance.[1]

Pesticide use has been suggested as one cause of the increased rates of child cancer in the last fifty years and the incidence of illnesses such as mild cognitive disorder in gardeners and farmers.[2] When you eat fruit and vegetables that have been sprayed, your body is able (by using up much of its precious energy) to detoxify to a certain extent, but many toxins accumulate in your body tissues. Eating non-organic meat is the worst thing you can do, because chemicals from sprayed grains concentrate in the flesh of animal tissue. Women's breast milk tends to have concentrated levels of pesticides, although vegetarian mothers have far lower levels than those who eat meat.[3]

Organic farmers spread manure and compost over the soil, which ensures that the nutrients that are taken out of it are put back in. Crop rotation prevents crops from draining the soil of minerals needed to grow those crops. Pests are kept away with natural, harmless methods—for example, fruit orchards are kept free of whitefly with the use of beetles that eat the flies but not the fruit, while hedgerows encourage the presence of birds and insects, which feed on pests. Healthy crops grown in rich soil are also more able to resist disease.

The result is bountiful yields and soil that is fertile in the long term. Organically grown food is better for health and has more flavor than food produced by modern farming methods because it contains more nutrients. The soil in Bama, for example, has been found to be high in manganese and zinc, and hair analysis tests have shown that these same minerals are at the right levels for optimum heart health in the Bama people. It takes a few years for nonorganic farms to feed their soil back to its original richness, and our farmers in the West have only just begun. However, according to The Soil Association in the UK, "research comparing the nutrient contents of organic and non-organic fruit and vegetables reveals a strong trend towards higher levels in organic produce."

Organic produce still has a way to go. It is more expensive than nonorganic produce and it is not as widely accessible as it could be. The amount of money governments put into promoting organic farming is miniscule compared with how much is invested in more modern, high-tech farming methods. Yet organic farming is often best for the consumer, the farmer, and the environment, especially in the long term. By buying organic when you can, and encouraging your local supermarket to promote organic foods, you will help improve your own health and that of the planet.

FEEDING THE WORLD WITH "FRANKENFOODS"

Genetic modification (GM), in which scientists take genes from one organism and put them into another, is a very complicated process with unknown effects. "We're right at the very beginning of this incredible set of scientific advances," Robb Fraley, the chief technology officer for Monsanto, recently proclaimed.[4] They certainly are. GM science is still in its infancy, and much more experimentation needs to be done before it is fully understood— if it is ever fully understood. It is we and the natural environment, which took millions of years to evolve in a very specific way, which will be the guinea pigs in this vast, unpredictable experiment. At least we can wash pesticides off under the tap; we cannot do this with genes.

Most studies on GM foods have been undertaken by the GM companies themselves, and have been kept from the public. However, information on these studies has been leaked, showing troubling findings. Secret research carried out by GM giant Monsanto showed that rats fed GM corn had smaller kidneys than other rats, as well as blood abnormalities. According to Dr. Michael Antoniu of Guy's Hospital in the UK, these findings were "very worrying from a medical point of view."[5] In another study by the GM company Aventis, chickens fed with GM corn were twice as likely to die as those fed non-GM corn.[6]

If these are the effects of GM foods on rats and chickens, what might they do to human beings? In 2003, 101.5 million acres of GM crops were planted in the U.S., according to the U.S. Department of Agriculture, and 75 percent of processed foods in the U.S. are estimated to contain some GM ingredients. Most GM food crops grown in the U.S. are corn, canola, and soybeans, as well as cotton, papaya, and squash. Eighty percent of soy grown in the U.S. is genetically modified, so if you buy anything containing soy you are likely to be ingesting a GM product.

What are GM crops for, anyway? The people discussed in this book certainly have no use for them. Neither do the commercial Asian farmers who have become disillusioned with them.[7] GM crops have nothing to do with feeding the world, and everything to do with the billions of dollars they are worth annually. Even the GM companies themselves admit as much: Steve Smith of GM giant Novartis recently said, "If anyone tells you GM is going to feed the world, tell him that it is not. To feed the world takes political and financial will, it's not about production and distribution. It may produce more for less and create more food, but it won't feed the world."

Many GM crops currently being developed are weedkiller-tolerant, which means that heavy doses of chemicals can be used to spray the fields they are in, killing the weeds but not the crops. There is widespread concern that the use of weedkiller-tolerant GM crops will encourage the evolution of "superweeds"— triffid-like weeds that adapt to survive the sprays and cause environmental havoc such as the eradication of native bird species.[8]

Research shows that GM crops can interbreed with wild plants and contaminate them with their genes.[9] GM crops are thought to be able to contaminate non-GM crops up to 5.6 miles away. This means that if GM farms are set up near to organic farms, those organic farms will go out of business. GM crops also have a nasty habit of entering the food chain in unpredictable ways. In a disastrous case in the United States in 2000, StarLink, a variety of GM corn intended purely for animal feed, due to concern that it might cause allergic reactions, somehow found its way into taco shells on supermarket shelves.

If you want to avoid the potential health risks of pesticides in your body, buy organic food when you can, or grow your own if you have spare time and space. Limit the amount of meat and dairy products you eat, especially nonorganic, as these contain the most concentrated levels of pesticides and antibiotics. Make sure you scrub fruit and vegetables well under the tap before eating them. Supermarkets listen to their consumers—they need to—so encourage your local supermarkets and grocery stores to stock organic produce and nonorganic produce treated only with pesticides that do not leave residues.

To avoid eating GM produce, check the labels on foods carefully. Soy, corn products, and foods containing rapeseed oil are the most likely foods to contain GM produce, especially processed foods. Shopping at health-food outlets may be the easiest way for you to avoid eating GM produce. If you wish to campaign against the growing GM revolution, contact one of your local conservation or environmental groups and ask what you can do.

❧ 30 ❧

Chew

All the healthy food in the world will have limited value for you if you don't chew it. As the nineteenth-century American health guru Horace Fletcher said, "Nature will castigate those who don't masticate." Chewing sets off a chain reaction essential for the proper digestion and assimilation of your food, and has some other health benefits as well. All of the people in this book take the time to chew their food in a relaxed manner. The Hunzakuts in particular have been noted for it.

Several well-known historical figures have enthused about the importance of chewing. The British prime minister William Gladstone recommended chewing each mouthful thirty-two times—once for each tooth. Horace Fletcher, otherwise known as The Great Masticator, went a step further and said that each mouthful should be chewed until the food became a liquid and swallowed itself—extreme chewing subsequently became known as "Fletcherizing." Fletcher has been reported to have lost forty-two pounds just by chewing, although skeptics claim this was simply due to calories lost as a result of exercising his jawbone. Mahatma Gandhi, the great chewing expert (and Indian leader) agreed with Fletcher, however, saying you should "eat your drinks and drink your food."

Some truly dramatic health benefits have been attributed to chewing. Concentration camp prisoner Antonio Stanchich claimed to have survived a Nazi camp simply by chewing his food. He found that "chewing" his cold water to warm it up seemed to give him more energy, so he then tried chewing his food. He started chewing 50 times per mouthful, then 75 times, gradually increasing it until he found that the "magic number" for chewing was 150 times. He noticed that this gave him more energy and that he was less apt to become sick than his fellow inmates. He taught his chewing technique to two other prisoners, and of all the thirty-two men in his original ship's crew who were imprisoned together, they were the only three to survive. The experiences of Antonio Stanchich are described by his son Lino in his bestselling book, *Power Eating Program: You Are How You Eat.*

The process of digestion actually begins before you even start chewing. It is important to take a few minutes to concentrate on your food so that this process can start—in today's hurried world it is easy to neglect this part of eating. The people in this book love cooking and eating, and they make and eat their food with care; this undoubtedly has a good effect on their digestion. Start by looking at and breathing in the delicious aroma of your salmon noodles or roast vegetables with herbs, or whatever it is you are having. This will send a message to the brain to galvanize your saliva, digestive juices, enzymes, and digestive hormones into action. Hopefully you will not be staring at a white roll in plastic wrap, which will probably not have the same effect.

Put the first forkful in your mouth, and start chewing. Taste the delicious flavors as they flood through your mouth. Chewing helps produce saliva, which contains amylase enzymes that are needed to break down carbohydrates. Saliva is also antibacterial and antiviral; the AIDS virus, for example, is disabled by saliva. Chewing also reduces the surface area of the food so that the digestive enzymes can break it down more efficiently. A chain reaction will be started in which the stomach registers that it must produce hydrochloric acid, which in turn stimulates the digestive process farther on down the intestinal tract. Chewing also ensures that the message that the stomach is full gets to the "satiety center" in the brain so that you don't overeat.

One sign of aging is lowered production of hydrochloric acid, although a great many younger people also have low stomach acid, partly as a result of not chewing. Hydrochloric acid is important because it kills pathogens, it is needed for protein digestion, and it liberates minerals from food. Signs of low stomach acid include a bad taste in the mouth, an itchy rectum, and flatulence. If food, especially animal protein, is not broken down properly by chewing and stomach acid, it encourages the proliferation of putrefactive bacteria in the digestive tract, which causes flatulence and foul-smelling stools as well as creating toxic by-products.

Chewing also has other advantages. It is a good workout for your jawbone, and it activates the circulation of blood in the area, bringing nutrients and oxygen to muscles and the brain. This is one reason why macrobiotics gurus teach that chewing can help bring about a state of bliss. Lino Stanchich, macrobiotics expert and son of Antonio Stanchich, recommends closing your eyes while chewing, for additional therapeutic and energy-giving benefits.

You will find it easier to chew your food if you relax while you eat, as the people in this book do, and try to get out of the mind-set of being in a hurry. Sit down when you have your meal, and don't forget to breathe. If possible, avoid eating at the computer or at the wheel of your car. (I once read about a man who was arrested on Christmas for negotiating a traffic circle using his elbows to turn the steering wheel while he demolished a turkey carcass.) Try also to minimize stress, which reduces the digestive enzymes and hydrochloric acid, and depresses the immune system, which is needed to maintain a healthy digestive tract. After eating, try to avoid getting up for fifteen minutes. Breathe in and feel your breath entering your abdominal area, relaxing the stomach as you do so. This may help with any anxiety-related digestive problems. Most people could benefit from chewing a lot more than they do. Unless you happen to be eating an oyster, try chewing each mouthful between twenty and fifty times. If this helps you to stay younger for longer, then it will, after all, save you time in the end.

31

Beware the Pastry Counter

When it is 11:00 A.M. at the office and we are feeling tired, we often reach for a sugary doughnut or bagel and a cup of coffee to provide instant relief. Once inside us, the doughnut or bagel is broken down very quickly into glucose, which gets into the bloodstream and causes an abrupt rise in blood sugar levels. Glucose floating around in the veins is toxic, so the pancreas quickly releases a large amount of insulin to tether the glucose away safely in cells. In its haste, the pancreas lets out too much insulin—the body was not designed to take in so much sugar at once—and glucose levels fall too low. Some time after eating the doughnut, we feel a dip in energy, and crave something else to pick us up. We reach for the cookie jar or sandwich section, and the whole cycle begins again. These swings in blood sugar levels are called hypoglycemia, and a great many of us suffer from it.

After many years of this, our cells tire of answering insulin's knock to let in glucose; this is called insulin resistance. The insulin is forced to take glucose off to fat cells instead, causing us to become overweight. We also now have excess insulin circulating in the bloodstream. Insulin, like glucose, is damaging, and aging, to cells and tissues and can cause a variety of illnesses. People who are insulin resistant continually feel tired, as the cells have less of the energy they normally get from glucose. The end result of excess insulin, or hyperinsulinemia, and excess glucose is adult-onset diabetes. Seventeen million people in the United States have adult-onset diabetes, and you have a one in three risk of getting it during your lifetime.[1]

Here is a brief outline of what glucose does in the veins. Sugar is sticky, and it likes to stick to, or form complexes with, the proteins in our bodies, which make up most of our tissues and also our genetic material. This process is called glycation, or glycosylation, and the unsavory result is "advanced glycosylation end-products," appropriately known as AGEs. These are a tangle of cross-linked structures that gum up the works in the affected tissue, accumulating over the years and causing gradual deterioration of the organ. They cause collagen, which keeps our skin elastic, to stiffen; our eyes to grow cataracts; and harmful LDL cholesterol to linger in our arteries. The brains of Alzheimer's patients have been found to have unusually large clumps of AGEs.

Excess circulating insulin speeds up the aging process, as it causes our genetic material, DNA, to turn over more quickly. It also lowers production of the "youth hormone," DHEA (dehydroepiandrosterone). Excess insulin triggers the release of inflammatory substances called eicosanoids, which increase the risk of heart disease, cancer, and arthritis. It damages the body's antioxidants and raises levels of free radicals, a deadly combination. Studies have shown that insulin, like glucose, can also stimulate the growth of cancer cells.[2] As diabetics are aware, hyperinsulinism is the most reliable predictor of atherosclerosis, because insulin raises levels of bad LDL and very bad VLDL (very low density lipoprotein) cholesterol.[3] It also causes blood vessels to become thickened and stiffened, it makes blood clot, and it raises blood pressure. Even small rises in glucose and insulin levels are closely related to diseases of aging such as heart disease, cancer, and diabetes.

The people featured in this book would probably eat fast-burning foods if they had access to them—after all, they are addictive and convenient—but in the main, they avoid them. Neither do they eat the high-meat diets that are fashionable today. Eating a high-meat diet is not the answer, since large amounts of saturated fats can damage cell membranes and increase their insulin resistance. The diet of long-lived people consists of a balance of vegetables, vegetable proteins such as beans, nuts, and seeds, some fruit, whole grains, fish, lean meat, and healthy fats such as olive oils and essential fatty acids. This is the best type of diet to eat if you want to balance your blood sugar levels.

You can use the glycemic index (GI) to choose slow-burning foods. The GI is a system used to measure how fast glucose enters the blood stream after a certain carbohydrate is eaten. Pure glucose, the highest, measures 100 on the scale. Those carbohydrates which are low on the glycemic index are the slowest-burning. By eating slow-burning foods, you can prevent and even reverse those "diseases of aging" caused by an overzealous insulin response.

GLYCEMIC INDEX OF COMMON FOODS

High Glycemic Index Foods (70-100): Restrict
- Baked potatoes, mashed potatoes (up to 100)
- French baguette (95)
- Sugar, honey, sweets, cakes, cookies
- Cooked carrots
- White bread, English muffins
- Whole-wheat bread
- White rice, brown rice
- Sugary drinks
- Most commercial breakfast cereals such as corn flakes
- Dried fruits and bananas

Medium Glycemic Index Foods (40-70): Include
- Boiled potatoes, sweet corn, raw carrots, sweet potato
- Pasta
- Barley bread, rye bread
- Mixed whole-grain bread and seed breads
- Basmati rice
- Oatmeal, bran cereals, muesli
- Pita bread
- Grapes, mangos, figs, kiwifruit

Low Glycemic Index Foods (0-40): Enjoy
- Beans and legumes
- Nuts and seeds
- Apples, peaches, oranges, plums
- Most vegetables, including broccoli, cauliflower, salad, mushrooms, leeks, tomatoes
- Dairy products
- Meat and fish
- 70 percent-cocoa chocolate (enjoy in small quantities only)

You will see that baked potatoes are high on the GI, but eating them with vegetable protein or salad will lower the overall score of the meal, otherwise known as the "glycemic load." Eating the skin will also slow down the rate of digestion and therefore of glucose release (buy organic potatoes, which don't have pesticide-soaked skins). Campodimelani often eat their pasta with low-GI beans in soup or stew; Okinawans eat their rice with fish. Avoid heaping your plate with too much of anything, which will bring the score up: none of the people in this book eat large amounts at one meal. Low-GI foods tend to satisfy the appetite more than high-GI foods, anyway, as they linger for longer in the digestive system, which has the additional benefit of keeping you slim. If you wish to learn more about the GI and the effects of glucose on the body, an excellent book to read is *Syndrome X*, by Jack Challem, Burton Berkson, and Melissa Diane Smith.

Since even whole grains cause a rise in insulin levels, if you have severe blood sugar swings and are addicted to carbohydrates, it is a good idea to avoid them for a few weeks. You will see that brown rice, for example, is high on the GI. Eat mainly vegetables with fish, chicken, and a little vegetable protein (such as lentils or soy) to return blood sugar levels to normal before gradually introducing small amounts of whole grains back into your diet.

You can slow down your rate of digestion in other ways. Avoid using more than a tiny amount of salt, as salt speeds up digestion; strong condiments should also be limited for the same reason. Putting lemon juice or vinegar on food helps slow absorption of starches, so make a dressing from lemon, olive oil, and garlic, and include a dressed salad with your meal. Do not go for long periods without eating and then binge at mealtimes, because this will mean a large glycemic load all at once; you can regulate blood sugar levels by snacking on low-GI foods such as avocado, fruit, nuts, or salads during the day. Try to drink green tea rather than coffee, as caffeine stimulates an insulin response. A little wine with a meal may be beneficial, as studies have shown that it can stop the formation of AGEs.[4]

I have yet to meet someone who does not achieve much higher energy levels after giving up sugar and refined carbohydrates. It may be difficult for the first few days, or weeks, because blood sugar swings are a vicious cycle that is hard to get out of. If you don't want to go cold turkey, cut down on sugar and refined carbohydrates gradually over two or three weeks. You will find you want them less and less, and that you feel increasingly good for it. Most importantly, to a large degree, you will have taken control of your health and rate of aging.

*\$ 32 *\$

Have a Glass of Red Wine with Dinner

The answer to life—or long life at least—may turn out to be at the bottom of the glass after all. One thing all five populations in this book have in common is a fondness for drink—enjoyed in modest amounts only, of course, and always with a meal. Even the Hunzakuts—the healthiest population in an otherwise unhealthy teetotal nation—enjoy a nice glass of *vin rouge*, or a somewhat rough version of it known locally as "Hunza water," on a regular basis.

In Campodimele, grapevines grow on trellises outside every

house in the village, and each household makes around three hundred to four hundred liters of white and red wine every year. In Symi, wines are drunk either with a meal or with small dishes of *mezzedhes* (appetizers) such as tsatsiki or grilled octopus. The Hunzakut version of red wine, a rough, potent, sugar-free drink, is brought out for meals or on "special occasions"—special occasions being quite frequent in Hunza.

Fermented rice wine, or sake, is brewed by the Okinawans and the people of Bama. The Okinawans make their own version of sake called awamori, which is used for cooking and seasoning or drunk from a tiny earthenware mug. Bama villagers sip sake from glazed bowls throughout the day, and they also make snake wine, a fermented rice or maize wine bottled with snakes preserved in the alcohol.

This doesn't mean that we can leap to hasty conclusions about alcohol being a necessary part of a life-lengthening lifestyle. In large amounts, it undoubtedly shortens life. However, red wine has some important health-giving properties that should not be overlooked, and there is some research to show that sake may also bring benefits, when drunk in conjunction with a healthy diet.

The secret of red wine lies in the powerful antioxidants contained in the skin of the grape, especially red grapes. Two antioxidants in particular, resveratrol and quercetin, are thought to be especially beneficial. These protect against heart disease by preventing plaque from forming on artery walls, which is thought to be one reason why the wine-loving French have low rates of heart disease, despite their love of fatty foods. Resveratrol and quercetin also act together to lower levels of bad cholesterol in the blood, reduce high levels of harmful insulin, and prevent high blood pressure. Wine can also protect against cancer—when cardiologist Serge Renaud studied 34,000 middle-aged men in France, he found that the death rate from all causes, including heart disease and cancer, was reduced by up to 30 percent in moderate wine drinkers.

The antioxidants in wine keep the arteries to important organs such as the heart and brain elastic and youthful, and also protect brain cells from aging. Studies from the National Institute of Longevity in Japan show that those who drink moderate amounts of either grape or rice wine (such as awamori or sake) have an IQ on average 3.3 points higher (for men) or 2.5 points higher (for women) than teetotalers.[1] Those who drink over a pint a day, however, have lower IQs.

If you had a choice between caloric restriction and a steak with a glass of red wine, which would you choose? New research from Harvard indicates that wine may not only be beneficial to health but actually extend maximum life span in the same way that caloric restriction can. The Harvard studies show that resveratrol, like caloric restriction, stimulates a family of enzymes called sirtuins, which act like little mechanics in cells, repairing DNA damage and influencing the behavior of genes.[2] Yeast, worms, and fruit flies all had their lives extended, with yeast enjoying an extra 70 percent of life in its Petri dishes. Ongoing studies will determine whether resveratrol can have similar effects in human cells, although there is some controversy about this; it is thought to work best with quercetin, as in red wine. Whether or not we can attain the heights of yeast, one thing for certain is that resveratrol and quercetin can help us enjoy what life span we do have by reducing the risk of diseases of aging such as heart disease and diabetes.

Beware the law of diminishing returns, since a high intake of alcohol—more than two drinks daily—is associated with many illnesses, including liver damage, accelerated brain aging, increased blood pressure, and cancer. One recent study has shown that drinking just one glass of wine daily increases a woman's chances of getting breast cancer by about 6 percent, due to raised estrogen levels.[3] However, the long-lived women featured in this book drink moderately and have very low rates of breast cancer, so other factors need to be taken into account. For example, they eat large amounts of detoxifying fruit and vegetables, and the high fiber content of their diet ensures the removal of excess estrogen from the body. The possible benefits of drinking red wine, therefore, need to be seen in the context of the rest of the nutritional advice given in this book. If you think you have high estrogen levels or are at risk of breast cancer, then it may be best for you to avoid alcohol.

If you do not want to drink alcohol, you can get resveratrol and quercetin from red grapes and grape juice, although they are more concentrated in wine. Alternatively you can use wine to cook recipes such as risotto or casseroles, in which most of the alcohol evaporates. If you do drink or cook with red wine, buy organic if possible, to avoid pesticide residues. Sake, although it may not have such powerful health benefits as red wine, is free at least of the harmful sulfites used as preservatives in red wine. Always drink alcohol with meals, to avoid harming the stomach lining, and dilute red wine with a little water, as the Greeks and Italians do, if you wish. Treat yourself to an expensive bottle, sip it slowly, and really enjoy it.

33

Make Time for Tea—Green Tea

New studies are showing something that the Okinawans and other Asians have known for a long time—that you can stall aging with several cups of green tea daily. The Okinawans enjoy theirs scented with jasmine flowers. The ancient Chinese believed it should be sipped slowly in a pavilion, next to a lily pond, in the company of a beautiful woman. Today's gerontologists give it to their test subjects in a capsule. However you take your green tea, it is thought to prevent everything from constipation to cancer, so if you want to live long, make having it a part of your daily routine.

If anyone asks you why you are drinking a lot of green tea all of a sudden, just tell them it contains the fat-soluble antioxidant epigallocatechin-3-gallate. EGCG, as it is known, is a powerful substance that gets into our fatty brain cells and protects them from aging. EGCG is even more effective than both fat-soluble vitamin E (another important anti-aging antioxidant) and resveratrol, the antioxidant in red wine.

EGCG is also an important anticancer agent. It was recently noticed that areas devoted to green tea production in the Shizuoka Prefecture of Japan had significantly lower cancer rates than elsewhere, and that those people of the area who drank their green tea in the highest concentrations had the lowest cancer rates of all. Studies on green tea and EGCG in particular show that mice given extract of green tea had a marked reduction in tumor growth and were 50 percent less likely to develop certain induced cancers.[1] EGCG has also been found to kill cancer cells in human tissue.[2] It is thought to be especially protective against cancers of the bladder, prostate, esophagus, and stomach, as well as the lung, breast, colon, and skin.[3]

Ounce for ounce, green tea contains more disease-preventing antioxidants, including vitamin C and vitamin E, than any other food or drink. One cup, for example, contains more vitamin C than an orange. Green tea also contains antistress, energy-making B vitamins. It is very low in caffeine, so makes a good replacement for tea and coffee, which dehydrate the body, use up B vitamins, and drain the body of important minerals such as calcium.

The benefits of green tea do not stop there. It has antibiotic properties, and has long been used as a remedy for diarrhea, since it kills pathogenic bacteria while leaving the "friendly" bacteria in the intestine alone. Green tea is also antiviral, and promising new research is looking at the uses of green tea against the AIDS virus. It has been found to lower blood sugar in diabetic mice, it contains a natural form of fluoride that may help keep teeth strong, and it is said to relieve constipation. Green tea has also been found to protect against heart disease by controlling high blood pressure and reducing the buildup of bad LDL cholesterol.[4]

There are some studies that have failed to show such clear benefits of green tea as those described above, which may indicate the importance of drinking green tea along with a healthy diet. The Okinawans, who have an exemplary diet, drink only three cups daily on average, and seem to get the benefits. Mainland Japanese drink an average of six cups a day, which could be one reason why they have lower levels of lung cancer than they should, considering the high rate of cigarette smoking.

What is the best way to drink green tea? Researchers recommend a minimum of four cups daily to get the benefits. According to ancient Chinese tradition, the leaves should first be collected by virgins from the rainforest at the start of the harvest. With any luck, these tea leaves will end up for sale in your nearest health-food shop or Asian supermarket. High-quality loose green tea leaves taste the best, but you can also buy teabags. If using loose leaves, put them in a teapot and let the tea brew for five minutes. You can also add jasmine or lemongrass for taste.

34

Drink Water—the Most Essential Nutrient

Water is arguably the most essential nutrient there is. We can go without food for forty days and more, but without water it would all be over in three to five days. To stay in optimum health, it is absolutely essential that you drink enough water.

Water transports nutrients around the body and flushes wastes out—without it, we would drown in a stagnant pool of our own metabolic waste. Water is essential for helping the liver with its taxing job of detoxification, and it is also needed for digestion, circulation, absorption, and excretion. Water will also keep your skin hydrated and looking younger. Chronic dehydration may cause aging and disease in the organs and tissues of the body. If you don't drink enough water, the body takes water from the colon to use, which causes constipation and hard, dry stools. Toxins in the colon water also get reabsorbed, causing lethargy and headaches.

The people in this book do not drink soft drinks of any kind, but they do drink plenty of pure, natural spring water. The Okinawans drink calcium-rich local water, which helps prevent osteoporosis and keeps the body alkaline, which is how it likes to be. The Campodimelani have traditionally drunk pure mountain spring water piped down from nearby Mount Faggeta, source of a local brand of bottled water. The Hunzakuts have irrigation channels cutting through the near-vertical rock faces to bring icy, pale glacier water full of beneficial minerals down to the valley. Bama villagers get their water for cooking and drinking from the pure, clear Panyang River that flows into the valley; Panyang water has been found to be high in the manganese and zinc our bodies need.

These people are lucky to have a ready supply of water from natural sources; we are lucky to be able to buy bottled versions in the supermarket. Unfortunately, this comes at a price to the environment. Buying water in recyclable bottles is one alternative; another is to use tap water. Tap water is often polluted, however— a recent study found that U.S. tap water samples contained lead, pathogenic bacteria, carcinogenic by-products of chlorine treatment, arsenic, radon, rocket fuel, and other toxic chemicals.[1] Carbon filters remove chlorine and heavy metals from tap water, and they are inexpensive and easy to use, so they are a good option for some, although they may not remove all bacteria and toxins.

The minerals in mineral water are in an inorganic form, which means they cannot be absorbed by the body, so some believe that distilled water, which contains nothing but hydrogen and oxygen, is a better option. However, it is thought that friendly intestinal flora can convert the minerals in water into their organic, absorbable form, whereas distilled water may leach minerals out of the body. The people in this book drink natural mineral water, which suggests this may be best for our health, especially as this is the type of water we have adapted to during evolution. If you are detoxifying or fasting, it may be a good idea to choose low-surface-tension mineral water. Geologists studying Hunza water believe that its low surface tension is beneficial to health, since this enables it to carry nutrients to and toxins from cells efficiently.

How much water should we be drinking? The standard advice from nutritionists is to drink eight to ten glasses daily; more specific advice given by some experts is to drink one ounce per two pounds of body weight. This, plus the water that is contained in the food we eat (especially fruit and vegetables), should provide us with the amount we need—around 2.5 liters for women, and

3.7 liters for men daily. If you drink a lot of juices and eat soups, you can get much of your daily quota of water that way. Some people, such as athletes, or those living in hot climates, may need more water, while others may need less. Remember that too much water can be as dangerous as too little, and a number of athletes are reported to have died from drinking excess water.

Drink your water away from meals, so as not to dilute the digestive juices, and sip it slowly for maximum absorption. Avoid ice-cold water, which is not compatible with the temperature inside your body. If you are not used to drinking water, you may not be aware of your thirst, but as your body gets tuned in to water drinking, you may start to desire it more. You may be able to tell how much you need by looking at your urine—it should not be too yellow, but if it is the color of water, you may be drinking too much.

You are probably the best person to gauge exactly how much water you need, but remember that thirst is often one of the last signs of dehydration. If you drink alcohol or caffeine, they will dehydrate your body and cause you to urinate, so drink extra water to make up for it. If you find you forget to drink water, keep a bottle near you at all times to remind yourself to stay hydrated.

🌿 35 🌿

Combine Your Foods

If you suffer from digestive problems such as constipation and bloating, this secret is for you. It outlines a way of combining foods that should speed up stool transit time and enable more efficient assimilation of nutrients and expulsion of toxins. This should help you to feel more energetic and gain clearer skin and more radiant looks. It may also enable you to avoid more serious illness. The long-lived populations in this book do not consciously combine their foods "correctly," but, as is explained below, they unknowingly follow some of the principles of food combining, which may explain in part their healthy digestive systems, so fundamental to good overall health.

The concept of food combining was born in the early 1900s, when a doctor named William Howard Hay found himself, at the age of forty, seriously overweight and suffering from a chronic kidney condition, high blood pressure, and an enlarged heart. He was told by physicians that he would almost certainly never regain his health. However, Dr. Hay proved them wrong by correctly identifying the source of his problems— faulty digestion. "Death begins in the colon," he announced, and set to work devising a new way of eating. Within a relatively short time, Dr. Hay had lost fifty pounds and eradicated his health problems, as well as those of many of his patients whom he put on the diet.

The basic principle of the Hay diet is to improve the digestion by eating certain foods separately—most crucially, starches (such as bread and potatoes) and proteins (especially the richest proteins, animal products). Just as you cannot brush your teeth while combing your hair, so the body cannot break down proteins at the same time as it breaks down starch. By combining foods correctly, the body can work much more efficiently to absorb the nutrients it is given and use spare energy for detoxification and metabolism.

Practitioners of food combining claim that patients who are overweight, underweight, arthritic, diabetic, insomniac, anxious, depressed, hypertensive, hypoglycemic, constipated, or suffering from headaches, Crohn's disease, heart disease, Raynaud's disease, colitis, indigestion, migraine, premenstrual tension, and irritable bowel syndrome (just for a start) find their energy returning and their symptoms disappearing when they combine their foods properly.

Dr. Hay made the important observation that people with an acidic system—the familiar grouchy, irritable, paunchy types who go out for steak and fries at lunchtime and follow it up with a handful of indigestion tablets—tend to suffer more from illness than other people. A slightly alkaline system is the ideal environment for good health. Cancer cells thrive in an acid environment, but dislike an alkaline one. Dr. Hay recommended eating mainly fruit and vegetables, which keep the system alkaline, while meat and carbohydrates create acid conditions. According to Dr. Hay, when carbohydrates are eaten, these should be whole grains rather than refined carbohydrates, for better digestion.

Long-lived peoples do a moderated form of the Hay diet. They sometimes combine vegetable proteins with starches, but they do not eat much meat, so do not commit the ultimate Hay crime of combining rich animal protein with starches. They also eat an alkaline-forming diet based on fruit and vegetables, and they eat whole grains rather than refined carbohydrates.

Below is a guide to food categories, as well as recommended and forbidden combinations on the Hay diet. You can also consult one of the more detailed books that are available on the subject.

FOOD CATEGORIES

Proteins: Animal, fish, dairy, eggs, nuts, seeds, beans, and legumes

Fats: Animal and vegetable fats, butter, cream, oils, avocadoes

Starches: Grains, potatoes, starchy root vegetables

Green and nonstarchy vegetables: Leafy green vegetables, cabbage, onion, seaweed, broccoli, etc.

Fruits: Sweet fruit, subacid fruit, and melons

COMBINATIONS

1. AVOID starch + protein, especially rich proteins (e.g., steak) and rich starches (e.g., fries)

2 AVOID protein + fats (fats coat the stomach wall and prevent gastric juices from working properly)

3. AVOID carbohydrates + acid fruits (e.g., tomato, orange), as the fruits inhibit the enzyme ptyalin, which is needed for carbohydrate digestion

4. Eat fruit alone, as it breaks down quickly and ferments in the stomach if kept waiting

5. AVOID carbohydrates + refined sugar

6. Fats + acid fruits may be combined (e.g., yogurt + strawberries)

7. Consume milk alone or not at all, as it curdles if combined

8. COMBINE protein + nonstarchy vegetables

9. COMBINE carbohydrates + nonstarchy vegetables + fats and oils

The Hay diet may be best viewed as something to try when suffering from digestive problems, rather than something to do all the time. The regime is quite strict and not easy to follow over a lifetime. However, I have included the details above for your information, as strict food combining may be of help to you, at least as a temporary measure.

❧ 36 ❧

Spring-Clean with Juices and Saunas

The best anti-aging doctor in town is your own body. Nature is capable of many extraordinary feats, and the human body has a powerful ability to heal itself, *when given the right conditions.* Unfortunately, modern living means that, for most of us, those conditions are not there. Every time you breathe in car exhaust, feel stressed, consume additives, take medicine, use shampoo, or eat barbecued food—to name but a few instances—you add to your body's toxic load. Our bodies also produce their own "endogenous" toxins merely as a result of eating and breathing.

The poor overworked liver frantically tries to disarm all the millions of free-radical-producing toxins and expel them through the skin, urine, mouth, breast milk, mucus, bowel, or any other outlet it can find, sometimes causing pimples, mouth ulcers, bad breath, a coated tongue, or boils. Our livers were never designed to have such a full in-box, and because most people are nutritionally deficient, the body also lacks the materials needed for detoxification. The toxins end up getting into the bloodstream, which dumps them around the body, in fat and connective tissue, to be sorted out another time.

This turns us into disease time bombs, ticking away for years or decades until, eventually, inevitably, something has to give. Some of the greatest physicians in history have firmly believed that disease—*all* disease—results from a body that has become clogged by toxicity. "There is but one disease," said the one-time British royal surgeon Sir Arbuthnot Lane, "and that is deficient drainage."

The long-lived people described in this book avoid toxins from cigarettes, processed food, meat, pesticides, and alcohol in excess. They also tend to live in rural mountainous or coastal areas where there is very little pollution. Most of the toxins they do acquire can be eliminated through their nutritious, fibrous diet. They take plenty of exercise, which gives them an opportunity to sweat out their toxins and boost circulation. The Hunzakuts have always traditionally fasted during the lean weeks between winter and spring, before the new harvest came in, which is thought to be one reason for their extreme good health.

Like the people in this book, you can create balance in your body, expelling as many toxins as are taken in, so that you remove the conditions for degenerative disease. By giving your body a good spring-cleaning in the ways outlined in this secret, you can cleanse your blood and tissues and give your body time to sort out its "in-box."

WATER-ONLY FASTING

The most extreme form of fasting is the water-only fast. Fasting gives the body the chance it so desperately needs to cleanse itself and begin healing. For the first three days of a fast, toxins are expelled and the blood is cleansed. Enzymes, no longer needed by the stomach, go to the bloodstream and start destroying pathogens, diseased cells, and toxins. At around five days, healing and rebuilding of the immune system begins. From ten days on, disease begins to be reversed and prevented. Serious illnesses and other conditions begin to disappear at around thirty days. Some time after this, the body signifies when it is time to end the fast with a return of appetite, sweet breath, a clear tongue, and a feeling of enormous well-being.

Water fasting is a controversial method of detoxifying that has been reported to reverse many signs of aging and to dramatically improve elevated cholesterol, high blood pressure, edema, rheumatoid arthritis, cysts, benign tumors, appendicitis, digestive problems, obesity, alcoholism, heart disease, backache, headache, kidney stones, insomnia, prostatitis, hernia, fibroids, eczema, gallstones, sterility, mental illness, arthritis, ulcerative colitis, multiple sclerosis, and supposedly terminal illnesses. One of the most well known practitioners of water fasting was an American called Herbert Shelton, who supervised around 35,000 fasts between 1925 and 1970 at his clinic in San Antonio, Texas.

Today, it is thought that because of the high levels of pollutants in our environments, it may be unwise to do a water-only fast, as this may put too great a burden on the liver too quickly. If you are considering such a fast, it is essential that you do it under the supervision of a reputable practitioner. It may be preferable, however, to do a short juice fast on a regular basis, as described below.

JUICE FASTING

Juices have an effective cleansing effect, with health benefits comparable to those of water-only fasts. Juices have the additional benefit of providing enzymes for detoxification that our stressed livers may require in extra amounts. A juice fast of three days will cleanse the blood and help the body to eliminate toxins, while a five-day fast will have further-reaching benefits. Fasting on juice for one day a week is also highly recommended. Apple, carrot, grape, beet, celery, and cabbage are all good for use during a juice fast; avoid orange or tomato juice, which are too acidic for use in fasting. For more details on how to do short juice and other fasts, consult one of the many books available on the subject, or see a practitioner. It is important that you prepare yourself correctly by removing stressors and cutting out toxic foods and other substances from your diet in the periods before and after the fast.

EAT DETOXIFYING FOODS

You can give your body a mini-spring-cleaning on a daily basis by eating foods that sweep the intestine clean. This means fibrous foods such as fresh fruit and vegetables, whole grains, and beans. Fiber is best retained when cooked as little as possible, so try to eat fruit and vegetables raw, or steamed for just a minimum of time.

Certain foods contain substances that will aid your liver in the process of detoxification by providing enzymes and other molecules. Some of the most useful are cruciferous vegetables (such as broccoli, cabbage, and cauliflower), garlic and onions, amino acids (from high-quality protein sources), and green tea. If you are very sensitive to alcohol or paint fumes, or have very low tolerance to alcohol, these are possible signs that your liver is not detoxifying efficiently; these foods will give it a helping hand.

COLONIC IRRIGATION

Colonic irrigation seems to be an effective way of getting out substances that might otherwise have stayed there to the (early) grave. Items such as a blue marble, fatty lumps, brown stringy objects, rubbery nuggets, and gristle have variously been reported as appearing in the post-irrigation debris.[1] Hardened mucus builds up in our colons when we eat foods that are hard to digest, such as most of those in the SAD, namely: cooked meat, white flour, sugar, and fats. Colonic irrigation is a quick way to get rid of this black rubbery mucus, and pieces of it as long as twenty-seven feet have reportedly been removed from the human gut. People have reported health benefits such as shedding mysterious lumps, getting rid of allergies, gaining high energy levels, losing sinus problems, and having clear skin and bright clear eyes as a result of combining fasting with colonic irrigation.[2]

The subject of colonic irrigation is a hotly debated one, and nutritionists tend to fall between two stools (poor things) as to whether or not it should be done. Some nutritionists object to it on the grounds that washing out your colon strips it of the mucosal lining and friendly flora. You will have to make your own decision, based on talking to a health practitioner, reading about the subject, or perhaps trying it out once and seeing how you feel.

SWEAT IT OUT

In her book *Poisoning Our Children*, Nancy Sokol Green writes of her extraordinary experience of sweating out toxins: "On the fourteenth day of detox, I started experiencing allergic symptoms, such as eyelid swelling, while I was in the sauna! . . . I was actually beginning to reek of the pesticides that had been sprayed in my home. . . . Several of the patients at the clinic who were sensitive to pesticides had to stay away from me as I triggered adverse reactions in them."[3]

As Green found, we can sweat out copious quantities of waste through the skin, which is why this wonderful organ of detoxification is sometimes called the "third kidney." In her book *Digestive Wellness*, Elizabeth Lipski recommends low-temperature saunas and steam baths as the most effective way of sweating out deeply embedded toxins, such as pesticides and pharmaceutical drugs, from our fatty cells. Another benefit of saunas is that cancer cells dislike heat and die at around 104 degrees Fahrenheit, whereas healthy cells survive.

For detoxification, the sauna needs to be at a fairly low temperature of between 110 and 120 degrees Fahrenheit—enough for you to be able to stay in for about forty-five minutes, sweating slowly and steadily, without getting too hot. You should do this three to five times weekly so as to keep the momentum going. Exercise will also help to sweat out toxins, as well as stimulating the lymph function and circulation, which are both important components of our detoxification systems. Longevity populations do not use saunas, but they live in warm climates and they take a lot of exercise, so they get plenty of opportunity to sweat. Avoid using a sauna if pregnant, and consult a health practitioner if you are in doubt for any other reason.

DRINK WATER

Whether or not you are fasting, it is absolutely essential that you drink plenty of water, as all of the populations in this book do. Water flushes toxins out of the body, helps prevent toxicity from constipation, and transports nutrients needed for detoxification to the cells. You should drink around eight to ten glasses of water daily, and more when taking exercise, sweating, or detoxifying. See Secret 34 (page 171) for more about water.

EXERCISE REGULARLY

Exercise gets the waste drainage system in your body working properly, and also helps you to sweat out toxins. No detoxification program would be complete without it, and you should aim to get thirty to sixty minutes of exercise two or three times weekly. Secret 38 (page 192) explains more about why regular exercise is essential for health and longevity.

🌾 37 🌿

Supplement Your Diet

It is hard for us to get everything we need in order for our bodies to function as they should. An orange you buy in the supermarket today can actually contain zero vitamin C, while the magnesium levels in carrots have dropped by up to 75 percent in the last few decades, due to the impoverishment of soil by modern farming methods. You need a minimum of 400 grams of vitamin C daily to help ward off colds and more serious illnesses such as cancer and heart disease; if you have low magnesium levels, as the average American does, you are at risk of suffering from heart irregularities, high blood pressure, PMS, insomnia, and others.

The populations featured in this book do not take vitamin and mineral supplements. They don't need to, because their soil is so rich, as they farm on a small scale using organic compost, and everything they take out of the soil goes back in. The soil in Bama, for example, has been found to have excellent levels of minerals and trace elements such as zinc, manganese, and copper, which have also shown up in hair mineral analyses of the villagers.

In order for our bodies to function optimally, we need at least seventeen minerals and thirteen vitamins, in addition to protein, fiber, carbohydrates, and the right fats. The average American is deficient in most of these. In 1988, the American surgeon general concluded in his *Report on Health and Nutrition* that around 75 percent of deaths in the United States involved nutritional deficiencies. Most fruits and vegetables in the supermarkets are picked before they are ripe, so that they do not have time to acquire all their vitamins and minerals, and they then travel long distances to the supermarket, so that vitamins deteriorate along the way. Unless you get your vegetables from mineral-rich soil that has been carefully fertilized with natural composts and manures for many years, as the people in this book do, you almost certainly need to take a vitamin and mineral supplement for optimum health.

ANTI-AGING SUPPLEMENTS FOR OPTIMUM HEALTH

Following is an outline of some of the main anti-aging vitamins and minerals available in supplement form. If you take a good multivitamin and mineral supplement, you can get a good range of essential vitamins and minerals, including these, without having to think about which one is supposed to do what. Remember that supplements are just that—they are supposed to supplement a balanced diet, not replace it. A cheeseburger, fries, and milkshake followed by a handful of vitamins will not lead to optimum health.

If you have ever looked at the RDA (recommended daily allowance) amounts on the side of a jar of vitamins, you will notice that the suggested dosages given there are *much* higher than those given below. RDA levels are set by government scientists, and are based on how much of a given nutrient is needed to prevent serious deficiency diseases such as scurvy and beriberi, rather than on how much is needed for optimum health. Doses given below are for an average healthy adult.

VITAMIN C

Vitamin C is a potent immune-boosting antioxidant that is absolutely essential for our good health in many ways. The champion of vitamin C, Nobel prizewinner Dr. Linus Pauling, claimed that we could add twelve to eighteen years to our lives if we took 3–12 grams of vitamin C daily; he himself claimed to have lived an extra twenty years because of the large doses of vitamin C he took.

Vitamin C quenches carcinogenic free radicals and protects DNA from being damaged. According to Gladys Block, PhD, cancer epidemiologist at the University of California, Berkeley, people who eat the highest amounts of vitamin C are only half as likely to get cancer as people who are deficient in the vitamin.[1] Vitamin C also builds collagen and protects arteries from damage. A study published in the *British Medical Journal* showed that men who had low levels of vitamin C were three and a half times more likely to have a heart attack than others.[2]

Suggested optimal dose: 1,000–3,000 milligrams (1–3 grams) is recommended; 400 milligrams at the very minimum. Use magnesium ascorbate for best absorption, and spread the dose throughout the day.

Caution: No known toxicity, although very high doses cause temporary diarrhea. If taking an oral contraceptive, 10 grams daily may render it ineffective. Vitamin C aids absorption of iron, so if you have a disorder in handling iron (such as hemochromatosis), consult a doctor.

Some food sources of vitamin C: red peppers, berries, citrus fruits, and cruciferous vegetables, eaten raw.

VITAMIN A/BETA CAROTENE

Once known as the "anti-infective vitamin," vitamin A, and its precursor, beta carotene, are a major factor in immune health. Vitamin A is a powerful fat-soluble antioxidant that protects cell membranes and mucus membranes such as those lining the lungs and digestive tract.

More than a hundred studies have shown that people with high levels of vitamin A are about half as likely as others to develop various cancers, especially lung cancer. Beta carotene prevents LDL cholesterol from being oxidized; diets high in beta carotene have been found to lower the risk of heart attack by up to a half.[4]

Suggested optimal dose: 5,000–50,000 IU of beta carotene or 7,500–20,000 IU of vitamin A. For best absorption, beta carotene and vitamin A should be taken with beneficial fats such as those found in oily fish or olive oil.

Caution: Vitamin A can be toxic in very high doses (more than 50,000 IU daily). Do not take more than 2,000 IU of vitamin A in pregnancy, as it can be toxic to the fetus, although the fetus does need some vitamin A for proper development. You can take much higher levels of beta carotene, as the body will only convert the amount it needs. Beta carotene is nontoxic, although very high levels can cause a slight yellowing of the skin, which is temporary and is thought to be completely harmless.

Some vitamin A food sources: dark green, orange, and red fruits and vegetables (beta carotene); cod liver oil and liver (vitamin A).

VITAMIN E

Vitamin E has been dubbed the "fountain of youth" for its heart-protective properties. This powerful fat-soluble antioxidant boosts the immune system and protects against heart disease and cancer; high blood levels are associated with health and longevity.[5]

Studies show that low blood levels of vitamin E make people 50 percent more susceptible to all kinds of cancer.[6] Vitamin E also protects the heart by thinning the blood and preventing LDL cholesterol from oxidizing; a major study showed that it can reduce the risk of heart attack by 40 percent.[7]

Suggested optimal dose: 40–800 IU daily; take with vitamin C, which recycles "spent" vitamin E.

Caution: If you are taking anticoagulant drugs, consult your doctor. Vitamin E can replace blood-thinning drugs, but this must be done gradually and with care. If you have high blood pressure, consult your doctor before using vitamin E.

Some vitamin E food sources: nuts, fish oil, olive oil, and avocado.

SELENIUM

Selenium rejuvenates the immune system; studies show that the immune systems of older people given selenium behave like those of younger people.[8] It is also a powerful antioxidant; studies have found that cancer death can be reduced by half by taking selenium supplements.[9] High levels of selenium in soil in some places (Norfolk in the UK and Rumania are two examples) are associated with a reduced risk of cancer, while areas with low selenium levels in the soil have been found to have higher cancer and virus levels.[10]

Selenium protects the heart by boosting the function of the mitochondria, the powerhouses of heart cells. In a large-scale study in Finland, it was found that those with the lowest blood levels of selenium were three times more likely to die from heart disease than those with the highest levels.[11]

Suggested optimal dose: 100–200 micrograms daily.

Caution: Selenium can be toxic in high doses of 2,500 micrograms daily (liver damage, joint inflammation). Japanese fishermen have around 500 micrograms per day without any apparent damage; keep to 200 micrograms daily to be on the safe side.

Some selenium food sources: Brazil nuts straight from the shell (one or two of these provide enough for a day). If you buy preshelled nuts, you need more, as they come from a different part of Brazil with lower selenium levels. Selenium is also found in garlic, asparagus, seafood, and whole grains.

ZINC

Zinc deficiency is very common, especially in the elderly. Look at your fingernails—if you have more than two small white spots in the fingertip part, you are likely to be zinc deficient. Zinc-deficient animals have been found to have 15–20 percent higher levels of free radicals in their bodies than animals with normal levels.[12] Zinc regulates normal cell death and "tells" problem cells to commit suicide, which prevents them from dividing uncontrollably—an important anticancer mechanism. Zinc also has a seemingly miraculous ability to rejuvenate an aging thymus gland, responsible for overseeing our all-important immune systems.

Suggested optimal dose: 10–30 milligrams daily. Zinc gluconate is the best-absorbed form.

Caution: Do not exceed 50 milligrams, as high doses may interfere with absorption of other nutrients.

Some zinc food sources: oysters, meat, poultry, garlic, whole grains, green leafy vegetables, and nuts and seeds.

COENZYME Q10

Coenzyme Q10 (CoQ10) is a powerful anti-aging antioxidant that is the subject of much exciting new research, particularly with regard to its ability to boost heart health.[13] It is one of the few antioxidants that can get inside the mitochondria, the powerhouses of our cells that are highly susceptible to free radical damage, particularly in the heart and brain.

Studies show that CoQ10 rejuvenates the immune system in aging people.[14] It also has antiviral, antibacterial, and antitumor effects, with some cancer patients showing complete regression. Fifteen mice given CoQ10 stayed younger for longer and were more active in old age, according to studies conducted at UCLA.[15, 16]

Suggested optimal dose: 50–100 milligrams or more daily.

Some CoQ10 food sources: sardines, mackerel, and organ meats.

GLUTATHIONE

Glutathione is a potent antioxidant that regenerates immune cells and makes them superefficient. Known as the "master antioxidant," it is needed by every cell in our bodies. It is also a crucial part of our liver detoxification systems. It is abundant in most foods and is produced in our cells, but people who are even moderately deficient are more likely to age prematurely, as free radicals are left unchecked.[17] Levels drop with age: in one study, elderly patients who were given 75 milligrams daily had a dramatic increase in immune cell activity, and they felt healthier and more energetic.[18]

Suggested optimal dose: 50–100 milligrams daily. Five hundred milligrams daily of vitamin C boosts glutathione levels.

Some glutathione food sources: raw fruit and vegetables, especially avocado, watermelon, asparagus, and cruciferous vegetables such as cauliflower and broccoli.

ALPHA LIPOIC ACID

This is a very potent antioxidant that is being increasingly viewed as a "miracle cure." It is both water- and fat-soluble, so is able to protect both fatty and watery areas of the body and can regenerate both vitamin E and vitamin C. Alpha lipoic acid also boosts the body's own production of glutathione. It lowers blood glucose and insulin levels, and can be very useful for counteracting insulin resistance. It is made in small amounts by the body, but supplementation is probably necessary in order to counteract our polluted, low-nutrient environment and lifestyles.

Suggested optimal dose: 100–300 mg daily.

Some alpha lipoic food sources: dark green leafy vegetables such as broccoli, spinach, and amaranth.

CALCIUM

Calcium is necessary for bone health, although it cannot work without magnesium and vitamin D. (Vitamin D is synthesized in the body from sunlight, and is also found in seafood. Supplementation with vitamin D should not be necessary; however, you do need to ensure adequate magnesium intake.)

Suggested optimal dose: 500–1,000 milligrams, taken with magnesium. You may be getting enough from your diet; it is often lack of magnesium that is a problem, rather than lack of calcium. Too much calcium also depletes levels of magnesium (see below).

Caution: More than 2,000 milligrams can be toxic; too much can cause constipation.

The best food sources of calcium: cruciferous vegetables (such as broccoli), nuts, and seeds, as these also contain magnesium. Other sources include kale, yogurt, alfalfa sprouts, legumes, fish (especially soft bones in canned fish, such as sardines), seaweed, and tofu. Cheese is not the best source of calcium, as it lacks magnesium and can cause leaching of calcium from the bones—see Secret 9 (page 86).

MAGNESIUM

Magnesium protects the mitochondria in our cells from free radical damage, a process that is thought to be at the core of the aging process. According to French researchers, animals that are deficient in magnesium are almost perfect specimens of accelerated aging.[19]

Magnesium gives us youthful flexibility. It relaxes and dilates blood vessels and keeps muscles, including the heart muscle, flexible; people who die suddenly from heart attacks have been found to have low levels of magnesium.[20] It can also work as a mild laxative by relaxing the smooth muscles lining the colon. Magnesium works with calcium to maintain bone health.

Suggested optimal dose: 400–800 milligrams, depending on your calcium intake—you need half as much magnesium as calcium.

Caution: Magnesium relaxes the bowel, so avoid large doses if you have diarrhea. Do not take if you have severe kidney problems or heart failure.

Some magnesium food sources: whole grains, green leafy vegetables, broccoli, and nuts and seeds.

CHROMIUM

Dr. Gary Evans, of Bemidji State University, Minnesota, says: "I call chromium the geriatric nutrient because everybody starts to really need it past age thirty-five." Chromium deficiency, which is extremely common, causes premature aging; rats given chromium have been found to live longer and have more vitality than others. The main function of chromium as an anti-aging agent is in forming glucose tolerance factor (GTF), which is involved in getting blood glucose into cells. In one study of people with adult-onset diabetes, those given 200 micrograms of chromium picolinate daily had their blood sugar levels lowered as effectively as with orthodox medication.[21]

Suggested optimum dose: 200 micrograms daily in chromium picolinate form.

Some chromium food sources: nuts, seeds, and whole grains.

B VITAMINS

You need to take the whole complex of B vitamins in order for your body to metabolize nutrients, make energy, and make immune cells. Especially important are vitamins B_6, B_{12}, and folic acid. B vitamin deficiency is linked with various illnesses of aging, including cancer, heart disease, senility, and multiple sclerosis. Vitamin B_6 protects the heart by metabolizing homo-cysteine, while B_{12} deficiency symptoms include memory loss, neurological problems, and pernicious anemia. Folic acid defi-ciency increases the risk of cancer.[22]

Suggested optimal dose: A good supplement will give you levels far higher than the RDAs; choose a good brand for sufficient dosages.

Some vitamin B_6 food sources: seafood, whole grains, nuts, soy, sweet potatoes, prunes, poultry, and bananas.

Some folic acid food sources: meat, fish, poultry, grains, nuts and seeds, soy, green leafy vegetables, potatoes, legumes, organ meats, mushrooms, and cruciferous vegetables.

Some vitamin B_{12} food sources: meat, fish, and poultry.

38

Exercise, Exercise, Exercise

You will be hard-pressed to find exceptionally long-lived people who don't take plenty of regular exercise. The people discussed in this book all lead an outdoor life, farming, getting in the day's catch, doing housework, and climbing up and down the rugged terrain in which they live. They are also fond of sports—the

Okinawans practice martial arts, for example, while the Hunzakuts enjoy regular dancing sessions along with their home-brewed alcohol. Even the supercentenarians in these places are mobile and able to take part in some physical activity most days.

According to a recent study, inactivity is an even stronger predictor of death risk than high cholesterol levels, high blood pressure, diabetes, and heart disease.[1] Exercise is so important for good health that it can even negate some of the harmful effects of smoking. According to a 1996 report in the *Journal of the American Medical Association*, smokers who are moderately fit live longer than sedentary nonsmokers. The real benefits occur, however, when you combine a nutritious diet with regular exercise.

Exercise makes you look and feel better and benefits every part of your body. It reduces the risk of cancer, and, according to one study, it particularly reduces the risk of colon cancer in men and breast cancer in women.[2] It lowers blood pressure, homocysteine levels, and LDL cholesterol levels, thus reducing the risk of heart disease; according to a Harvard study, men who run for an hour or more each week lower their risk of heart disease by 42 percent.[3] All of the muscles in your body, including the heart and those lining the colon, need regular exercise in order to function well.

Exercise boosts the circulation, so that more nutrients get to your cells, and it improves lymphatic function so that your waste drainage system works properly. Exercise improves the immune system by boosting white blood cell performance and ridding the body of toxins through sweat. For women, exercise can help prevent a difficult pregnancy and labor, and reduces the risk of osteoporosis.[4] Of course, exercise will also help you lose weight, through boosting the metabolism as well as burning off a few calories.

There are numerous studies to show that regular, aerobic exercise can add several years to your life. On average, those who live to be one hundred walk an hour a day, or get the equivalent amount of exercise.[5] Growth hormone, associated with youthfulness, is stimulated by exercise. Studies show that regular exercise slows the aging process by lowering blood glucose levels, which prevents the age-inducing cross-linking of skin and tissues (see Secret 2, page 53) and insulin damage to blood vessels.

Even if you aren't overweight, a sedentary lifestyle increases your chances of developing glucose intolerance and diabetes; inactive men are almost four times as likely as active men to get diabetes.[6] People who exercise regularly are also less likely to become disabled in later life.[7] It is never too late to start exercising regularly; one study by W. J. Evans showed that even ninety-six-year-olds can increase their strength and muscle size by beginning an exercise program.

Exercise is good for mental health and happiness. Studies show that it improves mood, reduces anxiety and depression, and gets rid of stress.[8] It can even raise your IQ; in one study, older adults who walked for forty-five minutes three times a week performed better in psychological tests than people who merely did stretching and toning exercises.[9]

HOW TO EXERCISE

Half to One Hour Daily

For those of us who have no gardening to do or messages to deliver on the other side of a mountain, the only opportunity for incidental exercise we get may be strolling over to the office water cooler from time to time. Some of us even glide to the water cooler on our swivel chairs. We tell ourselves there is "no time" to exercise, but it's strange how easy it can be to fit in several hours' worth of TV viewing after work, instead. You can incorporate regular exercise into your busy life easily, so long as you have the willpower. Experts recommend half to one hour of reasonably strenuous exercise most days of the week, in order to get the benefits. It is best to consult a health practitioner before starting any exercise program.

Walk Briskly

The best kind of exercise works on the whole body simultaneously, including the muscle groups, skeletal system, circulatory system, nervous system, respiratory system, and immune system. Brisk walking for half an hour meets all these criteria, and because it is a weight-bearing exercise, it strengthens bones and so helps prevent osteoporosis.

Brisk walking can be done anywhere, anytime—try walking to work instead of taking the bus. Brisk walking is probably better for you than jogging, which can cause knee injuries and has also been found to reduce immune cell levels.[10] The best longevity-promoting exercise mimics the kind of movements our bodies make naturally; weightlifting alone, for example, will not improve your health as much as walking or swimming, although it will tone your muscles; a combination of strength training and aerobic exercise may be of optimum benefit.

Explore Aerobic Exercise

The true benefits of exercise will only occur when the exercise is aerobic. The deeper breathing brought about by aerobic exercise helps oxygen and nutrients get to the places where they are needed and boosts heart function.

Types of aerobic exercise include brisk walking, swimming, dancing, climbing uphill, riding, rollerblading, rebounding (jumping on a special trampoline called a "rebounder"), tennis, football, and martial arts—anything that makes you out of breath. Belly dancing, although not especially aerobic, is good for stiff backs and the pelvic area, and seems to create extra amounts of endorphins. Yoga is an excellent form of exercise that acts like aerobic exercise by oxygenating the tissues through deep breathing. Yoga can benefit internal organs and improve lymph and blood flow, and there are yoga exercises for specific complaints such as constipation and flatulence.

Don't Overdo It

Do not be tempted to overexercise. This increases levels of age-inducing free radicals and suppresses the immune system, which is why professional athletes tend to have short careers and often have to retire as a result of health problems, especially immune-related illness. Too much exercise increases levels of the stress hormone cortisol, another factor in aging. One of many studies in this area showed that high-mileage runners eating a low-fat diet had suppressed immune systems and raised levels of cortisol and inflammatory prostaglandins.[11] For the best results, combine regular, moderate exercise with a diet based on whole foods and the right kind of fats.

Take One Step at a Time

There is no need to totally overhaul your life in order to include a major exercise program. If you are not in the habit of getting any exercise at all, start with just a few minutes a day and work gradually upward—you will soon find you don't feel right without your daily bit of exercise and that you want more and more.

You could begin by walking or cycling to places that are near enough, or even walking to the supermarket and carrying the bags back instead of driving. If you don't want to move away from the TV or stereo, you can do step aerobics on a step at home, in front of the TV, or buy a rebounder and jump around for ten minutes to music. In this day and age, there are many ways to explore exercise—from joining a gym to reading any one of the number of books out there, to seeking out videos/DVDs for at-home workouts. The key is finding something you enjoy.

🦋 39 🦋

Get Your Daily Dose of Sunshine

We are often told to cover up and keep out of the sun, but it is equally important that we get enough sunlight. People who live in cloudy regions of the world are more apt to get TB, cancer, high blood pressure, osteoporosis, multiple sclerosis, and depression.[1] Studies also show that not getting enough sunshine while pregnant increases the unborn child's risk of schizophrenia, crooked teeth, and myopia later in life. The people in this book all live in sunny climates, which may well be a factor in their low rates of these and other diseases.

The condition known as seasonal affective disorder (SAD) affects sufferers during the dark winter months, most likely because more of the sleep-related hormone melatonin is made during this time, which can cause depression. Spending an hour in the winter sunlight or using phototherapy helps those with SAD, since sunlight suppresses the manufacture of melatonin. Being outside during the day also helps our biological body clocks to keep in tune with night and day, thus aiding our quality of sleep.

Sunlight provides us with good levels of vitamin D, a vitamin and also a hormone with several functions, which is thought to help protect us from cancer, TB, osteoporosis, multiple sclerosis, hypertension, and possibly some as-yet unknown diseases. Vitamin D is manufactured from cholesterol when skin is exposed to ultraviolet rays from the sun, and it is difficult to get enough from diet alone. *The Third National Health and Nutrition Examination Survey (NHANES III)*, conducted in the U.S. (1988–1994), found that up to 40 percent of the U.S. female population has hypovitaminosis D (low blood levels of vitamin D); African-American women are particularly at risk, since those with dark skins make less vitamin D. People whose cultures encourage them to cover up their bodies are also prone to low levels of this very important hormone.

The most well known result of severe vitamin D deficiency is rickets, a disease causing crippling bowlegs, which occurs in children deprived of sunlight. This is because vitamin D is necessary for the proper absorption of calcium and magnesium, needed for good bone density. In adults, vitamin D deficiency disease is known as osteomalacia and is caused by an inability to absorb both calcium and phosphorus, for which vitamin D is necessary. Rickets is supposed to be obsolete in modern civilization, yet cases have recently been appearing in the U.S. Rickets may just be the tip of the iceberg, indicating more widespread deficiency of vitamin D, and indeed 25 million adults in the U.S. are estimated to either have or be at risk of developing osteoporosis, while 50 percent of women hospitalized with hip fractures have been found to have low levels of vitamin D.[2]

Vitamin D has recently become known as an effective anti-cancer agent, and it has been known for decades that there is an inverse correlation between sun exposure and cancer mortality.[3] Vitamin D is associated with lower colon, prostate, skin, and breast cancer, and women with breast cancer have been found to be twice as likely to have a fault in the gene that enables the body to use vitamin D. This anticancer activity of vitamin D may be due to its ability to inactivate certain oncogenes, genes that instruct ordinary cells to become cancer cells. In one recent study, mice given tumors were split into two groups, one treated with radiation alone and another treated with both radiation and a derivative of vitamin D called EB1089. The second group had approximately 50 percent lower final tumor volume, indicating that vitamin D may actually be able to shrink tumors.[4]

The adequate intake for vitamin D as set by the Institute of Medicine of the National Academy of Sciences is 200 IU daily for children and adults up to the age of fifty, 400 IU for those fifty-one to seventy years old, and 600 IU for those seventy-one to eighty years old, because the older we get, the less we are able to manufacture it. The upper limit is set at 1,000 IU for infants up to a year old, and 2,000 IU daily for children, adults, and pregnant and lactating women. However, it is probably not advisable to have more than 800 IU daily, since excess vitamin D is toxic and can cause nausea, vomiting, loss of appetite, constipation, weakness, and weight loss. You can have a blood test for vitamin D levels, which will tell you how much vitamin D it is safe for you to have.

Vitamin D can be obtained from the diet, but not very easily. Milk and some breakfast cereals sold in the U.S. are fortified with vitamin D, but many people cannot digest milk well, and breakfast cereals often have unhealthy additives. Eggs contain vitamin D, but you would need to eat ten eggs to get 200 IU. The best source of vitamin D is fish oil, as the sun-deprived Inuit well know. A three-ounce portion of canned salmon provides 530 IU of vitamin D. One tablespoon of cod liver oil has 1,360 IU, so a smaller dose in the winter months will provide you with enough; it may be better to avoid it during the summer, if you are getting a lot of sunlight. Make sure you buy a good brand that has had toxic dioxins removed, and avoid cod liver oil when pregnant, due to high levels of vitamin A, which can harm the developing fetus. Vitamin D is no use with a completely fat-free diet, since it is a fat-soluble substance needing fat for transport; fish oils are a healthy fat to include in the diet.

Spending ten to twenty minutes outside two or three times a week in summer is thought to give us adequate vitamin D. Those with dark skins may need more, and you may need to take supplements in winter if you live in a cloudy region. It is interesting that vitamin D protects us from precancerous changes to skin cells when they are exposed to the sun's UVB rays. When we use sunscreen, vitamin D is not made, since UVB rays are blocked, but the UVA rays still get through and raise the risk of skin cancer. Spending many hours in the sun is not a good idea, with or without sunscreen, but, contrary to today's advice, you may well benefit from a short time in the sun without sunscreen before you cover up. Make sure it is only a short time, however; do not go out in strong sunshine without sunscreen, and consult with your health practitioner if you are pale-skinned or have any other concerns.

❦ 40 ❧

Jog Your Memory

What did you do last weekend? Can you remember what you had for supper last night? If you have children, you may need to ask them, because our memory starts to decline from our midtwenties onward, and the rest of our cognitive function along with it. For many, wandering the house searching for our keys, thinking our car has been stolen then remembering we parked it somewhere else, and forgetting what we were about to say halfway through a sentence become an increasing reality as we age.

However, this aging of the brain is not at all inevitable. We do lose brain cells as we get older—around 50,000 a day—but, since we start with 100 billion of them, this only amounts to a very small percentage of the total. In addition, mental exercise such as doing crossword puzzles and other mind games strengthens neural networks in the brain and improves cognitive ability, whatever your age. Studies show that keeping the brain active can protect against senile dementia, and that when older people are given mental tasks to do, they can become as good or better at the tasks than younger people after just six months.

Like a muscle, the brain can even grow with exercise. London taxi drivers have been found to have a larger part of the brain where maps and street names are stored in memory, compared with other people, according to a UK survey. The cab drivers had an enlarged posterior part of the hippocampus, and the longer they had been taxi drivers, the more pronounced was the difference.[1] The rest of their brains, of course, were no bigger than anyone else's.

If you hate jogging, take heart from the fact that sitting comfortably on a sofa while exercising the mind may help you to live longer. Professor George Singer of the La Trobe University School of Psychology, Australia, says that studies have shown that crosswords improve the immune system by boosting antibody production, which means fending off degenerative disease.

The old and super-old Okinawans do not retire but keep busy, even in their nineties or hundreds, gardening, socializing, working in the fields, or maintaining cottage industries making handicrafts. This sense of purpose in later life is thought by gerontologists to maintain vigor and promote longevity. Staying active after retirement has been found to have a major impact on the rate of aging, and intricate work with the hands, such as weaving fabric, may stimulate the brain to keep it fresh.

In Bama, weekly folk-singing competitions are held, with competitors aged up to one hundred, and older, pitting their wits against each other by singing impromptu songs. These competitions are considered by locals to keep their brains alert and youthful; they also keep villagers young in other ways (see Secret 45, page 213).

In all of the five longevity hot spots in this book, there is no conception of "retirement," so older people never reach a cutoff age when their brains start to become useless. In the West, where older people constitute an increasingly large proportion of the population, and there will be fewer young people to support the older generations as time goes on, it may become necessary for older people to carry on working. In some countries, there are already plans for the retirement age to be raised in anticipation of this.

If you aren't one already, you are almost certainly going to be one of those people, so don't forget to do your brain exercises. Find a mental activity you enjoy, as this releases brain chemicals called endorphins, which make us feel happy and combat stress. Brain exercises you can do include going to a concert; playing stimulating games such as chess, bridge, Scrabble, or backgammon; socializing; memorizing a poem; and learning a language. Music also has a powerful ability to retard the aging process, and is covered in the next secret.

🙼 41 🙼

Breathe—and Hum

Breathing is the first thing we do after we are born, and the last thing we do before we die. We can't live without doing it for more than a few minutes. In some ways, the nutrition we get from the air is even more important than that which we get from food. As with food and water, breath can be of bad or good quality. By improving your breathing, you can enhance your digestion and circulation, to get nutrients around the body where they are needed, which can have a deep impact on your health.

When we are stressed, we tend to take shallow breaths using only the chest. This prevents proper exhalation of stale air and toxins and efficient oxygenation of tissues. When stressed, breathing may be the last thing on your mind, but next time you find yourself feeling anxious, try remembering to breathe deeply, using not only the chest but also the diaphragm and abdomen. This will improve heart rate and blood pressure, and help melt away the tension.

Proper breathing may reduce the risk of cancer, since cancer cells are the only cells in the body that do not like oxygen. Dr. Otto Warburg won the Nobel Prize in 1931 for this discovery, and oxygenation treatments have been used to kill cancer cells as a result. Conversely, depriving cells of oxygen is thought to increase the likelihood of their turning cancerous. Low oxygen levels in the body also encourage acid conditions, increasing the risk of disease, including cancer, whereas good breathing will encourage alkalinity and therefore good health.

Oxygenation treatments get oxygen to cells by using hydrogen peroxide, which is water with an extra oxygen molecule attached. It is interesting that breast milk and colostrum are high in hydrogen peroxide, which is thought to be because it stimulates immunity and enzyme systems in the baby's body.[1] Hydrogen peroxide is also produced by vitamin C, which is thought to be one way in which vitamin C fights infections.[2]

The people discussed in this book get plenty of aerobic exercise, and they have very low stress levels, so they are not prone to shallow breathing and insufficient oxygenation, as we often are in the Western world. It helps also that they live in places by the sea or in the hills, with well-oxygenated, clean air. Some of them also practice meditation, which improves the breathing (see the following secret for more on the power of meditation). Eating a healthy diet that is low in saturated and trans fats and high in antioxidants from fruit and vegetables also helps their oxygenation by keeping their arteries clear.

A simple deep-breathing exercise is as follows: Sit cross-legged in loose clothes, keeping your spine straight. Relax. Inhale and exhale smoothly. Notice your breathing, and expand your chest and lower abdomen as you breathe. Feel your powerful diaphragm moving in and out. Do this several times. Feel the fresh air coming in and the stale air going out. Doing aerobic exercise such as walking briskly or doing yoga is also an excellent way of improving breathing. As a result of doing deep-breathing exercises such as these, your normal everyday breathing should also improve.

You can also try humming. Humming dramatically improves the efficiency of the gas exchange between the sinuses and nasal passages, and is thought to help reduce upper respiratory tract infections and sinusitis. Humming also increases nitric oxide levels, which helps dilate capillaries and increase blood flow.[3]

You should not breathe deeply all day long, but there are certain times of day when it may be helpful to do so. After eating, breathe in and feel your breath enter your abdominal area. Relax. This should help with anxiety-related digestive problems you may have. Other times when it may be helpful to breathe deeply are during moments of stress, when you are feeling tired, or when you feel unhappy or depressed. Try it, and notice the difference.

❧ 42 ❧

Sit Still and Do Nothing

There is a practice that has been found time and again to keep away illness and preserve the youth and beauty of those who engage in it. It is incredibly effective, and does not involve preparing healthy food, spending any money, or exercising. It involves nothing more than sitting still and doing nothing, and it has been practiced for thousands of years. This technique is otherwise known as meditation.

Meditation can lower blood pressure, relax the muscles, raise levels of the "youth hormone" DHEA, lower age-inducing cortisol levels, and generally rejuvenate the body. One form of meditation in particular, known as transcendental meditation (TM), is thought to be especially beneficial. According to studies, people who practice TM have 55 percent less cancer and 80 percent less heart disease than nonmeditators.[1] Another study of 2,000 people showed a more than 50 percent reduction in use of medical facilities among those practicing TM. For the over-forties, reduction was more than 70 percent. This included heart, respiratory, and gastrointestinal diseases.[2]

TM has been found to actually lower biological age. In one study, three key biomarkers of aging—blood pressure, close-object vision, and auditory skills—were used to measure "real age." Those who practiced TM long-term were found to be physiologically twelve years younger than their chronological age, while those who practiced TM short-term were five years younger. Diet and exercise were controlled for, in the study, showing that it was TM alone producing the benefits.[3]

The word "transcendental" in "Transcendental Meditation" implies an ability to transcend, or go beyond, activity. The body goes into a profound state of restfulness similar to that experienced in the deepest sleep; this state of being is the exact opposite of "fight or flight," and could be called the "rest and repair" state. TM helps combat the aging effects of stress such as muscle tension, raised cortisol levels, and acidity. Lymph starts to flow better, so that toxins are drained, and oxygenation of tissues becomes more efficient. Meditation can also enhance your natural beauty by smoothing out lines on the face. It also helps insomniacs to sleep and improves the quality of sleep—an important part of the rejuvenation process.

The Okinawans, Hunzakuts, and people of Bama achieve serenity and low stress levels with regular meditation sessions. The Okinawans were introduced to meditation by the ancient Chinese text *The Bubishi*, which was brought to Okinawa hundreds of years ago; the Centenarian Study researchers' book, *The Okinawa Program*, contains several methods of meditation practiced by the Okinawans.

Meditation consists simply of putting the attention on the breath, focusing on nothing—or on *now*—and letting thoughts come in and then out of the mind, neither giving them attention nor pushing them away. This takes practice, and it is only after some time that the true benefits start to take effect, and thoughts start to lose their hold on the mind.

If you want to practice meditation, there are hundreds of different techniques, so it should be easy to find one that suits you. There are also thousands of TM teachers in the U.S., who can be found in phone books or on the Internet. Meditation can be done alone at home or in a class. A simple technique for you to do at home is described on the following page.

SIMPLE TEN-STEP MEDITATION TECHNIQUE

1. Find a quiet place to sit for thirty to forty minutes.
2. Find a comfortable position in which you can sit upright without straining your back. Try sitting cross-legged on the floor or against a wall.
3. Keep your back straight and your neck in line with your spine, so your head is tilted slightly forward.
4. Keep perfectly still.
5. Half-close your eyes—this will prevent both fantasies and objects in the room from distracting you.
6. Relax your shoulders.
7. Slightly constrict the sphincter to preserve internal energy circulation.
8. Exhale the stale air from your lungs with a few breaths, then take a few deep breaths. Then start to breathe normally, with smooth soft breaths, and focus on your breath.
9. Focus on internal sounds and ignore external sounds.
10. Stray thoughts will start to come. Let them pass through. Don't focus on them, and don't try to push them away, either. Let your internal dialogue get weaker and weaker, and do nothing.

Try doing this exercise every day and observe how it affects your physical and mental health. Meditation can be hard—it is difficult to prevent one's thoughts from straying to the grocery shopping or more serious worries—but learning to let these thoughts pass through is where much of the benefit of meditation lies. Meditation becomes easier with practice, and if you make it a part of your routine in the long term, it should have a long-term, profound impact on your state of being.

🎵 **43** 🎵

Have Faith

Being religious may or may not give you eternal life, but it is very likely to lengthen it. A meta-analysis of forty-two studies examining 125,826 people, published by the American Psychological Association in 2000, found that attendance at a place of worship, whether it be church, synagogue, mosque, or temple, can add eight years to the average life span and significantly improve health. One study also showed that religious people were one-third less likely to die after open-heart surgery than nonbelievers. Private personal faith was found to be important, but worshipping in a public place provided the most striking correlation between faith and good health.[1]

Having spiritual beliefs may enhance health in several ways. Worshipping in a public place provides social contact and a strong support network, which can significantly reduce stress levels. Frequent churchgoers have also been found to be less obese and more likely to stop smoking and drinking and to take up exercise than others. One study showed that those attending religious services were half as likely to have excess blood levels of the pro-inflammatory immune component, interleukin-6, indicating healthier immune systems than non-worshippers.

Having spiritual beliefs may also improve health by giving people a sense of meaning. Finding meaning in difficult circumstances may lower stress levels and create a greater sense of fulfillment, which can have beneficial effects on the body, such as improving immunity. When sociologist Aaron Antonovsky studied aging Holocaust survivors, he found that those who felt that life had meaning had a longer life expectancy after the Holocaust than those who did not.

All of the people discussed in this book have strong spiritual beliefs, no matter what their religion. The Hunzakuts embrace a more liberal form of Islam than the rest of the country, but they have a powerful sense of spirituality. The Okinawans share their problems with gods and ancestors, and their spirituality is also expressed by a reverence for nature and a blend of Taoist and Confucian influences. When Okinawans are ill they consult a shaman as well as a doctor, knowing their spiritual health to be an important part of the overall picture.

Okinawan women, who are particularly in touch with their spiritual beliefs, have an enhanced sense of well-being as a result, according to the Centenarian Study researchers. The researchers speculate that a spiritual awareness and strong sense of social integration may explain why women tend to live longer than men in Okinawa and elsewhere in the world.

Prayer can have an amazing impact on health. For one thing, praying lowers breathing and heart rate, and can reduce blood pressure, according to studies from the National Institutes of Health. It also lowers levels of age-inducing stress hormones such as cortisol. Yet prayer also seems to have more extraordinary powers than this. In a study of 393 cardiac patients at San Francisco General Hospital, it was found that those who were prayed for by others needed fewer drugs and antibiotics and spent less time on ventilators. This was a scientifically conducted double-blind study in which none of the patients or nurses knew which patients were being prayed for.

Another recent study at the California Pacific Medical Center in San Francisco showed that of forty AIDS patients, those who were prayed for visited their doctors or were hospitalized less than those who were not, and also described their mood as "much improved." Again, none of the patients knew who was in the prayed-for group and who was in the control group. Those who were praying included people from a wide range of faiths, including Buddhism, shamanism, and Judaism.

A leading expert in the power of prayer on health, Dr. Larry Dossey, has conducted and reviewed many experiments on healing through prayer. He has found that prayer, whether or not subjects know they are being prayed for, can improve conditions such as high blood pressure, wounds, heart attacks, headaches, and anxiety, and that a range of biological processes, including enzyme activity, mutation rates of bacteria, tumor size, and wound healing rate, are also influenced. Even more incredibly, Dossey has found, in experiments that rule out any possibility of knowingly being prayed for, that prayed-for rye grass grows taller, and prayed-for yeast resists the toxic effects of cyanide.

Around thirty medical schools in the U.S. now provide courses in faith and medicine, and many doctors believe that praying with patients helps recovery from serious operations. Whether the effects of prayer and faith are to do with measurable biological functions, types of energy transfer we do not yet fully understand, some other force, or all of these, these are powerful methods of healing that we cannot afford to ignore.

✲ 43 ✲

Laugh It Off

It is often observed that happy people are less apt to get sick than unhappy people. There is a scientific basis for this, since stress is thought to contribute to up to 80 percent of all major illnesses, including cancer, heart disease, and back problems. Conversely, people who live long tend to have "stress-resistant personalities," according to the New England Centenarian Study.[1] Jeanne Calment, the Frenchwoman who lived for a world-record 122 years, was known for being unflappable and immune to stress. Perhaps this is why the Okinawans use a single word, *genki*, for "happy and healthy."

Chronic stress, whether it is caused by a belligerent boss, a difficult relationship, a death in the family, or daily traffic jams, causes harmful physiological changes We release the hormones adrenalin and cortisol, blood glucose goes up, cholesterol levels rise, and free radicals are formed. Digestion and immune response are put on hold. All of these things cause accelerated aging.

Laughter is a highly effective way of relieving stress. The health craze for laughter was born in the U.S. in the 1960s, when *Saturday Review* editor Norman Cousins made an extraordinary recovery from illness. He was diagnosed with a painful autoimmune disease called ankylosing spondylitis, from which he was told he had a 1 in 500 chance of recovering. He was sent to a hospital, where he was given thirty-eight painkillers daily, as well as sleeping pills and codeine.

Worried about the effects of this medication, along with the abysmal food he was given, Cousins decided that hospitals were no place for sick people and had himself discharged. Aware of the negative effects of stress on health, he reasoned that the opposite must also be true, and set about inventing his own laughter cure.

Every day Cousins watched Marx Brothers films from his bed and had his nurse read amusing books to him. He soon found that if he had a good ten-minute belly laugh each day, he was able to have two hours of pain-free sleep. Within a relatively short space of time, Cousins was well enough to return to his job full-time.[2] He was ridiculed for his methods at the time, but his findings have since been backed up by several scientific studies.

For example, in 1996, Dr. Lee Berk and Dr. Stanley Tan of Loma Linda University, California, studied the effects of laughter on the immune system by giving ten healthy males a funny video to watch. It was found that levels of immune-boosting T-cells, cancer-fighting natural killer cells, B-cells, and other components of the men's immune systems were raised, with the effect lasting into the next day.[3]

Laughter is sometimes called "inner jogging." Laughter gives your heart, diaphragm, abdomen, and facial muscles a good workout, and it triggers the release of endorphins, the body's natural painkillers. "One hundred laughs is equal to fifteen minutes on a stationary bicycle," says Dr. Diane Snustad, a geriatrician at the University of Virginia. Laughter also discharges tension and so reduces levels of the stress hormones, adrenaline and cortisol.

In Bombay, Madan Kataria has established more than eighty Laughing Clubs to help people heal. During each session, members stand in the park, raise their arms in the air, and laugh. People who attend the sessions report dramatically reduced depression, weight loss, and other beneficial health effects. The health-promoting effects of laughter have now been noted by medical experts in the U.S., and humor programs are being developed in many medical institutions and considered for use in cancer therapies.

The long-lived people of this book have relatively stress-free lives, and they also tend to have happy, strong dispositions. For those of us who encounter many potential stressors during the day, laughing not only has physiological benefits, but it is also empowering and makes us feel in control of situations we find ourselves in. Even if you don't want to raise your arms in the air and go "ha-ha, ho-ho," looking for the funny side of a situation will help you to get things in perspective and reduce stress. Laughter is also free, and has no known side effects, so you have nothing to lose by increasing your daily dose.

❧ 45 ❧

Sing in the Shower

Music is the food of love—and longevity. The use of music in therapy is not new, and it has long been a common experience that listening to or making music can be soothing or stimulating, and is also a good way to express—literally to "squeeze out"—feelings that may otherwise be bottled up. This can have a powerful effect on health.

A recent study from Ohio State University at the James Cancer Hospital showed that when patients listened to music, they had lowered stress levels, and their immunity was enhanced. In the study, musicians played to patients who were in their beds, enabling many of the patients to relax enough to fall into a gentle sleep, although one man got out of bed and started to dance with his wife. In another study from Austria, postoperative patients for whom music was played got more rest than the control group and reported substantially less pain.

One of the favorite pastimes in Bama is folk singing. Any excuse will do—weddings, funerals, meetings, or doing the household chores. Every week, thousands of people attend a singing competition at Jiazhuan town in the Panyang River Valley, with people gathering along the riverbanks to cheer on the competitors, who range in age from children to a hundred years old and over. Singing contests are partly a social activity, and are also a test of intellect, with competitors required to make up songs on the spot.

Researchers studying Bama believe that singing is an important part of the local menu for longevity, since it relieves stress, keeps the brain active, and enhances immunity. Two sisters aged

105 and 103 told researchers they had been singing since they were children, and out of 135 singers in Bama, 3 were over 100 years old, while 44 were over 71. One 112-year-old said he liked to sing while resting or doing household chores in order to express his feelings. Common topics for songs are feelings about work, love, and nature.

In Okinawa, villagers sing on their way to work in the fields at dawn, and in the evening they gather on each other's porches to sing and make music. In Hunza, dancing to music is an important part of the nightly entertainment, and the Symiots are also very fond of music and dancing, Greek style, with the aid of a glass of wine or two.

Music helps us to relax, which puts the body in parasympathetic nervous system mode, in which heart rate is slowed and we feel calm. Music affects the brain, which can have a powerful impact on the rest of the body, as the brain is directly linked to the digestive tract via a system known as the "gut-brain axis," and it is also directly linked to the immune system. One study has shown that listening to music raises levels of secretory immunoglobulin A (sIgA)—an important part of the intestine's immune system that protects the lining from toxins—by 55 percent.[1] Music also helps counteract negative feelings that stimulate the production of the pro-aging stress hormone, cortisol, while at the same time raising levels of the "youth hormone," DHEA.

Listening to music, going to concerts, singing in the shower, or humming on the way to work are all ways of incorporating music into your life. Taking up an instrument or joining a band takes more commitment but can be deeply rewarding, as well as giving focus to a social evening. If you are feeling ill, tired, or stressed, try listening to some music for a cheap, effective medicine without any harmful side effects.

❦ 46 ❧

Give Help to Others

Selfish people die younger than helpful people, according to a recent study. University of Michigan researchers followed a group of older people for five years and found that those who were helpful to others reduced their risk of dying by 60 percent, compared to those who weren't. In another study, scientists at the Boston University School of Public Health found that being hostile is an even better predictor of heart disease than unhealthy living habits such as drinking and smoking.[1]

Giving help, in the University of Michigan study, included nothing more spectacular than assisting with housework and childcare, running errands, or providing help with transportation. It also involved giving emotional support to spouses, for example by listening if they needed to talk. Giving help may extend life for several reasons, including, in this case, creating motivation to stay alive, providing a sense of empowerment, enabling elderly people to feel a part of a community, and reducing loneliness. In the University of Michigan study, being on the receiving end made no measurable difference, suggesting that society should look at ways for the elderly to help others, and not just to receive help.

The people featured in this book live in communities where young and old assist each other on a regular basis. Some Bama centenarians interviewed have cited "doing good deeds" as a reason for their longevity, while the Okinawans have a special expression, *yuimaaru*, meaning "mutual aid and reciprocity." Although the Okinawan elderly often live on their own and enjoy a healthy sense of independence, they are actively involved with their friends and family, and neighbors will often leave food on each other's doorsteps if it is needed. The other communities described in this book have similar traditions of helping each other out. The Campodimelani, for example, all join in to help get in the harvest, and when people are short of something, or old and infirm, their neighbors and family make sure they are provided for.

In the places featured in this book, old people often contribute as much as the younger people. In Hunza, for example, it is the elders who are the decision makers for the community. They are not made to feel "helpless," because they themselves are being helpful. In contrast, elderly people in Western societies are often made to feel somewhat useless and unimportant after they retire and more youthful people take over. This seems like a real waste of knowledge and experience, especially since elderly people are a rapidly growing section of the population, with 77 million baby boomers currently nearing retirement in the U.S. What are they going to do with the eighteen-odd years left after they retire? Rather than making them feel as if they have nothing to contribute, Westerners should take cues from the people in the longevity zones. Not only are elders revered, but clearly they have much to teach younger generations.

For those who do not live in small village communities such as those described in this book, organized volunteer work can be a good way for retired and elderly people to get involved with others in the neighborhood. Some studies conducted in the U.S. show that people who volunteer for as little as two hours a week are likely to benefit from lowered blood pressure and heart rates, reduced stress, and increased self-esteem. Volunteer work does not have to mean stuffing envelopes, although this apparently mundane task may in itself have the power to keep aging away. There are also many types of volunteer opportunities publicized on the Internet to match specific skills to needed jobs. Giving is receiving, so be selfish and help someone today.

🌿 **47** 🌿

Marry—or Get a Dog

Marriage can be for better *or* worse health. One recent study showed that married people live longer and enjoy better health—although if you aren't married, read on, as there is another side to the coin. The study, conducted by Warwick University in the UK, showed that married people, especially men, live up to three years longer than unmarried people. Merely living together, however, was not found to have such a health-promoting effect.[1] In the United States, mortality rates from all causes have been found to be significantly higher for divorced, single, and widowed people, according to author and medical researcher James J. Lynch.

Reasons for the longevity-promoting effects of marriage are thought to include a sense of security and having someone to talk to about your problems, which men can find difficult to do outside of marriage. Married couples also tend to watch out for each other's health: a 1987 study published in the *Journal of the American Medical Association* showed that unmarried men and women who got cancer were more likely to be diagnosed at a more advanced stage and have a lower survival rate.[2]

Another reason could be sexual healing: according to neuropsychologist Dr. David Weeks, sex three times a week between long-term partners makes them look up to ten years younger, partly because it produces growth hormone in women.[3] Sex three times a week outside a stable relationship, however, was found to age single women. It was suggested that one possible reason for this might be that it can cause feelings of insecurity. While sex can provide all the benefits of exercise, sex outside marriage may not be so health-promoting, according to one study. A survey done at St. Thomas's Hospital in the UK showed that 75 percent of heart attack deaths during sex strike people having affairs or one-night stands.

It is the quality of the marriage that counts, however. Scientists at Ohio State University have found that couples who are nasty and sarcastic to each other during fights have weakened immune systems, with women being more susceptible than men. The researchers gave each partner a small blister on the arm and then asked them to discuss a marital issue they wished to change. They found that if the interaction was positive, levels of stress hormones such as cortisol were lower, causing healing compounds to be delivered to the wound more quickly, and vice versa.

Another disadvantage of being married, according to British Nutrition Foundation dietician Sarah Schenker, is that marriage makes women fatter, as they tend to take on their husband's bad eating habits, such as eating potato chips.[4] Male partners also disrupt women's sleep, especially if they snore. Women also find it easier being alone than in an unhappy relationship, whereas men are thought to find it harder, and often choose to remain in an indifferent marriage rather than be single. The Warwick study also found that cancer rates are highest among divorcees, with the cost of divorce lawyers, in the neighborhood of three hundred dollars and up per hour, contributing to the stress caused.[5]

The people studied in this book come from societies where marriage is considered desirable, and divorce rates are low. In one study in Bama it was found that a man had recently married at the age of ninety-seven. However, these people also live in supportive extended family networks, and do not have unrealistic expectations about marriage, so are less likely to suffer from marital rifts.

While having a spouse can help you to stay young, there are other ways of having health-promoting close relationships.

Keeping a pet, for example, has been found to prolong life span, and helps to keep blood pressure down, perhaps because pets provide unconditional love and do not answer back. University of Warwick researchers found that getting a dog also makes you three times more likely to meet people of either sex. As the following secret shows, having a good network of friendships and social life can also boost health, so if dogs and romantic partners are not what you want in your life, read on.

🎋 48 🎋

Invite a Friend

If you are planning to have fries and ice cream for dinner, despite everything, make sure you invite a friend. Loneliness shortens life span, while having plenty of friends improves health and prolongs youth, according to numerous studies. In a Harvard University study, it was found that men and women who had few social contacts were two to three times more likely to die during the following nine years than those with more social connections, and that even having a healthy lifestyle did not fully counteract the effects of loneliness.[1] Of course, the study also showed that the longest-lived people of all had both a healthy lifestyle and good social networks.

The long-lived people described in this book all have strong social networks. Symi is often described by locals as being one big neighborhood, where everyone knows everyone else, and people sleep with their doors open without fear of crime. Families are large and loving, so that members benefit from knowing they have an unconditional support system. In Campodimele, there is always some kind of community event going on—five or six generations of young and old might come out and stand on the walls to cheer on a mountain bike race, or just gather outside their houses to chat and watch life go by. The village even has its own small amphitheater cut into the side of the hill, which has a performance every night during the summer.

In Okinawa, *Ichariba chode* is an expression that means to interact with everyone as though they were your own kin, so that everyone feels loved and wanted. People socialize frequently, dropping in on each other for breakfast or playing music on each other's porches in the evenings. According to the authors of *The Okinawa Way*, yuimaaru extends life span and protects from illness, partly by boosting the immune system.

Living in extended families provides a loving environment where duties are shared and everyone is looked after. In Bama up to five generations can often be found living under one roof, which seems to contribute to their longevity. Researchers have found that the majority of the very long-lived in Bama live in large families of seven or eight people, and in a survey of those aged over ninety, it was found that they all lived with their families.[2]

It may be that having plenty of friends can lengthen life because of the practical support friends provide, such as recommending doctors or helping with the children. Having friends or joining social organizations may also promote healthy activities such as hiking or cycling. Friendships and social events also lower levels of pro-aging stress hormones such as epinephrine, norepinephrine, and cortisol. One 1993 study showed that when subjects did a stressful task with a friend, their blood pressure rose less than if they did it alone.[3]

Joining clubs, holding bridge evenings, going to church, visiting family members, or just inviting friends to dinner are all ways of having stress-reducing friendships. Counseling groups and therapy sessions can also help in coping with problems. Discussing a problem with a friend will usually help to put it into perspective, while hearing about a friend's problems in return can often make one's own seem less difficult. Laughing, another health-boosting activity, also tends to happen more in the company of others—problems can often become something to laugh about rather than to worry about. So don't wait for someone to call you—invite a friend to share your gourmet wild fish and organic vegetables and get double the benefits.

❦ 49 ❦

Avoid the SAD— the Standard American Diet

The Standard American Diet, otherwise known as the SAD, is almost opposite to the diets eaten by the long-lived people featured in this book. The SAD, which is eaten by the average North American, consists primarily of meat, dairy, sugar, salt, and refined carbohydrates. It is low in nutrients and high in "empty calorie" foods that are fattening but do not feed the body. The SAD is implicated in causing the high rates of degenerative disease, such as heart attack, cancer, diabetes, and stroke, in the U.S.

today. Even children, many of whom are eating the SAD, are now starting to get these diseases, once thought of as diseases of aging.

Here is an example of the type of daily diet you should avoid. Combine this diet with a high-stress, low-exercise lifestyle, and you have the ultimate formula for ill health and accelerated aging. More details on some of these foods are given in Part Three and in earlier sections of this book.

Saturated fats: One or more servings of meat, especially red meat, and full-fat dairy—a large part of the SAD diet.

Fast foods: One or more meals from fast food outlets.

White flour and white rice (refined carbohydrates): One or more servings of white bread, white rice, cookies, cakes, or pastry.

Altered fats: One or more servings of foods containing hydrogenated fats such as ready-made meals, packaged cakes and cookies, or foods fried in vegetable oil, such as french fries.

Coffee and carbonated drinks: One or more cups of coffee and/or canned sodas and other sweet carbonated drinks.

Candies and sugar: One of more servings of chocolate, cake, candies, or cookies.

Excess alcohol: More than two glasses of alcohol daily, especially hard alcohol.

If these foods form a large part of your daily diet, and you think you cannot enjoy life without them, don't panic. Start by cutting down on these foods, and feel pleased that at least you know about the dangers they pose to your health. Find healthy substitutes you enjoy, based on the information given in this and other books on nutritious eating. Take comfort from the fact that much ill health is reversible through a change in diet, and that the more you do to eat well, the more you can improve your health. Aim ultimately to have these foods as occasional "treats" rather than letting them form the bulk of your diet. It may be easier than you think.

❀ 50 ❀

Sleep

It has been well established that good sleeping habits improve health and extend life span. Edward L. Schneider, of the Leonard Davis School of Gerontology, UCLA, says, "To age successfully, you must get a good night's sleep." Deep, refreshing sleep is particularly important for hormone production, immune function, digestive function, and energy.

How much sleep do we need? Some people seem to function fine on five or six hours, others need ten or more. Received wisdom has long been that the majority of people operate at peak performance during the day if they get eight hours of sleep. However, one recent study of 1.1 million Americans indicated that seven hours' sleep is best for adults, with people getting eight hours having a 12.5 percent greater risk of dying than those sleeping for seven hours.[1] As with all studies, it may be that other factors need to be taken into consideration. Ultimately you yourself are likely to be the best judge of exactly how much sleep you need.

Most members of the populations in this book get plenty of good sleep every night, and the University of Rome study of the Campodimelani found that they sleep eight hours a night on average. Because they tend to work outside, these people are also very much in tune with their natural body clocks, going to bed soon after dusk and rising at dawn. This ensures that their bodies make the right amounts of melatonin, an anti-aging, antioxidant hormone that is secreted cyclically by our bodies in response to the fall of darkness and which promotes proper sleep.

Good sleeping patterns are a reflection of our physical and mental health generally, which may be another reason for the link between sound sleep and long life. An unhealthy diet full of stimulants, refined carbohydrates, and fats is likely to impair sleep because of digestive problems and blood sugar swings. Deep sleep is also encouraged by regular exercise and relaxation techniques such as meditation.

Millions of people have sleep disorders, and one in ten Americans has chronic insomnia. The two main types of insomnia are being unable to fall asleep and waking up in the night and being unable to get back to sleep. The first may be caused by blood sugar disturbances, caffeine, sugar, antidepressants, or high cortisol levels caused by stress. The second is often caused by a lack of magnesium and calcium, which help relax the muscles. Restless leg syndrome (RLS), in which the legs twitch involuntarily in bed, and muscle cramps are also signs of low magnesium and calcium levels, so if you suffer from insomnia as well as these, you may benefit from a calcium and magnesium supplement.

The body likes to have a regular rhythm because hormone production depends on a twenty-four-hour clock, so if you have problems sleeping, try to go to bed and get up at roughly the same time each day. Melatonin supplements can help, but these should be taken with the advice of a doctor, since melatonin is a powerful hormone and is contraindicated in some cases, for example in pregnancy.

If the problem is excess cortisol caused by stress and worry, relaxation techniques such as meditation may help. Alcohol helps with relaxation initially, but it can also cause insomnia, as it is a stimulant and it unbalances blood sugar levels. Vitamin C, magnesium, and calcium can all help to reduce stress. Taking plenty of exercise during the day also helps reduce stress, as well as making the body physically tired; exercise is best taken earlier in the day for best effect.

A final word before you doze off snoring partners and city sounds can disturb sleep, so you may wish to invest in a good set of ear plugs.

PART THREE

Putting It
All Together

The final section of this book summarizes the information in the earlier parts and includes some further useful tips on healthy eating and other factors that help to increase longevity and, more importantly, help you feel good today.

The Secrets of Living Long in Summary

What are the secrets of living long and staying young, in a nutshell? The secrets of long-lived populations described in this book are encapsulated below, along with a suggestion for an ideal daily intake of different types of food that will help you to stay young.

If you follow the outlined suggestions, the likely benefits to you should include:

- Prolonged youth
- Long life
- Plenty of energy
- Youthful looks
- Slender figure
- Positive outlook
- Higher IQ
- Happy bowels
- Trouble-free menstruation
- Clear skin
- Shiny hair

- Robust immune system
- Healthy offspring
- Less likelihood of serious chronic disease such as cancer, heart disease, stroke, diabetes, and Alzheimer's disease

THE IDEAL DAILY DIET PYRAMID

Your ideal daily diet should be as similar as possible to the diets of the people who were described in Part One. It should incorporate the following each day:

(Note: One serving is equivalent to 100 grams (4 ounces) of grains, one large carrot, or one slice of bread.)

Fruits and vegetables: Five to ten servings of fruits and vegetables—preferably one to two servings of fruit and the rest vegetables, mainly raw or lightly steamed.

Whole grains: Three to five servings of whole grains—e.g., brown rice, whole wheat, oats, corn, quinoa, hemp, millet.

Protein: Three to five servings of protein daily from the following sources: vegetable protein from tofu, quinoa, lentils, or other beans or legumes (daily); organic cheese (preferably sheep's or goat's) in small amounts; moderate amounts of live yogurt; three or four free-range organic eggs (weekly); lean meat in small to moderate amounts (one small serving three or four times weekly); fish two or three times (weekly).

Essential fats: A handful of nuts and seeds *or* one tablespoon cold-pressed nut and seed oils *or* one heaped tablespoon ground seeds *or* fish oil supplements (daily) *or* oily fish (twice weekly).

Drinks: Eight glasses of water daily, plus one to five cups of green tea.

Aging Substances to Avoid

Here is some supplementary information on the pro-aging "foods" and substances you should avoid. All of these are notably absent from the diets of the people discussed in this book.

FAST FOODS

These speed up the aging process with artery-hardening fats, salt, and free radicals, so even if they save time in the short term, you will pay in the end. An example of the ideal pro-aging meal might be a hamburger or fried chicken on a white bun, accompanied by french fries or potato chips and a sugary carbonated drink or milkshake, followed by a heavily sweetened snack or pie.

CIGARETTES

Smoking a pack of cigarettes a day is believed to add around eight years or more to your biological age. If you stop, you can undo much of the damage; in five years you can reverse most of the accelerated aging that has taken place. If you smoke, you have a one in two chance of dying an unpleasant, premature death as a result.

EXCESS ALCOHOL

A small amount of wine, especially red wine, can be good for you, and is drunk in moderation by many long-lived people. However, more than one (for women) or two (for men) drinks daily, especially of hard liquor, will significantly speed up the aging process—alcoholics nearly always look much older than they really are. And it's not just on the outside. According to Dr. Gene-Jack Wang, of Brookhaven National Laboratory in New York, "the brain of a thirty-year-old alcoholic looks like the brain of a fifty-year-old." Limit your drinking to moderate amounts of wine, preferably red, drunk with a meal. The liver has incredible powers of rejuvenation, so don't ever feel that it is too late to change your bad drinking habits.

PHARMACEUTICAL DRUGS

Drugs are potentially harmful, which is why they are to be kept out of reach of children, and they should not be regarded as cures, because they merely suppress symptoms. While some medications compensate for the body's inability to produce certain substances naturally, others can inhibit the body's efforts to heal itself and maintain its normal, balanced condition. They cannot be metabolized easily, and the body expends valuable energy in trying to process them. They create pro-aging free radicals and cause side effects, many of which are harmful to the liver.

Even a drug as seemingly innocuous as aspirin, which is touted as helping to prevent heart disease, can cause damage to the stomach and intestinal lining, which leads to digestive problems and hence to various illnesses. Long-term use of nonsteroidal anti-inflammatory drugs (NSAIDS) such as aspirin and ibuprofen causes twenty thousand deaths in the United States each year.

If your doctor has prescribed drugs, make sure you discuss the prescribed medications with him or her. You do not want to take any drugs unnecessarily or in excess dosages. It is also a good idea to discuss potential side effects of medications with your doctor.

SUGAR

Refined sugar is probably the most degenerated food there is. Commercial sugar is a bleached product that is almost a pure carbon, and forms carbonic acid in the body. Carbonic acid is toxic to tissues, and must be neutralized with any spare mineral reserves the body has, so that these reserves become increasingly depleted the more sugar is eaten.

Sugar stresses the adrenal glands, causes acne, and promotes yeast and fungal overgrowth in the body. It is high in calories and is converted to saturated fat in the body. It can increase your risk of developing conditions such as heart disease, varicose veins, kidney disorders, arthritis, diabetes, obesity, migraines, and high blood pressure. It also feeds cancer cells, and particularly increases the risk of getting breast cancer or cancer of the colon. The average North American eats just over 125 pounds of sugar annually, in the form of cookies, cakes, sweets, soft drinks, ketchup, jams, and jellies.

Sugary foods seem very pleasant because they are addictive. However, like all addictions, a sugar addiction can be reversed by simply avoiding any sugar for a few days. Try substituting a piece of ripe fruit or a handful of dried fruit if you really want a sweet snack. If you like chocolate, choose dark semisweet chocolate that is made from 70 percent cocoa solids and raw cane sugar, and that does not contain hydrogenated vegetable oil or vegetable fat.

CAFFEINE

The link between coffee drinking and degenerative disease is becoming increasingly clear. According to studies, drinking coffee and other caffeinated drinks may increase the risk of diabetes by impairing insulin function, while it contributes to high blood pressure by raising blood homocysteine and triglyceride levels.[1] Caffeine also halves the amount of micronutrients absorbed with a meal.

Caffeine, like sugar, is addictive, and it is possible to get rid of the addiction by avoiding coffee for a few days. If you really can't give up your coffee, try to get your intake down to one cup a day, and drink it away from a meal, so that you still get your nutrients. After a while you will notice you feel quite jittery and unpleasant if you have more than this. Tea is better than coffee, as it contains slightly less caffeine and also contains antioxidants. Green tea has anti-aging properties and the least caffeine content, and is drunk by some of the populations discussed in this book.

SALT

Those who are not used to cooking without salt often say that salt gives food "taste"; to others, it just makes the food taste like salt. Salt increases blood pressure and therefore raises the risk of heart disease. It also undermines health in other ways, as discussed in Secret 28 (page 148).

HEAVY METALS AND PLASTICS

Canned food, tap water, mercury amalgam fillings, and contaminated meat are all sources of toxic heavy metals, which accumulate in the body and cause degenerative disease. Canned tuna fish, for example, contains high levels of mercury, while aluminum foil, aluminum pans, and antacids may all cause a buildup of aluminum in the body, which has been linked to illnesses such as Alzheimer's disease. Children's teeth braces made with nickel are associated with above-normal levels of appendicitis, for an unknown reason. The most common heavy metals found in human tissue at potentially harmful levels are cadmium, mercury, lead, aluminum, arsenic, and nickel, which come from our polluted environment, including our water supply.

Plastic wrap and plastic packaging contain hormone-disruptive chemicals that are linked with conditions such as infertility and hormone-related cancers. Try to avoid using plastic wrap at home—you can put food in a bowl with a plate on top, instead, or cover it in such a way that the plastic wrap does not touch the food. Hard plastic, such as that used in plastic boxes and bags, is preferable to soft plastic such as that used in plastic wrap and many supermarket wrappings.

Tips for Using the Secrets

I t is one thing to buy a book about health food, and another to actually do what it tells you. If you want to benefit from the invaluable information available in nutrition books today, you have to get into the habit of eating healthy food *almost always*, rather than just now and again. The occasional deviation won't kill you, but eating the wrong way all the time might.

Many of us do not eat healthily, but think we do. This is hardly surprising—healthy eating isn't taught at home or in schools, and much of the information put out is confusing and conflicting. Sugary cereal with milk for breakfast, and chicken sandwiches on half-brown bread with a tiny bit of iceberg lettuce, washed down with orange juice or coffee and a vitamin pill for lunch, is not healthy eating, even if it seems like it. If you eat this way, and wonder why you still get pimples, unshiftable love handles, PMS, and headaches (for example), you will be amazed by how much better you look and feel when you eat *really* healthily.

ENJOY COOKING AND EATING YOUR FOOD

You don't have to think about the concepts behind healthy eating if you don't want to. You can just cook it, enjoy it, and feel the energy and health miraculously coursing into your grateful body, just as the excess pounds fall off. Eating should not be punishing or sacrificial. You are making a commitment, however, and this will mean putting in the work that a change of habit requires.

You will have to make time to go to the supermarket or health-food shop and to prepare the food. You will probably soon find, however, that not only is this extra effort well worth it, but that the effort itself—choosing and preparing food—becomes a rewarding part of your day. As you begin to explore new ingredients, impress your friends with your new cooking skills, feel and look better, and be complimented on how well you look to the point where it bores you, you won't look back.

When using the principles of this book, make things easy for yourself by discovering which foods you like best, and which are easiest to shop for and make, then use them regularly. There is no point in having soy every day for a week and tomatoes the next week, then never having either of them again. The people in this book eat their health foods on a regular basis, in moderate quantities, so that they get the cumulative benefits over a lifetime. If you particularly like green tea and buckwheat, make those some of your staples, and using them will become a habit. Try also to eat a good range of healthy foods, instead of always repeating the same meal.

When planning meals, shop adventurously, remembering that there are dozens of different kinds of fruit, vegetables, whole grains, fish, and other healthy foods around. Avoid the central aisles of the supermarket, which is where the cakes and cookies tend to be, and spend more time in the vegetable section. Explore different kinds of food that you like at the health-food shop. Invent your own recipes using the principles of healthy eating, and try using Asian and Mediterranean cookbooks to expand your repertoire, as well as the recipes in this book.

Each of us is unique, and people respond to different types of food in their own ways. Experiment to find out which foods suit your digestive system and give you energy, and which do not. When you start eating healthily, your body becomes more able to discern what it does and does not thrive on, and you should become able to spot the signs. You may feel lethargic or flatulent after eating bread, for example, which you may not have noticed before if you were feeling lethargic or gassy all the time.

ONE STEP AT A TIME

If you hate the idea of missing out on doughnuts and chips, then set a goal of eating healthily for one month only, and focus on what you would like to improve about your health. At the end of the four weeks, you will probably feel so much better that you will want to continue eating this way. When you eat clean, healthy food, your body detoxifies and your taste buds become more appreciative, so you may lose your taste for doughnuts and chips anyway.

Like cigarettes, these "foods" are cleverly manufactured to be addictive, and after a brief period of withdrawal they often lose their appeal. In fact, research has shown that once people get away from their established tastes, they start enjoying health-giving foods. One of my favorite foods used to be take-out pizza, but I remember vividly having my first fast-food pizza after several months of strict healthy eating, and I was amazed to find that the pizza tasted like cardboard and rubber.

Whatever you do, don't "diet." Make sure that you always satisfy your appetite and that you make your food as delicious as possible. Keep healthy snacks, such as fruit or nuts, around to eat between meals if you get hungry. At mealtimes, if you are having a salad, don't make it from watery, tasteless iceberg lettuce and tomato, because you will just be wishing you were having something else. Throw in lightly roasted sesame seeds, olives, herbs, and anything else you can find to make it interesting, nutritious, and very tasty.

OCCASIONAL INDISCRETIONS

The benefits of lightly steamed vegetables or poached fish will be severely compromised if you follow them up with a bowlful of ice cream, even if it is eaten surreptitiously, with your head inside the freezer. However, if you do stray into the arena of unhealthy eating from time to time, try to adapt sensibly. If you find you have just had three pints of beer and a cheeseburger before you even knew what you were doing, don't think you have ruined everything and then eat hamburgers and pizza for the rest of the week, in an orgy of guilty masochism. Just forget what happened and get back on track by continuing as before.

If you love red meat or white bread, and you would rather not live a long time if it means going without them, then let yourself have them from time to time. Change the ratios around so that you have more of the vegetables and less of the unhealthy food, and try not to indulge too often. I find that men generally seem to like meat more than women do, so if you are a health-conscious woman cooking for a man who just wants his meat (or vice versa), you can deceive him by making a vegetable-based dish flavored with small amounts of meat, which is how the people in this book eat theirs. If you love a warm white baguette or foccacia bread, try to eat it as a special treat only, and stick to whole grains at other times.

EATING OUT

If you are going to a restaurant, or you don't feel like cooking and want take-out, try to stick to the principles of healthy eating as far as possible. If you can, persuade the people you are meeting to go to a Japanese restaurant or one that does vegetarian food, and there is bound to be an option that suits you. If you have to go somewhere where there is nothing you want on the menu, order the best option and ask if you can have an extra helping of steamed green vegetables or a salad on the side. Most restaurants keep food in the kitchen that isn't on the menu and will be happy to oblige. You can then concentrate on the vegetables, and leave some of the main dish.

If you are eating dinner at someone's house, whoever is cooking may well show hospitality and fondness for you by trying to give you severe indigestion. Your plate is heaped high, you are urged to eat a second or third helping, an enormous mound of apple pie is placed firmly in front of you. If this is a rare occasion, and you decide to treat yourself, then enjoy it. Otherwise, you must forget everything your mother taught you and leave something on your plate. This is your health, after all, and you have been asked for your company, not your ability to save your host the inconvenience of leftovers.

THE OFFICE LUNCH

It can be hard to find anything to eat other than sandwiches around the office, so, if you are dedicated enough, you might have to make your own lunch and bring it in. I remember starting at a new job and cautiously lifting the lid off my Tupperware box (containing brown rice, soy sauce, garlic, and seaweed with broccoli and beans), slightly embarrassed by the garlicky smell that wafted out. I was surprised when two or three people stopped on their way past my desk to ask what I was eating. One of them was inspired to start doing the same herself at lunchtime, and the other placed an order with me to make lunch for her, too, which I did every day from then on.

STOCKING UP

Stock up on a range of foods that you can incorporate into your healthy eating plan, so that they are always ready to be cooked at home. Rather than putting them at the back of the cupboard where you might forget them, you can put them in glass jars on a shelf where they will look attractive and remind you of their presence. Do not leave them in open bags, which will decrease shelf life and may attract health-conscious insects and rodents.

Items you can stock up on:

- Extra-virgin olive oil
- Organic whole grains, beans, and legumes (brown rice, brown rice cakes, whole-grain flour, polenta, oatmeal, lentils, a variety of beans)
- Nuts and seeds for snacks (unsalted, uncooked nuts, sunflower seeds, sesame seeds, and pumpkin seeds)
- Dried fruit for snacks (apricots, dates, figs)
- Asian noodles (e.g., somen and udon noodles, available in health-food shops and Asian supermarkets)
- Kombu seaweed for making *dashi*—see recipe section (available in packages from health-food shops and Asian supermarkets)
- Bonito flakes (packets of dried fish flakes available in Asian supermarkets) for making dashi
- Miso soup (available in packets from health-food shops and supermarkets)
- Tofu
- Garlic
- Growing herbs
- A selection of dried herbs
- Green tea
- Herb tea

Finally, *enjoy* eating healthily. Try to make food you like and engage in exercise and relaxation practices that are within your reach, so that you can stick with it. Set your sights on the here and now, and appreciate the immediate benefits of the "secrets"— after all, even more important than living longer is feeling good *today.*

Recipes

OKINAWA RECIPES

Dashi

This is a classic Japanese stock made from seaweed and dried fish flakes from the bonito fish. It is a staple of many dishes—see the following recipes—and is also used as a medicinal soup to maintain and restore vigor. Use it as a versatile base for your own invented recipes using noodles, soy, and vegetables.

2 strips kombu seaweed
1 large pinch of bonito flakes (available in packets from
    Asian supermarkets)
$^3/_4$ tablespoon soy sauce (use the traditionally brewed,
    low-salt kind)

1. Boil the kombu for 3–4 minutes in a small pan of water (use about half a pint of water). Remove from the heat.
2. Add the bonito flakes and return to the heat. Remove from heat just as the water returns to the boil.

3. Allow to stand for 5 minutes, or until bonito flakes sink. Strain and keep the liquid. Discard the solids (if you are making dashi again soon, you can reuse them).
4. Add the soy sauce. Serves 2-3.

Pork Noodles with Dashi

This is extremely easy to make and delicious—you will be amazed by the authenticity of the flavor, which comes from the dashi. Eat it with some steamed vegetables on the side, or add a few sliced vegetables such as cabbage or broccoli after Step 2.

> 4 ounces cooked pork slices or salmon
> 1 tablespoon olive or canola oil
> $^{1}/_{2}$ clove garlic
> 1 tablespoon dashi
> 1–2 teaspoons soy sauce
> $^{3}/_{4}$ teaspoon sake or sweet white wine
> 1 cup stock (pork, or vegetable if using salmon)
> 4 ounces Asian noodles, preferably udon noodles (buckwheat udon noodles are available in Asian groceries)
> 3 stalks green onions, chopped very fine

1. If using pork, boil the meat in about a pint of water for 25 minutes. Skim the fat off the top of the water and keep the rest of the water to use as stock.
2. Heat the oil in a wok or frying pan. Add the garlic and fry gently for a minute or two, without letting it brown. You can bring down the frying temperature by adding a tablespoon of stock.
3. Add the pork or salmon and stir for a few seconds.
4. Add the dashi, soy, sake, and stock, and bring to a boil.
5. Add the noodles and heat.
6. Garnish with the onion and serve. Serves 1–2.

Sautéed Tofu and Vegetables

You can use any leftover vegetables for this, such as broccoli, cauliflower, green peppers, or bok choy.

1–2 tablespoons olive or canola oil
1 onion, chopped
1 clove garlic, chopped (optional)
1 teaspoon fresh ginger, chopped (optional)
1/2 cup GM-free tofu, diced
1 carrot, sliced
1 cup cabbage, sliced
1 cup bean sprouts
1–2 teaspoons soy sauce
1 tablespoon dashi (optional)

1. Heat the oil in a frying pan or wok, and cook the onion on a fairly high heat for a few minutes, stirring continually until it is soft but not brown. Add the garlic and/or ginger, if you are using them.
2. Add the tofu, then the carrot, then the cabbage or other vegetables, then the bean sprouts. Keep stirring for 3–4 minutes.
3. Add soy sauce to taste, and/or dashi if you are using it. Cook for another 2 or 3 minutes, so that the vegetables are cooked but still retain some bite, and serve. Serves 2.

Grilled Fish with Greens and Baked Sweet Potato

There is no particular Okinawan recipe for this. When they eat fish, they usually just grill it and eat it with vegetables and rice or sweet potato.

1 sweet potato
11 ounces or more oily fish (e.g., salmon, fresh tuna, mackerel, or fresh sardines)

Juice of 1 lemon
1 tablespoon extra-virgin olive oil or canola oil
5 ounces spinach or bok choy

1. Bake the sweet potato in the oven at 375 degrees F for about 40 minutes.
2. Grill the fish with a little lemon and the oil, for 5–10 minutes on each side, until cooked (it should be just cooked through—not raw, but not dry).
3. Steam the greens over boiling water for a couple of minutes, and serve with the rest. Serves 1.

Pork and Vegetable Soup with Sake

Okinawans make this when someone is unwell, but it can be enjoyed anytime. If pork is not available, they sometimes use fish. If you want to use fish, boil it for just a few minutes, and make sure you use really fresh fish.

11 ounces pork
11 ounces pork liver (optional)
Sake or awamori (fermented rice wine)
3 potatoes, diced
1 carrot, diced
1–2 spring onions, cut into thin "matchsticks"
1 tablespoon miso (soy paste)
1–2 teaspoons chopped ginger

1. Cut the meat into small pieces and marinate in a bowl of sake or awamori for 20 minutes.
2. Boil the meat in a pan of water, just covering the meat (the amount you use depends on how watery you want your soup to be). Skim any fat from the top of the water as it forms.

3. After 15–20 minutes, add the potatoes and carrots, then continue cooking for about 10 minutes, until the potatoes and carrots are fairly soft but not overcooked.
4. Remove from heat and stir in the miso.
5. Garnish with the spring onions, and serve soup with a glass of warm sake. Serves 4.

Rice with Seaweed

This is used as a side dish for fish and/or vegetables. You can use kombu seaweed and cut it into strips, or hijiki seaweed, which comes in tiny dark strips.

$1^1/_2$ cups brown rice
2 strips kombu seaweed/hijiki seaweed
1 onion, chopped small
1 clove garlic, chopped small
1 tablespoon extra-virgin olive oil or canola oil
1 teaspoon sesame oil
1 tablespoon soy sauce

1. Wash and cook the rice.
2. If using kombu seaweed, boil for 20 minutes, then cut into matchstick-size slivers, using scissors or a knife. If using hijiki seaweed, soak it for 15 minutes in warm water, then drain.
3. Gently cook the onion and garlic in the olive or canola oil, until the onions are just starting to go yellow (this can take up to 10 minutes, if you are cooking gently), add the cooked rice and stir, then add the seaweed.
4. Add the sesame oil and the soy sauce, and stir for another minute or two. Serves 2.

SYMI RECIPES

Rustic Bread with Olive Oil and Sesame Seeds

Bread is easy and satisfying to make, and it fills the house with a delicious, welcoming smell. Once you have made it, you will find you want to do it regularly, and no other bread will taste as good.

About 1 tablespoon yeast
4 fluid ounces tepid water
5 cups whole-wheat flour (or other whole-grain flour)
2 teaspoons sea salt
2 tablespoons extra-virgin olive oil
1–2 teaspoons sesame seeds

1. Dissolve the yeast in 1 cup of tepid water.
2. Mix the flour and salt together and put in a pile on a clean, dry surface. Make a well in the middle and add the dissolved yeast water, a little at a time. Each time you add it, swirl the yeast into the flour, using circular movements with four fingers, until the yeast is thoroughly mixed in.
3. Keep adding water and mixing together until you have a moist dough. Knead the dough for 5 minutes until it is springy—the Symiots claim that, when done, it should feel like a woman's breast. If the dough is too dry or too sticky, you can add more water or flour as required.
4. While kneading, add the olive oil a teaspoon at a time.
5. Shape the dough into a roundish shape and put on a baking sheet. Score the top with a knife—this helps it to rise (and makes it look professional). Cover with a dishtowel and leave to rise in a warm place for 40 minutes to 1 hour, until it is roughly double its original size.
6. Remove the loaf from the sheet, punch the air out of it, and knead for a couple of minutes. Reshape into a loaf and allow it to rise a second time, for about 20–30 minutes.

7. Sprinkle the top with the sesame seeds, and bake at 435 degrees F for about 25 minutes or until done (it should be going brown on the outside, and sound hollow when tapped on the base).

8. Serve warm with a small bowl of extra-virgin olive oil for dipping.

Greek Salad, Symi Style

Wait for a summer day, then make this with the freshest, best-quality ingredients you can find, and enjoy it out in the sunshine.

    2 tablespoons extra-virgin olive oil
    1 tablespoon white wine vinegar
    1–2 cloves garlic, chopped small
    4 fresh tomatoes, sliced
    1 cucumber, sliced
    1 onion, sliced thin
    15–20 black olives
    3 tablespoons parsley, chopped
    1–2 teaspoons oregano
    1 ounce capers (with leaves and stalks, if you can get them)
    5 ounces organic feta cheese
    2–3 large fresh sardines, skinned and boned (the Symiots salt
        theirs and marinate them in white wine vinegar first)
    Sea salt and freshly ground black pepper

Mix the oil, vinegar, and garlic together to make a dressing. Mix together the other ingredients, except the fish, and sprinkle with the dressing. Lay the fish on top and add a little salt and pepper to taste. Serves 3.

Fish Soup

This has a beautiful rust color and a succulent flavor, and is an excellent hangover remedy. Have it with a Greek salad and homemade bread.

For the fish stock:
Fish for boiling, including the heads and bones (turbot, halibut, or monkfish heads and bones are best)
5 cups water
1 onion
2 sticks celery
1–2 carrots
2 bay leaves
6 peppercorns
A few stalks of flat-leaved parsley
1 teaspoon sea salt

For the soup:
2 tablespoons extra-virgin olive oil
1 onion, chopped
2–3 cloves garlic, chopped
3 stalks fennel, chopped small
1 pound of fish for boiling, filleted (such as fresh sardines or monkfish—ask your grocer for a recommendation)
2 cups white wine
2 large tomatoes, chopped small
1 tablespoon tomato paste
Juice of 2 lemons
Sea salt and freshly ground pepper
1 large pinch of saffron
1–2 large potatoes, peeled and sliced thick
A few sprigs of parsley

1. For the fish stock, put all the ingredients together in a large pan of water, and boil for about an hour, until the liquid is reduced by half. Strain, throw out the solids, and keep the liquid.
2. To make the soup, heat the oil gently in a heavy-based pan, and sweat the onions (cook them gently with the lid on, so

that they stay moist in their own juice), garlic, and fennel, keeping the heat low. Add a spoonful of the fish stock.

3. Put in half of the fish and stir it around in the vegetables.
4. Add the wine, turn the heat up, and cook for about 10 minutes, or until the wine has reduced by half.
5. Add the tomatoes, tomato paste, and lemon juice, and continue cooking for several minutes.
6. Cover with the fish stock and simmer for about 20–30 minutes, until the liquid has reduced by half.
7. Taste and add salt, pepper, and more lemon if desired.
8. Add a large pinch of saffron.
9. Put in the sliced potatoes and the rest of the fish, and cook for about 10 minutes.
10. Garnish with parsley and serve. Serves 3.

Baked Fish in Wine

1 large fish for baking (use one whole fish such as salmon, trout, or monkfish if small enough)
Sea salt and freshly ground pepper
2–3 tablespoons parsley, chopped
(1–2 large cloves garlic, chopped (to taste)
1 lemon
5 or 6 ripe, red tomatoes
2 onions, sliced
1 green pepper, 1 red pepper, 1 yellow pepper, cut into strips
1 cup extra-virgin olive oil
1 large glass white wine (for cooking—keep another for drinking)

1. Clean and wash the fish, if necessary.
2. Put a little salt on both sides of the fish, stuff the belly with the parsley and garlic, and squeeze the lemon over the fish. Refrigerate for 1 hour.
3. Put half of the tomatoes, onions, and peppers in a small baking

dish in a single layer, put the fish on top, then make a second layer of the vegetables on top of the fish. Pour the oil over it.

4. Bake at 400 degrees F for 15 minutes, then baste the mixture with the juices. Add the wine, and bake for another 15 minutes. Serves 2–3.

Spicy Tuna Salad

For the salad:

1 6-ounce can of tuna in olive oil

4 free-range eggs, hard-boiled and cut in quarters

2 ounces capers, chopped very small

4 ounces gherkins, chopped very small

3 potatoes, boiled and diced

2 onions, sliced very thin

3 tomatoes, chopped

2 ounces small black olives

5–6 anchovy fillets

1–2 green peppers and 1–2 red peppers, chopped

Lettuce (mixed organic greens, romaine)

Dressing 1 (shaken together):

2 tablespoons extra-virgin olive oil

1 tablespoon white wine vinegar or apple cider vinegar

1 teaspoon Dijon mustard

1–2 cloves garlic, chopped small

Sea salt and freshly ground black pepper

Dressing 2 (mixed together):

5 tablespoons mayonnaise (preferably homemade)

1 tablespoon mustard

Sea salt and freshly ground black pepper

Make a bed of the lettuce. Combine the salad ingredients and put them in the middle of the lettuce. Drizzle with the dressing of your choice. Serves 3.

Tsatsiki

This is very quick to make and is a far superior version of the kind you can buy ready-made in the supermarket. You can vary the amounts according to taste:

$1/2$ cucumber
2–3 cloves garlic
1 small pinch of sea salt
12 ounces Greek yogurt
1 tablespoon white wine vinegar
2–3 tablespoons extra-virgin olive oil
1 tablespoon chopped mint or dill

1. Peel and grate the cucumber and squeeze out as much of the moisture as possible.
2. Mash the garlic with the salt, using a mortar and pestle.
3. Mix together the cucumber, garlic, and yogurt.
4. Slowly stir in the vinegar and olive oil.
5. Add the mint or dill and stir in.

CAMPODIMELE RECIPES

Pasta and Bean Soup

This rich-tasting, full-bodied soup, eaten with a salad, is a meal in itself.

1–2 cloves garlic, chopped small
3 tomatoes, chopped small
2 tablespoons extra-virgin olive oil
5 cups pork or vegetable stock
1 cup beans (fagioli or cannelloni beans are best, presoaked or canned)

1 pinch chili pepper (optional)
4 ounces pork, in small pieces
4 ounces fettuccine, broken into short strips
2 tablespoons Parmesan or other cheese, grated
Basil leaves (for garnish)

1. Cook the garlic and tomatoes gently in the olive oil, with the lid on, so they stay moist.
2. Add the stock, then the beans, and a pinch of chili pepper if desired. Put in the raw meat and simmer until the beans are cooked. If using uncooked beans, cook for 45 minutes to 1 hour, adding more liquid if necessary. If using canned beans, add them in Step 3 when the pasta is almost cooked.
3. Add the fettuccini and cook until it is done (al dente), following the cooking time given on the package.
4. Serve with a drizzle of olive oil and the grated cheese. Garnish with the basil leaves. Serves 2.

Gnocchi with Porcini Mushrooms

A mixed green salad makes an excellent accompaniment to this dish.

5 ounces gnocchi (preferably freshly made from an Italian delicatessen, but available in supermarkets)
1–2 tablespoons extra-virgin olive oil
$1^1/_2$ ounces (when dry) dried porcini mushrooms, soaked in a little warm water
1 large pinch thyme
1–2 cloves garlic, chopped small
Sea salt
2 teaspoons parsley, chopped
1 very small pinch chili pepper
2 tablespoon, Parmesan or goat's cheese

1. Put on a pan of water to boil for the gnocchi. Meanwhile, heat

the olive oil and add the porcini mushrooms with a pinch of thyme. Cook for a minute, then add the garlic and a small pinch of salt. Cook for another 2–3 minutes, then add the parsley and a very small pinch of chili pepper, stir for a minute, and remove from the heat.

2. When the pan of water is boiling, add the gnocchi and cook for a couple of minutes until they float.

3. Drain gnocchi and serve with the mushroom sauce, a little cheese, and an extra dribble of olive oil. Serves 1.

Pasta with Roasted Red Peppers
Again, this goes perfectly with a mixed green salad.

4 red peppers
2 tablespoons extra-virgin olive oil
1 clove garlic, chopped
Sea salt
7 ounces penne pasta

1. Grill the peppers until black all over, seal in a plastic bag, leave to cool for 20 minutes, then skin them, remove the insides. Alternatively—a healthier option—you can slice each pepper into 3–4 pieces and roast them in olive oil in a slow oven for 30–45 minutes.

2. Toss the peppers with the olive oil, garlic, and a small pinch of salt. Serve immediately with freshly cooked pasta. Alternatively, you can eat on toast or on their own. Serves 2.

Mixed Salad with Sesame Seeds and a Garlic and Olive Oil Dressing
For the salad:

4 ounces green beans
4 ounces broccoli

1 lettuce (romaine, butter lettuce, bibb lettuce, arugula, wild organic greens—anything but iceberg)

10 black olives

4 ounces feta cheese

Sesame seeds (not a Campodimele staple, but these dramatically enhance the taste of any salad)

For the dressing:

1 teaspoon mustard

1 teaspoon vinegar (balsamic, white wine, or apple cider vinegar)

1 clove garlic, chopped

2 tablespoons extra-virgin olive oil

Sea salt and freshly ground black pepper

1. Make the dressing by shaking the mustard with the vinegar to dissolve it, then adding the garlic and olive oil. Add a very small pinch of salt and some pepper.
2. Cut the beans and broccoli into bite-size pieces and steam for 3 or 4 minutes, so that they are still crunchy.
3. Mix the greens together and add the black olives. Crumble in feta cheese.
4. Gently roast the sesame seeds for a few minutes in a dry frying pan over low heat, stirring them continuously to keep them from burning.
5. Pour the dressing over the salad, and then immediately add the sesame seeds—they should crackle slightly and give off a delicious smell as they fuse with the salad dressing. Toss and serve. Serves 2.

Fettucine with Asparagus

1 bunch (about 5 ounces) asparagus (Campodimelani use thin, wild asparagus; use baby asparagus or else cut the stems into shorter pieces)

7 ounces fettuccine

2 tablespoons extra-virgin olive oil

1 clove garlic, chopped small

2–3 tablespoons parmesan

Sea salt and freshly ground black pepper

1. Steam the asparagus for 5–10 minutes, until tender but still reasonably firm. Meanwhile, boil the pasta.
2. Heat the olive oil with the garlic and toss together with the asparagus.
3. Serve the asparagus with the fettuccine, with some parmesan grated over the top. Add a very small amount of salt and a good grind of pepper. Serves 2.

HUNZA RECIPES

The Hunzakuts use crushed apricot kernels and their oil for cooking; you can use extra-virgin olive oil instead.

Chapattis

Hunzakuts eat these at almost every meal, and they also double as spoons. They go well with the stew, spinach, and dahl recipes that follow.

5 cups whole-grain flour (e.g., wheat, rye, millet, buckwheat)

Water at room temperature

Olive oil for cooking, if necessary

1. Mix together the flour and a little water (enough so that the flour mixes with the water without becoming sticky) to make dough, and knead for 5 minutes.
2. Take a small handful of dough and mold into a sphere. Roll out with a rolling pin to make a small circular shape. Slap the dough from palm to palm to enlarge and thin it (this may take a little practice).

3. Heat a heavy-bottomed frying pan or griddle, then cook the chapatti for a minute or two on each side. Lubricate the pan with a little olive oil if necessary. Makes 5 chapattis.

Lamb, Feta, and Pasta Stew

Known locally as daudo, *this is a favorite dish in Hunza, and is served on special occasions. It contains meat, but the meat is boiled, and the fat is removed from the meat stock. There is also a healthier bean-based option, which follows.*

8-10 ounces lamb, cut in chunks
1 onion, whole
3 bay leaves
3 tablespoons extra-virgin olive oil
1 onion, chopped very small
3 cloves garlic, chopped
1 rib celery, chopped very small
6–8 tomatoes, chopped very small
2 tablespoons tomato puree
4 ounces pasta (the Hunzakuts use chapattis cut into small short strips, like short tagliatelle)
2 teaspoons oregano or mixed herbs
5 ounces organic feta cheese (the Hunzakuts use an ancient, crumbly cheese that looks like small rocks and tastes exactly like feta)
Sea salt and freshly ground pepper to taste

1. Boil the lamb in a pan of water with the whole onion and bay leaves for about an hour, to create stock. Put the meat aside and keep the stock. Remove the fat from the surface of the stock.
2. Gently heat the olive oil in a heavy-bottomed saucepan over a low flame—you can also add 2 tablespoons stock to keep the temperature down. Gently cook the onion, garlic, and celery in

the olive oil until soft, but don't let them go brown. Add the meat and cook for a few minutes, then add the tomatoes with the tomato puree and gently cook for 5–10 minutes.

3. Put in enough stock so that the liquid level is about an inch above the solids. Simmer with the lid on for about an hour. Add more juice if necessary (or a glass of red or white wine).
4. Add the pasta and cook until it is al dente.
5. Add the oregano or mixed herbs.
6. Serve with the feta cheese crumbled over the top. Serves 2–3.

Bean, Lamb, and Feta Stew

This is a variation on the previous recipe. Use 12 ounces of beans as well as, or instead of, the lamb (you can use less lamb or just use some mutton to make the stock and then throw the meat out or give it to the dog). Choose brown or red beans, such as kidney beans, soaked overnight or canned—these go very well with the lamb stock. Add them after Step 2, and simmer the stew for about 1¹/₂–2 hours, or until the beans are cooked. You can either include or leave out the pasta, as you prefer.

Spinach with Onions and Feta

   1¹/₂ pounds of spinach, washed and chopped
   1 large onion, chopped very small
   2 tablespoons extra-virgin olive oil
   4 ounces organic feta cheese

1. Steam the spinach for 1–2 minutes in a steamer or colander over boiling water and drain.
2. Gently cook the chopped onion in the oil in a frying pan or saucepan for a few minutes. Add the spinach and cook for 1–2 minutes.
3. Serve with a little feta cheese crumbled over the top. Serves 2.

Dhal with Lemon and Cilantro

7 ounces lentils (any color—the Hunzakuts use brown, black, or yellow)
1 large onion, shredded
2 tablespoons extra-virgin olive oil
3 tomatoes, chopped very small
2 tablespoons tomato paste
2–3 fresh green chilis, chopped small
2 teaspoons garam masala or curry powder
Sea salt (optional)
2 lemons
1 bunch cilantro, chopped
Brown bread or brown rice

1. Wash the lentils well. Put them in a pan with 2 cups water, bring to a boil, and cook for about 15 minutes, until soft but not mushy.
2. In the meantime, use a heavy-bottomed pan to gently cook the onion in the olive oil, until soft and starting to turn yellow. Add the tomatoes, tomato paste, and chilis, and cook for a few minutes until soft. Add the garam masala and a little salt.
3. When the lentils are cooked, add them to the mixture and simmer for 5 minutes. Add extra tomato paste and/or water if you want the dhal to be more liquid.
4. Squeeze in the juice of 1–2 lemons to taste.
5. Add the cilantro at the last minute and stir it in. The Hunzakuts crumble homemade brown bread into theirs; alternatively, you can eat it with brown rice (using either combination makes this a complete protein meal). Serves 2.

Crudités

The Hunzakuts eat a lot of raw vegetables. They just pick a carrot or cauliflower, wipe off the soil, and eat it as it is.

Instead of eating potato chips and salted nuts with your predinner glass of wine, eat cut-up pieces of raw vegetables such as carrots, cauliflower, cucumber, and celery, dipped in hummus or guacamole.

Oatmeal with Almonds and Apricots

For a cholesterol-lowering, beta-carotene-raising breakfast, make oatmeal with water and soy milk, stir in a spoonful of honey, and sprinkle almonds and apricots over the top. Try to get the dark orange, organic apricots—these contain the most nutrients and are by far the best-tasting (you can buy Hunza apricots in health-food shops, but these have been whitened and are not quite the same as those eaten by the Hunzakuts).

Sprouted Wheat Bread

1. Soak 3 cups wheat berries (grains) in mineral water overnight.
2. Spread out the seeds thinly in some wide-bottomed sieves (the kind used for sifting flour are ideal), cover with napkins, and keep in a dark place.
3. Rinse with water 3 times daily.
4. After 2–4 days, depending on the temperature (in very hot countries, one day is usually enough), the wheat berries will have little white sprouts about a quarter of an inch long. The berries are now ready to make into dough. Do not let the sprouts grow any longer, or the dough will taste sour.
5. Put the sprouted berries in a blender and blend until you get a claylike dough.
6. Knead the dough for 5–10 minutes.
7. Shape into 2 loaves, long oval shapes, and put on a greased baking tray.
8. Bake at 325 degrees F maximum for 2 hours, or longer at a cooler temperature. Serve warm with the spread of your choice. Makes 2 small loaves.

You can also add seeds, dried fruit, banana, carrots, coconut, or honey to the dough.

Fruit and Nut Bar (Sultan Coq)
    7 ounces apricot kernels or almonds
    7 ounces walnuts
    7 ounces dried mulberries or golden raisins
    2 tablespoons water

1. In a coffee grinder, grind the apricot kernels or almonds and walnuts, then add the dried mulberries or raisins and grind.
2. Put in a bowl and mix together with water to make a thick paste. Roll the paste into a ball, then shape into cookie or pancake shapes.

BAMA RECIPES

Hemp Oil Salad Dressing
    2–3 tablespoons hemp oil (buy from darkened, refrigerated containers in health-food shops)
    1 tablespoon balsamic vinegar
    1 teaspoon lemon juice
    1 clove garlic, chopped very small
    Sea salt (a small pinch) and freshly ground pepper

Mix together the ingredients, and serve liberally with salads.

Sweet Potato and Salad
This is an easy recipe that makes a very good multicolored antioxidant lunch.

    1 organic sweet potato
    Green salad leaves (e.g., romaine, organic mixed greens, arugula, watercress, spinach)

1 cooked sliced beet
2 thinly sliced tomatoes
1 avocado, sliced
Handful basil or cilantro leaves, chopped
10 black olives, sliced
Sesame seeds
Olive oil or Hemp Oil Dressing Salad

1. Scrub the potato under running water and bake it for 30–40 minutes at 350–400 degrees F until done.
2. Mix up the other ingredients, except for the sesame seeds, and add the olive oil or Hemp Oil Salad Dressing but do not toss.
3. Heat the sesame seeds in a dry pan for 2 or 3 minutes, then add to the dressed salad and toss. Serves 2.

Sweet Potato and Carrot Soup

This is an excellent beta carotene soup, perfect for winter. The Bama people do not use cardamom or cumin in their cooking, but I have added them because they taste good and have their own health benefits. You can also make this soup with pumpkin.

2 or 3 sweet potatoes
4 or 5 large carrots
2 tablespoons extra-virgin olive oil
1 teaspoon cumin
1 pinch of ground cardamom seeds
$1^1/2$ pints chicken or vegetable stock

1. Peel and chop the sweet potatoes and carrots.
2. Heat the olive oil in a heavy-bottomed pan and add the vegetables.
3. Add about a teaspoon of cumin powder and a pinch of ground cardamom seeds, stir in, and sweat the mixture gently for a few minutes.

4. Add enough stock to cover the vegetables and simmer until they are soft (about 5 minutes).
5. Put in a blender or food processor and blend—if the soup is too solid, you can add more stock.
6. Return to the pan for a few seconds, just to heat the soup through, and serve. Serves 2.

Hemp Pasta with Pesto

Hemp pasta is delicious and very versatile—it goes well with any pasta sauce. Hemp pasta and hemp pesto are both available from health-food shops and some supermarkets.

5–7 ounces hemp pasta
1 tablespoon basil or hemp pesto

Boil the pasta for the length of time specified on the package (this varies according to the shape of pasta). Drain and return to the pan. Add the pesto, stir, and heat through.

Serve with a salad. Serves 1.

Grilled Polenta with Spinach

There is no Parmesan in Bama, and although it isn't health food, it goes very well with polenta—use organic cheese if possible.

$2^{1}/_{2}$ cups water
1 cup polenta flour
3 tablespoons grated Parmesan cheese
Sea salt and freshly ground pepper
2 tablespoons extra-virgin olive oil
14 ounces spinach
1 clove garlic, chopped

1. Bring the water to a boil in a heavy pan. Pour in the polenta slowly, in a steady stream, whisking it at the same time. Turn the heat down as low as possible, and simmer very gently for a few minutes, until it is of the same consistency as oatmeal (cooking times vary, so refer to the instructions on the package). Stir in the Parmesan cheese, a little salt, and pepper to taste. Transfer to a small, shallow dish and leave to cool and harden.

2. Cut the polenta into wedges, brush a little olive oil on both sides, and grill for a few minutes on each side until it is starting to go golden.

3. Meanwhile, steam the spinach for 1 or 2 minutes until just wilted. Heat the olive oil in a pan on medium heat, add the garlic, cook for a few seconds, then toss the spinach in the pan for a few seconds. Serve with the polenta and a few extra shavings of Parmesan cheese. Serves 1–2.

ACKNOWLEDGMENTS

Thanks to Matthew Lore, Kylie Foxx and Renée Sedliar at Avalon.

Many thanks also to the following for their invaluable help with each of the places:

OKINAWA:
Tariq Wasir Khan, Yumi Kashiba, Dr. Akihiri Yomo
Dr. Hiroto and Junko Miyagi (for their recipes)
Kagumi Yamagami and Masa Yamagami (for their interviews)

SYMI:
Chrisa Karagianni
Irene Petridi (for her interviews)
Fottini Attiti (for her recipes)
Georgios Papadopoulos

CAMPODIMELE:
Paola Masi
Guiseppina Grossi (for all her invaluable help)
Marino Pecchia (for his advice and recipes)
Dr. Pietro Cugini

HUNZA:
Jalal Haider Khan
Air Commodore Naunehal Shah, Dr. Salman
Nusrat Shah, Arifa Shah, Muhammec Dost Khan, Qudsia Shah

BAMA:
Ji Yang, Yuan Ye

ENDNOTES

Introduction

1 G. Kaati, L. O. Bygren, and S. Edvinsson, "Cardiovascular and Diabetes Mortality Determined by Nutrition During Parents' and Grandparents' Slow Growth Period"; *European Journal of Human Genetics* 10, no. 11 (November 2002): 682–688.

2 Office of Statistics and Programming, National Center for Health Statistics/National Vital Statistic System.

3 Dr. Michael Colgan, www.miraclehealth.com/goodnews.3.htm (accessed 2002)

4 The Cancer Cure Foundation Web site, www.cancure.org.

5 Barbara Starfield, MD, MPH, "Is U.S. Health Really the Best in the World?" *Journal of the American Medical Association* 284, no. 4 (July 26, 2000): 483–485.

PART ONE

Chapter 1—Okinawa

1 Bradley Willcox, Craig Willcox, and Makoto Suzuki; *The Okinawa Way* (London: Penguin Books, 2001).

Chapter 2—Sym

1 S. Karagiannis, N. Karagiannis, E. Grigoriadis, and M. Telonis; "Comparison of Morbidity and Causes of Death Between the Province of Rhodes and the Rest of Greece, During the Decade 1981–1990" (paper presented at the 14th Panhellenic Gastroenterology Conference, Athens, November 16–20, 1994).

2 *Epidemiology* (February 18, 1998).

Chapter 3—Campodimele

1 *Alimentazione, Nutrizione, Invecchiamento;* 2a Campodimele Conference, Obiettivo Longevita (Rome: Edizioni L. Pozzi, 1995).

2 *Alimentazione, Nutrizione, Invecchiamento;* 2a Campodimele Conference, Obiettivo Longevita (Rome: Edizioni L. Pozzi, 1995).

Chapter 4—Hunza

1 Sir Robert McCarrison, 1925 article.
2 Jay M. Hoffman, *Hunza: Secrets of the World's Healthiest and Oldest Living People* New Win Publishing, 1996.
3 Sir Robert McCarrison (Mellon Lecture, University of Pittsburgh School of Medicine, Pittsburgh, 1922).
4 Dudley White and Edward Toomey, "Longevity of Aged Hunzas," *American Heart Journal* (December 1964).
5 Renee Taylor, *Hunza Health Secrets for Long Life and Happiness* (New Canaan, Connecticut: Keats Publishing 1964).
6 Alexander Leaf, "Search for the Oldest People" *National Geographic,* 143, no 1. (January 1973).
7 J. I. Rodale, *The Healthy Hunzas* (:Rodale Press, 1948).

Chapter 5—Bama

1. *China Geriatrics Magazine* 11, no. 2 (1982).
2. Ze Yang, "Systematic Research and Analysis of the Factors Associated with Longevity in Bama Population" (1981); Zhi-Chien Ho, "A Study of Longevity Protein Requirements of Individuals 90–112 Years Old in Southern China," *Journal of Applied Nutrition* 34, no. 1 (1982).
3 Ze Yang, "Systematic Research and Analysis of the Factors Associated with Longevity in Bama Population 1981."
4 *European Journal of Human Genetics* 10 (October 31, 2002): 682–688.
5 Zhang Yan et al., 1994
6 Ze Yang, "Systematic Research and Analysis of the Factors Associated with Longevity in Bama Population."
7 Health Longevity Survey in China, conducted by Peking University and China National Research Centre on Aging.

PART TWO

Secret 1: Eat Until You Are Only Eight Parts Full

1 M. Suzuki, M. Akisaka, and S. Inayama; "Medicobiological Studies on Centenarians in Okinawa, Measuring plasma Lipid Peroxide, Proline, and Plasma and Intracellular Tocopherol." *Recent Advances in Aging Science,* edited by E. Beregi, I. A. Gergely, and K. Rajczi. (Bologna: Monduzzi Editore, 1993).
2 Self, *New England Journal of Medicine,* November 1995.
3 *The Week,* issue 360 (January 6, 2002).

Secret 6: Eat Meat As a Treat

1 P. Krohn, "Rapid Growth, Short Life," *Journal of the American Medical Association* 171, (1959): 461.

2 J. W. T. Dickerson et al., "Disease Patterns in Individuals with Different Eating Patterns," *Journal of the Royal Society of Health* 105 (1985): 191–194.
3 B. Reddy and E. Wynder, "Large Bowel Carcinogenesis: Fecal Constituents of Populations with Diverse Incidence of Colon Cancer," *Journal of the National Cancer Institute* 50 (1973): 1437.
4 Obituary Column, *Riverside Herald* (March 14, 1982), C 11.
5 Colin Campbell, MS, PhD, *Nutrition Advocate* ? 1, no. 6 (December 1995).

Secret 7: Prepare Your Meat Right

1 S. A. Bingham et al., "Are Imprecise Methods Obscuring a Relation Between Fat and Breast Cancer?" *The Lancet* vol 362, issue 9379, 212–214 (July 19, 2003);
    E. Cho et al., 'Premenopausal Fat Intake and the Risk of Breast Cancer," *Journal of the National Cancer Institute* 95, No. 14 (July 16, 2003): 1079-1085.
2 M. S. Sandhu et al., "Systematic Review of the Prospective Cohort Studies on Meat Consumption and Colorectal Cancer Risk: a Meta-Analytical Approach," *Cancer Epidemiology Biomarkers & Prevention* 10, no. 5 (May 2001): 439–446.

Secret 8: Choose Organic Goat's and Sheep's Cheese

1 H. M. Dosch, "Interview with Hans-Michael Dosch: An Update of the Ig-G-mediated Cow's Milk and Insulin-Dependent Diabetes Connection, Part 2," *The Immunological Review* 2, no. 3 (Spring 1994).
2 A. Walker, "The Human Requirement of Calcium: Should Low Intakes Be Supplemented?" *American Journal of Clinical Nutrition* 25 (1972): 518.

Secret 11: Find Good Fats in Fish

1 Johanna Budwig, *Flax Oil As a True Aid against Arthritis, Heart Infarction, Cancer and Other Diseases* (Vancouver: Apple Publishing, 1994).
2 A. E. Stoll et al., "Omega-3 Fatty Acids in Bipolar Disorder: A Preliminary Double-Blind Placebo Controlled Trial" *Archives of General Psychiatry* 56 (1999): 407–412.
3 Artemis Simopoulos, Omega-3 Fatty Acids in Health and Disease and in Growth and Development, *American Journal of Clinical Nutrition* 54 (1991): 438–463.

Secret 14: Beware of Fats in Disguise

1 R.P. Mensink and M.P. Katan Effect of Dietary Trans Fatty Acids on High-Density and Low-Density Lipoprotein Cholesterol Levels in Healthy Subjects *New England Journal of Medicine* 323, no. 7 (1990): 439-445.

Secret 15: Use Garlic and Onions—Nature's Healers

1 R. Munday and C.M. Munday, "Low Doses of Diallyl Sulfide, a Compound Derived from Garlic, Increase Tissue Activities of Quinine Reductase and Glutathione transferase in the Gastrointestinal Tract of the rat" *Nutrition and Cancer,* 1999; 34 (1) 42-48

2 Mishiyama N., Moriguchi T., Saito and H., Beneficial Effects of Aged Garlic Extract on Learning and Memory Impairment in the Senescence-Accelerated Mouse *Experimental Gerontology* 32 (1997): 149-160.
3 W. C. You et al., "Allium Vegetables and Reduced Risk of Stomach Cancer" *Journal of the National Cancer Institute* 81, no. 2 (January 18, 1989): 162–164;

Secret 16 Discover the Power of Crunchy Vegetables
1 Ansher, SS, Federation of Chemistry and Toxicology, vol.24, p405, 1986.

Secret 17: Keep Aging Away with a Salad a Day
1 Leslie and Susannah Kenton, *Raw Energy* (London: Guild Publishing, 1984), 89.

Secret 19: Enjoy Pizza . . . Guilt Free
1 E. Giovannucci et al., "Intake of Carotenoids and Retinol in Relation to Risk of Prostate Cancer," *Journal of the National Cancer Institute* 87 (December 6, 1995): 1767–1776.
2 J. Van Eenwyk, F. G. Davis, and P. E. Bowne; "Dietary and Serum Carotenoids and Cervical Intraepithelial Neoplasia," *International Journal of Cancer* 48 (1991): 34–38.

Secret 20: Snack on Apricots and Apricot Kernels
1 Ernst Krebs Jr. (speech, second annual Cancer Convention, Los Angeles, 1974). Cited in Phillip Day, *Cancer: Why We're Still Dying to Know the Truth* (Tonbridge, England: Credence Publications, 1999).

Secret 24: Choose Soy—the Traditional Way
1 Hidemi Todoriki, Japan Public Health Center Database. Cited in Bradley Willcox, Craig Willcox, and Makoto Suzuki, *The Okinawa Way* (London Penguin Books, 2001), Chapter 2, note 45.
2 Mark Messina and John W. Erdman Jr. "First International Symposium on the Role of Soy in Preventing and Treating Chronic Disease *Journal of Nutrition* 125, no. 3 (March 1995): 606S–611S.
3 M. Rice, "Soy Consumption and Bone Mineral Density in Older Japanese American Women in King County, Washington: The Nikkei Bone Density Study". University of Washington (doctoral dissertation, 1999)
    D. L. Alekel et al., "Isoflavone-Rich Soy Protein Isolate Attenuates Bone Loss in the Lumbar Spine of Perimenopausal Women," *American Journal of Clinical Nutrition* 72 (2000): 844–852.
4 Lon R. White et al., "Brain Aging and Midlife Tofu Consumption," *Journal of the American College of Nutrition,* vol 19, no. 2 (2000): 242-255.

Secret 26: Eat Magical Mushrooms

1   N. Kodama, K. Komuta, N. Sakai, and H. Nanba; "Effects of D-Fraction, a Polysaccharice from *Grifola frondosa* on Tumor Growth Involve Activation of NK Cells," *Biological & Pharmaceutical Bulletin* 25, no. 12 (December 2002): 1647–1650.

Secret 28: Don't Pass the Salt

1   J. V. Joossens et al., "Dietary Salt, Nitrate and Stomach Cancer Mortality in 24 Countries," *International Journal of Epidemiology* 25, no. 3 (June 1996): 494–502.

Secret 29: Go Organic and Avoid "Frankenfoods"

1   John Robbins *Diet for a New America* (Tiburon, California: H. J. Kramer, 1987).
2   BBC news online, "Child Cancer Rates Increasing." http://news.bbc.co.uk/ (Accessed on December 18, 2001.)
3   *New England Journal of Medicine* (March 26, 1981).
4   Maastricht Aging Society, Netherlands, *The Lancet* (september 2002).
5   *The Independent on Sunday* (May 22, 2005).
6   "Genetically Modified Crops and Food," Friends of the Earth briefing, note 10.
7   "Genetically Modified Crops and Food," Friends of the Earth briefing, note 29.
8   "Genetically Modified Crops and Food," Friends of the Earth briefing.
9   Fred Guterl, "The Fear of Food," *Newsweek* (January 27, 2003).

Secret 31: Beware the Pastry Counter

1   K. M. Venkat Narayan, James P. Boyle, Theodore J. Thompson, Stephen W. Sorensen, and David F. Williamson, "Lifetime Risk for Diabetes Mellitus in the United States," *Journal of the American Medical Association* 290 (2003): 1884–1890.
2   Beezy Marsh, "Findings from Bristol Royal Hospital for Sick Children," *Daily Mail*, (September 28, 2002).
3   Jean Carper, *Stop Aging Now!* (New York: HarperCollins, 1995): 284.
4   S. E. Hankinson et al., "Circulating concentrations of Insulin-Like Growth Factor-I and Risk of BreastCancer," *Lancet* 351 (1998): 1393–96;
        E. Giovannucci, "Insulin and colon cancer," *Cancer Causes Control* 6, no. 2 (1995): 164–179;
        J. Chan, M. Stampfer, and E. Giovannucci, "Plasma insulin-like growth factor I and prostate cancer risk: A prospective study," *Science* 279, no. 5350 (1998): 563–566.

Secret 32: Have a Glass of Red Wine with Dinner

1   As reported in the *Daily Mail* (November 27, 2000).
2   K. T. Howitz et al., "Small Molecule Activators of Sirtuins Extend *Saccharomyces cerevisiae* lifespan," *Nature* 425 (September 11, 2003): 191–196. Published online, August 24, 2003.
3   Valerie Beral, *British Journal of Cancer* (November 12, 2002).

Secret 33: Make Time for Tea—Green Tea

1 I. Oguni and ShuJun Cheng, *Annual Report of the Skylark Food Science Institute*, no. 3.57 (1991).

2 N. Ahmad et al, "Green Tea Constituent epigallocatechin-3-gallate and Induction of Apoptosis and Cell Cycle Arrest in Human Carcinoma Cells," *Journal of the National Cancer Institute* 89, no. 24 (1997): 1881–1886.

3 Y. T. Gao et al., "Reduced Risk of Esophageal Cancer Associated with Green Tea Consumption," *Journal of the National Cancer Institute* 85 (1994): 855–858;
   S. K. Katiyar and H. Mukhtar, "Tea in Chemoprevention of Cancer: Epidemiologic and Experimental Studies," *International Journal of Oncology* 8 (1996): 221–238.

4 K. Goto, S. Kanaya, and Y. Hara, *Proceedings of the International Symposium on Tea Science* (Shizuoka, Japan: The Organizing Committee of ISTS, August 1991), 314.
   Y. Hara, T. Matsuzaki, and T. Suzuki; *Nippon Nogeikagaku Kaishi* 61,803 (1987), 49.

Secret 34: Drink Water—the Most Essential Nutrient

1 Natural Resources Defense Council "Study Finds Safety of Drinking Water in U.S. Cities at Risk." www.nrdc.org/water/drinking/uscities.asp.

Secret 36: Spring-Clean with Juices and Saunas

1 Ian Belcher, "The Enema Within," *The Guardian*, London (September 3, 2002).

2 Ian Belcher, "The Enema Within," *The Guardian*, London (September 3, 2002).

3 Nancy Sokol Green, *Poisoning Our Children* (Chicago: Noble Press, 1991).

Secret 37: Supplement Your Diet

1 Jean Carper, *Stop Aging Now!* (New York: HarperCollins, 1995): 51.

2 Kristiina Nyyssonen, et al; "Vitamin C Deficiency and Risk of Myocardial Infarction: Prospective Population Study of Men from Eastern Finland," *British Medical Journal* 314 (1997): 634–638.

3 Carper, *Stop Aging Now!* (New York: HarperCollins, 1995): 60.

4 K. Klipstein-Grobusch et al., "Dietary Antioxidants and Risk of Myocardial Infarction in the Elderly: the Rotterdam Study," *American Journal of Clinical Nutrition* 69 (1999): 261–266.

5 Diplock 1994

6 Jean Carper, *Stop Aging Now!* (New York: HarperCollins, 1995): 44.

7 Stampfer et al, "Vitamin E Consumption and the Risk of Coronary Heart Disease in Women" *New England Journal of Medicine*, 328: 1444-1449 (June 1993).
   Stampfer et al, 'Vitamin E Consumption and the Risk of Coronary Heart Disease in Men," *New England Journal of Medicine*, 328: 1450-1456.

8 Jean Carper, *Stop Aging Now!* (New York: HarperCollins, 1995): 119.

9 L. C. Clark et al., "Effect of Selenium Supplementation for Cancer Prevention with

Carcinoma of the Skin: a Randomised Controlled Trial," *Journal of the American Medical Association* 276 (1996): 1957–1963.

10. Study by Professor Harold Foster, University of Victoria, British Columbia, as reported in Lorna R. Vanderhaeghe and Patrick J. D. Bouic, *The Immune System Cure* (London: Cico Books, 2001).

11 P. Suadicani, H. O. Hein, and F. Gyntelberg; "Serum Selenium Concentration and Risk of Ischaemic Heart Disease in a Prospective Cohort Study of 3000 Males," *Atherosclerosis* 96 (1992): 33–42.

12 Jean Carper, *Stop Aging Now!* (New York: HarperCollins, 1995): 119.

13 As reported by Burton Goldberg, *Heart Disease, Stroke and High Blood Pressure* (Tiburon, California: Future Medicine Publishing, 1998),118.

14 K. Folkers, *Clinical Investigator* (1993) as reported in Vanderhaeghe and Bouic, *The Immune System Cure.*

15 Lockwood et al., as reported in Vanderhaeghe and Bouic, *The Immune System Cure.*

16 Jean Carper, *Stop Aging Now!* (New York: HarperCollins, 1995): 144.

17 Maydani et al. (1995)

18 Vanderhaeghe and Bouic, *The Immune System Cure.*

19 Y. Rayssiguier, "Magnesium and Aging. I. Experimental Data: Importance of Oxidative Damage," *Magnesium Research* (1996).

20 D. A. Wood et al., "Adipose Tissue and Platelet Fatty Acids and Coronary Heart Disease in Scottish Men," *Lancet* 2, no. 8395 (July 1984): 117–121.

21 According to Dr. Richard Anderson of the Beltsville Human Nutrition Research Center, Maryland, 180 patients with Type II diabetes were given 200 micrograms of chromium piccolinate daily, and their blood glucose levels were lowered, results that were comparable or even better than those for most medication used for Type II diabetes. Reported in *Diabetes*, November 1997.

22 Jean Carper, *Stop Aging Now!* (New York: HarperCollins, 1995): 75.

Secret 38: Exercise, Exercise, Exercise

1 Stanford University study reported in *Newsweek* (January 20, 2002).

2 I. Thune et al., "Physical Activity and the Risk of Breast Cancer," *New England Journal of Medicine* 336, no. 1267 (1997): 1269–1275;

   R. Tang, J. Y Wang, S. K. Lo, and L. L. Hsieh, "Physical Activity, Water Intake and Risk of Colorectal Cancer in Taiwan: a Hospital-Based Case-Control Study," *International Journal of Cancer* 82 (1999): 484–489.

3 M. Tanasescu et al., "Exercise Type and Intensity in Relation to Coronary Heart Disease in Men," *Journal of the American Medical Association* 288 (October 2002): 1994-2000.

4 J. F. Clapp, "Exercise and Fetal Health," *Journal of Developmental Physiology* 15 (1991): 14.

5 J. E. Pierog, "Recipe for Longevity," Healthlinks net newsletter. www.healthlinks.net./archive/ageing.html [date accessed - current]

6   M. Wei et al., "The Association Between Cardiorespiratory Fitness and Impaired Fasting Glucose and Type 2 Diabetes Mellitus in Men," *Annual of Internal Medicine* 130 (1999): 89–96.

7   S. G. Leveille et al., "Aging Successfully Until Death in Old Age: Opportunities for Increasing Active Life Expectancy," *American Journal of Epidemiology* 149 (1999): 654–664.

8   S. S. Lennox, F. R. Bedell, and A. A. Stone, "The Effect of Exercise on Normal Mood," *Journal of Psychosomatic Research* 34, no. 6 (1990): 629–636;

     E. R. Braverman, "Sports and Exercise: Nutritional Augmentation and Health Benefits," *Journal of Orthomolecular Medicine* 6 (1991): 191–200.

9   A. F. Kramer et al., "Aging, Fitness and Neurocognitive Function," *Nature* 400 (1999): 418–419.

10   S. Shore et al., "Immune responses to training: How Critical is Training Volume?" *Journal of Sports Medicine and Physical Fitness* 39 (1999): 1–11.

11   J. T. Venkatramen (presentation, Fourth International Symposium of the Society for Exercise and Immunology, Rome, May 1999).

Secret 39: Get Your Daily Dose of Sunshine

1   E. D. Gorham et al., *International Journal of Epidemiology* 20 (December 1991): 1145;

     E. S. Lefkowitz et al., *International Journal of Epidemiology* 23 (December 1994): 1133;

     C. F. Garland et al., *Lancet* (November 18, 1989): 1176;.

     M. J. Barger-Lux, *Journal of Nutrition* 124 (August 1994): 1406S.

2   I. R., "The Roles of Calcium and Vitamin D in the Prevention of Osteoporosis," *Endocrinology and Metabolism Clinics of North America* 27 (1998): 389–398.

3   R. P. Heaney, "Long-Latency Deficiency Disease: insights From Calcium and Vitamin D" *American Journal of Clinical Nutrition* 78 (2003): 912–919.

4   *Cancer Chemotherapy Pharmacology* 51, no. 5 (May 2003): 415–421.

Secret 40: Jog Your Memory

1   Eleanor Maguire et al, "Navigation-Related Structural Change in the Hippocampi of Taxi Drivers," *Proceedings of the National Academy of Sciences* vol 97, no. 8 (2000): 4398–4403.

Secret 41: Breathe—and Hum

1   Proceedings of the International Conference on Bio-Oxidative Medicine 1989, 1990, 1991.

2   "Vitamin C Helps Fight Infections by Producing Hydrogen Peroxide," *Infectious Disease News* 91 (August 8): 5.

3   Lars Olaf Cardell, M D, PhD; "The Paranasal Sinuses and a Unique Role in Airway Nitric Oxide Production?" *American Journal of Respiratory and Critical Care Medicine* 166, no. 2 (2002): 131–132.

Secret 42 Sit Still and Do Nothing

1   D.W. Orme-Johnson, "Medical Care Utilisation and the Transcendental Meditation Program," *Psychosomatic Medicine* 49 (1987): 493–507.
2   R. K. Wallace, M. Dillbeck, E. Jacobe, and B. Harrington; "The Effects of the Transcendental Meditation and TM-Sidhi Programme on the Aging Process," *International Journal of Neuroscience* 16, no. 1 (1982): 53–58.
3. D.W. Orme-Johnson, "Medical Care Utilisation and the Transcendental Meditation Program," *Psychosomatic Medicine* 49 (1987): 93–507.

Secret 43: Have Faith

1   Michael E. McCullough et al., "Religious Involvement and Mortality: A Meta-Analytic Review," *Health Psychology* 19, no 3. (2000).

Secret 44: Laugh It Off

1   T. T. Perls and M. H. Silver, *Living to 100* (New York: Basic Books, 1999).
2   N. Cousins, *Anatomy of an Illness As Perceived by the Patient* (New York: W.W. Norton & Co, Inc., 1979).
3   Lee Berk and Stanley Tan, "The Laughter-Immune Connection," *Humor and Health Journal* 5, no. 5 (1996).

Secret 45: Sing in the Shower

1   R. McCraty (report of study, Proceedings of the Tenth International Montreux Congress on Stress, Montreux, Switzerland, February 28–March 6, 1999).

Secret 46: Give Help to Others

1   Avron Spiro III et al, "Hostility, the Metabolic Syndrome, and Incident Coronary Heart Disease," *Health Psychology* vol 21, no. 6 (November 2002).

Secret 47: Marry—or Get a Dog

1   Andrew Oswald and Jonathan Gardner, "Is it Money or Marriage That Keeps People Alive?" August 2002. www.oswald.co.uk.
2   J. S. Goodwin, W. C. Hunt, C. R. Key, and J. M. Samet; "The Effect of Marital Status on Stage, Treatment and Survival of Cancer Patients," *Journal of the American Medical Association* 31 (1987): 25–30.
3   David Weeks, *Secrets of the Superyoung* (New York): Villard Books, 1998.
4   Andrea Thompson, "Does Marriage Make You Healthier?" *Glamour* (November 2002).
5   Oswald and Gardner, "Is It Money or Marriage That Keeps People Alive?"

Secret 48: Invite a Friend

1   L. F. Berkman and S. L. Syme, "Social Networks, Host Resistance and Mortality: A Nine-Year Follow-Up Study of Alameda County Residents," *American Journal of Epidemiology* 109 (1979): 186–204.

2 Ze Yang, "Systematic Research and Analysis of the Factors Associated with Longevity in Bama Population" (1981).

3 S. Lepore, K. Allen, and G. Evans; "Social Support Lowers Cardiovascular Reactivity to an Acute Stressor," *Psychosomatic Medicine* 55 (1993): 518–524.

Secret 50: Sleep

1 Study led by Daniel Kripke at the University of California at San Diego. See Daniel Kripke et al., "Mortality Associated with Sleep Duration and Insomnia," *Archives of General Psychiatry* 59 (February 15, 2002).

PART THREE

Aging Substances to Avoid

1 Kiejzers et al., *Diabetes Care* (2002) Thong et al., *Diabetes* (2002). Grubben et al., *American Journal of Clinical Nutrition*, (2002): 480-4

INDEX